African American Cultural Theory and Heritage

Series Editor: William C. Banfield

The Jazz Trope: A Theory of African American Literary and Vernacular Culture, by Alfonso W. Hawkins Jr., 2008.

In the Heart of the Beat: The Poetry of Rap, by Alexs D. Pate, 2009.

George Russell: The Story of an American Composer, by Duncan Heining, 2010.

Cultural Codes: Makings of a Black Music Philosophy, by William C. Banfield, 2010.

Willie Dixon: Preacher of the Blues, by Mitsutoshi Inaba, 2011.

Willie Dixon and Keith Richards, Chicago, 1989. Photo by Paul Natkin.

Willie Dixon

Preacher of the Blues

Mitsutoshi Inaba

African American Cultural Theory and Heritage

THE SCARECROW PRESS, INC.
Lanham • Toronto • Plymouth, UK
2011

Published by Scarecrow Press, Inc.
A wholly owned subsidiary of The Rowman & Littlefield Publishing Group, Inc.
4501 Forbes Boulevard, Suite 200, Lanham, Maryland 20706
http://www.scarecrowpress.com

Estover Road, Plymouth PL6 7PY, United Kingdom

British Library Cataloguing in Publication Information Available

Library of Congress Cataloging-in-Publication Data

Inaba, Mitsutoshi, 1964–
  Willie Dixon : preacher of the blues / Mitsutoshi Inaba.
      p. cm. — (African American cultural theory and heritage)
  Includes bibliographical references and index.
  ISBN 978-0-8108-6993-6 (hardback : alk. paper) — ISBN 978-0-8108-6994-3 (ebook)
  1. Dixon, Willie, 1915–1992—Criticism and interpretation. 2. Blues (Music)—
History and criticism. 3. Blues (Music)—Analysis, appreciation. I. Title.
  ML410.D68I63 2011
  781.643092—dc22   2009033237

For everyone who taught me the beauty of black music and to love the blues
For my wife and very best friend, Pam, and my lovely daughter, Aria

In memory of
Shirli Dixon (1963–2003)
Arthur "Butch" Dixon (1959–2004)
Koko Taylor (1928–2009)

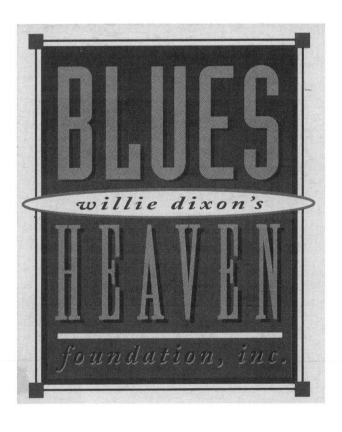

~

Contents

~

Foreword

Willie Dixon is hailed in the music world for his many classic songs and the incomparable studio work he did with the legendary figures of Chicago blues. But he felt he was on a higher mission, as Mitsutoshi Inaba ably chronicles in this unique and exhaustive study. Growing up in Japan, "Mit" never saw or met Willie Dixon, but fortunately, Dixon left not only a legacy of lyrics and music but also one of spoken words of wisdom about the meaning of his songs, imparted in conversations and interviews that were often transcribed and published in books, newspapers, and magazines. Time and again, Dixon explained and defined the blues as "the facts of life"—not just the hard times, heartbreaks, and troubles but also the triumphs, joys, boasts, and celebrations, and many things in between. The central theme of Mit's treatise here is the role of Dixon as a preacher of the blues, a stance Dixon adopted for himself as well as for the blues artists who most effectively sang his songs, especially Muddy Waters, Howlin' Wolf, and Koko Taylor. It was Dixon's intent to imbue even songs like "Hoochie Coochie Man," "I Just Want to Make Love to You," "Back Door Man," "I'm Ready," and "Little Red Rooster" with messages of wisdom deeper than the lyrics may have seemed on the surface. Dixon also shaped the public personae of many performers, carefully choosing which song to place with which singer (even though some singers often disagreed with the material he picked for them). A keen observer of life, Dixon took into account their vocal styles, personalities, and even their physical traits to match the singer to the message of the song.

In his work at Chess and Cobra Records, Dixon was positioned as a middle man between the blues artists he recorded and the record companies; on one hand, he was an African American blues artist too, subject to usual practices of the record labels, but he was also an employee of the label owners, which meant he was sometimes viewed with distrust by the artists for being part of the system. Dixon was no stranger to hustling and did what he could to feed his family (actually, two families in his case) and make his way in the world—but all along, I believe, he maintained a vision of a better way for the world.

I must have learned who Willie Dixon was in the same way Mit and countless others did—by seeing his name in the songwriters' credits on Rolling Stones records. Once the blues bug bit me, it didn't take long to realize what a crucial position Dixon occupied in the hierarchy of the blues. I was fortunate enough to see him perform, interview him several times, visit his home and his studio (where I would buy 45s and LPs on his Yambo label in the 1970s), travel with him to festivals in Mexico City and Berlin, and join him in a 1990 program at the Old Capitol building in Jackson, Mississippi, where he (of course) wanted only to deliver his message about the blues as the facts of life, happy to be able to do it as a guest of honor in a state where he had been incarcerated and abused in his youth.

The first time I ever talked to Dixon was in 1969, in a phone interview when I was a journalism student at Northwestern University doing an article on Chicago blues. What better source on blues could there have been than Willie Dixon? The next year, I and a group of blues aficionados in Chicago founded *Living Blues* magazine, which gave us plenty of reasons to keep in touch with Dixon and report on his activities. Chess Records was in its twilight in Chicago, but Dixon was operating independently with his own record label and publishing company. He rented his studio out on occasion, and when blues enthusiast Steve Wisner rented it to pursue his project of "recording the unrecorded" artists on the Chicago blues scene, Dixon voluntarily stepped out on the floor to give encouragement and suggestions to the musicians (see photo in this book). I was always impressed by the ease with which he handled his authority.

In 1976 Dixon called with an offer to write an "I Am the Blues" column in *Living Blues*. He wrote the first installment, an elaboration on the "blues is the facts of life" theme. In a way he was preaching to the converted by choosing *Living Blues* as his medium; when we offered to ask him questions from readers in subsequent columns, the questions usually pertained to specific recordings and musicians. In the course of our discussions, Dixon sometimes asked me questions in return. *Living Blues* always tried to keep up with the musicians active on the Chicago blues club scene, and when Dixon was seeking to fill slots in the changing personnel of his Chicago Blues Allstars, I was flattered, and a bit stunned, when he asked, "Hey, man, do you know a good harmonica player?" (or, another time, "a good guitar player?"). Always looking for opportunities to market his work to a larger audience, he also once confided his hopes for one of his songs: "You know, man, we could make a million if we could get a fay [white] chick to record this song."

But more often, it was just the purpose of the blues he liked to talk about, with me and everyone else. Through his lyrics and through his words and those of his wife, Marie, and children, Shirli and Butch, Mitsutoshi Inaba has been able to probe the underlying truths Dixon conceived in his songs, and the varied and fascinating ways in which the musical backing enhances the messages. To Dixon, the blues was a multifaceted tool: a means of survival, a belief system much like a religion unto itself, a declaration of pride and self-assertion, a forum for philosophy and education, a song of romance, an instrument of erotic persuasion and desire, a communal voice of the African American experience and the collective memory of a people, a pressure valve to release tensions, a prescription for therapy and healing, a voice of social and political commentary, a journey into magic and superstition, a preservation of folklore and oral history, a mirror of everyday existence, a probe into human heart and mind, a siren of warning, a stage for both comedy and melodrama, a parable for lessons in life, a petition for peace and justice, and a road to wisdom.

Dixon's message was still being preached at his funeral, where Louis Farrakhan, invited by the Dixon family, delivered a stirring eulogy on Dixon and the blues. (Dixon did not know Farrakhan personally but admired him.) After the service, I marched along with the first New Orleans jazz-style funeral procession ever held in Chicago.

Willie Dixon wanted the whole world to understand the blues as he did. It was a difficult challenge, but he did show the way, and through the vast body of music he left, the work of Marie Dixon and the family with the Blues Heaven Foundation, and now through *Willie Dixon: Preacher of the Blues*, his messages of wisdom live on.

Jim O'Neal
Cofounder, *Living Blues* magazine
Research Director, Mississippi Blues Trail

~

Acknowledgments

This book is a reworking of the doctoral dissertation I submitted to the University of Oregon in 2005. Writing a Ph.D. dissertation and re-creating it as a commercial publication was a very long process. In addition, having been born in Japan in the mid-1960s, I had to educate myself—not just in speaking English, but in the depth of African American folk culture surrounding the blues. Beyond the cultural differences, many people guided me through my journey with their hands, eyes, feet, thoughts, and voices.

This work would not have been developed without the cooperation of Willie Dixon's Blues Heaven Foundation. I thank Kevin Mabry and Andrew J. Tribble of Blues Heaven for their assistance in arranging my meetings with Willie Dixon's family. I would like to express my most sincere appreciation to Dixon's family members: Shirli Dixon, Arthur "Butch" Dixon, Jacqueline Dixon, and Marie Dixon. Thank you for spending hours with me and sharing your family stories.

I want to thank Dr. Anand Prahlad, whose African American literature class gave me the basic concept for this work—the significance of the preacher in African American culture. Much gratitude is expressed to my dissertation committee: Dr. Anne Dhu McLucas, Dr. Mark Levy, Dr. Ben Saunders, Dr. Marian Smith, and Professor Carl Woideck. I also thank Dr. Ed Coleman, who ensured that I was on the right path in the final phase of writing a dissertation.

I thank all of the research participants: Billy Branch, Bo Diddley, Vernell Jennings, Bob Koester, and Koko Taylor. I give special thanks to my peer reviewers: Dr. Kip Lornell, Dr. Barry Lee Pearson, and Dr. David Evans. Their profound knowledge and constructive criticism provided me with some of the most valuable information on my work.

For their contribution in obtaining documents, inspiration, and warm friendship, I thank Naoaki Arima, William E. Anderson, Sumito Ariyoshi, Greg Drust, Les Fancourt, Martha Gomez, Chuck Haddix, Mark Hoffman, Takeshi Imura, Fernando Jones, Raenie Kane, Fred Murschall, Kenji Oda, Karl Payne, Masaru Saeki, Matthew "Sarge" Sargis, Greg Sutherland, and Roger Williams.

I would like to thank Peter Amft, whose photo for the cover of the book has made this work very special. For their generosity to donate their photo collections, I thank Mary Katherine Aldin, Paul Natkin, Scott Shigley, and Roger Williams and Matthew Genthe of Chicago Public Library.

My special thanks goes to Jim O'Neal, for his kindness to share his knowledge, as well as his collection of Willie Dixon documents: unpublished interviews, photos, rare records, and many e-mail correspondences.

My very special gratitude is extended to the editors at the Scarecrow Press—Stephen Ryan, Dr. William Banfield, Corinne Burton, and Jessica McCleary—and copyeditor Gail Fay. I also thank publisher and editorial director Edward Kurdyla; designer Neil Cotterill; Jared Hughes in marketing; and Lisa McAllister, Sam Caggiula, and Emily Todd in publicity. I appreciate all of your help to give my work a life after dissertation. Thank you.

Most of all, I would like to thank my parents, Terumi and Shuko Inaba. Your encouragement, understanding, and constant support are greatly appreciated.

And to my wife, Pam, and daughter, Aria—you two are my true inspiration. Thank you for putting up with me over the years and listening to my stories. There will be more.

This work is 100 percent my responsibility. I am still finding new information with which I will update this study. I would highly appreciate your thoughts, opinions, and any stories regarding Willie Dixon and his fellow musicians. Please contact me through the Scarecrow Press or mit64@comcast.net.

Permissions

"21 days in Jail" (*Willie Dixon and L.P. Weaver*)
© 1965 (Renewed 1993) HOOCHIE COOCHIE MUISC (BMI)/ADMINISTERED BY BUG MUSIC and ARC MUSIC CORPORTATION (BMI)
All Rights Reserved Used by Permission
Reprinted by permission of Hal Leonard Corporation

"Built for Comfort" (*Willie Dixon*)
© 1959 HOOCHIE COOCHI MUSIC (BMI) ADMINISTERED BY BUG MUSIC

"Catfish Blues" (*Robert Petway*)
Copyright © 1941, 1947 SONGS OF UNIVERSAL, INC.
Copyright Renewed
This arrangement Copyright © 2011 SONGS OF UNIVERSAL, INC.
All Rights Reserved Used by Permission
Reprinted by permission of Hal Leonard Corporation

"Catfish Blues" ("Rollin' Stone") (*McKinley Morganfield*)
© 1960 (Renewed 1988) WATERTOONS MUSIC (BMI)/ADMINISTERED BY
   BUG MUSIC
This arrangement © 2011 WATERTOONS MUSIC (BMI)/ ADMINISTERED BY
   BUG MUSIC
All Rights Reserved Used by Permission
Reprinted by permission of Hal Leonard Corporation

"Choo Choo Ch' Boogie" (*Vaughn Horton, Denver Darling, and Milton Gabler*)
© 1945 (Renewed) RYTVOC, INC.
Reprinted by permission of Hal Leonard Corporation
This arrangement © 2011 RYTVOC, INC.
All Rights Reserved Used by Permission
Reprinted by permission of Hal Leonard Corporation

"Close to You" ("Close to Me") (*Willie Dixon*)
© 1984 HOOCHIE COOCHI MUSIC (BMI) ADMINISTERED BY BUG MUSIC

"Cool Kind Woman" (*Willie Dixon*)
© HOOCHIE COOCHI MUSIC (BMI) ADMINISTERED BY BUG MUSIC

"Crazy Love" (*Willie Dixon*)
© 1990 HOOCHIE COOCHI MUSIC (BMI) ADMINISTERED BY BUG MUSIC

"Crazy Mixed Up World" (*Willie Dixon*)
© 1984 HOOCHIE COOCHI MUSIC (BMI) ADMINISTERED BY BUG MUSIC

"Dead Presidents" (*Willie Dixon and Billy Emerson*)
© 1964 (Renewed 1992) HOOCHIE COOCHIE MUISC (BMI)/ADMINISTERED
   BY BUG MUSIC and ARC MUSIC CORPORTATION (BMI)
All Rights Reserved Used by Permission
Reprinted by permission of Hal Leonard Corporation

"Hoochie Coochie Man" (*Willie Dixon*)
© 1957 HOOCHIE COOCHI MUSIC (BMI) ADMINISTERED BY BUG MUSIC

"I Ain't Superstitious" (*Willie Dixon*)
© 1970 HOOCHIE COOCHI MUSIC (BMI) ADMINISTERED BY BUG MUSIC

"I Am the Blues" (*Willie Dixon*)
© 1984 HOOCHIE COOCHI MUSIC (BMI) ADMINISTERED BY BUG MUSIC

"I Am the Lover Man" (*Willie Dixon and Eleanor Broadwater*)
© 1955 (Renewed 1983) HOOCHIE COOCHIE MUISC (BMI)/ADMINISTERED
   BY BUG MUSIC and ARC MUSIC CORPORTATION (BMI)
All Rights Reserved Used by Permission
Reprinted by permission of Hal Leonard Corporation

"I Can't Quit You Baby" (*Willie Dixon*)
© 1970 HOOCHIE COOCHI MUSIC (BMI) ADMINISTERED BY BUG MUSIC

"I Don't Care Who Knows" (*Willie Dixon*)
© HOOCHIE COOCHI MUSIC (BMI) ADMINISTERED BY BUG MUSIC

"I Don't Play" (*Willie Dixon*)
© 1984 HOOCHIE COOCHI MUSIC (BMI) ADMINISTERED BY BUG MUSIC

"I Got a Razor" (*Willie Dixon*)
© 1959 HOOCHIE COOCHI MUSIC (BMI) ADMINISTERED BY BUG MUSIC

"I Got All You Need" (*Willie Dixon*)
© 1991 HOOCHIE COOCHI MUSIC (BMI) ADMINISTERED BY BUG MUSIC

"I Got My Brand on You" (*Willie Dixon*)
© 1984 HOOCHIE COOCHI MUSIC (BMI) ADMINISTERED BY BUG MUSIC

"I Got What It Takes" (*Willie Dixon*)
© 1984 HOOCHIE COOCHI MUSIC (BMI) ADMINISTERED BY BUG MUSIC

"I Just Want to Make Love to You" (*Willie Dixon*)
© 1962 HOOCHIE COOCHI MUSIC (BMI) ADMINISTERED BY BUG MUSIC

"I Love the Life I Live, I Live the Life I Love" (*Willie Dixon*)
© 1984 HOOCHIE COOCHI MUSIC (BMI) ADMINISTERED BY BUG MUSIC

"Rattin' and Runnin' Around" (*Willie Dixon and Eddie Boyd*)
© 1953 (Renewed 1981) HOOCHIE COOCHIE MUISC (BMI)/ADMINISTERED
  BY BUG MUSIC and ARC MUSIC CORPORTATION (BMI)
All Rights Reserved Used by Permission
Reprinted by permission of Hal Leonard Corporation

"Same Thing (The)" (*Willie Dixon*)
© 1984 HOOCHIE COOCHI MUSIC (BMI) ADMINISTERED BY BUG MUSIC

"Seventh Son" (*Willie Dixon*)
© 1970 HOOCHIE COOCHIE MUSIC (BMI) ADMINISTERED BY BUG MUSIC

"Sit and Cry" (*Willie Dixon*)
© 1991 HOOCHIE COOCHIE MUSIC (BMI) ADMINISTERED BY BUG MUSIC

"Spoonful" (*Willie Dixon*)
© 1970 HOOCHIE COOCHIE MUSIC (BMI) ADMINISTERED BY BUG MUSIC

"Spoonful Blues" (*Charley Patton*)
© 1998 EMI LONGTITUDE MUSIC
All Rights Reserved International Copyright Secured Used by Permission
Reprinted by permission of Hal Leonard Corporation

"Still a Fool" (*McKinley Morganfield*)
© 1959 (Renewed 1987) WATERTOONS MUSIC (BMI)/ADMINISTERED BY
  BUG MUSIC
This arrangement © 2011 WATERTOONS MUSIC (BMI)/ADMINISTERED BY
  BUG MUSIC
All Rights Reserved Used by Permission
Reprinted by permission of Hal Leonard Corporation

"Tail Dragger" (*Willie Dixon*)
© 1984 HOOCHIE COOCHIE MUSIC (BMI) ADMINISTERED BY BUG MUSIC

"Tell That Woman" (*Willie Dixon*)
© 1990 HOOCHIE COOCHI MUSIC (BMI) ADMINISTERED BY BUG MUSIC

"Third Degree" (*Willie Dixon / Eddie Boyd*)
© 1952, 1953 (Renewed) HOOCHIE COOCHIE MUSIC (BMI)/ADMINISTERED
  BY BUG MUSIC and ARC MUSIC CORP. (BMI)
ARC MUSIC CORP. ADMINISTERED BY BMG CHRYSALIS for the world ex-
  cluding Japan and Southeast Asia
All Rights Reserved Used by Permission
Reprinted by permission of Hal Leonard Corporation

Introduction

It would have taken 10 guys to do the things he did.

—Keith Richards, on Willie Dixon's contributions to the
modern blues and American popular music scenes[1]

As a songwriter, arranger, producer, and bassist for Chess Records (1953–
1956 and 1958–1971) and Cobra Records (1956–1958), two of the most
important record companies in the Chicago blues scene, Willie Dixon
(1915–1992) was an innovative force in the development and maturation
of postwar electric Chicago blues. Yet, as Barry Lee Pearson and Bill Mc-
Culloch claim in their book *Robert Johnson: Lost and Found* (2003), "Dixon's
songs, most of which were written for other Chess artists, have never been
put under a microscope the way [Robert] Johnson's have."[2] My intention
with this book, which was originally a doctoral dissertation submitted to the
University of Oregon (2005), is to do just that.

As a house songwriter, Dixon provided songs for artists such as Muddy
Waters, Howlin' Wolf, Little Walter, Sonny Boy Williamson, Bo Diddley,
Willie Mabon, Buddy Guy, Otis Rush, and Koko Taylor. Dixon's composi-
tions premiered by these artists include "(I'm Your) Hoochie Coochie Man,"
"I Just Want to Make Love to You," "I'm Ready," "Spoonful," "Back Door
Man," "Little Red Rooster," "My Babe," "Bring It on Home," "You Can't
Judge a Book by Its Cover," "The Seventh Son," "Let Me Love You Baby,"
"I Can't Quit You Baby," and "Wang Dang Doodle." The commercial and

artistic success with these songs was a testament to Dixon's ability to capture the performers' personalities in song.

Yet the compositions were only a part of what made Willie Dixon who he was. Dixon was also the man with the standup bass, calling the shots as an arranger and producer. Dixon's bass was an indispensable backbone in the Chess studio sounds. His assistance not only helped blues artists but also propelled rock 'n' roll classics such as Chuck Berry's "Maybellene" and "Roll Over Beethoven."

Then there was Willie Dixon, ambassador of the blues, who, through his work for the American Folk Blues Festival in Europe in the early 1960s, strongly influenced the British popular music scene. Here, his compositions became important in the repertoires of the bands leading the scene then: the Rolling Stones, Cream, Jeff Beck Group (with Rod Stewart), and Led Zeppelin. It was through these artists' interpretations in studio recordings and live performances that many rock music listeners got to know Dixon's works. I am no exception. One of the first blues songs I ever heard was Dixon's "Little Red Rooster," included in the Rolling Stones' live album *Love You Live* in 1977. At the time, I was a junior high school student in the small town of Hiroshima, Japan.

It goes without saying that Dixon was a commercial songwriter. But in time, he became much more: a blues philosopher, a blues educator, and a blues visionary. Around the beginning of the 1960s, he became aware of the importance of documenting and spreading what the blues meant for him. During his lifetime, Dixon left a considerable number of interviews and two books: his autobiography, *I Am the Blues* (1989), and a collection of his representative compositions, *Willie Dixon: The Master Blues Composer* (1992).

A part of Dixon's passion for talking about the blues arose from his feeling that many books about the blues—written by the scholars of the time—failed to discuss what he felt the blues truly meant for African Americans. In an unpublished interview for *Living Blues*, Dixon told editor Jim O'Neal,

> It's a wide range that's in [the blues] that nobody that have [sic] been touching it has been able to say anything about. . . . And they all think blues means hard times and troubles and all this kind of stuff. That's just a part of it. But the better part of the blues, world don't know, because the blues has caused the black man to survive through all the humiliations and all this [sic] various things been going on in America ever since there's been an America.[3]

My intention in this book is to discuss the meaning of Dixon's compositions in an African American cultural context. In this sense, the main idea of this work is somewhat similar to the Robert Johnson book by Pearson and McCulloch in which they present interpretations of Johnson's songs based more on African American cultural and folklore studies.[4]

To Dixon's mind, "The Blues is the true facts of life expressed in words and songs with feeling, inspiration and understanding. The most important aspect of the Blues is its wisdom."[5] In light of this statement by the one who assertively claimed, "I am the blues," and considering how influential he was in the blues scene, it is difficult to find descriptions and interpretations of his songs that reflect such a deep appreciation. For example, how do we reconcile the quest for wisdom with such Dixon creations as "Hoochie Coochie Man"? The song "I Just Want to Make Love to You" is apparently about machismo, but is blatant sexual appetite all that Dixon wanted to express through Muddy's performance? While song lyrics can be interpreted in many different ways, what does this particular song mean in an African American cultural context upon understanding their concept of sexuality? What made Dixon decide to give a didactic song like "Spoonful" to Howlin' Wolf, the same man he cast as an ominous figure in "Back Door Man"? These are some of the questions I seek to answer in this book.

The blues consists of a complex worldview. Folklore researcher Bruce Bastin writes, "The blues emerged from violent socio-cultural changes; at the turn of the century a cultural change in the life-style of the lowest class of blacks found expression in a new musical direction."[6] Similarly African American study researcher Clyde Woods writes, "The blues courageously explores the origins, varieties, and consequence of life lived in a brutal and loveless society. It is also the voice of those who are dedicated to the preservation of their humanity."[7]

While the blues is a musical phenomenon that occurred around the turn of the twentieth century, it has much deeper roots, going all the way back to the origins of the slave trade. In the documentary *The Full Moon Show with Robbie Robertson*, Willie Dixon discusses the African tradition of story telling as one of the important roots of the blues:

> It [the blues] actually didn't spring out of the ground of [the Mississippi Delta]. They say heritage that was created generations ago, and people brought it here from Africa. And this particular heritage, as you know, many generations ago, African people were always told stories. They, people, was always anxious to let the world know exactly what was going on.[8]

In African culture, as in many others, storytelling does not function simply as entertainment. A far more important role is to pass on lessons that they learned in the past—to impart wisdom. Media study researcher William Barlow writes that cautionary folktales played an important role in early blues:

> They [blues songs] were a mix of personal sentiments and collective memory. They were focused on the present, but they were framed in the folklore of the past. Many rural blues were "cautionary folktales" designed to uphold traditional values and foster group cohesion: they were commonsense lessons on how to survive in America as have-nots.[9]

In communities where illiteracy was the norm and oral forms were the principal means of education, blues performers often served an especially important role—that of educators. While religion and the blues have often been at odds with one another—particularly with regard to the content of songs—some blues performers have seen themselves, and have been seen by others, as serving roles with interesting parallels to African American preachers, another kind of educator in the black communities. This was certainly the case with Willie Dixon. His daughter, the late Shirli Dixon, defined her father as a blues preacher: "He was a blues preacher. He was a life preacher. And he also believed that he was a minister of the blues."[10]

Although I had never heard the term *blues preacher* until Shirli Dixon said it to me, folklorists, poets, theologians, and researchers have long discussed the religious nature of the blues. African American theologian James H. Cone's "The Blues: A Secular Spiritual" in *The Spirituals and the Blues: An Interpretation* (1972) and African American folklorist Jon Michael Spencer's *Blues and Evil* (1993) are some of the most representative studies of the religious function and theological understanding of the blues in African American communities, although some scholars disagree with their studies.[11]

According to Cone, "The blues are 'secular spirituals.' They are secular in the sense that they confine their attention solely to the immediate and affirm the bodily expression of black soul, including its sexual manifestations. They are spirituals because they are impelled by the same search for the truth of black experience."[12]

In his book, Spencer discusses a characteristic Southern folk belief that he sees in Delta blues, which he calls "blues-based ethics"[13] or "blues belief,"[14] in which existentialism and Christianity coexist. Spencer summarizes, "Thus, the blues was *not* of church, but 'blues belief' (and therefore blues people) existed only on the periphery of the doctrinal enclave of Christianity."[15] In this sense, singing blues was an attempt to come to grips with a world ruled by a good god where evil is allowed to exist.[16]

Dixon shares a similar perspective. He compares the function of blues with that of spirituals:

> The blues can be about anything pertaining to the facts of life. The blues call on God as much as a spiritual song do [sic]. The blues calls on love as much as a love song do. The blues call on happiness and understanding. The blues calls on the sadness as prayer do. The blues calls on working—even working on the railroad and chopping cotton, they could always build a rhythm up to this that made it the blues.[17]

Willie Dixon's songs, too, are located along the continuum of the blues beliefs, and there is a strong parallel between his religious view and that of the Delta blues performers whom Cone and Spencer discuss. Understanding this is a key to reading Dixon's songs.

As research has shown, the origin of Chicago blues was in Delta blues. That is, the musical tradition of the Deep South was transported to the North via the massive migration of African Americans in the first half of the twentieth century. And the musical tradition that they brought was eventually transformed by the urban environment through the electrification of instruments and the absorption of narratives about city life.

Much of this transition can be seen directly in the work of Willie Dixon, who, coming from Vicksburg, Mississippi, to Chicago, applied what he inherited from the rural South blues tradition to the postwar electric blues.

In order to present this comprehensive study of Willie Dixon, I have relied not just on historical research but also on fieldwork and interviews with people who had personal and/or professional relationships with him. Especially, two of Dixon's children, Shirli and Arthur "Butch" Dixon—both of whom passed recently—spent hours with me sharing stories that their father told them, their memories of life with him, and insights into his work.

Throughout the book, I will make use of Dixon's own words, but the sources I quote from the most are the less common ones. This book is not intended to be a basic introduction to Willie Dixon. Such an introduction already exists in the form of his autobiography *I Am the Blues* as well as in numerous blues history books and dictionaries.[18]

The musical analysis and examination of Dixon's arranging and production techniques discussed in this book are based on the available recordings. I have avoided extremely detailed musical notation, such as indicating slight pitch bends or the rhythmic nuances heard in Muddy Waters' vocal lines, because the level of meaning I am describing is not revealed in such precise musical analysis. I limit myself to showing the core ingredients of a composition—such as characteristic riffs, hooks, and verses consisting of the repetition of a few pitches—that Dixon often uses. For greater subtleties of interpretation, readers should turn directly to the recordings themselves.

The transcriptions of lyrics are mostly based on listening to recordings, unless printed versions are available. I have tried to transcribe as precisely as possible, but some parts were unintelligible as I marked in the transcriptions. In some cases, I have corrected sections of printed versions when I discovered discrepancies from my listening. My transcriptions of lyrics follow standard English practice, but I also observe obvious vernacular variations; for example, *walkin'* instead of *walking*, and *womens* instead of *women*.

Because the focus of this book is Willie Dixon, it does not include all the compositions recorded by the artists he worked with, such as Muddy Waters and Howlin' Wolf. In addition, the discussions and analyses of Dixon's songs are meant to be informed by his particular point of view, as documented by his own writings and by interviews with his close associates. This book is a cultural study and an aesthetic-historical study, from the point of view of one important composer of the Chicago blues tradition. And this book is also a collection of memories of the Chicago bluesman as told by his family members and fiends.

I hope that my research on Willie Dixon will contribute to revealing the spirit of his blues classics and that the following chapters will lead us to a new appreciation of one segment of American culture that has often been overlooked. As Dixon once wrote, "When I go to the source, the root of all American music, I find out it was the blues to begin with. All American music comes from the blues. We put the roots down. It was like discovering America."[19]

Notes

1. Keith Richards, quoted in *Willie Dixon's Blues Heaven Foundation's Record Row Festival* [concert brochure] (Chicago: Willie Dixon, 2002).

2. Barry Lee Pearson and Bill McCulloch, *Robert Johnson: Lost and Found* (Urbana: University of Illinois Press, 2003), 69.

3. Willie Dixon, interview by Jim O'Neal, December 6, 1978.

4. Pearson and McCulloch, *Robert Johnson*, 70–86.

5. Willie Dixon, *Willie Dixon: The Master Blues Composer* (Milwaukee: Hal Leonard, 1992), 8.

6. Bruce Bastin, *Red River Blues: The Blues Tradition in the Southeast* (Urbana: University of Illinois Press, 1986; repr., 1995), 19.

7. Clyde Woods, *Development Arrested: The Blues and Plantation Power in the Mississippi Delta* (New York: Verso, 1998), 288.

8. *The Full Moon Show with Robbie Robertson* [broadcast] (Hollywood: One Heart Productions, Video Arts Japan, Japan Satellite Broadcasting, 1991).

9. William Barlow, *Looking Up at Down: The Emergence of Blues Culture* (Philadelphia: Temple University Press, 1989), 4.

10. Shirli Dixon, interview by the author, September 23, 2002.

11. For example, blues researcher David Evans is one of the scholars who disagrees with this concept. He wrote in the review for my manuscript, "'Secular spirituals' is an awkward concept. Why not then call spirituals 'religious blues'? There is actually a term 'gospel blues' used by some scholars to describe gospel songs—though not usually describe spirituals. I find it equally awkward. There are, of course, commonalities, but most performers of blues or spirituals make sharp distinctions between them." David Evans, "A Review for Mitsutoshi Inaba's Manuscript," June 10, 2008, p. 2.

12. James H. Cone, *The Spirituals and the Blues: An Interpretation* (New York: Seabury Press, 1972; repr., Maryknoll, NY: Orbis Books, 2000), 100. Citations are to the Orbis Books edition.

13. Jon Michael Spencer, *Blues and Evil* (Knoxville: University of Tennessee Press, 1993), xxiii.

14. Ibid.

15. Ibid.

16. Ibid., 69.

17. Willie Dixon, with Don Snowden, *I Am the Blues: The Willie Dixon Story* (New York: Da Capo Press, 1989), 2.

18. Some representative books include Lawrence Cohn, ed., *Nothing but the Blues: The Music and the Musicians* (New York: Abbeville Press, 1993); Francis Davis, *The History of the Blues: The Roots, the Music, the People from Charley Patton to Robert Cray* (New York: Hyperion, 1995); Vladimir Bogdanov, Chris Woodstra, and Stephan Thomas Erlewine, eds., *All Music Guide to the Blues: The Definitive Guide to the Blues*, 3rd ed. (San Francisco: Backbeat Books, 2003).

19. Worth Long, "The Wisdom of the Blues—Defining as the True Facts of life: An Interview with Willie Dixon," *African American Review* 29, no. 2 (Summer 1995): 212. Obviously not "all American music comes from the blues." This exaggerated statement by Dixon reflects his political view that was nurtured through his experiences as an African American. As I will discuss, Dixon believed black heritage and its contribution to American culture were often disregarded.

~

CHAPTER ONE

Dixon's Youth: The Cultural Basis for the New Interpretation of Dixon's Compositions

Willie James Dixon was born on July 1, 1915, in Vicksburg, Warren County, then the second-largest city in Mississippi and an important trade base located between Memphis and New Orleans. According to the 1910 U.S. census, the population of Vicksburg was 20,814—8,754 European Americans; 12,053 African Americans; and 7 from Asian countries (India and China).[1]

Dixon's family lived in the north end of this city. His mother was Daisy A. Dixon (née McKenzie, 1893–1974), and his father was Anderson "A. D." Bell (unknown birth year–1928); the name Dixon was taken from Daisy's first husband, Charlie Dixon, whom she married in 1903 and divorced in 1912. As he later memorialized in his song "The Seventh Son," Willie Dixon was the seventh of fourteen children, and one of seven who survived.

At times Daisy worked as a janitor for a local church, Spring Hill Baptist Church, and she also ran a restaurant and a laundry.[2] Willie's older sister Rose describes this restaurant as "some nice business,"[3] but the Dixons experienced living in severe poverty, as did many blacks in the rural South of the early twentieth century. Willie remembers there was a time his mother "made two dollars a week, and rent and everybody's food had to come out [of] that."[4] In order to help put food on the table, Willie and his siblings spent time scrounging for junk to sell.[5]

During Willie's youth, racism was an inevitable, everyday experience. White children were known to chase black children home from school, throwing rocks and bricks.[6] On one occasion, Dixon saw Ku Klux Klan members marching by his house dragging a black man. He also knew a local sheriff who raped a black woman with impunity.[7]

While many blacks in the rural South at this time had little opportunity to receive formal education, Daisy was literate. Her eagerness to educate her children, especially in language skills, played a large part in Dixon's growing interest in words and poetry. He remembers,

> My mother always wanted to teach us a speech as soon as we was big enough to walk on the stage. I was so small I couldn't even get up on a one-step platform to say the speech. They had to help me up there and the speech I said was, "Here I stand on two little chips / Please come kiss my sweet little lips." She taught me that when I was about four years old. The first thing I ever learned to say on my own was a poem so this could have been starting me towards getting poem ideas.[8]

Dixon's daughter, Shirli Dixon, says the most important nature her father inherited from his mother was a sense of optimism:

> To know her would be to know a person that really did not see any controversy. She always saw opportunity. One of the things that my dad used to tell me that she said to him as a kid was "There's something good in everything you look at." And so she'd point to, maybe some animal that had been hit or something, she'd say, "Look how white these teeth are." No matter what it was, she could find something positive.[9]

Daisy was a pious Christian. In her free time, she wrote prayer poems; one of them is included in Willie Dixon's funeral pamphlet:

> God is my refuge and my strength
> He is my all in all;
> He leads me each day I live,
> And hold me lest I fall.[10]

Dixon's father, Anderson Bell, did not live with Dixon's family. Daisy did not want him around her house because he provided little financial support. Moreover, he was a troublemaker with a fondness for guns; he was known to have shot at white people.[11] He accidently died when he was working at the sawmill. Willie was thirteen years old then.[12]

Regardless of Bell's less-than-positive influence and short life, Shirli Dixon associated her father's will to fight against racial inequality with her grandfather's struggles.

My dad often told me that my grandfather was a no-nonsense kind of a man.
. . . He thought he didn't hate people who were not of color, but he also did
not believe that they have a right to misuse it. He did speak often of his father
being very strong willed, and I believe that what may have been inherited from
my grandfather was the ability to operate in environments where black people
were not necessarily respected.[13]

Contrary to Daisy, Bell was skeptical about organized religion. Dixon's
son, Butch Dixon, speaks of the difference in his grandparents' religious
views:

His [Willie's] dad was one of those people who's cut and dried. What he said
was what he felt. My grandmother, on the other hand, was "If a preacher said
it, it had to be true." And my grandfather would always tell her, "A preacher
is no closer to God than any other man. He's a man like I'm a man. So what
makes any difference between what I say and what he says?"[14]

As was the case with Anderson Bell, during and even after slavery, not all
African Americans accepted Christianity for their spiritual and moral needs
for several reasons. Some African Americans knew that Christianity was initially imposed in part as a code to control slaves.[15] Dixon said of his father's
religious views, "He thought the Christian thing was just psychologizing
people so they could be under control."[16] Dixon recognized the hypocrisy of
Christian ideology for himself:

You know, the Black people in America had all their things they got from
white slave owners down there; and the owners would tell them anything
they wanted to, to *use* them with. They had to control the slaves anyway they
possibly could. And they wanted them to believe praying was going to help
them in the next world. They was brainwashing the Black people with spiritual
ideas—teaching them the Bible and telling them about how they could fly to
heaven and all this kind of stuff.[17]

In the process of assimilation, those African Americans who accepted
Christianity had more opportunities to enter mainstream American society
and become middle class. On the other hand, some working-class blacks
viewed the middle class as controlled or—as in Dixon's description—
"psychologized" by European Americans.

Although blacks generally accepted the doctrines of Christianity,
they understood that providing solutions for everyday reality, especially

life-threatening problems such as lynching, was not the church's main concern. As Albert Murray notes,

> The church is not concerned with affirmation of life as such, which in its view is only a matter of feeble flesh to begin with. The church is committed to the eternal salvation of the soul after death, which is both final and inevitable. Human existence is only a brief sojourn in a vale of trials, troubles, and tribulations to be endured because it is the will of the Creator, whose ways are mysterious.[18]

Another perceived problem of the church was that its ministers did not always practice what they preached. As Frank Stokes sang in the early 1920s, "Some folks said that a preacher wouldn't steal / I caught about eleven in a watermelon field."[19]

In addition, some blacks rejected organized religion based on the institution's ambivalent attitude toward sexuality. In particular, the Protestant church's insistence on the division of body and spirit was something not everyone in the African American community could accept, because they believed that God is responsible for the whole of creation, including the human body. Therefore, physicality is not sinful but is as sacred as spirituality. James H. Cone writes about the divine nature of the body for blacks:

> Indeed, for black people, existence is a form of celebration. It is joy, love, and sex. It is hugging, kissing, and feeling. People cannot love physically and spiritually (the two cannot be separated!) until they have been up against the edge of life, experiencing the hurt and pain of existence. They cannot appreciate the feel and touch of life nor express the beauty of giving themselves to each other in unity, in love, and in sex until they know and experience the brokenness of existence as disclosed in human oppression.[20]

Possibly for these reasons, the two opposite views of Christianity—holding to Christianity's values and skepticism toward such belief—caused disagreement in some members of the African American community, the Dixon family among them. Eventually, in trying to reconcile the differences between his parents, Dixon reached his own view of religion: "I have nothin' against no religion, but when you go to think about it, Baptist, Holy Roller, Presbyterian, Catholic, Saint Luke, Saint John, Jim Jones, snake kissers—all of them are supposed to be goin' to the same heaven. And yet, still, they fall out over two dollars down here. And they're goin' to a place where the streets are paved with gold!"[21]

Nevertheless, to say Dixon was an atheist would be an oversimplification.[22] While Dixon once mentioned that he did not believe "in any religion,"[23] it appears he meant that he did not belong to any religious organization. Shirli Dixon explains her father's religious views:

> My dad did not really believe [in] any form of organized religion because he felt that it only complicated matters, and that if we simply would obey God in the form of treating each other equally and respecting each other. . . . He had some difficulty with all of the different titles that came along with claiming to love and honor God and live right with each other as human beings.
>
> His childhood experiences may have initially had an impact on his worldview, but my dad loved people, and he loved life and he loved God. He was a true man of God. . . . My mom will tell you my dad made that reference all the time: "I belong to this world. God put me in this world." He never thought himself just as my dad or her husband or father of twelve children. He believed he belonged to this world.[24]

This tension between a religiously strict upbringing and a more liberal worldview would also have a lasting effect on Dixon's life philosophy as well as on his taste in music.

> I was raised up on blues and spirituals; but after you wake up to a lot of facts about life, you know, the spiritual thing start to look kind of phony in places. So this is one of the reasons I guess I took off to the blues. I like the blues and I stick to the blues, because the blues gives you a chance to express your feelings. And it's wrote on facts . . . not phony.[25]

While Willie Dixon had no trouble finding space in his life for both spirituality and the blues, his mother proved far less flexible. Butch Dixon recalls,

> She thought the blues had no place for anyone to listen to. It was bad music or sad music. It told a story about either man cheating or woman cheating. . . . My dad's view of blues was, however, what he experienced in life. My dad used to always say, "The blues are the true facts of life expressed in songs. If you have some problems in your life, whether be good or bad, that's the blues."[26]

Shirli Dixon explains that her father and grandmother's disagreement over the respective virtues of the blues and gospel music came down to one core difference:

> One of the things that my dad taught me about gospel music as opposed to blues music was . . . actually both of them called on the Lord just as much as

the other. One of them called for relief in life, and another one for relief after life. . . . It took many many years before she was even accepting it. I was a kid when I remembered my dad finally saying . . . (we called her Big Mama), "I think Big Mama is finally going to accept the reality of the blues." I think she was like ninety years old by the time he was able to actually feel that she was accepting him.[27]

Willie Dixon's view of the blues that it expresses "the life here and now"[28] and his existential philosophy—"the experience you receive on earth was the only thing you had to go on because nobody had the experience of heaven"[29]—correspond well to what James H. Cone writes of the key to understanding the blues:

Historical experience, as interpreted by the black community, is the key to an understanding of the blues. Black people accepted the dictum: Truth is experience, and experience is the Truth. If it is lived and encountered, then it is real. There is no attempt in the blues to make philosophical distinctions between divine and human truth. That is why many blues people reject the contention that the blues are vulgar and dirty.[30]

Similarly, Angela Nelson writes about the importance of truth telling in African American culture, arguing that it is one of the ethical values traditionally held most dear, that it "is used as a way of maintaining self-dignity and holding at bay the oppositional myths the oppressors have used to control African Americans."[31]

Although there is a clear-cut difference between the philosophy of the blues and that of gospel music, the sacred and secular have often been combined in practice. For Dixon, the blues and sacred scriptures were inextricably linked:

I know many people think most of the Blues began with a particular song or artist. But I believe the Blues has been inside of us since human beginnings. According to the oldest history, when man was created, he became blue and lonesome, so woman was created to relieve man of these feelings. . . . So after man and woman increased the population, rules and laws were set up to control the people. From then on man ruled by either force and/or laws. When man wanted to continue to dominate the world he carried his laws, rules, messages and teachings to the next generation. . . . Most of these holy books were combined to make one holy book—what we call The Holy Bible. All the holy books of the various nations talked about giving good advice and this advice was made in statements, in the form of clichés and poems. . . . Now most of these various clichés and poems express the need to have a better understanding for a better future.[32]

Dixon saw the blues as generally the same educational function as scripture that provides knowledge and insight for leading a good life. For this reason, he often made a point of embedding bits of wisdom in his compositions. William Barlow writes that the nature of the wisdom contained in the blues text "focused on the everyday lives of the black masses—their working conditions, living conditions, prison experiences, travels, and sexual relationships. The texts fall into two broad categories: cautionary folktales—lessons on how to survive in a hostile environment—and prideful songs of self-assertion."[33]

To the extent that some blues musicians—like Willie Dixon—saw themselves as educators of their community, their role in many ways paralleled that of the preachers of organized religious institutions. Dixon's longtime wife, Marie Dixon, concurs with Shirli Dixon's vision of her father as "a blues preacher."[34]

> He could quote anything in the Bible, because that's the way he was raised by his mother . . . but he was considered a blues minister. His mother wanted him, on the other hand, to be a gospel minister talking about once you're gone. He wanted to talk about why we are here. . . . We all agree on the same thing—he was a blues preacher. If there was a blues, he just was a man of knowledge that understood the world. And he wanted to put it in the music form so people could sing about it and enjoy. He wanted you to be loved, and he wanted you to understand the facts of life. I heard of him saying in many interviews that if peoples analyze what he say, it will be a better world.[35]

In African American popular music performances, the charisma and showmanship of Pentecostal/holiness/sanctified preachers has constructed an idiomatic model for performers.[36] One important quality of the blues performer was his or her ability to uplift, just like an enthusiastic preacher would do to his congregations. As Ralph Ellison notes of Bessie Smith,

> Bessie Smith might have been a "blues queen" to the society at large, but within the tighter Negro community where the blues were part of a total way of life, and a major expression of an attitude toward life, she was a priestess, a celebrant who affirmed the values of the group and man's ability to deal with chaos.[37]

These qualities observed in city blues performance were also very much present in the Delta blues. Referring to early Delta blues, music writer Robert Palmer writes, "Blues musicians were well aware that their singing was comparable to preaching, both in style and in the effect it could have had on an audience."[38] Muddy Waters saw clear analogies between his mentor, Son House, and a Baptist preacher: "That guy could preach the blues . . . sit down there and sing one thing after 'nother, like a preacher."[39] In fact, House's singing style was highly influenced by Reverend J. M. Gates, a popular preacher from the mid-1920s through the early 1940s. Over time, this "preaching" tradition was carried on from the Delta blues to the electric Chicago blues. Even some religious figures recognized the similarities. Muddy's cousin, Elve Morganfield, recollects that his father, Lewis Mathews Morganfield, a Baptist minister, frequently told Muddy "he was gon' preach, because if you notice, he had a lot of that in his singing."[40]

Some blues artists believed that blues was, like gospel music, not just a musical exercise. Muddy recognizes its therapeutic power:

The blues are an expression of trouble in mind, trouble in body, trouble in soul. And when a man has a trouble, it helps him to express it, to let it to be known. When a person thinks he's the only one in hot water, he's miserable. But when he gets to realize that others have the same kind of trouble—or even worse—he understands that life isn't just picking on him alone.[41]

And Dixon states that one of the functions of the blues is a communication tool: "The people, regardless of what condition an individual is in, they want to be in better shape. They believe in letting somebody know what condition they're in, in order to help themselves. Whether it's good, whether it's bad, right, or wrong."[42]

Koko Taylor, who sees Dixon as her mentor, also talks about a healing power of the blues in her performing context:

In my career, my singin', a lot of people ask me, "What is the blues?" To me, my music is like a therapy. My music is healin', you know? It's healin', it's therapy, it's encouragement. I try to sing the type of songs that make people happy. I try to sing a song that's gonna touch somebody, to make them look up, pep up, feel good about themselves, encourage them—have a lyric that will encourage them in some way or another.[43]

Dixon remembers that he first discovered the therapeutic power of blues and its function as a communication tool while serving a yearlong sentence

in Ball Ground County Farm, located in the north of Vicksburg. When he
was twelve years old (1928), he was caught stealing plumbing fixtures from
an abandoned house to put into his own:[44]

> That's when I really learned about the blues. I had heard 'em with the music
> and took 'em to be an enjoyable thing but after I heard these guys down there
> moaning and groaning these really down-to-earth blues, I began to inquire
> about 'em. I would ask guys why they sang these tunes and what does it mean
> and various ones would tell me. . . .
>
>   I really began to find out what the blues mean to black people, how it gave
> them consolation to be able to think these things over and sing them to them-
> selves or let other people know what they had in mind and how they resented
> various things in life. I guess it kind of rubbed off on me because after you see
> guys die and everybody living in hopes [sic].[45]

In the following year (1929), Dixon was again arrested, this time for
hoboing, and he was sent to Harvey Allen County Farm near Clarksdale.[46]
Violence was omnipresent here. Dixon saw a man beaten to death for the
first time, and one time Dixon was terribly whipped, which caused him to
lose hearing for nearly four years. Dixon remembers, "I go down there and
this guy took that damn strap and hit me upside the head and I stayed deaf for
almost four years. He knocked this big patch of skin off my face and I didn't
even know what the hell was up."[47]

Shirli Dixon heard from her father that this was an unforgettable experience:

> He told me that was very difficult existence. It was extremely difficult. He
> said that it took him years to stop remembering the screams and cries that he
> heard from the man that was beat to death. He said that destroyed great deal
> of his respect for the way that the government put together American lifestyle
> of people of color.[48]

Through these horrible experiences what Dixon discovered was that the
blues could serve as a survival tool:

> If it not been for the blues the black man wouldn't have been able to survive
> in the United States of America. Other people had other things to fight with.
> The black man didn't have nothin' but the blues and he survived much better
> than the majority. His thing has proved that blues has been understood by
> other people.[49]

Butch Dixon adds that the country farm was the place his father shaped his musical ideas:

> A lot of his thoughts from his old times and writings happened right there in the penitentiary cell. He would sing and whistle 'cause he could whistle better than anybody I ever heard in my life. He could sing and whistle his songs and keep them in his head. They didn't give him anything to write with because in those days you can't write. You weren't supposed to write down anything. You were black and you were inferior. . . . So some of those hardship and life experience he had, what helped him through in that penitentiary, there's one of those things helped him through was music.[50]

Dixon's experiences as African American man living in the rural South in the early twentieth century constructed the core of his compositions. His philosophy of the blues and its cultural background, the overlapping ideology of the blues and religion, and the quest for healing in real life provide the basis to interpret his works—the key to understanding Dixon's blues.

Notes

1. Department of Commerce, Bureau of the Census, *Thirteenth Census of the United States Taken in the Year 1910*, vol. 2, *Population 1910, Alabama–Montana*, Reports by States, with Statistics for Counties, Cities and Other Civil Divisions, director E. Dana Durand, Wm. J. Harris (Washington, DC: Department of Commerce, 1913), 1034.

2. Willie Dixon, with Don Snowden, *I Am the Blues: The Willie Dixon Story* (New York: Da Capo Press, 1989), 14.

3. Ibid., 15.

4. Anthony Connor and Robert Neff, *The Blues: In Images and Interviews* (Boston: D. R. Godine, 1975; repr., New York: Cooper Square Press, 1999), 39. Citations are to the Cooper Square Press edition.

5. Ibid.

6. Dixon, *I Am the Blues*, 20.

7. Ibid.

8. Ibid., 13.

9. Shirli Dixon, interview by the author, September 24, 2002.

10. *Blues Heaven Willie Dixon: Wednesday, February 5, 1992* [funeral pamphlet] (Chicago: Metropolitan Funeral Parlors, 1992), 17.

11. Dixon, *I Am the Blues*, 10.

12. Ibid.

13. Shirli Dixon, interview by the author, September 23, 2002.

14. Arthur "Butch" Dixon, interview by the author, September 23, 2003.

15. LeRoi Jones, *Blues People: The Negro Experience in White America and the Music That Developed from It* (New York: William Morrow, 1963), 38.

16. Worth Long, "The Wisdom of the Blues—Defining Blues as the True Facts of Life: An Interview with Willie Dixon." *African American Review* 29, no. 2 (Summer 1995): 208.

17. Connor and Neff, *The Blues*, 8–9.

18. Albert Murray, *Stomping the Blues*, 2nd ed. (New York: Vintage Books, 1982), 38. Bruce Bastin also writes,

> If the black intellectual was frustrated in his hopes, the lower-class blacks were no less so. Indeed, their frustrations frequently had no outlet except the church, which was often inadequate to relieve the repression that some blacks felt. Moreover, for some rural blacks, but perhaps even more for the young blacks who were forced to move in order to attempt to find work, the church was no answer.

Bastin, *Red River Blues: The Blues Tradition in the Southeast* (Urbana: University of Illinois Press, 1986; repr., 1995), 22.

19. William Barlow, *Looking Up at Down: The Emergence of Blues Culture* (Philadelphia: Temple University Press, 1989), 219.

20. James H. Cone, *The Spirituals and the Blues: An Interpretation* (New York: Seabury Press, 1972; repr., Maryknoll, NY: Orbis Books, 2000), 128. Citations are to the Orbis Book edition.

21. Anthony DeCurtis, "Willie Dixon and the Wisdom of the Blues," *Rolling Stone*, no. 548 (March 23, 1989): 112.

22. Blues researcher David Evans writes about the religious view of blues singers:

> There have been many surveys of the subject matter of blues texts. Two primary facts emerge from these: the blues are distinctly secular in outlook and they mainly deal with man/woman situations. They are secular in the sense that they do not hold out hope for escape from one's problems through organized religion. Yet, although blues singers may make fun of preachers and churchgoers in their songs, they are not necessarily opposed to religion as such. They are simply uncommitted to it as a way of life for themselves.

Evans, *Big Road Blues: Tradition and Creativity in the Folk Blues* (New York: Da Capo, 1982), 28.

23. Dixon, *I Am the Blues*, 160.

24. Shirli Dixon, interview by the author, September 23, 2002.

25. Connor and Neff, *The Blues*, 8.

26. Butch Dixon, interview by the author, September 23, 2002.

27. Shirli Dixon, interview by the author, September 23, 2002.

28. Willie Dixon, *Willie Dixon: The Master Blues Composer* (Milwaukee: Hal Leonard, 1992), 9.

29. Long, "The Wisdom of the Blues," 208.

30. Cone, *The Spirituals and the Blues*, 119.

31. Angela Nelson, "Rap Music and the Stagolee Mythoform," *Americana: The Journal of American Popular Culture* 4, no. 1 (Spring 2005): 6.

32. Dixon, *Willie Dixon*, 8.

33. Barlow, *Looking Up at Down*, 325.

34. Shirli Dixon, interview by the author, September 23, 2002.

35. Marie Dixon, interview by the author, September 24, 2004.

36. Ethnomusicologist Portia K. Maultsby writes, "All of the components—sound construct, interpretative devices, and performance style—that define the gospel tradition are found in its secular counterparts." Portia K. Maultsby, "Impact of Gospel Music," in *We'll Understand It Better By and By*, ed. Bernice Johnson Reagon (Washington, DC: Smithsonian Institution, 1992), 29. African American music researcher Teresa L. Read writes, "The terms Holiness, Sanctified, and Pentecostal are often used interchangeably or in conjunction with each other in many African American circles." Teresa L. Reed, *The Holy Profane: Religion in Black Popular Music* (Lexington: University Press of Kentucky, 2003), 16.

37. Ralph Ellison, *Shadows and Act* (New York: Random House, 1953; repr., 1964), 257.

38. Robert Palmer, *Deep Blues* (New York: Viking Press, 1981; repr., New York: Penguin Books, 1982), 81. Citations are to the Penguin Books edition.

39. Giles Oakley, *The Devil's Music: A History of the Blues* (New York: Taplinger, 1976), 216.

40. Muddy Waters, *Can't Be Satisfied* [VHS] (n.p.: Wellspring/Tremolo Productions, WHE 71315, 2002).

41. Sandra B. Tooze, *Muddy Waters: The Mojo Man* (Toronto: ECW Press, 1997), 116.

42. Long, "The Wisdom of the Blues," 210.

43. Michael B. Smith, "Koko Taylor," *Goldmine* 27, no. 2 (January 26, 2001): 16. African American writer Leonard Goines supports Taylor's view of the blues as therapy for African Americans:

> Blues, then functioned for the Black man in the same way that personal and social therapy functions for the white world. The therapist is not there to propose solutions to problems but to ask questions so that the patient can clearly come to see and understand the nature of his problem. It is assumed that once a problem can be clearly and simply defined, solutions will follow. The blues functions in the same manner, as an analysis of the lyrics clearly demonstrates.

Goines, "The Blues as Black Therapy," *Black World* (November 1973): 31. Blues pianist Roosevelt Sykes also states the doctorlike role of bluesman for his audience. His statement proves that the therapeutic function of the blues was not just a common belief within Dixon's inner circle:

> So blues is sort of a thing on people like the doctor. I'll put it this way—there's a doctor; he has medicine; he's never sick; he ain't sick but he has stuff for the sick people . . . "Call

the doctor."// "I'm the doctor." // "Oh, you're a sick man." // "No, I just work on the sick people." So the blues player, he ain't worried and bothered, but he got something for the worried people. Doctor: You can see his medicine; he can see his patient. Blues: You can't see the music; you can't see the patient, because it's soul. So I works on the soul and the doctor works on the body.

Barry Lee Pearson and Bill McCulloch. *Robert Johnson: Lost and Found* (Urbana: University of Illinois Press, 2003), 42.

44. Dixon, *I Am the Blues*, 25.

45. Ibid. What Dixon means by "blues" includes work songs and field hollers.

46. Shirli Dixon says one of Dixon's hobo mates was Roebuck "Pop" Staples of the Staples Singers. Staples told her that the reason her father was sent to the county farm was his large size. She says,

I had an occasion to talk with Pop Staples before he passed, and he told me that he and my dad were trying to leave the South together from Vicksburg. And my dad got caught, and put on to a county farm. Daddy was bigger. So that was a reflection of how they affected larger black boys and use them as workers.

Shirli Dixon, interview by the author, September 23, 2002.

47. Dixon, *I Am the Blues*, 27–28.

48. Shirli Dixon, interview by the author, September 23, 2002.

49. Bob Corritore, Bill Ferris, and Jim O'Neal, "Willie Dixon (Part 2)," *Living Blues*, no. 82 (September–October 1988): 31.

50. Butch Dixon, interview by the author, September 23, 2003.

CHAPTER TWO

~

Dixon's Early Musical Experiences

Willie Dixon's family was not particularly musical. No family members played instruments, and the young Dixon was not an exception. According to Shirli Dixon, the local school Dixon attended had music classes, but his report card from the second grade says that he failed music because his attendance was not satisfactory.[1] Dixon did not learn the acoustic bass until he settled in Chicago when he was twenty-four or twenty-five years old.

Nevertheless, music was everywhere in Dixon's early life, whether it was secular or sacred. Outside the house, he would hear field hollers or work songs from the fields. In a documentary film *Chicago Blues*, Dixon explains field hollers and sings one:

> Down South, most of 'em made up their songs as they went along. And if he was catching a mule to work with or somethin' . . . and the mules he had and been workin' with . . . [and] maybe his shoulder was sore from pulling to plough or pullin' a heavy load or somethin' like this. This is how these type of songs was made:
>
> > Ooh, oh, oh,
> > I done ploughed old Susie,
> > I done ploughed old Bell, you know,
> > I can't find a mule with a shoulder well.[2]

Figure 2.1.

As James H. Cone writes, "The work songs were a means of heightening energy, converting labor into dances and games, and providing emotional excitement in an otherwise unbearable situation."[3] From his own experience, Dixon knew this was true. He once said, "[If] you didn't have these various rhythms and things to carry on, why, it would make the task much harder."[4]

Work songs were not just a passive presence in Dixon's life; they became an important influence on his compositions. According to Shirli Dixon, her father learned the function of rhythms from work songs:

> From the very beginning, my dad told me he used to hear as a child the work songs in the field. They were almost like chants. Ongoing chants, chants, chants. He said it just moved him inside in a way he couldn't explain. No matter what they were saying, the rhythms would be moving his spirit. If they were awful or happy, or no matter what lyrical content, repetitive chants and repetitive rhythms and melodies just are feeding his spirit from the earliest he could remember.[5]

Some representative Dixon compositions—like "Hoochie Coochie Man" and "Spoonful"—clearly retain the practical effect of work songs. As we will see in the following chapters, one of the most distinctive characteristics of Dixon's blues songs is that rather than depending on a walking-bass pattern, he often utilizes a melodically and rhythmically characteristic riff consisting of two or three pitches. The riff is repeated over one chord, and vocal melodies that are based on a pentatonic scale are built upon the long duration of the repetition of the riffs, often exceeding twelve bars. This musical approach makes Dixon's music haunting and memorable. What he learned from work songs was the way he could extract maximum musical and psychological effect from a minimal musical device.

Following his mother's lead in making up rhymes, Dixon as a child would make up songs with his own words, but the only thing he could use as an instrument was a tobacco can.[6] Tapping out a rhythm is basically how Dixon composed songs and introduced them to musicians throughout his career. The documentary, *The Full Moon Show with Robbie Robertson*, captures a scene in which Dixon keeps rhythm by tapping his fingers against a sheet of paper held to his chest, while singing "I Just Want to Make Love to You."[7]

The only formal musical activity Dixon and his siblings engaged in was singing in the choir of Spring Hill Baptist Church where their mother, Daisy, had once worked as a janitor. Dixon was good enough to be assigned a solo in church services.[8]

Regardless of Daisy's dislike of the blues, however, the blues was too prevalent for Dixon to ignore. Besides listening to the blues records his father brought home, Dixon was exposed to live performances at his neighbor's house parties for which local musicians played. Although he was too young to join in the drinking, Dixon would go to listen to the music outside the house. He remembers,

> Oh, there was always blues around. Occasionally we used to be singing things and my mother would say, "Well, you can't sing those kind of songs." She called those old songs—those old songs that wasn't spiritual songs—they called them reels. They don't be singing the reels around the house, you know. Well, you take the average person that would be doing any kind of work, they'd be singing various blues songs.[9]

The term *reels*, or *reals*, which was used around the turn of the century— and at least up to the 1920s—to describe black secular music, was probably adopted from the dances, the "reels," brought by Irish and Scottish immigrants. According to David Evans, the word *reels* came to be applied generally to secular dance-oriented music before the term *blues* became common. As dancing to reels became less common in the twentieth century, the term came to be confused with *real*, especially because the new secular songs were grounded in ideas of "truth" and "reality."[10]

St. Louis–based blues pianist Henry Townsend remembers this term as the old name of the blues and what it meant. He says, "It was real because it made the truth available to the people in the songs—if you wanted to tell the truth."[11] Dixon recalls the terms *reel* and *evil music* being interchangeable: "Most whites did not like the music; in fact they labeled it reel music or evil music and convinced the blacks that it was bad as well."[12]

Among the offshoots of the reel, Dixon's favorite was Dudlow, which later became known as the boogie-woogie. Dixon explains, "That original 12-bar Blues was first arranged by a black man called Dudlow, from Dudlow,

Mississippi, who developed that left hand traveling bass which was later commercialized as Boogie Woogie."[13]

In Dixon's days, the Dudlow piano style was commonly heard in barrelhouses. In his own neighborhood, there were two such places: Curley's Barrelhouse (Khoury's Dry Goods), next door to his mother's restaurant, and Southside Park Club. One of the main performers in the style was pianist Little Brother Montgomery, whom Dixon saw for the first time when he was seven or eight years old (1922 or 1923). Dixon says Montgomery "was my first contact with music altogether."[14] It was Montgomery who ignited Dixon's interest in music. Butch Dixon says,

> What he told me about Little Brother Montgomery . . . he had something most piano players didn't have. He has a right hand doin' one thing and a left hand doin' something totally different. . . . When my dad was a little boy, he sneaked out to hear that. . . . It would make him dance and jump around like everybody in the juke joints would. He said, "One day if I can ever do that for people, I would do that for people."[15]

Dixon was an enthusiastic follower of Montgomery and his band. Montgomery also remembered Dixon as a child: "I knowed him ever since he was about eight years old—big, fat boy running around Vicksburg, Mississippi, following us and trying to hear us play."[16]

Born as Eurreal Montgomery in Kentwood, Louisiana, in 1906, Little Brother Montgomery had a long career, spanning from around 1918 or 1919 until his death in Chicago in 1985. As discussed in chapter 6, Montgomery and Dixon played together for the sessions for Otis Rush and Magic Sam on Cobra Records in 1957.

Montgomery learned piano from various players who visited his father's juke joint, including Jelly Roll Morton. From around 1918 or 1919 to the mid-1920s, Montgomery played mainly in barrelhouses in New Orleans and Mississippi. He temporarily settled in Chicago in the late 1920s, but in the 1930s, because the Depression affected his job as a pianist, he moved back to the South where he toured on the TOBA (Theater Owner's Booking Association) circuit.[17]

David Evans notes that Montgomery was "a superb craftsman on the virtual library of the styles performed by the many other obscure pianists who roamed this territory."[18] His playing demonstrates a unique combination of influences: Jelly Roll Morton and Delta blues guitar players Tommy Johnson, the Chatman Brothers (later to be called the Mississippi Sheiks), Skip James, and Johnny Temple.[19]

Montgomery's early recordings document his versatile artistry. "No Special Rider Blues" has a New Orleans boogie-woogie style.[20] "Louisiana

Blues" is a medium-tempo blues song that sounds like the work of the popular blues piano player of the time, Leroy Carr. "Mama You Don't Mean Me No Good" is a pop song. "Vicksburg Blues" is in a slow blues tempo with a double-time meter.[21]

"Vicksburg Blues," the song for Dixon's hometown, was one of Montgomery's two earliest recordings (another was "No Special Rider Blues"— both were recorded for Paramount in September 1930), but his popularity extended beyond Vicksburg. The tune was so popular that he recorded two more versions in 1931 and 1936. For Dixon, who was fifteen years old then, Montgomery was a hero.

In his autobiography, Dixon does not mention specifically how he was influenced by Montgomery, nor do there seem to be parallels between his and Montgomery's compositions, in terms of musical and lyrical elements. However, it's likely that Montgomery influenced Dixon in at least three ways: (1) Montgomery's versatility in styles is something Dixon shared, (2) both Montgomery's and Dixon's compositions rarely deviate from a firm musical structure, and (3) Dixon always chose a piano player as his musical partner throughout most of his career.

Throughout Dixon's career, one of his most salient strengths as a songwriter was his ability to adapt to different musical styles. When he developed himself as a composer for the Big Three Trio in the second half of the 1940s, he always tried to avoid being cast in a single mold. As we will see in the following chapter, his compositions ranged from the blues, to pop song in the Tin Pan Alley vein, to ballad, and even to melodrama. Furthermore, he often utilized different musical forms for blues-based compositions.

Another noticeable characteristic of Little Brother Montgomery is that no matter what styles he played, his music was easy to follow because the phrases were structurally clear. He did not insert irregular beats in a measure, in contrast to the styles of Delta blues guitar players such as Charley Patton, Son House, and Robert Johnson.[22] This clarity of structure is also found in Dixon's music, although vocalists for whom he provided songs sometimes unwittingly changed the beat. For an arranger, producer, and accompanist, understanding musical structure is a very important ability in helping musicians in the studio.

Although many writers on the blues tend to focus on Delta guitar players when they discuss forerunners of electric Chicago blues, it is noteworthy that Delta music was much more diverse than the guitar blues tradition. Butch Dixon notes,

> I think Little Brother Montgomery's music was more influential on my father than Robert Johnson or anyone else. He liked Little Brother Montgomery.

He didn't like a lot of other people. . . . He even had little, thick 78s of Little Brother Montgomery. He said he used to save little pennies up to get nickels, so he can go play it at the local soda shop.[23]

As another of Montgomery's likely influences, Dixon always chose a pianist as his musical collaborator once he became a professional musician. In two of his early groups, the Five Breezes and the Big Three Trio, Leonard "Baby Doo" Caston was Dixon's most important partner, and during his Chess Records period in the 1950s and 1960s, Dixon often chose Lafayette Leake as a collaborator in the studio, especially for the recordings released under his own name, and for the Koko Taylor sessions that Dixon produced. In the late 1950s, for his musical activity outside of Chess Records, Dixon teamed up with Memphis Slim.

Besides musical styles, what Dixon inherited from Little Brother Montgomery was philosophy. Montgomery was Dixon's spiritual mentor.

My father used to say, "If you don't learn nothing, you have nothing, you know nothing, and you do nothing." But Little Brother Montgomery used to say that everybody was born naked. When I first met him as a youngster, I used to ask him, "Why do you say that everybody was born naked all the time?" When I was older, and he and I were getting around together, he said that meant we all started the same way—you can gain if you want to, or lose, if you please, but ain't nobody came in here with nothing, and ain't nobody going to take nothing away. So get what you can while you're here, and be the best you can, and try to make arrangements for somebody else while you're here.[24]

As he grew older, Dixon gradually became involved in full-scale music making. According to his autobiography and other interviews, he composed songs and tried to sell them to local musicians. He was about fifteen or sixteen (1930 or 1931) then:

I used to write songs of all types and anything. In fact, I wrote a lot of poems and I was trying to sell those. I'd put them all in book form. I didn't have them typed up but nobody wanted them, anyway. So I started to make popular songs out 'em. I couldn't sell 'em as popular songs but I never stopped writing because I got a kick out of just writing poems. Then I started to converting them into blues things.[25]

Some of the earliest compositions he wrote around this period were in a pop novelty and country and western style: "Laundry Man," "Sweet Louise," and "West Ain't Wild No More." He later recorded "Laundry Man" and "Sweet Louise" with his first professional group, the Five Breezes. Other compositions from this period include "Signifying Monkey," which he recorded with the Big Three Trio, and "This Pain in My Heart," which he recorded as a solo artist on Chess Records.

In 1932 or 1933, when he was seventeen or eighteen, Dixon joined a semiprofessional five-voice gospel group, the Union Jubilee Singers.[26] This was his first formal musical group. The Union Jubilee Singers learned songs from the popular spiritual songbook *Gospel Pearls* and popular gospel records of the time. By 1934 or 1935, the group became so popular that they got a fifteen-minute regular show on the radio station WQBC. They also toured churches in Jackson, Utica, Greenwood, and Greenville, Mississippi.[27] The leader of the group was Theo Phelps. Dixon talks about Phelps' coaching on harmony:

> What I liked about Theo Phelps, he was so rough on us with that harmony situation. Anytime you harmonized with him, every note had to be perfect. We could get them chords to harmonize and blend so beautiful, boy, I hated to turn the chord loose. That harmony is so sweet and it makes you feel the music and gives you inspiration. Anybody can holler but you don't feel it.[28]

Dixon's musical experiences, especially singing the bass part for the Union Jubilee Singers, served as important training for his later vocal harmony groups, the Five Breezes, the Four Jumps of Jive, and the Big Three Trio. In addition, blending of voices, the technique he learned from Phelps to make harmonies, later became a valuable source for blending instruments in the recording studio.

Regardless of their importance to Dixon's development as a musician, the Union Jubilee Singers could never become more than a semiprofessional group. For the members, the group was naturally less a priority than their real jobs. Dixon, too, tried out a variety of professions—carpenter, boat crew member, working for the government experimental station for levee protection, and the Civilian Conservation Corps. Around this time he also tried his hand at boxing and wrestling, because he had gained confidence in his physical ability through his experience as a manual laborer.[29]

Dixon won some informal local fights, but the prize money he earned was not good enough to support himself. Probably in 1935 or 1936, when he was twenty or twenty-one, Dixon decided to leave Vicksburg. First he went to New Orleans, where he worked for an excursion boat shoveling coal all the way up to Rock Island, Illinois. When he arrived at Rock Island, Dixon decided to settle in Chicago, where his sister and her husband

lived. Shirli Dixon says her father was unsure about the success of his exodus from the South.

> When my dad left the South, he wasn't really sure what he should expect
> because he felt that there were misrepresentations. But he also believed like so
> many African Americans that were migrating, if he will, that there might be
> more opportunities. But I know he was very much heartbroken by the experi-
> ence that he saw African American people having as well as the experiences
> he had himself. If you read his book, you know, he was hit in the head and lost
> his hearing [in the penitentiary]. The story is a phenomenal story in that he
> was able to excel in music.[30]

Soon after he arrived in Chicago, Dixon joined Eddie Nichol's boxing
gym.[31] Under the name James Dixon, he fought in the 1937 Illinois heavy-
weight Golden Gloves Competition.[32] The *Chicago Defender*, on February
27, 1937, reported that Dixon was one of several impressive black fighters.

> Race lads played a conspicuous part in the early thrills afforded at the opening
> of the inter-city Golden Gloves Monday night at the Chicago Stadium. . . .
>   As early as the first round of opening night there was evidence that the
> Race boys would be tough to handle. . . . Another knockout saw James Dixon,
> Savoy, stop Lee Christians in two rounds.[33]

Besides boxing, Dixon was still pursuing music, joining three different vocal groups—one featuring gospel; another, the blues; and the third, popular
songs. One of the members of the pop song group was Bernardo Dennis, who
later became a member of the Big Three Trio. During this period, Dixon met
another future bandmate, his lifelong friend Leonard "Baby Doo" Caston.

Leonard Caston was born in Sumrall, Mississippi, in 1917. He was raised
up with Walter Sykes, famous blues pianist Roosevelt Sykes' brother. Being
inspired by Roosevelt's success, Caston moved to Chicago to be a professional musician in 1939.[34] He first worked with T-Bone Walker and regularly
played at Café Society.[35] Around this time, Caston formed a vocal group, the
Bumpin' Boys, which Dixon would join later.

Caston often visited the gymnasium where Dixon trained, and they soon
became kindred spirits. They enjoyed making music together in the breaks
during Dixon's training.[36] They modeled themselves on the popular vocal
groups of the time, the Ink Spots and the Mills Brothers, with Dixon taking
the bass lines.

After fighting four matches, Dixon was suspended for six months. Because
he found that he had been cheated out of his prize money, he and his man-

ager caused a scuffle at the boxing commissioner's office.[37] During this down time, Caston persuaded Dixon that he should focus on musical activity.[38] Caston opened the door for Dixon to become a professional musician.

Notes

1. Shirli Dixon, interview by the author, September 23, 2002.

2. *Chicago Blues* [DVD], produced and directed by Haley Cokliss (Tokyo: P-Vine Records, BMG Fun House, PVBP-953, 2003; original produced in London: IRIT Film Production, 1970).

3. James H. Cone, *The Spirituals and the Blues: An Interpretation* (New York: Seabury Press, 1972; repr., Maryknoll, NY: Orbis Books, 2000), 109. Citations are to the Orbis Books edition.

4. Bob Corritore, Bill Ferris, and Jim O'Neal. "Willie Dixon (Part 1)." *Living Blues*, no. 81 (July–August 1988): 25.

5. Shirli Dixon, interview by the author, September 23, 2002.

6. Willie Dixon, with Don Snowden, *I Am the Blues: The Willie Dixon Story* (New York: Da Capo Press, 1989), 18.

7. *The Full Moon Show with Robbie Robertson* [broadcast]. (Hollywood: One Heart Productions, Video Arts Japan, Japan Satellite Broadcasting, 1991).

8. Dixon, *I Am the Blues*, 14.

9. Corritore, Ferris, and O'Neal, "Willie Dixon (Part 1)," 18.

10. David Evans, "A Review for Mitsutoshi Inaba's Manuscript," June 10, 2008, p. 3.

11. William Barlow, *Looking Up at Down: The Emergence of Blues Culture* (Philadelphia: Temple University Press, 1989), 326. In Dixon's experience, "one group of people was calling it 'reel' because it was the real facts of life. . . . Other people were calling them 'reels' because it certainly wasn't about Christianity and going to get to heaven." Dixon, *I Am the Blues*, 4. Other artists remembered the term *reels*, like blind gospel singer Charles Haffer. When Alan Lomax asked Haffer about his career as a singer, he answered, "I reckon I might say I always was talented for singing. Before I was converted, I used to sing all the old jump-up songs—blues weren't in style then—we called them reels." Alan Lomax, *The Land Where the Blues Began* (New York: Pantheon Books, 1993), 55. Leadbelly also uses the term *reels* to describe "love songs and blues and one thing and another like that," and Mississippi Fred McDowell remembers "the earliest blues he heard" was called "reels." He also says what people referred to him: "Uh-uh! He ain't got nothin' I heard him play a reel, see." Mark Humphrey, "Holy Blues: The Gospel Tradition," in *Nothing but the Blues*, ed. Lawrence Cohn (New York: Abbeville, 1993), 129–30.

12. Willie Dixon, *Willie Dixon: The Master Blues Composer* (Milwaukee: Hal Leonard, 1992), 9.

13. Ibid. Dixon also told Karl Gert zur Heide, author of Little Brother Montgomery's biography *Deep South Piano*, about the precursor of the term *boogie-woogie*: "They

used to call boogie piano Dudlow Joes in Mississippi. I didn't hear it called boogie till long after. If a guy played boogie piano, they'd say he was a Dudlow player." Karl Gert zur Heide, *Deep South Piano: The Story of Little Brother Montgomery* (London: Studio Vista, November Books, 1970), 18. David Evans also notes that Lee Green, a mentor of Montgomery and Roosevelt Sykes, recorded the piano instrumental "Dud-Low Joe" in 1929. This composition contains many boogie-woogie riffs. The term is probably derived from "Todalo" (var. Toddle-O), a popular dance in the early twentieth century often associated with blues and boogie-woogie music. Evans, "A Review for Mitsutoshi Inaba's Manuscript," 3.

14. Dixon, *I Am the Blues*, 18.

15. Butch Dixon, interview by the author, September 23, 2003.

16. Anthony Connor and Robert Neff, *The Blues: In Images and Interviews* (Boston: D. R. Godine, 1975; repr., New York: Cooper Square Press, 1999), 18. Citations are to the Cooper Square Press edition.

17. Herzhaft Gerard, *Encyclopedia of the Blues*, 2nd ed., trans. Brigitte Debora (Fayetteville: University of Arkansas Press, 1997), 146.

18. David Evans, "Goin' up the Country: Blues in Texas and the Deep South," in *Nothing but the Blues: The Music and the Musicians*, ed. Lawrence Cohn (New York: Abbeville Press, 1993), 70. Blues historian Francis Davis also notes Little Brother Montgomery was "the most sophisticated of the barrelhouse crushers—though somewhat hesitant singer—whose rolling bass and chiming, melodic lines earmarked a highly personal synthesis of blues and jazz." Davis, *The History of the Blues: The Roots, the Music, the People from Charley Patton to Robert Cray* (New York: Hyperion, 1995), 149.

19. Evans, "Goin' up the Country," 146. According to Montgomery, in about 1922, he with two other barrelhouse pianists, Long Tall Friday and Dehlco Robert, developed a composition, which later became known as "Forty Four Blues" or "The Forty-Fours." This composition was passed on to another pianist, Lee Green, and Green passed it on to Roosevelt Sykes, who premiered it with OKeh Records in 1929. In 1930, Montgomery himself recorded this composition as "Vicksburg Blues," and Green also recorded it as "Train Number 44." Heide, *Deep South Piano*, 19–20.

20. The New Orleans boogie-woogie is a piano blues style featuring characteristic bass line that consists of two quarter notes played in the style of long-short (so-called swing). These steadily repeated bass patterns, which are one or two measures long, delineate the twelve-bar blues progression.

21. Montgomery says, "Vicksburg Blues [is] the hardest barrelhouse blues of any blues in history to play because you have to keep two different times going in each other hand." Heide, *Deep South Piano*, 20. As heard in the recording, Montgomery's right hand plays a fast shuffle pattern, while his left hand plays a slow blues pattern accentuated by a quick arpeggio figures.

22. For example, these guitar players often display a technique in which they insert a fifth quarter beat in a measure written in four-four time.

23. Butch Dixon, interview by the author, September 23, 2003.

24. Worth Long, "The Wisdom of the Blues—Defining Blues as the True Facts of Life: An Interview with Willie Dixon," *African American Review* 29, no. 2 (Summer 1995): 207.

25. Corritore, Ferris, and O'Neal, "Willie Dixon (Part 1)," 16–17.

26. Jubilee singers were groups of spiritual/gospel singers that originated with the Fisk University Jubilee Singers, established in 1871 by George L. White, for the purpose of fund-raising. They traveled not only to various places in the nation but also to some European countries until they disbanded in 1880. The term *jubilee* was also applied to smaller-sized vocal quartets or quintets, such as the Golden Gate Quartet (Golden Gate Jubilee Quartet) and the Norfolk Jubilee Quartet (Norfolk Jubilee Singers). Dixon's group was a reminiscent of such jubilee quartets.

27. Dixon, *I Am the Blues*, 34.

28. Ibid., 34–35.

29. Ibid., 37–38.

30. Shirli Dixon, interview by the author, September 23, 2002.

31. According to the newspaper article cited in note 34, Dixon moved to Savoy Athletic Club by the time he fought in the Illinois Golden Gloves.

32. Dixon, *I Am the Blues*, 46.

33. "Golden Gloves Bouts Begin," *Chicago Defender*, February 27, 1937, 14.

34. Jonas Bernholm, "Liner Notes," *I Feel Like Steppin' Out* [CD], recorded by the Big Three Trio (Czechoslovakia: Dr. Horse, RBD 804, 1985), 2. Around this time Caston was a guitar player but he later switched to piano.

35. Jeff Titon, ed., *From Blues to Pop: The Autobiography of Leonard "Baby Doo" Caston*, JEMF Special Series no. 4 (Los Angeles: John Edwards Memorial Foundation, Folklore and Mythology Center, University of California, 1974), 14.

36. Corritore, Ferris, and O'Neal, "Willie Dixon (Part 1)," 18.

37. Dixon, *I Am the Blues*, 47.

38. Ibid., 46.

~

CHAPTER THREE

Willie Dixon's Early Groups

By the mid-1930s, Chicago had become a blues capital.[1] Among the most popular blues artists playing in the Windy City around this time were guitarists Lonnie Johnson, Big Bill Broonzy, Tampa Red, and Memphis Minnie; pianists Memphis Slim, Big Maceo, Roosevelt Sykes, and Little Brother Montgomery; and harmonica player John Lee "Sonny Boy" Williamson. In addition to these professional artists, Chicago was thronged with amateur and semiprofessional musicians—like Leonard "Baby Doo" Caston—hoping to make their fortunes. Flush with talent, Chicago was also an important place for scouts and producers from record companies. For anyone looking to break into the business, the secret, as Dixon knew, was to first "find Mayo Williams, and if ya didn't find Mayo they tell ya to find Melrose."[2]

Mayo "Ink" Williams, formerly a producer of Paramount Records' race record division and a founder of Black Patti Records, was one of the most important behind-the-scenes men in the blues recordings in the 1920s and 1930s, producing artists such as Gertrude "Ma" Rainey and Ida Cox.[3] In the 1940s, Williams was affiliated with Decca Records. By the second half of the 1930s, Lester Melrose became more important than Williams for record deals in the blues market. It was with Melrose that Dixon established a very important relationship.

Lester Melrose, who provided artists mainly for Columbia Records and Victor Records, was responsible for popularizing the "Bluebird beat," a blues performing style designed to suit the taste of the new urban audience. Bluebird beat was "a mixture of older black blues and vaudeville styles and material with the newer swing rhythms."[4] It typically featured guitar, harmonica, and piano instead of the single acoustic guitar. It was often characterized by additions of bass and washboard to the ensemble. From the mid-1930s to the late 1940s, the Bluebird beat nearly dominated the blues record market.

The Bluebird beat from Victor's subsidiary Bluebird Records heralded what we have since come to call a house sound, the signature style by which a particular record label is known—like early Motown sounds from Motown Records. In order to maintain the same quality of style in the records, Melrose had his roster of artists—including Big Bill Broonzy, Sonny Boy Williamson, Tampa Red, and Washboard Sam—serve as each other's accompanists. Melrose also used the same sidemen, including drummer Fred Williams and bassists Ransom Knowling, Alfred Elkins, Bill Settle, and, later on, Willie Dixon.

Of equal importance, Melrose established a house songwriter system. Recognizing that song publishing was a lucrative business, he paid small fees for the rights of songs written by his musicians, and in return he received the royalties.[5] Reworking preexisting songs was still common practice in blues recordings, but writing new songs was more encouraged, because songs had to be original to be copyrighted—although there are numerous instances of songwriters copyrighting reworked songs as their own originals.[6] In addition to composing songs for themselves, the artists such as Tampa Red and Washboard Sam wrote pieces for their label mates to make records. This system urged Dixon to write songs for the Big Three Trio, although he did not write for other artists at this point.

There was another importance in Dixon's affiliation with Lester Melrose. Bob Koester, founder of Delmark Records, notes, "I'm sure he [Dixon] learned much of record production from Melrose, possibly a little bit from Mayo."[7] Dixon developed his studio techniques by visiting Tampa Red's house, where many of the Chicago blues musicians congregated and where Melrose found new talents and new songs to put on records. Dixon describes,

He [Tampa Red] had a place up over a pawnshop. And a lotta the musicians used to go up there and write songs, lay around in there, and sleep. Melrose always came there when he was in town. That was his kind of headquarters, like. . . . And we'd get to singing it and seein' how it sounds. If it sounded like it was alright, then Melrose would say, "Well looky here, we'll try it out and see what happens." And he'd write the name of it down—who was doin' it. And then after he would get so many of the songs and he would say, "Well, we gonna get a date to record and we gonna record this guy 'n' that guy and the other guy." He'd make a decision about who was gonna record next time.[8]

Jim O'Neal, former editor of *Living Blues*, relates,

> I think Willie learned a lot probably from Melrose and from being at Tampa Red's house. I think one of the first questions I asked Willie when I talked to him was about Tampa Red. . . . Lester Melrose had kind of a recording machine almost. He had stable of artists. He had people who would pick the artists to play on each other's records. They would even write for each other. And I think you can look at what happened to Chess. For Chess studio, Chess kind of had same stable musicians who recorded for everyone.[9]

The Five Breezes

In 1938 or 1939, Dixon became a member of Leonard "Baby Doo" Caston's vocal group, the Bumpin' Boys, whose other members were Eugene Gilmore, Dixon's nephew Lionel Douglas Turner, and Dixon's brother Arthur Dixon.[10]

Willie Dixon was an unofficial member of the group, vocalizing only the bass line, in a style similar to that of the Mills Brothers.[11] Even at this point, Dixon's role was more as an instructor to the group than as a member, presaging some of his future roles in recording sessions as producer and arranger.

Around 1938 or 1939, Dixon experienced his first recording session, when the Bumpin' Boys went into the studio for Decca Records with producer Mayo Williams. How the group signed with Decca is not clear. Caston said that he looked for Williams to find a record deal,[12] while Dixon said that he was introduced to Williams by Little Brother Montgomery.[13] The songs they recorded included Dixon's composition "Beat Her Out, Bumpin' Boys,"[14] but their recordings were never released. Dixon remembers, "Those big old thick waxes was expensive and by the time we ruined a couple, hell, they was about ready to get rid of us, anyway."[15]

Sometime after the Bumpin' Boys' unsuccessful recording, Caston and Dixon formed a new band with three other musicians, naming themselves the Five Breezes after the nickname of the main vocalist, Joe "Cool Breeze" Bell. Caston also called himself "Evening Breeze" and Dixon "Big Breeze."[16]

In addition to encouraging Dixon's involvement in his groups, Caston played another important role for Dixon's musical career; he suggested his friend should learn to play the bass, and they crafted Dixon's first instrument from an oil can. Dixon says,

> That oil can had an open bottom to it, and we put this stick on the back of it and made it like an African instrument. Then he made another thing like a fingerboard and put this one bass string on it, attached to the center of the

oil can and on top of the stick. And the stick had a little adjusting thing that he could wind up and down to play into whatever key we were playing in.[17]

The Five Breezes rehearsed their repertoire at Tampa Red's house, and finally Melrose scheduled them for a recording session. On November 15, 1940, the Five Breezes cut eight sides.[18] Dixon did not have the lead vocal part; the only segment that features his vocal contribution is spoken lines inserted in "Sweet Louise." Although none of the songs are copyrighted by Dixon, he was the composer of "Sweet Louise" and "The Laundry Man," which he had previously sold in Vicksburg.[19]

"Sweet Louise" is a slow country and western ballad, a monologue of a cowboy who falls in love with a girl he met a few days ago. He is trying to catch her attention with sweet words, but she is not interested in—a typical country and western song. The introduction uses guitar arpeggios, the Ink Spots' trademark. A romantic spoken part inserted between verses is also found in many of Ink Spots records. "Laundry Man" is an up-tempo novelty song.[20] This song is an advertisement of a hardworking laundry man who washes out anything as clean as it gets, though it can be sexually suggestive, depending on its interpretation.

Although Dixon was later known as a blues composer, his first recorded compositions were not blues in the sense of musical form and style. In fact, throughout his career, Dixon wrote many songs with a pop-song form, and he also combined a blues form with a pop-song form rather than utilizing a simple twelve-bar/a-a-b blues pattern. Artistically, "Sweet Louise" and "Laundry Man" are not important compositions, but they indicate the degree to which Dixon was already absorbing different styles and forms of music.

The Five Breezes could not become a popular recording group. While they were among the bluesiest "jive" vocal groups in the 1930s, their style was still too much like that of the Ink Spots. Caston remembers, "Anything you do, well, in those days you just didn't copy nobody and was successful."[21]

However, they were good enough to become a regular band at Martin's Corner on the West Side of Chicago. The steady work meant Dixon was now making more money playing music than boxing. As a side benefit, the club owner loaned Caston and Dixon their first formal instruments.[22]

Although a musical career was looking more attractive to Dixon, he nevertheless quit the band for a time, feeling he "didn't have very much hopes [sic] for the musical field at first."[23] However, by 1941, Dixon returned to the group, and in the same year Dixon joined the Chicago Musicians' Union.[24] By then the band members were earning more money.[25] In addition to performance fees of thirty-five dollars each per week, they were also being supplied fashionable stage uniforms, zoot suits "with the great big knees and the little small bottom and the coat was real long and you had a great big hat with a feather in it and a chain hanging down to your knees."[26]

Besides playing with the group, Dixon had begun bringing his bass out to the streets, where he played for tips and worked on improving his technique.[27] Dixon had another motivation. Stocked with song sheets, he and "Cool Breeze" Bell hawked the songs they were singing to passersby. Their performance already included the Big Three Trio's hit songs "You Sure Look Good to Me" and "Signifying Monkey."[28]

Although Dixon's musical activities began to take off, at the end of 1941 or the beginning of 1942, World War II intervened in his career. Like some other blacks, he refused to be drafted, questioning why he had to serve the government that had been oppressing his people for a number of years. He ignored a draft notice, and one day the authorities came to arrest Dixon at the club where the Five Breezes were performing.[29] This was the end of the group.

Dixon spent ten months in jail off and on, but he continued to be an outspoken opponent of the government's position. Afraid of the influence he might have over others, the authorities forbade him from having contact with reporters from black newspapers.[30]

Various racial experiences in the South and the political strife regarding military service made Dixon recognize what the government defined as patriotism was filled with contradictions. Shirli Dixon talks about her father's distrust for the government:

> Not only was he skeptical but he used the experiences that he not only seemed to have experienced himself but he saw often perpetuated on people of color. . . . He had quite a strong disdain for the way that Native Americans had been treated, and he felt that . . . there was a formal genocide being always cultivated and developed through the drug sales, and alcohol, and cigarettes and things, all of which many times were approved by this government that was supposedly designed to develop strong country.[31]

Finally, around the end of 1942, the authorities decided to drop the case.[32] While Dixon was involved in the dispute, Caston formed his new band—the Rhythm Rascals—and toured overseas for the USO (United Services Organization).[33] Dixon then took the opportunity to form his own band, the Four Jumps of Jive.

The Four Jumps of Jive

The Four Jumps of Jive—a group consisting of Dixon on bass, Gene Gilmore (from the Five Breezes) on piano and lead vocal, and Bernardo

Dennis and Ellis Hunter on electric guitar—was a regular act at Libby's in the Northwest Side. Although the group came together in 1942, their first opportunity for recording did not come until the end of the war, perhaps because of the 1942–1943 musicians' union strike against record companies or the shellac shortages experienced during the wartime. In 1945, the band made a contract with newly founded Mercury Records, and they were the label's debut recording group.[34] On September 12, they cut four sides, including Dixon's composition "Boo Boo Fine Jelly." This was the group's sole recording session.

The only recordings by the Four Jumps of Jive still available today are "Satchelmouth Baby" and "It's Just the Blues." "Satchelmouth Baby" features four-part vocal harmony, although the quality of their harmony is somewhat rougher than that of other popular "jive" vocal groups of the time, such as the Four Vagabounds and Three Sharps and Flats. Yet the interaction of the two electric guitars played by Hunter and Dennis gives the sound an exciting feeling.

In "It's Just the Blues," Dixon's contribution to the arrangement is apparent. He uses slap-bass technique, and the sound of strings hitting the fingerboard creates a delightfully percussive effect. Within the same walking-bass beat pattern, Dixon tries to change melodic patterns to add more variety to the arrangement.

Although the Four Jumps of Jive existed for only a short period, they were a fairly popular band. They were ranked as high as tenth in a "specialty artist" category of the *Chicago Defender*'s band polls in early 1946—the winner of this category was the Nat Cole Trio.[35]

A few months after the newspaper's vote, the band broke up. Dixon subsequently reunited with Baby Doo Caston, who had just returned from a USO tour. Together with Bernardo Dennis of the Four Jumps of Jive, they formed the Big Three Trio.

The Big Three Trio

"During the war the Big Three were Roosevelt, Stalin and Churchill," Leonard "Baby Doo" Caston says, "and that's where I got the name."[36] In spite of the name Big Three Trio, for recordings the band usually included a forth member, a drummer.

The Big Three Trio was a popular cocktail trio.[37] From 1946 to 1952, they had eleven recording sessions and cut fifty-four sides, including some duplicated songs for the Bullet Records and its subsidiary Delta label, and for Columbia and its subsidiary OKeh. They recorded eighteen Dixon compositions (including some co-compositions with members of the group), but these were only a fraction of the work Dixon assembled for the group. Caston admitted later that he had not properly valued Dixon's songs: "[I said], 'Man, don't nobody want to hear that junk you got'"[38] "When we turned around and somebody else was doing 'em, then we knew what we had bypassed."[39]

Soon after the band's formation, producer Lester Melrose visited them at their regular venue Sky Club. He scheduled the band's first recording session at the World Studio in the Wrigley Building on Michigan Street sometime in 1946. Around the same time, Jim Bulleit from Bullet Records of Nashville visited Melrose in Chicago, looking for a new talent. Melrose sold Bulleit Big Three Trio's "Lonely Roamin'," "You Sure Look Good to Me," "Signifying Monkey," and "Get up Those Stairs, Mademoiselle." All of these recordings were introduced in "Advanced Record Releases" of the May 10, 1947, issue of *Billboard*.[40]

"You Sure Look Good to Me" (aka "Wee Wee Baby") is not Dixon's composition, but it shows the Big Three Trio's principal performing style, which the band adopted in many other compositions. The most apparent characteristic is a blues song performed in a three-part vocal harmony with all the vocalists moving in the same rhythms (see figure 3.1).

Oh   wee   wee   baby,   you   sure   look   good   to   me.

Figure 3.1.

According to Caston, this performing style was a novel idea for the time, although there had been precedents in the 1920s:[41]

> Now what happened—all of the stars was singing single—and we got together and I arranged this song. . . . And it was the first time blues was played like that. And it was all over, everywhere. Well, the Mills Brothers was the first to sing pop tunes together, but I'm talking about the blues. . . . So after that it's been the Midnighters and the Clovers and Moonglows.[42]

"You Sure Look Good to Me" is a reworking of "Wee Baby Blues" by Big Joe Turner with Art Tatum (1939). Inspired by a woman whom the band members nicknamed Jessie Bellbottom, Caston turned it into a song of an appreciation of plus-sized beauty.[43] This was the only song by the Big Three Trio that made the *Billboard* race record charts, achieving tenth position on April 3, 1948.[44]

The flip side of "You Sure Look Good to Me" was Dixon's "Signifying Monkey," a composition that reflects his desire to compose something other than blues. While Dixon was trying to be artistically versatile—an influence from Little Brother Montgomery—he also knew that the group needed to fulfill the expectations of their audiences' broad musical tastes: "We pretty much were playin' what the peoples wanted to hear, you know. If it was blues, well, we played it, or standards, what they called novelty tunes, you know. Oh yeah, we was playin' it all."[45]

"Signifying Monkey" is one of the best known African American toasts, along with "Stackolee" and "Titanic."[46] Dixon heard this tale with illustrations from his schoolmate in Vicksburg:

> When I was in Vicksburg there used to be a boy in our room, his name was Eddy Cooper. He was some kin to another fella called Elmore Johnson. Eddy Cooper was a born cartoonist. . . . Even when he was third and fourth grade he could draw a picture very good. He would draw animals and put different heads on them. So, Eddy Cooper come up with this idea one day of this monkey and baboon and all this kinda stuff. Elmore, he used [to] say because I was fat I was the elephant. And another fella named T. W. Grier—he was tall and lanky— and he called him the monkey or something like that. And the teacher came back; I think everybody in the room got a whipping about it. Well, I couldn't get it out of my system. So after then I kept this particular cartoon and writing and I made this—I made that song about the Signifying Monkey.[47]

The toast "Signifying Monkey" had been used as material in black popular music prior to the Big Three Trio's recording: for example, Big Maceo's "Can't You Read" (1941) among others.[48] A primary characteristic of the toast is the verbal agility of the characters, in this case, the monkey, the lion, and the elephant. Like many of the transcriptions of the story, Dixon says his original version of the song was filled with vulgar expressions, but he "decided to clean it up and put it on record."[49]

The available transcriptions from traditional storytellers suggest that Dixon was well aware of the toast's history.[50] There are striking resemblances between some sections of his composition and excerpts from "The Lion, Monkey & Elephant" by Red Larrison (see table 3.1), which are included in the March 1946 issue of Indiana State Prison publication *The Lancer* (this transcription does not contain informal expressions because it was published in a state prison).[51]

Dixon composed "Signifying Monkey" in a ballad form.[52] He applied the four-line structure of the verse to an eight-measure phrase. Throughout the

Table 3.1. Dixon's "Signifying Monkey" (1947) and Red Larrison's "The Lion, Monkey & Elephant" (1946)

Dixon's Version	Larrison's Version
[Hook] You call yourself the jungle king, I found out you ain't a doggone thing.	"What overbearing, dull-witted, firehouse headed square John has the gall to gossip, about my folks that way, knowing I'm the king of the jungle?"
[Verse 1] Said the monkey to the lion on a bright summer day, There's a big fat (bad) cat livin' down the way, He talked about your folks in the heck of way, A lotta other things I'm afraid to say.	One bright sunny day Mr. Lion strolled leisurely through the jungle of his merry way when a pint-sized monkey in tree yelled: "Hey there brother lion, there's a big burly two-tailed bilikin down your way, and how he talks about you relatives. . . .
	"Hey you big dough-bellied ivory toter, I hear you've been beating up your gums about my people in a scandalous way." [No correspondent section]
[Verse 2] The lion jumps up all full of rage, Like a Harlem cat that's blown his gage, He meets the elephant up under the tree, He says, "Now, big boy, it's you or me."	
[Verse 3] The elephant looks at him from the corner of his eyes, Said-a find someone to fight your size, Lion jumps up and makes a fancy pass, But the elephant knocks him over in the grass.	The elephant grunted, raised his head, squinted out of the corner of an eye and replied: "Go on you big-pawed wing and pick on somebody your size."
[Verse 4] They fought all night and fought all day, I don't know how the lion really got a way, He come back to the jungle more dead than alive, That's when the monkey really started his jive.	The lion tussled with that thick-skinned jasper all day and all night. I still don't see how he survived that hectic fight. Nonetheless, early next A.M. he came slinking back through the jungle with his tail between his legs and as wobbly a new-born calf, and right then is when the monkey spotted him and started his signifying.

(continued)

Table 3.1. (*continued*)

Dixon's Version	Larrison's Version
[Verse 5]	
He waked up his temper when he jumpin' up and down,	Like a bolt of thunder and a silver streak, the lion lit on him with all four feet.
Then his foot missed the limb and his head hit the ground,	
Like a bolt of lightning and a streak of heat,	
The lion was on him with all four feet.	
[Verse 6]	
But the monkey looks up from the corner of his eyes,	The monkey began to weep and cry and he begged; "Now Mr. Lion, please let me apologize."
Says "Now Mr. Lion, I apologize,"	
The monkey on his back studies up a scheme,	
He's trying to trick that jungle king.	

verse, Caston keeps the same accompaniment pattern upon which the vocal melody is built. The principal musical structure of this song—building vocal melodies on the repetition of the short melodic-rhythmic figure (riff)—later became Dixon's most characteristic musical device, although this song lacks the truly catchy riff of the sort heard in "Hoochie Coochie Man" and "Spoonful."

In addition, "Signifying Monkey" lyrically foreshows Dixon's future works. At the point he composed this song, he simply used his favorite material to write a funny song. But conscious use of song subjects with which black audiences, especially those from the South, were familiar—that is, collective memories of his principal audience—became a highly important characteristic of his compositions.

The recording of "Signifying Monkey" also displays Dixon's musicianship. For example, he skillfully changes the intensity and dynamics of his voice: when he sings, "He talked about your folks in the heck of way," he gradually increases volume, and the next line, "A lotta other things I'm afraid to say," he sings much more quietly. For the line "He come back to the jungle more dead than alive," Dixon slurs words to suggest a beaten-up lion, and the following line, "That's when the monkey really started his jive," sounds joyous by contrast. Butch Dixon observes his father's vocal style: "He is not a good vocalist but a great expressionist."[53]

In addition, Dixon's bass playing is inventive. After the fourth verse, Baby Doo Caston and Bernardo Dennis take eight-measure solos by turn, while

Dixon occasionally accentuates a walking-bass pattern with a crisp triplet phrase. Without interfering with the soloist, Dixon tries to be musically creative and self-assertive.

The commercial success of the Big Three Trio's debut record on the minor label Bullet brought them a new record deal with a major company, Columbia. For the band, the major label distribution helped them gain more popularity than they had had before, while for producer Lester Melrose, the larger record deal meant the band would earn more royalties for him.

The Big Three Trio's first Columbia session was held on March 11, 1947. For this session, guitarist Bernardo Dennis was replaced with Ollie Crawford, a member of Caston's former group, the Rhythm Rascals. Reportedly, Dixon and Dennis did not always get along, although Dixon liked Dennis's vocal style.[54] The band rerecorded "Signifying Monkey" and "Lonely Roamin'," and two new slow blues compositions, Dixon's "Money Tree Blues" and "If the Sea Was Whiskey," which he cowrote with Caston.[55]

While "If the Sea Was Whiskey" is a reworking of three previously popular blues—"Divin' Duck Blues," "Match Box Blues," and "Milkcow Blues"—"Money Tree Blues" is Dixon's original, in which he uses rich sexual metaphors to describe the attraction of a woman:

[Hook]
My baby, she's got a money tree,
My baby, she's got a money tree,
If she don't shake for you, she'll surely shake for me.

[Verse 1]
A little money tree,
It ain't out in the wood,
But every time she shake it,
Makes me feel so good.

[Hook]
My baby, she's got a money tree,
If she don't shake for you, she'll surely shake for me.

[Verse 2]
Well I am goin' and get my tree,
If it don't bear green,
I'll be the meanest man,
That you have ever seen,
I'll cut the money tree down,
Dig up the trunk,

Cover up the hole,
Burn up the stump.

[Hook]
My baby, she's got a money tree,
If she don't shake for you, she'll surely shake for me.

[Tag]
I love my money tree, I love my money tree,
I love my money tree for my money,
I love my money tree, I love my money tree for my money,
I love my money tree, 'cause my money tree is so good to me.

Throughout the song, Dixon utilizes different text forms for different sections: an a-a-b form (three-line form) for the hook, a quatrain refrain text
form (four-line text followed by a refrain/hook) for the first verse, and a
modification of the quatrain form for the second verse. In the verses, along
with the quatrain form, the musical device that sounds very similar to a stop-
time riff creates rhythmic interest (see figure 3.2).

Figure 3.2.

The second verse with the strong accent on the first beat of each bar is
expanded to eight measures, making it a total of sixteen measures long until
the end of the hook. Prolongation of this riff causes extra tension. While the
accompaniment keeps the same pattern over the same chord, Dixon sings the
lines with very limited melodic movement, using only three pitches (E-flat,

F, and A-flat). In this way, Dixon effectively makes the music intense, as if he is trying to provoke sexual desire.

On June 10, 1947, three months after the first Columbia session, the Big Three Trio were hired as sidemen for singer Rosetta Howard. On September 3, 1947, they again backed up Howard, and also had their own session. The four songs the group recorded included "No More Sweet Potatoes," another of Dixon's important early compositions. The song is a slow blues based on an a-a-b form in the hook and a quatrain refrain form in the verses. Here again, Dixon uses two different forms in one song.

"No More Sweet Potatoes" is about the hard times of a farmer who has lost his crops because of bad weather. The first line "No more sweet potatoes, the frost done killed the vine" was probably a traditional expression.[56] What makes this song unique for Dixon is a catalogue of related words, in the case of this song, the brand names and personal names of food manufactures as seen in the following verses:

> [Hook]
> No more sweet potatoes, the frost done killed the vine,
> No more sweet potatoes, the frost done killed the vine,
> Hobos made a mulligan, now I'm left behind.
>
> [Verse 1]
> Henderson cooked the chicken,
> Cleanhead made the stew,
> Washboard Sam cooked cabbage green,
> Now what am I gon' do?
>
> [Hook]
> No more sweet potatoes, the frost done killed the vine,
> Hobos made a mulligan, now I'm left behind.
>
> [Piano solo]
>
> [Verse 2]
> Maxwell made the coffee,
> Lipton made the tea,
> Campbell made the tomato juice,
> And nothing left for me.
>
> [Hook repeated]

Dixon's creative ability was blossoming in this early stage of his career. All of the compositional techniques detailed previously are the key to making his famous songs distinctive, although he was not the first to use such techniques.

There were some reasons that Dixon tried to break away from the conventional writing formula. First, he was frustrated by Melrose's production strategy in which artists should retain the molded writing style. He explains, "Most of Melrose's things was 12-bar blues music. The artists were what they considered older types and all these guys had a straight 12-bar pattern with punchline and I couldn't get any of them to use introductions or melodic lines for their music."[57]

Another issue for Dixon was that the twelve-bar scheme was too short for many of the songs he liked to compose:

> I couldn't never see how they could use 12 bars to complete the story. And so naturally I began to try and put other bars and introductions to it. And it worked out pretty good and this is the way I began to write most of my songs. Where they would either have introductions or certain patterns that they had to go to. And I didn't have to use exactly the same 12-bar system all the time.[58]

For the December 30, 1947, session, the Big Three Trio cut eight titles. This unusually large number was due to the record company's desire to secure enough materials to make records prior to a musicians' union strike that started two days after this session.[59]

Dixon was not the sole composer of any of these recordings. The two instrumental numbers, "Big Three Boogie" and "88 Boogie," are credited to Dixon and Baby Doo Caston. "Big Three Boogie" begins with a cascading sequence played by Caston, after which the members sing a short line, which became the title of the song, in their characteristic three-part harmony. After the repetition of the theme, Caston takes a solo. He is a strong piano player; while playing a typical boogie-woogie left-hand part with mainly chromatic figures, his right hand is hitting powerful chords. After Caston, Dixon plays a bass solo, incorporating a walking-bass pattern with syncopated phrases, slap-bass technique, and melodic ascents and descents. Another number, "88 Boogie," also features all the members' solos. The band is trying to create a locomotive feel, common in boogie-woogie.

Having started playing a handcrafted oil can bass, Dixon became an accomplished bass player, and as early as 1945—just after the Five Breezes broke up—he became a regular sideman of the Melrose production. According to Dixon, the recording sessions for which he played as a sideman include John Lee "Sonny Boy" Williamson's "Elevator Woman" (recorded on July 2, 1945).[60] Here, Dixon is playing a walking-bass that leaves him in the background, but he still shows creativity within a limited framework by adding a series of triplets in the chord change sections and turnaround. Dixon continued session work after he became a member of the Big Three Trio. In early 1947, he played the bass for Memphis Slim's records, including "Kilroy Was Here" and "Rockin' the House." Slim and Dixon later worked as a blues duo.[61]

In live performances with the Big Three Trio, Dixon included flamboyant gimmicks in his bass playing, like "spinning the bass around, laying all down on the floor with the bass, and rid[ing] it like a horse."[62] He remembers he was also a loud bass player:

> I wasn't playing what the media was callin' correct bass but I was the flashiest bass player and loudest one. Years ago, when a guy played the bass, nine times out of ten you couldn't hear him. I always did tell people, "I don't care what you're playing, give me a solo. When it comes my time, I wanted to be seen and heard."[63]

Butch Dixon talks about his father's unique bass techniques:

> My dad had extremely large hands. . . . For him to play the bass, he had to really narrow his fingers down to pluck the strings. Because his hands were so big, he can pluck the strings and stop the bass at the same time, and he goes with the drummer. . . . A lot of times if you listen to some of his records, you can hear he's actually slapping the bass at the same time.[64]

While Dixon once said, "I was never influenced by any bass players at all,"[65] Bob Koester notes that much of Dixon's bass techniques came from his observation of Ransom Knowling, who was Melrose's preferred bassist: "Dixon learned a lot from Ransom, too. I'm sure he learned from Ransom helluva lot at Tampa Red's house."[66]

In the 1948, Dixon branched out from Melrose's operation. Sometime in September, Dixon joined guitarist/vocalist Robert Nighthawk's session as a bassist. This was Dixon's first work for Chess Records before his involvement became full scale in 1953.

The Big Three Trio did not have any recording sessions in 1948, probably because of the musicians' union strike. This was also the year that RCA Victor and Columbia started to reduce their recordings of blues artists. John Lee "Sonny Boy" Williamson's accidental death on June 1 marked the clear decline of the Bluebird beat. By the end of 1949, RCA stopped making blues records and finally dropped the Bluebird label in 1950. This change in musical trends affected Columbia. Memphis Minnie had her last session for Columbia in 1949, and in April 1950 the label halted its 30000 blues series from which the Big Three Trio's records were issued.[67] On the other hand, in April of 1948, the inclusion of Muddy Waters' "I Can't Be Satisfied" and "I Feel Like Going Home" on Aristocrat/Chess initiated a new trend of Chicago blues featuring greater distortion in the guitar sound than ever.

Although musical trends in Chicago had started to change, 1949 was a big year for the Big Three Trio. They constantly toured cities in the Midwest, including Austin, Minnesota; St. Louis, Missouri; Omaha, Nebraska; Denver, Colorado; and Cheyenne, Wyoming. They were a popular band. Caston relates an episode in St. Louis where women were chasing them in the hotel.

> And the peoples found out who we was and man they come in that place and we had a heck of a time after that. Man, we lived it up in St. Louis. We lived five years in a week's time in St. Louis, man! 'Cause they'll kill you with kindness, you know. And man, the girls was coming in there trying to get next to me; and my wife and I was there and we were staying at the hotel and they would come in there with Willie Dixon and Ollie Crawford and the girls would come in there.[68]

They had good publicity, and newspapers carried their gig announcements, sometimes with group portraits. The *Chicago Defender* national edition issued on April 23, 1949, published the first article about the band, which appeared with their picture:

> Big Three Trio, currently wowing 'em at the Turf Bar, Austin, Minnesota, is wowing 'em all across the country with the latest Delta release, "Till the Day I Die," penned by Russ DeBow. . . . The popular unit is expected to hit the top with this tune, which is backed by "Don't Let the Music Die," written by Willie Dixon, bass man.[69]

The review for their performance at the Turf Bar is vivid evidence of their hot show:

> There's rhythm and action in every beat of music at Bob and Jake's Turf Bar in Austin these days as the "Big Three Trio" turns out tunes at a terrific clip. . . . In their specialty numbers "Baby Doo" Caston, the leader, shoves his piano around like a toy, while 330 pound "Big Jump" Dixon spins his bass and slaps it until the instrument practically comes to life. Holding his own between these two human dynamos is Ollie Crawford, the third member of the trio, who joined the group about a year and a half ago.[70]

In addition to the massive touring, they had three recording sessions in 1949. On February 18, they were in the studio for first time since the end of 1947 and cut six titles, none of which were Dixon's solo compositions. "I Ain't Gonna Be Your Monkey Man No More" is credited to Dixon and Caston, and the two instrumentals, "Big Three Stomp" and "Hard Notch Boogie Beat," are credited to all three members of the band.

In "Hard Notch Boogie Beat," Dixon again shows his virtuoso bass playing by changing beat patterns. First his solo is based on a walking-bass line, but he inserts a peppy sixteenth-note phrase here and there, and then, after the first turnaround, he uses more sixteenth-note phrases to construct melodies. In another instrumental, "Big Three Stomp," Ollie Crawford had a larger contribution, providing a guitar riff that serves as a main theme for the track.

Caston-Dixon's "I Ain't Gonna Be Your Monkey Man" is a fast shuffle with three-part harmony, the group's trademark. The lyrics and the feel of the music are somewhat inconsistent, because while the music is highly energetic, the words are a man's lament, expressing hatred toward the woman whom he serves.

Sometime in April 1949, the Big Three Trio was in the studio again. For this session, the band recorded seven compositions, including Dixon's "Don't Let That Music Die." Strangely, these recordings were published by the Delta label, their former record company, Bullet's subsidiary. For some reason, the May 7 *Defender* carried an advertisement for "Till the Day I Die" coupled with "Don't Let That Music Die," though it was extremely rare for a newspaper to carry an advertisement for an individual record around this time.[71]

"Don't Let That Music Die" is another example of Dixon's non-blues compositions. This is a simple pop song in which instrumental solos based on the vocal melody are inserted after each verse.[72]

There were no Baby Doo Caston compositions for this session, although he had been considered the group's main composer. From this session to their last session in December 1952, Caston provided only one song, "It's All Over Now."

On December 16, 1949, the Big Three Trio cut four sides for Columbia, including Dixon's "Practicing the Art of Love" and a rerecording of "Don't Let That Music Die." "Practicing the Art of Love" is an example of a Dixon song in the Tin Pan Alley style. The song opens up with a series of block chords lightly played by Caston's piano. This is followed by a Mills Brothers–like introduction (singing wordless, three-part harmony), and then Dixon sings the lyrics of lovemaking in a soft, crisp, and rhythmical way:

> [Verse 1] (A1)
> If you see me in my room,
> And I'm makin' a funny tune,

> With a gal I think something of,
> I'm practicing the art of love.
>
> [Verse 2] (A2)
> And if you see the lights go out,
> Then you hear me scream and shout,
> And call the Lord above,
> I'm practicing the art of love.
>
> [Bridge] (B)
> I'm gonna take my baby in my arms,
> Rockin' in the morning, midnight, and dawn,
> I love that gal 'cause she's so sweet,
> The way she'll rock you off of your feet.
>
> [Verse 3] (A3)
> If you see I'm in the mood,
> Then you know I'm in the groove,
> We'll hurdle like a turtle dove,
> Practicing the art of love.
>
> [Guitar solo]
>
> [Bridge and Verse 3 repeated]
>
> [Tag]
> Practicing the art of love.

In the instrumental section, both the guitar and the piano play a riff based on the vocal melodies. This section sounds very similar to the performing style of Nat Cole Trio, one of the most popular cocktail trio groups in the late 1940s. Although it is not included in any currently available Big Three Trio CDs, this recording is charming.

The rerecording of "Don't Let That Music Die" is basically the reproduction of the previously recorded version for Bullet/Delta with some minor changes. The new version is somewhat faster, and it features solos by all of the members.

After the December 16, 1949, session, the Big Three Trio did not have a recording session until May 29, 1951, almost eighteen months later, when Columbia's subsidiary OKeh was revived.[73] For this session, Dixon provided three different types of compositions: "Tell That Woman," "Violent Love," and "Lonesome."

"Tell That Woman" is another ballad-type composition. The material for the narrative was derived from Dixon's experience, although there had been prewar blues recordings with the similar theme, such as Johnny Temple's

"Big Boat Whistle" (1935). Working as a roustabout on the Mississippi River, Dixon saw many women waiting for their men to return home with fortunes, although their wish usually went unfulfilled. Dixon mentions, "If a man went up the river and a woman didn't have no way to survive, sometimes she'd come down every day hoping to hear a boat blowing and coming back in. You take these facts of life and make them into songs."[74]

[Verse 1]
I went up to the river just to pack some sacks,
I thought I'd bring some of my money back,
(The) big boat up the river and she won't come down,
My woman on the levee just a-acting a clown, but

[Hook]
Somebody tell that woman,
Somebody tell that woman,
Somebody tell that woman,
Big boat up the river and she won't come down,
Big boat up the river and she won't come down.

[Verse 2]
Big boat up the river on a bank of sand,
If she don't hit the big water she won't never land,
My woman just a-shakin' and a-clappin' her hands,
She thinks she's gonna quit me for some other man, but

[Hook repeated]

[Piano solo]

[Verse 3]
The paddle on the big boat turnin' around and around,
My woman on the levee hoppin' up and down,
She thinks that you'll have some money when you come to town,
She gonna tail me down just like natural hound, but

[Hook repeated]

[Verse 4]
The big boat up to the river blowin' long and sad,
My woman on the levee feeling mighty glad,
She should've kept the money that you once have had,
When I get home, it's gonna be too bad, but . . .

[Hook repeated][75]

"Tell That Woman" is one of the two minor-key compositions of all the recordings discussed in this chapter. Caston's introductory phrases, which are based on the boogie-woogie piano, imitate the sound of a steamboat. This intro gives an uncomfortable feeling to listeners, as if it is telling them that this is not a happy song (see figure 3.3).

Other musical elements help create the gloomy mood. Dixon again uses his compositional technique of having the verse sung over the short riff on the tonic chord—similar to his musical approach in "Signifying Monkey." But in the case of "Tell That Woman," the riff played by Ollie Crawford's guitar is a chromatic descending phrase (see figure 3.3).

Figure 3.3.

Throughout the song, there are almost no chord changes, except when Crawford plays the dominant chord briefly at the end of every four bars.

When Dixon sings the verses, he tries to stay on the same pitch in his lower range, and he uses the same rhythms until all three singers sing the hook an octave higher. Such a stoic set of musical elements helps to depict the narrator's assurance: he knows that this woman will not meet the man she expects, but the chorus "Somebody tell that woman" indicates that he cannot tell her the truth.

Unlike "Tell That Woman," another composition for the May 29 session—"Violent Love"—projects a happy feeling in spite of its title. This is another Tin Pan Alley–style like "Practicing the Art of Love."[76]

Dixon also provided a slow twelve-bar blues song "Lonesome" for this session. This is typical of the Big Three Trio's blues records featuring three-part vocal harmony—their musical trademark.

Dixon says in his autobiography that 1951 was the beginning of the end of the Big Three Trio, because Baby Doo Caston's marriage problems began interfering with the band's gig schedule.[77] However, the year 1951 seems to be misremembered by Dixon. The musicians' union fee record shows that the group had public performances in this year, at least in Chicago.[78] Furthermore, the group actually continued recording until the end of 1952. But it is true that sometime in 1952 Caston was replaced by a new piano player, Lafayette Leake, who later became Dixon's partner for many sessions for Chess Records. While Dixon continued the Big Three Trio after this personnel change, he also became more involved with Chess Records.[79]

The Big Three Trio had three sessions for OKeh through December of 1952. On January 3, 1952, they cut only three sides, without any compositions of the band members. Almost six months after this session, on June 16, they were back in the studio to cut five sides, including Dixon's "Cool Kind Woman" and "My Love Will Never Die."

For "Cool Kind Woman," Dixon took the same lyrical and musical approach as he did to "Money Tree Blues." It is in an a-a-b/twelve-bar blues pattern, but there is a section in a quatrain refrain form combined with a stop-time riff—the words here consist of a catalogue of related words, Dixon's signature way to organize lyrics; in the case of "Cool Kind Woman," the words relate to the woman's actions. Such a rhythmical-lyrical device gives a clever effect to the composition (see figure 3.4).

> [Verse 1]
> She's cool and easy, time you went a home,
> She's cool and easy, time you went a home,
> But every time she shakes, some poor men's money's gone.

[Verse 2]
I just can't get it when you keep on snatchin' it back,
I just can't get it when you keep on snatchin' it back,
When you serve me right, I get just what I like.

[Verse 3]
She took my love,
She ran around,
She play everybody in the one-horse town.

[Hook]
[She's] cool and easy, time you went a home,
But every time she shakes, some poor men's money's gone.

[Verse 4]
Gone, good bye, cash is gone,
Gone, good bye, cash is gone,
That cool kind chick has made uh-many man leave his home.

Figure 3.4.

One unusual feature in "Cool Kind Woman" is that Dixon is not taking the lead vocal, the usual role for the composer. Instead, Crawford sings the vocal solo, and the other sections are in three-part harmony.

"My Love Will Never Die" is unique in that the musical style is derived from melodrama—a type of drama in which spoken words alternate with or are accompanied by passages of music that heighten their dramatic effect; melodrama often appears in vaudeville shows and movies.[80] It is also unique in exploring death, a theme Dixon generally avoided. And this is the second of two minor-key compositions discussed in this chapter ("Tell That Woman").

This song is in an open form. Instead of setting the exact tempo, Dixon sings words in tempo rubato, and his vocal melodies are sung over occasional chord changes by Baby Doo Caston's piano and Crawford's guitar. In the beginning, Caston plays a dramatic introduction that sounds similar to the startling opening of Edvard Grieg's piano concerto. When Dixon sings the statement "My love will never die," he exaggerates the vowels in the words with a smooth glissando and vibrato. Then Dixon softly speaks the next lines as if he is playing a character in a drama in which his death is about to separate him from his woman:

> [Melody]
> My love will never die.
>
> [Spoken]
> My love has found home,
> Deep down in your heart,
> And God knows it will never, never die.

The following section is a little more melodic than the narrative in the previous section:

> [Melody]
> If you see them put me in my grave,
> You maybe see them carry my body away,
> Lift up your head, honey please, don't cry,
> My love for you will never die,
> My love will never die.

For our ears, "My Love Will Never Die" sounds like an overdone tearjerker (because of that it is even funny), but Dixon says that this was a popular tune for their gigs: "I remember one time we played it out in Cheyenne, Wyo., Miles to Climb Club. Big Three was playing out there. We played this particular tune and everybody liked it."[81] Dixon later offered it to Otis Rush, and Dixon's melodramatic writing became an important technique for "Tollin' Bells," presented to Lowell Fulson, and "Tail Dragger," for Howlin' Wolf.[82]

On December 16, 1952, six months after the June 16 session, the Big Three Trio had another recording session for OKeh. This was their final recording session. The band cut four titles, including "Torture My Soul" and "Too Late" by Dixon, but no recordings from this session have ever been released.

One of the most salient characteristics of Dixon's early compositions is that he composed non-blues more than blues-form songs. In addition, as

Table 3.2.   Dixon's Non-blues Songs for His Early Groups

Title	Style	Form	Song Subject
Sweet Louise	Country and western	A-A-B-A pop-song form	Romantic love song
Laundry Man	Novelty	A-A-B-A pop-song form	Advertisement Work song (possibly obscene song)
Signifying Monkey	Ballad	One-part form	Narrative
Don't Let the Music Die	Jive	One-part form	?
Practicing the Art of Love	Tin Pan Alley pop	A-A-B-A pop-song form	Romantic love song
Violent Love	Tin Pan Alley pop	A-A-B-A pop-song form	Romantic love song
Tell That Woman	Ballad	Binary form	Narrative
My Love Will Never Die	Melodrama	Open form	Romantic love song

table 3.2 shows, Dixon's non-blues songs have a wide variety in forms, styles, and song subjects.

Although the non-blues song topics are varied, none of them include blatantly sexual themes. Two out of three blues compositions, on the other hand, are filled with graphic sexual metaphors. Dixon had a sense that certain song contents were suited to certain forms and styles.

What table 3.2 ignores, however, is that in Dixon's mind, there was no distinction between writing blues and writing other kinds of music. The labels to indicate different musical styles meant nothing to him. Shirli Dixon stresses,

> He thought it [pop song] was all blues. . . . My dad's philosophy . . . is "the blues are the roots, and everything else is the fruit." As far as he was concerned . . . it was all the blues . . . so, in his mind, Big Three Trio was just as much blues as was Muddy Waters or any other.[83]

The first ten years of Willie Dixon's career was a remarkable period. He developed his core musical techniques—some of his signature compositional techniques—as we have observed. This was also a time that he established himself as an accomplished bass player: as Butch Dixon describes, "Remember, he went from a tin can with sticking strings to four string bass fiddle."[84]

Notes

1. Blues historian Mike Rowe writes about the rise of Chicago's musical entertainment industry:

The fourteen years of Prohibition spanned the halcyon days of the prosperous '20s right through to the depressed '30s, but what was left after repeal was a network of crime organized on the lines of big (and very big) business. The musical result was the establishment of a lusty and vigorous club scene that asserted Chicago's claim to be the home of the blues.

Mike Rowe, *Chicago Blues: The City and the Music* [originally entitled *Chicago Breakdown*] (London: Eddison Press, 1973; repr., New York: Da Capo Press, 1975), 40. Citations are to the Da Capo Press edition.

2. Bob Corritore, Bill Ferris, and Jim O'Neal. "Willie Dixon (Part 1)," *Living Blues*, no. 81 (July–August 1988): 21.

3. The role of the record producer—also called the A&R (artist and repertoire) man—before the 1950s was different from that of today. The prime responsibilities included talent scouting, choosing materials for recording, organizing sessions, and giving advice to musicians. The technology of those days did not allow them to process sounds, and they could not even edit recordings until the invention of magnetic tape in the late 1940s.

4. Robert Palmer, *Deep Blues* (New York: Viking Press, 1981; repr., New York: Penguin Books, 1982), 135. Citations are to the Penguin Books edition.

5. Willie Dixon, with Don Snowden, *I Am the Blues: The Willie Dixon Story* (New York: Da Capo Press, 1989), 62. Benjamin Filene, *Romancing the Folk: Public Memory & American Roots Music* (Chapel Hill: University of North Carolina Press, 2000), 80.

6. David Evans disusses the causes of the emergence of professional blues songwriters who could write original songs. By the time blues recording resumed after the Depression, many of traditional blues lyrics and musical elements had already been recorded. Over the years folk blues performers had continued to incorporate songs learned from records into their repertoires. Evans, *Big Road Blues: Tradition and Creativity in Folk Blues* (Berkeley: University of California Press, 1982), 81.

7. Bob Koester, interview by the author, September 20, 2004. Koester continues, "But Mayo usually relied on musicians and engineers to deal with producer responsibilities. . . . There was Mayo and Lester, and then there was Willie."

8. Corritore, Ferris, and O'Neal, "Willie Dixon (Part 1)," 20.

9. Jim O'Neal, interview by the author, September 18, 2003.

10. Corritore, Ferris, and O'Neal, "Willie Dixon (Part 1)," 21.

11. Dixon, *I Am the Blues*, 48.

12. Jonas Bernholm, "Liner Notes," *I Feel Like Steppin' Out* [CD], recorded by the Big Three Trio (Czechoslovakia: Dr. Horse, RBD 804, 1985), 5.

13. Corritore, Ferris, and O'Neal, "Willie Dixon (Part 1)," 21.

14. Dixon says, "I'd made a song called 'Beat Her Out, Bumpin' Boys.'" Dixon, *I Am the Blues*, 49.

15. Ibid. Although their debut session was unsuccessful, Caston and Gilmore made solo records with Williams. Gilmore recorded two sides ("Brown Skin Woman" and "Charity Blues") on September 29, 1939, and he recorded another two sides

("She Got Something There" and "The Natchez Fire") on June 4, 1940, on which Caston was a sideman playing the piano. On this same day, Caston recorded two sides ("I'm Gonna Walk Your Log" and "The Death of Walter Barnes").

On October 23 1939, the Royal Rhythm Boys (Slam Stewart, Billy Moore, and Jimmy Prince) recorded "Beat It Out Bumpin' Boy" for Decca, a composer credit of which was shared by Gilmore and Mayo Williams. David Evans notes that probably Williams liked the song but not the Chicago group and gave it to Stewart's group to record. Evans, "A Review for Mitsutoshi Inaba's Manuscript," June 10, 2008, 3.

16. Bernholm, "Liner Notes," 3.

17. Worth Long, "The Wisdom of the Blues—Defining Blues as the True Facts of Life: An Interview with Willie Dixon," *African American Review* 29, no. 2 (Summer 1995): 209.

18. Complete recordings of the Five Breezes are available in CD: *Chicago Blues: Complete Recorded Works and Alternate Takes*, vol. 2, *1939–1944* (Vienna: Document Records, DOCD-5444, 1996).

19. "Sweet Louise" is copyrighted to Gene Gilmore, and "Laundry Man" is copyrighted to Robert Brown (Washboard Sam). BMI Repertoire, repertoire.bmi.com/TitleSearch.asp?querytype=WorkName&page=1&fromrow=1&torow=25&keyname=Signifying%20Monkey&blnWriter=True&blnPublisher=True&blnArtist=False&blnAltTitles=False (accessed December 3, 2004). The author could not have permission to include the lyrics of these songs.

20. "Laundry Man" can be classified as an odd pop song or a silly song written that way on purpose, mainly because the term *novelty song* is used in a very loose way.

21. Jeff Titon, *From Blues to Pop: The Autobiography of Leonard "Baby Doo" Caston*, JEMF Special Series no. 4 (Los Angeles: John Edwards Memorial Foundation, Folklore and Mythology Center, University of California, 1974), 14.

22. Dixon, *I Am the Blues*, 50.

23. Corritore, Ferris, and O'Neal, "Willie Dixon (Part 1)," 18.

24. Dixon's payment record is included in the Blues Archive of the Harold Washington Library (Chicago). According to the record, Dixon made his first payment to the union on May 31, 1941.

25. Dixon, *I Am the Blues*, 50.

26. Titon, *From Blues to Pop*, 14.

27. Dixon, *I Am the Blues*, 52.

28. Ibid., 53.

29. Ibid., 54–55.

30. Ibid., 54.

31. Shirli Dixon, interview, by the author, September 23, 2002. Dixon maintained this political view for his entire life. Dixon told *Rolling Stone* about his invitation from George H. W. Bush to play at the inauguration ceremony:

Asked if he voted for Bush, Dixon shakes his head and says simply, with a half smile, "No." His voice was a hoarse but friendly bass growl. Dixon continues: "You know, anything can change. . . . We have always had to go along with whatever the program was, because you go with what you got until you can get what you want."

Anthony DeCurtis, "Willie Dixon and the Wisdom of the Blues," *Rolling Stone*, no. 548 (March 23, 1989): 112. Shirli Dixon said that during the ceremony, Dixon had a Jesse Jackson button on his tuxedo.

32. Regarding the reason the authorities dropped the case, Dixon says, "I don't know why they let me out. I guess they must have felt like I would be better off for them on the outside because I'd have to hustle like hell for a living." Dixon, *I Am the Blues*, 55.

33. For the Rhythm Rascals, Caston and Ollie Crawford (a future member of the Big Three Trio) played guitar, and Alfred Elkins played bass. In Frankfurt, the Rhythm Rascals, Alberta Hunter, and two other musicians formed a group, Rhythm and Blues Unit 47, and they had a special performance for Eisenhower and Zhukov. The entertainment section of the *Chicago Defender* issued on January 5, 1946, introduced them as the 3 Rhythm Rascals. Joseph "Cool Breeze" Bell also continued to play. He formed the Four Breezes and now became a bassist. On September 19 and November 21, 1953, the entertainment section of the *Chicago Defender* had gig advertisements that included a portrait of him holding an upright bass.

34. Dick Shurman, Billy Vera, and Jim O'Neal, "Liner Notes," *The Mercury Blues 'n' Rhythm Story, 1945–1955* (New York: Mercury Records, 314 528 292-2, 1996), 4.

35. In the February 16 edition of the *Chicago Defender*, the Four Jumps of Jive only had 998 votes, but by the end of counting on April 20, they had increased their number of votes, which put the group at the tenth position in the "special artists" category: February 23—1,290; March 9—7,164; March 23—12,055; April 20—40,165. *Chicago Defender*, February 16, 1946, 16; February 23, 1946, 16; March 9, 1946, 16; March 23, 1946, 16; April 20, 1946, 16.

36. Bernholm, "Liner Notes," 4.

37. "Cocktail trio" was the musical style that was also known as "cocktail music" or "club blues" in white and black clubs respectively in the 1930s and 1940s. As seen in the Nat "King" Cole Trio, the most famous of the genre, the ensemble typically consisted of piano, guitar, and bass, and members also took a lead vocal and backup vocals. Their music generally functioned as background music for conversation with drinks. Portia K. Maultsby, "Rhythm and Blues" in *African American Music: An Introduction*, ed. Mellonee V. Burnim and Portia K. Maultsby (New York: Routledge, 2006), 251.

38. Willie Dixon, *I Am the Blues* [DVD] (Huntingdon Cambs, England: CJ Productions and Quantum Leap Group, DRB-1345, 2002).

39. Dixon, *I Am the Blues*, 69.

40. "Advanced Record Releases," *Billboard*, May 10, 1947, 122. In this issue, "Get up Those Stairs, Mademoiselle" with "Lonely Roamin'" (Bullet 274) and "You Sure Look Good to Me" with "Signifying Monkey" (Bullet 275) are listed. Because "records listed are generally approximately two weeks in advance of actual release date," the actual release date was probably around the end of May 1947.

41. Although Caston says, "It was the first time blues was played like that," there were blues recordings featuring vocal harmony in the 1920s: for example, "Jelly Roll Blues" and "Preacher Man Blues" by Norfolk Jazz Quartet (1921) and "Pleading Blues" by Monarch Jazz Quartet of Norfolk (1929). Caston quote is from Titon, *From Blues to Pop*, 18–19.

42. Ibid.

43. Butch Dixon, interview, by the author, September 23, 2003.

44. Joel Whitburn, *Top R&B Singles, 1942–1999* (Menomonee Falls, WI: Record Research, 2000), 31. In Paramount Record Shop's mail-order service advertised in the July 31, 1948, issue of the *Chicago Defender*, this song was listed for the first time in the best-seller section; *Chicago Defender*, National Weekly Edition, July 31, 1948, 10. In the September 11 edition, the song also appeared among "Old Favorites and Newest Releases in Stock" advertised by Essex Record Shop; *Chicago Defender*, National Weekly Edition, September 11, 1948, p. 9. In the September 25 edition, another company, Harlem Hit Parade Inc., listed this song in the catalogue; *Chicago Defender*, National Weekly Edition, September 25, 1948, p. 9. From then on, "You Sure Look Good to Me" was in the mail-order lists of those shops throughout 1948 and the first half of 1949; *Chicago Defender*, National Weekly Edition, February 25, 1950, p. 21.

45. Mary Katherine Aldin, "Liner Notes," *The Big Three Trio*, recorded by Willie Dixon (New York: Columbia Records Inc., CK 46216, 1990), 5.

46. Folklorist Bruce Jackson writes, "The best known toasts are 'Signifying Monkey,' 'Titanic,' and 'Stackolee.' Most toasts come from black folk tradition, but sometimes poems from other sources are adopted—poems from popular anthologies, hobo tradition, and parodies of well-known poems turn up with regularity." Jackson, "Liner Notes," *Get Your Ass in the Water and Swim like Me! Narrative Poetry from Black Oral Tradition* (Cambridge, MA: Rounder Records, Rounder CD 2014, 1998), 3.

47. Corritore, Ferris, and O'Neal, "Willie Dixon (Part 1)," 17.

48. Roger D. Abrahams, *Deep Down in the Jungle: Negro Narrative Folklore from the Streets of Philadelphia* (Hatboro, PA: Folklore Associates, 1964; 1st rev. ed, Chicago: Aldine Publishing Company, 1970), 145. Citations are to the Aldine Publishing Company edition.

49. Dixon, *I Am the Blues*, 53.

50. See Abrahams, *Deep Down in the Jungle* and Bruce Jackson, *Get Your Ass in the Water and Swim like Me: Narrative Poetry from Black Oral Tradition* (Cambridge, MA: Harvard University Press, 1974). A companion CD to *Get Your Ass in the Water* is also available (Rounder CD 2014, 1998). This CD includes two versions of "Signifying Monkey," and its variations "Partytime Monkey" and "Poolshooting Monkey."

51. Red Larrison, "The Lion, Monkey and Elephant," *The Lancer* 3, no. 3 (March 1946): 37. The Big Three Trio's "Signifying Monkey" was released in May of 1947. Therefore, their record was most likely not a source for Larrison's version.

52. Ballad form—derived from the British/American tradition—tells sequential stories which invites comparison, and the subjects were usually focused around a

single incident or the depredations of a single individual." Paul Oliver, *Songsters &
Saints: Vocal Traditions on Race Records* (Cambridge: Cambridge University Press,
1984), 229.

53. Butch Dixon, interview, by the author, September 23, 2003.

54. Martin Hawkins, "Liner Notes," *A Shot in the Dark: Nashville Jumps: Blues &
Rhythm on Nashville Independent Labels* (Hambergen, Germany: Bear Family Records,
BCD 15864 HL, 2000), 169.

55. The record "If the Sea Was Whiskey," coupled with "Signifying Monkey" (Columbia 37358) was introduced in "Advanced Record Release" of the *Billboard*, June 7,
1947, issue. "Advanced Record Release," *Billboard*, June 7, 1947, 117.

56. Country blues artist Robert Pete Williams, who was rediscovered during the
blues revival era in the late 1950s, sings the line "No more sweet potatoes, the frost
done killed the vine / Blues ain't nothing but a good woman on your mind" in his
recording "No More Sweet Potatoes." In this recording (made in Baton Rouge,
on April 28, 1963), Williams sounds as if he is building an improvisation around
traditional lyrics. Robert Pete Williams, *Poor Bob's Blues*, notes by Elijah Wald (El
Cerrito, CA: Arhoolie Records, Arhoolie CD 511, 2003).

57. Dixon, *I Am the Blues*, 62. For example, a series of John Lee "Sonny Boy"
Williamson's early recordings for Bluebird label sound very similar to one another.

58. Bob Corritore, Bill Ferris, and Jim O'Neal, "Willie Dixon (Part 2)," *Living
Blues*, no. 82 (September–October 1988): 24.

59. From this session on, Barnardo Dennis was replaced by Ollie Crawford, and
then Crawford became a permanent member of the group until it broke up.

60. Dixon, *I Am the Blues*, 59.

61. Dixon's collaboration with Memphis Slim will be discussed in chapter 7.

62. Dixon, *I Am the Blues*, 64.

63. Ibid.

64. Butch Dixon, interview, by the author, September 23, 2003.

65. Dixon, *I Am the Blues*, 64.

66. Bob Koester, interview, by the author, September 20, 2004.

67. Rowe, *Chicago Blues*, 76–78.

68. Titon, *From Blues to Pop*, 21.

69. *Chicago Defender*, National Weekly Edition, April 23, 1949, 16.

70. Bernholm, "Liner Notes," 8.

71. *Chicago Defender*, May 7, 1949, 25. These records were also released from
Columbia. Possibly because Lester Melrose was related to both companies, he could
have sold the original masters to Bullet, or the Big Three Trio could have made
up the unfulfilled contract with Bullet. It is also possible that Columbia and Bullet
fought over the ownership of these recordings, and Jim Bulleit tried to hold it. The
wording of the advertisement—"Everybody's Buying Their Delta Recording of 'TILL
THE DAY I DIE' AND 'DON'T LET THAT MUSIC DIE,' ASK FOR DELTA
202"—may be encouraging fans to avoid buying the same records from Columbia.

72. Dixon later offered this song to guitarist/singer Jimmy Reeves Jr. Producing Reeves' album was one of Dixon's final projects for Chess Records. Their collaboration is discussed in chapter 7.

73. OKeh was revived and replaced the Columbia 30000 series. The *Chicago Defender* carried the following article about relaunching OKeh:

> A number of top flight artists will appear on the revived OKeh record label, a subsidiary of Columbia records which has been inactive since 1942, it was learned here last week. . . . Although the present talent roster features for the most part quality semi-name artists, the list, however, does include big names such as Duke Ellington, and the Ravens. Others already lined up for the label are Arnett Cobb, Al Russell, the Do Re Mi Trio, Sugar Tones, the Treniers, Big Three Trio.

"To Revive OKeh Label: Many Top Names on Discs," *Chicago Defender*, June 23, 1951, 21.

74. Dixon, *I Am the Blues*, 32–33.

75. Peter, Paul, and Mary recorded this song under the title of "Big Boat" for their 1963 album *Moving*. They learned this song from folk singer Brother John Sellers' album *Big Boat up the River* (1954). While most of the lyrics and musical phrases are taken from Dixon's composition, Seller claimed he was the composer. Dixon took action to retrieve his royalty. The details are found in Dixon, *I Am the Blues*, 164–65.

76. "Violent Love" was rerecorded for Chess Records sometime in 1952, and Dixon offered this song to Otis Rush in 1956.

77. Dixon, *I Am the Blues*, 76.

78. Dixon made payments for February 2, May 23, and October 2 (two performances). Dixon's payments for June 19 and December 10, 1952, are also recorded.

79. Dixon, *I Am the Blues*, 76.

80. Anne Dhu Shapiro, "Melodrama," in *The New Grove Dictionary of American Music*, vol. 3, ed. H. Wiley Hitchcock and Stanley Sadie (New York: Grove's Dictionaries of Music, 1986), 202. One model for this type of writing is found in Bessie Smith's film *St. Louis Blues* (1929), which features a typical melodramatic scene.

81. Corritore, Ferris, and O'Neal, "Willie Dixon (Part 2)," 22.

82. Otis Rush's version is discussed in chapter 6. Dixon's work for Lowell Fulson is discussed in chapter 5 and Howlin' Wolf in chapter 7.

83. Shirli Dixon, interview by the author, September 23, 2002.

84. Butch Dixon, interview by the author, September 23, 2003.

CHAPTER FOUR

~

Willie Dixon and Chess Records

In 1953, Willie Dixon contracted with Aristocrat/Chess Records. He worked as an indispensable staff member for the company. From his first Aristocrat session with guitarist/vocalist Robert Nighthawk in 1948 until 1956, when he temporarily contracted with Cobra Records, Dixon was bassist in about seventy documented productions.

More importantly Dixon became a house songwriter for the company after his January 1954 success writing "Hoochie Coochie Man" for Muddy Waters. Other Chess artists who recorded Dixon compositions during this period included Eddie Boyd, Little Walter, Howlin' Wolf, Lowell Fulson, Willie Mabon, Jimmy Witherspoon, Bo Diddley, and Jimmy Rogers. Leonard Chess, one of the co-owners of the label, once described Dixon as "my right arm."[1]

Aristocrat Records was an independent record company owned by brothers Leonard and Philip (Phil) Chess, who were Polish Jewish immigrants born in 1915 and 1917, respectively, in the area known as White Russia. After graduating from a technical high school, Leonard took several odd jobs, then started a liquor business in the South Side of Chicago. He got to know its burgeoning black community and their love for music. He began working at the Congress Buffet in South Cottage Grove, and subsequently he bought the place and renamed it Macomba Lounge. Phil, after being released from the army in 1947, helped with his brother's business.

While Macomba became a well-known musical spot, Leonard hated the club business because of frequent—sometimes life-threatening—troubles with customers. Noticing that record company agents from as far away as the West Coast came to scout for artists who regularly played in the South Side clubs, and that radio broadcasts demonstrated the popularity of those artists' records, Leonard began to think that the recording business could be a new source of revenue.[2]

Counting on the Jewish community in Chicago, Leonard contacted Evelyn Aron. In the spring of 1947, Evelyn and her husband, Charles, had started a record company with another couple, Fred and Mildred Brount. They named the company Aristocrat Record Corporation. The company released its first record, with "Chi-Baba Chi-Baba," by Sherman Hayes and his orchestra, and "Say No More," by Wyoma. Sometime in the second half of 1947, Leonard became a sales representative, offering to Aristocrat the popular musicians playing in Macomba.

Toward the end of 1940s, social changes in Chicago's African American community transformed the black popular music scene of the city. By the time Aristocrat released Muddy Waters' "I Can't Be Satisfied" with "I Feel Like Going Home" in 1948, there were some black audiences looking for something new—something that would replace the currently popular black music, represented by the Bluebird beat (see chapter 3).[3] Most of those who supported Muddy's records were lower-working-class people who had recently arrived in Chicago and settled in the South Side. Muddy's music was alternative music that small independent record companies targeted at the new audiences.

Although Aristocrat originally recorded both black and white artists, along with Muddy's success it became an almost exclusively black music label. *Billboard* notes, "The growing demand for platters in Negro urban areas and in the South and Southwest and . . . the discovery of the idiom by the general record buying public."[4] Mississippi-native radio personality Al Benson eagerly promoted the music that suited the new audience's musical taste.[5]

Around this time, Aristocrat changed its business structure. Leonard bought out his business partners' share.[6] By the end of 1949, Evelyn Aron left the company, mainly because she did not like Leonard's rough manner. He still owned Macomba but decided to focus on the recording business, because this business occupied a great amount of time and his club was destroyed by fire sometime in 1950. In June 1950, Buster Williams, an owner of a record press plant in Memphis who pressed records for Aristocrat, recommended that Leonard change the label name to Chess Records, which was not only their family name but also sounded "crisp like the downbeat that kicks off a song."[7]

In September 1948 (specific date is not known),[8] about half a year after Muddy's successful record, Willie Dixon joined an Aristocrat recording session for the first time as a sideman for Robert Nighthawk and Ethel Mae's "Return Mail Blues" and "My Sweet Lovin' Woman." Dixon was still a member of the Big Three Trio. In most of the label's early sessions, Ernest "Big" Crawford was a regular bassist. It is not known why Dixon substituted for Crawford for this occasion; it could have been that Dixon and Nighthawk had known each other, because both belonged to Lester Melrose's production.

For the next Nighthawk session on July 12, 1949, Dixon again played the bass. This session included Nighthawk's famous "Black Angel Blues" (aka "Sweet Black Angel") and "Annie Lee Blues" (aka "Anna Lee"). Dixon's third Aristocrat session was again for Nighthawk on January 5, 1950.

When the Big Three Trio broke up in 1952, Dixon looked for a new source of income, and at the same time, Leonard Chess was looking for an assistant; his business was becoming too big to handle with only a limited number of people. The Chess brothers were responsible for every element of the business—record production, promotion, exploring new artists, and accounting.

The most immediate reason for Dixon to become a full-time employee was his session work for vocalist/pianist Eddie Boyd on October 10, 1952. This session was followed by another session in May 1953 (the specific date is not known), for which Dixon provided Boyd with a composition, "Third Degree." Boyd remembers,

> I mean I got Willie Dixon that job with Chess. I'm the man who introduced him to Leonard. Dixon wrote that tune "Third Degree" [Chess 1541] and "Rattin' and Runnin' Around" [Chess 1576] that I recorded. But he wasn't working for Chess at that time. . . . And then Leonard took him over there and he was doing some little, well, handyman work and helping some artists who didn't have material, and they just kept on until they put him on the staff as A&R man.[9]

Dixon made a formal contract with Chess Records sometime in 1953. From the following year, his name regularly appeared as a bassist on log sheets for recording sessions.

Dixon describes his work for Chess Records: "They [the Chess brothers] insisted that I assist them in everything they'd do."[10] There were four main capacities in which Dixon contributed to the label: as bassist, record producer, songwriter (although his talent as songwriter was not recognized immediately), and regular employee who helped with miscellaneous business chores.

At the early stage of his involvement with the label, the area of the company in which Dixon was most helpful was record production. The Chess brothers, even though they had already produced Muddy's hit records, were still developing their knowledge about recording. They needed someone like Dixon.[11] Malcolm Chisholm, engineer for Chess Records' sessions at Universal Studios from 1955 to 1958, recalls how he was educated by Dixon, not by the Chess brothers:

> What I know of blues other than the simple musical aspect, I learned from Will. He trained his own engineer as it were and, because of that, when I worked with Will it got to the point very quickly where our tastes in many things ran very similar. It got into an ideal situation—which doesn't happen frequently between producer, musicians and engineers—where we didn't have to talk to each other.[12]

By the time Dixon met the Chess brothers, he had gained a solid knowledge of studio operation by experiencing recording sessions with the Big Three Trio and as a sideman for Lester Melrose's production. Also Dixon had an ability to understand the structure of a composition. When musicians were confused in the middle of a recording session, Dixon could give them appropriate instructions.[13] In addition, Dixon was good at setting a mood to help musicians extract their best performances in the studio—an important role as a record producer. He explains,

> And in producin,' you feel, at its best level, if you can get the artist in the mood, that's one of the things. Get 'em in the mood to see what the song say and how the song feel, and if you have a bit of experience about some of the things that he singin' about, why, this inspires him a bit to do his best.[14]

According to Chess Records executive Dick LaPalm, "There wasn't a blues recording made by Leonard and/or Phil where Willie Dixon wasn't present in the studio or the control room. In spite of whoever is credited as producer, when you get right down to it, Willie was the guy. Very few blues things were done without him, even after the bass went electric."[15] Shirli Dixon also says, "110 percent of the time he was involved on the session, arranging the session, producing the session, rewriting the words for the artist."[16] She has observed her father's involvement in the studio by listing to outtakes:

> I have listened to outtakes. MCA Records recently decided to add my father as a producer of all of the Chess blues pieces. . . . They were able to determine

just from listening to the outtakes, every decision regarding the formation of these songs is coming through his voice. As a song is being stopped and started, he's modifying this part of the song, rewriting this part of the song right in the session. So why wasn't he acknowledged as a producer? Why was it always produced by this guy and that guy?[17]

Also, as a producer with an outspoken nature, Dixon made an important contribution to creative decision making. He was not a "yes man" for Leonard. And for Leonard, Dixon was an important artistic barometer:

Well, Leonard didn't know one thing from another; he'd accept the other people's word for it if it sound good. . . . He would always ask me about, "What's about this or that or the other." Different questions about producin' the thing. He had a lot of confidence in what I was sayin'. Everything that I had involved myself in turned out pretty good. So he accepted it. Why, up until the last he always said I was the only one that was 90 percent right (laughter). Because a lot of guys would just say—because he's the boss, "Ya see this is a good tune." I was always, "Hey man, I don't like this, it won't sell," or something. And then finally one day he was askin' different people about the tune, and I told him it wouldn't last. He played his song to death tryin' to make it happen and it wouldn't happen. So he'd come to me, say, "Go on, tell me I told you so." I say, "About what?" He'd say "You know it didn't work."[18]

Another factor that attracted the Chess brothers was that Dixon had strong and broad connections with blues musicians in Chicago. This may have been something he acquired at Tampa Red's house—the Chicago blues musicians' hangout. Chess' biographer Nadine Cohodas writes, "He [Dixon] had a terrific network of contacts throughout the city's blues community, and when it came time to go into the studio, he could find an errant musician. . . . Dixon not only knew them but also knew their friends, their girlfriends, and their habits."[19]

Appendix B lists the documented recording sessions that Dixon was involved in as a bass player from 1948 to 1971. On average, Dixon participated in about twenty sessions a year from 1954 to 1956. For each session, recording four or five compositions was not unusual, while some days produced as many as eight cuts. From the beginning of the 1960s, the number of sessions with Dixon diminished, mainly because of the adoption of the electric bass.

Besides working with blues artists, Dixon participated in almost every Chuck Berry session. "You Can't Catch Me" (1955), for example, captures Dixon's superb ability as a sideman. What creates the fast running feel, the backbone of this recording, is Dixon's bass as well as Johnny Johnson's piano and Eddie Harding's drums. At every end of measure, Dixon compliments Chuck's vocal phrase with a crisp sound of bass strings hitting a fingerboard.

Dixon not only put sessions together but also rehearsed in his home, where he had transformed one room into a rehearsal studio in the mid-1960s. Shirli Dixon explains,

> My bedroom was right over my father's rehearsal studio. So I'd hear the song starting one way, and then listen to them continuously work the song until it was ultimately what we would hear on a record, 45 or LP. So if they [the Chess brothers] made changes to it, I don't know when they were able to do it because my dad would generally work the song over a good portion of the time before they even come into the studio. . . . I'm sure they ultimately had the final business decision. I don't know if they had the final creative decision. I know for a lot of those Chuck Berry things, they absolutely didn't have it. Not only because of Chuck's bubbling personality, but then they had to have a structured musician that was there to make sure that Chuck didn't go too far out of the way on some of the material. So Chuck's sessions, I think, were probably challenging.[20]

Regarding Chuck Berry, Dixon was one of the people who suggested Chuck should shape up the original idea for his debut song "Maybellene" (1955). Dixon recognized "Maybellene" could be an instant hit, but it sounded similar to a country and western tune called "Ida Red" by Bob Wills and His Texas Playboys (1938). Dixon remembers,

> We discussed it pro and con for two or three days. I knew Chuck probably got angry because things weren't really going as he thought they should. I'd say, "But, man, this is too great a song to let it get away with another person's tune," because if it went over, whoever was involved with "Ida Red" would come running.[21]

As a record producer, talent scout was another important job. Sometime in 1953, Dixon arranged for Albert King to audition for disc jockey Al Benson; subsequently, King made his debut records for Benson's Parrot Records.[22] In 1953, with Memphis Slim, Dixon arranged Junior Wells' first session for States Records. In 1956, Dixon also scouted Otis Rush, but because Chess Records turned him down, Dixon brought Otis to Cobra Records (see chapter 6). In 1964, Dixon discovered Koko Taylor (see chapter 7).

Dixon was also a recording artist himself on Chess' subsidiary Checker label. The archive shows that he made four dues payments to the Chicago

Musicians' Union in 1954—this payment record does not include his per-formance outside Chicago.[23] Although the Big Three Trio did not make any records after 1952, they still played at clubs, as their performance was advertised in the September 4, 1954, issue of the *Chicago Defender*.[24] Dixon also performed as Big Dixon in 1955 and as Willie Dixon and His Blues Walkers in 1957.[25]

Besides acting as sideman, session organizer, producer, songwriter, and tal-ent scout, Dixon "did everything from packing records to sweeping the floor and answering the telephone to making out orders."[26] Dixon's robust body and his previous experience as a fighter may have been helpful for heavy labor as well. Peter Guralnick briefly writes, "If there are VIPs in town he [Dixon] shows them the clubs. If there are feelings to be smoothed over Wil-lie does that, too."[27] Shirli Dixon talks about her father's miscellaneous jobs:

> What did he do, I was told every single thing under the sun. My mom would tell you how she and my dad run the musicians to the airport to go on tours. How often telephones were turned off when bills weren't paid, how we went without all of our needs met, but he never stopped being diligent and commit-ted to getting the job done. My mom said that when records were sent to dif-ferent radio stations, [he would] ask the deejays or pay the deejays to perform. He didn't own the record company, so he should not have to do those types of thing. But he believed strongly getting music to the street, so whatever it took, he had the "just do it" kind of attitude.[28]

For Dixon's wife, Marie, being a musician's wife and a mother of several children was sometimes difficult. She recollects when her husband came home late in the evening with some musicians and food:

> I can remember many times that kids were disturbed, and we were disturbed, because of food being brought in. . . . That was always a problem and I was always upset. Willie wanted kids to be educated, but he also wanted to feed and [be] close to children. And it was difficult for him to separate their time of sleeping and [the time] he could get artists in there and do what he need to do, 'cause lots of artists had jobs, you know, a day job. So if it'd take him to midnight to get in with artists, unfortunately kids had to see consequences by not getting rest. And food again, he was always geared to food. It was time he'd come in and start cooking. And kids were waken to the aroma of food and couldn't get back to sleep. You know, they was kids. And we always had misunderstanding with that.[29]

The business relationship between Willie Dixon and the Chess brothers was strained. Dixon (as well as many other ex-Chess musicians) wrote bitter criticisms of them in his autobiography. As was the case of the relationships between other musicians and the label owners, the two sides had opposite opinions; Dixon thought that he was exploited, while the brothers thought that they treated him fairly by the rules of the time.

In spite of his dedication to the company, Dixon claimed that his salary was never satisfactory, and financial dissatisfaction was a constant cause of trouble between him and the label owners. Dixon says, "But they weren't giving me much of a pay thing. They promised to give me so much a week against my royalties and then every week, I'd have to damn near fight or beg for the money."[30]

Butch Dixon describes how his father's work relationship with the label owners became negative:

> In the beginning he was probably happy, because he had a place to exhume his creative idea. He had a place to say, "Well, you know I can go there to do this, and I can do that." In the way he found out "Records being played, people buying my records, but I'm not being paid. I have a family, mouths to feed, children and wife." You know, that became a tough one. They never gave him a straight answer to what he wanted to hear. So a three-hundred-pound ex-fighter is pretty upset with you. Instead of using his face and physical ability, he left.[31]

The fees from session work became one of the most problematic areas. While late payment of session fees was a common practice of the time, especially when it came to a small independent record label, Dixon complained the payment was not only late but also often inconsistent.[32] Dixon states that he "did not receive a penny for any arrangements of all the things he produced for the company."[33]

Royalties from compositions was another controversial realm between Dixon and the label. In 1953, Gene and Harry Goodman (Benny Goodman's brothers), the owners of a successful publishing company in New York, came to meet the Chess brothers. They were told to establish their own publishing company to deal with the compositions that first appeared on the label. Subsequently, they started Arc Music, which was affiliated with BMI. According to Cohodas, the following was the general agreement between the Chess brothers and the Goodman brothers:

> The four Arc principals [the Chess brothers and the Goodman brothers] agreed that Chess would pay the one-penny "mechanical" fee on the sale of these records directly to the writer. But Arc would not get the other penny even though it was the publisher of the song. That penny per record remained at Chess and Checker. One provision on the early Arc songwriting contracts said

specifically that "no royalties are to be paid on these recordings" for Chess and Checker labels. The writer would get mechanical royalties through Arc only from the sales of subsequent versions of a song on other labels.[34]

Soon Dixon's compositions for the label's top artists made the R&B (rhythm and blues) charts and regular rotation for radio airplay. He strongly felt that he was cheated, because "I didn't have $2 a lot of times to have a copyright paper on a song into Congress."[35]

On the other hand, from the point of view of his business experience as a blues record producer, an owner of a record company, and a record store, Bob Koester observes that royalties that songwriters received were legitimate:

> Blues records don't sell well. They never have. If a blues record would sell a hundred thousand, that would be a big hit. Artists say because it's selling well in the black community on the South Side, it's selling everywhere. And it's very easy for them to think that there is more money involved than it really is.
>
> Consider the economics of single record, a 45 or a 78 cost anywhere from twenty odd cents to thirty odd cents to press. Then the music publisher takes two cents each side [and a writer takes one cent each side]. The records are sold to distributer for thirty-five to forty cents. The distributer sells it to stores for fifty cents, fifty-five cents, something in that range. And store sells it for seventy-five cents to a dollar, depending on which period.
>
> But there's not much room there to cover recording cost, publicity, rent, light, heat, maybe air conditioning if you like, overhead. These are costs that nobody thinks about. They think record companies exist without paying rent. That kind of thinking persists today. People say, "Why do I have to pay fifteen dollars for a CD when it only costs seventy-five cents to press?" Because of all these other costs! . . . And it takes time to do it right. And if you hire somebody to produce a record, whatever you do with him, that's a part of overhead.
>
> Muddy Waters was on the chart. I don't think it was pop charts. He was on blues charts or R&B charts. That was kind of phenomenal, because during the '50s, most of the artists on the charts were not bluesmen. That was sax bands and trios and doo-wops and things. So that was a pretty good accomplishment. Blues was alternative music. It's a tiny part of the record business. . . . I mean you can't figure that a hit by Muddy Waters in the R&B charts gonna sell as well as a hit by Frank Sinatra on the pop charts.[36]

Dixon actually states that blues recording was not a big business: "Chess would never get over 1,000 or 2,000 records on anybody, but when we first cut that Chuck Berry number ['Maybellene'], I think he [Leonard Chess] put 10,000 on the floor at the first shot."[37]

Leonard's son Marshall Chess consistently justifies his family's work policy: "My father, my uncle, Chess Records, they weren't angels. If they were angels, they couldn't have survived, dealing even with the artists, who weren't angels, either. Period."[38] He also says,

> I don't think there was any ripping off at all. We paid *low* royalties, but everyone did, you know. I used to see my father go through all the royalty statements, and all I ever saw him do was *once* take money from one artist and give it to another because *he* needed the money to *live*. But I'll say this: they were 2–3 percent artists' royalties, all these cheap royalties.[39]

Cohodas also evaluates Chess brothers' business practices at that time:

> They played by the rules of the time, not questioning whether their practices and those of every other independent stacked the deck against the artist. Race was an element in the conflict, not because of Leonard and Phil's behavior toward their musicians but because of what it meant to be black in the mid-fifties, particularly for a migrant from the South in Chicago. There had been little opportunity for formal education and no training in the intricacies of business. In their place were strong and creative ways of surviving and thriving in a white-dominated world. It was a day-to-day proposition, celebrating the joy of the present with not much thought for the future. The money these musicians made was often the most they had ever seen. It could slip through their hands in a day.[40]

Cohodas' statement that "race was an element in the conflict" is actually not the whole picture. For instance, the fact that the publisher or record company takes advantage of musicians' ignorance of copyright is a matter of morality regardless of their racial differences. John Lennon and Paul McCartney, whose publisher was an English entrepreneur, renounced their copyrights from compositions at an early stage of their career without knowing what they were singing. On the other hand, there were savvy black musicians like W. C. Handy and Sam Cooke who established their own publishing companies.

Regardless of being black or white, in the recording industry, typically in the first half of the twentieth century, songwriters often had no idea about copyright, or they would assume that the copyright system was too complicated. To this day, it is not unusual that songwriters and publishers have disputes over royalties, while many songwriters hire capable lawyers to avoid such problems. The bottom line is that there are no laws that dictate that publishers need to explain copyright law to musicians. If a musician has no idea about copyright, it is likely to cause disagreement, and that person will possibly feel that he or she is being exploited. This was very true in the 1950s, especially when the copyright fee was generally one cent per side but not based on a percentage of record sales, no matter how the price of a platter along with other prices increased by degrees.

Frequent financial disagreements between Dixon and the Chess brothers eventually developed into Dixon's resignation from Chess Records. He moved to Cobra Records in the summer of 1956, though he still attended Chess sessions occasionally. He had also started his own booking agency, the Ghana Booking Agency, and in 1957 this developed into a publishing company, which was registered with BMI and was responsible for publishing his songs in Europe. In 1977, Dixon and Muddy Waters, with the aid of their business manager at the time, Scott Cameron, sued Arc Music. Dixon retrieved his songs and started Hoochie Coochie Music.

In fairness to Willie Dixon, other Chess musicians, and the label owners, their statements all seem to contain elements of truth as well as self-vindication and varying degrees of exaggeration, depending on each different point of view. There may have been times that musicians were exploited, while at other times the label owners treated musicians fairly and helped them with their financial needs.

Whether Chess Records was a good place to be or not, there could have been various reasons why artists stayed with the label. Most musicians who came out of the rural South needed an income to survive in the big city. Even though some felt they were being cheated, the payments they received were better than factory jobs or agricultural labor. There was no guarantee that a different label would treat them with any more respect. Fame could have been another motivation for artists to stay with the label. By being with Chess Records, the musicians obtained good publicity. In some cases, it took the artists some years to figure out the copyright system. For instance, Dixon did not find out that the Goodman brothers and the Chess brothers received the bulk of his royalties until the late 1950s.[41] More important, making music could have been a positive reason for staying. This was certainly true for Dixon.

What made Willie Dixon commit to Chess Records' productions was his strong belief that the music they created with the artists on the label was meaningful for the community. He believed that he was on an important mission to deliver their creation. For Dixon, Chess Records "was a workplace, a means to an end, and was a way for him to get these messages out there through a number of voices even if it wasn't going to be his own." Shirli Dixon stresses,

> I know that my dad was very much abused by the Chess family in that he did everything and very much underrepresented. But his goal was greater than being recognized for everything that he was doing. His goal was really to share these real life experiences that he had through music. He always told me that . . . music was a therapy for us. We had artistic therapy, had to continuously offer for the world to begin to understand each other.[42]

> The business operation he thought was horrible. And he knew that they were . . . trying to survive, trying to build the business. But one of the things that he told us was "You gotta get the record played and pressed." A lot goes into before one guy has a chance to hear it, and sometimes people don't realize that. So, because of that, there's a lot on the front end, but he knew that there was more available than they were getting. And it was demeaning to him to put in so much. He would've never done anything that he couldn't be a 100 percent, you see? So, it was demeaning to him.
>   While he liked them [the Chess brothers] overall in the idea of someone championed the blues, people from outside the blues coming in and wanting to champion the blues for the whole world to hear. He loved that concept. He appreciated anyone that loved what he loved and appreciated this art form. But he was heartbroken at the mistreatment that the musicians would get and him as well. He just didn't think he deserved it. And they called him for everything, to stop arguments, fights and walk out the sessions, and sometimes the guys were intoxicated. He'd have to come in whatever kind of an environment, but he loved this music, and he wanted everybody to win from it.[43]

Notes

1. Nadine Cohodas, *Spinning Blues into Gold: The Chess Brothers and the Legendary Chess Records* (New York: St. Martin's Press, 2000), 83.

2. Ibid., 34.

3. Blues historian Pete Welding explains why the shift of musical trends from Bluebird to Chess blues occured:

> As a result of the major record firms' concentration of recording activities in one city, coupled with the rise of what might be considered a bloc of reliable, versatile studio musicians who in varying combinations performed on by far the major portion of the blues records made there, the Chicago blues recordings of 1935–1945 tended toward a type of polished regularity that was suave and supple at best, bland and predictable at worst. Closed as the self-perpetuating studio blues scene was to new ideas, stagnation inevitably set in and the way was paved for the new synthesis of country and city that [Muddy] Waters and his followers set in motion right after the war.

Pete Welding, "Muddy Waters: Gone to Main Street," in *Bluesland*, ed. Pete Welding and Toby Byron (New York: Dutton, 1991), 134.

4. Cohodas, *Spinning Blues into Gold*, 42.

5. Ibid., 45.

6. Ibid., 43.

7. Ibid., 56.

8. This recording date is taken from the most updated discography: Les Fancourt and Bob McGrath, *The Blues Discography 1943–1970* (Canada: Eyeball Production, 2006), 420. In old sources, a different date, November 10, 1948, was given to this session. Les Fancourt, *Chess Blues: A Discography of the Blues Artists on the Chess Labels, 1947–1975* (Faversham, Kent, England: L. Fancourt, 1983; repr., 1989), 31. Michael Ruppli, *The Chess Labels: A Discography*, vol. 1 (Westport, CT: Greenwood Press, 1988), 6.

9. Jim O'Neal and Amy van Singel, *The Voices of the Blues: Classic Interviews from Living Blues Magazine* (New York, London Routledge, 2002), 250.

10. Willie Dixon, with Don Snowden, *I Am the Blues: The Willie Dixon Story* (New York: Da Capo Press, 1989), 82.

11. Although many musicians and music writers criticized Leonard Chess' production ability, his interest in music and his way of producing records should not be underrated. Bob Koester, who produced many significant blues records for Delmark Records in Chicago, corroborates: "I think it would be a mistake to underestimate Leonard's interest in music and his brusque and mother-fucking way of getting performances out of musicians. Because he did produce some pretty good records before Willie Dixon was much on the scene." Bob Koester, interview by the author, September 20, 2004. On the other hand, as Benjamin Filene points out, it is true that "Chess was savvy enough not to rely on his own musical instincts but to keep a close watch on the reactions of his African American market." Filene, *Romancing the Folk: Public Memory & American Roots Music* (Chapel Hill: University of North Carolina Press, 2000), 94–95.

12. Dixon, *I Am the Blues*, 95.

13. The actual example of Dixon's giving instruction in the middle of recording session is found in the section on Little Walter in next chapter.

14. Bob Corritore, Bill Ferris, and Jim O'Neal, "Willie Dixon (Part 1)," *Living Blues*, no. 81 (July–August 1988): 25.

15. Mary Katherine Aldin, "Liner Notes," *Chess Blues* [CD] (Universal City, CA: Chess/MCA, CHC4-9340, 1992), 21.

16. Shirli Dixon, interview by the author, September 23, 2002.

17. Ibid.

18. Corritore, Ferris, and O'Neal, "Willie Dixon (Part 1)," 23–24.

19. Cohodas, *Spinning the Blues into Gold*, 93.

20. Shirli Dixon, interview by the author, September 23, 2002.

21. Dixon, *I Am the Blues*, 90. In spite of Dixon's statement "We discussed it pro and con for two or three days," Chuck Berry mentions in his autobiography that he

immediately changed the title of "Maybellene" from "Ida Red" at the point of the session. Chuck Berry, *The Autobiography* (New York: Harmony Books, 1987), 103. The refrain of "Maybellene" was also inspired by "Oh Red" by The Harlem Hamfats (1936).

22. Lee Hildebrand, "Liner Notes," *Windy City Blues* (Berkeley: Stax Records/ Fantasy, 2004).

23. Payment record is included in the Blues Archive of Harold Washington Library (Chicago).

24. *Chicago Defender*, September 4, 1954, 31.

25. *Chicago Defender*, October 29, 1955, 28; *Chicago Defender*, January 26, 1957, 13.

26. Dixon, *I Am the Blues*, 82.

27. Peter Guralnick, *Feel Like Going Home: Portraits in Blues and Rock 'n' Roll* (New York: Outerbridge & Dienstfrey, 1971; repr., New York: Harper & Row, 1989), 229. Citations are to the Harper & Row edition.

28. Shirli Dixon, interview by the author, September 23, 2002.

29. Marie Dixon, interview by the author, September 25, 2004.

30. Dixon, *I Am the Blues*, 83.

31. Butch Dixon, interview by the author, September 23, 2003.

32. See Dixon, *I Am the Blues*, 98–101.

33. Ibid., 193.

34. Cohodas, *Spinning the Blues into Gold*, 80.

35. Dixon, *I Am the Blues*, 100.

36. Koester, interview by the author, September 20, 2004.

37. Dixon, *I Am the Blues*, 91.

38. Muddy Waters, *Can't Be Satisfied* [VHS] (n.p.: Wellspring/Tremolo Productions, WHE 71315, 2002).

39. George R. White, *Bo Diddley Living Legend* (Surrey, England: Castle Communication, 1995), 159.

40. Cohodas, *Spinning the Blues into Gold*, 96.

41. Dixon, *I Am the Blues*, 118.

42. Shirli Dixon, interview by the author, September 23, 2002.

43. Ibid.

CHAPTER FIVE

∼

Dixon's Compositions in the First Chess Records Period (1953–1956)

This chapter details Dixon's compositions for Chess artists recorded from 1953 to the summer of 1956. The artists that are discussed here are Eddie Boyd, Muddy Waters, Little Walter, Jimmy Witherspoon, Lowell Fulson, Willie Mabon, Bo Diddley, and Jimmy Rogers. Dixon's performances of his own compositions are also included in this chapter. The compositions for Muddy and Walter that were recorded after Dixon's return from Cobra Records are discussed in chapter 7. Dixon's compositions for Howlin' Wolf are also discussed in chapter 7, because most of those were recorded after 1959.

While Willie Dixon's compositions help intensify the character of the artists,[1] he did not usually compose a song with an assumption about the particular artist for whom he was writing. In other words, many of his songs are not really so-called tailor-made or custom-made songs, although there are some exceptions. Preparing a large stock of various kinds of compositions, Dixon was always ready to provide a suitable song whenever a vocalist needed one. When he chose a song for an artist, he observed the artist in order to have advance knowledge of the performer. Dixon talks about his knack for providing hit songs:

> Whenever I work with an artist or group, I like to hear them and get a feeling about the style that people like to hear them sing. I could make a song on the spot sometimes that would fit the individual just by watching his action. There are certain ways people act and music just fits what they're doing. . . .[2]

The thing most people don't realize about recording artists is the music itself is the background that makes the artists sound good. There are certain little angles of things that can attract more attention to the artists and a lot of people playing the music don't know about it. When you're getting ready to go out of the musical part, you have to focus people's minds on the singer again and blues itself has to be properly emphasized. You have to get the point over what you're trying to express.[3]

Dixon's observation of an artist is based on two angles that are inseparable from each other: the artist's individual characteristics and commercial considerations. The former includes (1) overall appearance, such as age, height, weight, facial features, and vocal quality; (2) performing style, which can be characterized by words like *traditional, modern, wild, smooth, sophisticated, serious, humorous, energetic,* and *laid-back*; and (3) a type of song subject the artist is good at, such as violence, sexuality, urbane or country imageries, humor, blue feelings, or romanticism/sentimentalism.

Commercial considerations include (1) the type of hit records the artist has made in the past; (2) the general performing context; and (3) the overall type of audience for the artist, such as male or female, young or old, working class or middle class.

For example, Dixon could have observed the following characteristics of Muddy Waters: he had a commanding stage presence; he was boastful and had a spirit of fortitude; he was a smart dresser; his hit records included country imageries and sexuality; and his main audience members were working-class individuals in their thirties or older living on the South Side of Chicago. On the other hand, what Dixon could have observed in Little Walter is that he was younger than Muddy; he was a fairly small figure; he had an energetic performing style; he had an audience of mainly younger women, as opposed to Muddy's middle-aged fans; and his hit records included fast-tempo instrumentals.

For each artist, the extent of an established performing style that Dixon could use existed at different levels. Some artists had already formed their public images, and Dixon strengthened the established basics. For example, when Dixon gave songs to Muddy and Walter, both were already popular artists with hit records. On the other hand, Otis Rush, Buddy Guy, and Koko Taylor were brand new artists. Dixon had to create their personae from the beginning, while considering their individual artistic potential.

In any case, Dixon compositions for those artists were commercially successful and became important pieces in their repertoires. The popularity of their records contributed to developing and enforcing their personae, and their images were impressed on the audience's awareness through hit songs for which Dixon was responsible in many cases. For example, five out of the thirteen Muddy Waters songs that made the *Billboard* R&B (rhythm and blues) charts were Dixon's,[4] and three out of twelve cuts on *The Best of Muddy Waters* (1957) were by Dixon.[5] One of Little Walter's two number-one R&B hits was "My Babe" by Dixon.[6] Dixon's impact on artists should not be underestimated, while acknowledging that his creation developed from what these artists originally embodied in varying degrees.

It should be noted that these artists also performed their own material besides Dixon's songs, and their own song choices did not necessarily follow Dixon's style in music and words. Clearly he did not control every aspect of these artists. Therefore, the following discussion and analysis of his songs and their relationships with the performing personae of the artists is based on Dixon's point of view, as interpreted from his statements, his writings, and from the songs themselves.

Eddie Boyd

Pianist/vocalist Eddie Boyd was the first Chess artist who recorded Dixon compositions. Boyd was responsible for Dixon's full-time engagement with Chess Records, as discussed earlier.

Edward Riley Boyd was born in Stovall, Mississippi, on November 25, 1914. In 1941, he settled in Chicago and started his career as a club piano player. He soon became one of the accompanists for John Lee "Sonny Boy" Williamson. Williamson's recommendation to producer Lester Melrose opened the door for Boyd to be a recording artist. Boyd and Dixon started their relationship around this time. A discography shows that Dixon was a bassist for Boyd's debut session for RCA Victor on April 3, 1947.[7]

Boyd only had moderate success with RCA, and because RCA stopped making blues records in 1950, Boyd had to look for a new label. In 1951, trying to change his luck, he went to Chess Records, but he was turned down. Boyd then went to J.O.B. Records, another label in Chicago. From J.O.B. "Five Long Years" became the number-one hit on the *Billboard* R&B charts in 1952.[8] This hit was phenomenal enough for Chess to reconsider an exclusive contract with Boyd. With Chess he recorded another hit, "24 Hours," in 1952. Dixon's "Third Degree" was for Boyd's follow-up session in May 1953.

"Third Degree" was Dixon's first experiment in providing songs for other artists. As he had already become a versatile songwriter for the Big Three Trio, he wanted to try the song-providing pattern that would come to success with Chess, but he didn't have enough authority to convince producer Lester

Melrose.[9] However, Dixon's first experiment worked well. "Third Degree" was ranked third on the *Billboard* R&B charts on July 4, 1953.[10]

Dixon explains the necessary procedure to provide songs for other artists:

> Well most of the time the fellas that I write for I've heard 'em play or sing. You learn how to get it over to 'em. And you learn a lot of the phrases that they do and the things that they like in their singing. But at the same time you have another job because you have to find out what the studio people like or the recording company likes.[11]

The analysis of "Third Degree" shows that Dixon learned this lesson early on. As Dixon says, "You learn a lot of phrases that they do," and "Third Degree" is clearly based on Boyd's previous hits "Five Long Years" and "24 Hours." As seen in the titles, numeric words "Five," "24," and "Third" give these songs a consistency. Plus, all of these have a similar atmosphere; they are slow low-down blues, featuring Boyd's wail-like piano as well as Little Sax Crowder's mournful tenor saxophone.

The form that both composers use is similar. Boyd's "Five Long Years" combines twelve-bar/a-a-b form (first verse) with a quatrain refrain text form (second verse):

[Verse 1]
If you ever been mistreated, well, you know just what I'm talking about,
If you ever been mistreated, you know just what I'm talking about,
I worked five long years for one woman, then she had the nerve to put me out.

[Verse 2]
I got a job at a steel mill,
Truckin' steel like a slave,
Five long years,
Every Friday I went straight home with all my pay.

[Hook]
If you ever been mistreated, you know just what I'm talking about,
I worked five long years for one woman, then she had the nerve to put me out.

Dixon similarly uses a quatrain pattern in "Third Degree." But probably this choice of form was Dixon's own decision, because he rarely used the simple a-a-b form anyway:

[Verse 1]
Got me 'cused of peeping,
I can't see a thing,

Got me 'cused of petting,
I can't even raise my hand.

[Hook]
Bad luck, bad luck is killing me,
Now I just can't stand no more of this third degree.

[Verse 2]
Got me 'cused of murder,
I never harmed a man,
[They?] got me 'cused of forgery,
I can't even write my name,

[Hook repeated]

[Verse 3]
Got me 'cused of taxes,
I don't have a lousy dime,
Got me 'cused of children,
Ain't nary one of them are mine,

[Hook repeated]

The structure of these lyrics is Dixon's favorite formula: listing similar concepts (words), as discussed in relation to his compositions for the Big Three Trio, "No More Sweet Potatoes" and "Money Tree Blues." More curiously, what seals the lyrical interest of this song is the impressive use of two black code words: *third degree* and *bad luck*. *Third degree* means a severe accusation typically by the authorities, and *bad luck* traditionally refers to the cultural evil caused especially by discrimination and poverty.[12]

Dixon rarely wrote such depressing contents and made reference to racism, but this is the result of his observation of Boyd's personality and what in his music attracted record buyers. Dixon actually mentions that Boyd had been through various kinds of experiences: "Eddie was one of those guys that got into the blues because he'd sing blues things that reminded him of different things in his life."[13]

Following the successful formula, Dixon wrote another slow blues, "Rattin' and Runnin' Around," for Boyd's follow-up session on September 24, 1953. This song is a monologue of a man who notices his woman's unfaithfulness:

[Verse 1]
I'd rather be beat by an alligator,
Scratched by a grizzly bear,

Go home in the morning,
And can't find my baby nowhere.

[Hook]
I know she's out rattin,'
Yeah, she's rattin' and running around,
If my baby don't do no better,
I'll be forced then to put her down.

[Verse 2]
I'd rather be bit by a little snake,
Kicked by a Missouri mule,
Go home late in the evening,
And my baby done broke my rule.

[Hook repeated]

[Verse 3]
I'd rather jump from the Empire State Buildin',
Bust the atom bomb with my knee,
Than to go home early in the morning,
My baby been cheatin' on me.

[Hook repeated]

Dixon could not provide another hit for Boyd, but "Third Degree" was an important achievement that was apparently proven by the high ranking on the R&B chart. Nevertheless, he still had to wait to get full recognition as a songwriter until "Hoochie Coochie Man." Shirli Dixon recounts,

> He always said, "I've got hits, they just don't realize." He also knew that Chess brothers did not know music, so that it's just a matter of time before that would become obvious to them. . . . He had such a strong self-confidence without any elegance, which is unusual. He knew who he was, and it's just the matter of them figuring out. They had to catch up to him in that regard.[14]

Muddy Waters

From 1954 to 1956, Muddy Waters recorded eleven compositions by Willie Dixon: "(I'm Your) Hoochie Coochie Man," "I Just Want to Make Love to You," "Oh Yeah," "I'm Ready," "I Don't Know Why," "This Pain," "Young Fashioned Ways," "I Want to Be Loved," "I Got to Find My Baby," "Don't Go No Further," and "I Love the Life I Live, I Live the Life I Love."

At a glance, most of these songs are depictions of a macho womanizer. However, such a surface-level interpretation of these songs is obviously contradictory to Dixon's intention: "the most important aspect of the blues is its wisdom." In order to examine the contents of these songs, it is important to understand Dixon's blues philosophy and its cultural background, as discussed in chapter 1. In essence, Dixon casts Muddy as a powerful communal hero as well as a sexy womanizer. And Muddy is also taking a role to deliver wisdom of real life situations, as if he is a preacher in the secular context.

Born McKinley A. Morganfield in 1913 in Jug's Corner in Issaquena County, Mississippi—the nearest town is Rolling Fork, which he usually referred to as his home—Muddy Waters spent his childhood and youth in Stovall's Plantation outside Clarksdale. Because he lost his mother when he was three years old, Muddy was raised by his grandmother, who gave him the nickname Muddy Waters because he played in the mud puddles near the Mississippi River. He was strongly influenced by Delta bluesman Son House. In 1941 and 1942, the researchers of the Fisk University–Library of Congress Coahoma County Study visited Muddy and recorded his performances.[15] As Muddy heard the playback of his own performances for the first time, his ambition to be a professional musician became unshakable. In 1943, he joined the exodus to the Northern cities, and he based his life in Chicago since then.

After having made some records with Mayo Williams for 20th Century Records and with Lester Melrose for Columbia Records in 1946—Williams released only one cut from this session under another artist's name, and the Columbia recordings were unissued—Muddy got another recording chance from Aristocrat Records in 1947. Eight recordings from two sessions were only good enough to secure a further session, but his subsequent record from the third session in April 1948, "I Can't Be Satisfied" with "I Feel Like Going Home," became an unprecedented success both for Muddy and Aristocrat.

Muddy as a person and as an artist is described in very positive terms. For example, Marshall Chess, who knew Muddy from early on, says, "Muddy Waters was a chief. If he had been born in Africa, he would've been a chief of the tribe. He was a regal leader of men."[16] Peter Guralnick writes, "He is, it is obvious, an extremely proud man, and sometimes it is not difficult to imagine that the titles which have been bestowed upon him for his singing were not in fact his earlier possession. For Muddy Waters carries himself with all the dignity of a king."[17]

On the other hand, the songs Muddy recorded before he worked with Willie Dixon are not strongly related to such a charismatic personality. As seen in the titles and contents of songs such as "I Feel Like Going Home," "I Can't Be Satisfied," and "Screamin' and Cryin'," one of the most visible themes in his early records is blue feelings, which are subdivided into frustration in a new urban environment, nostalgia for the South, and lost love. Another outstanding theme is womanizing—that is, sex with someone else's woman—as heard in "Rolling Stone," "Honey Bee," and "She Moves Me."

While Muddy made his music within the traditional perspective of the Delta blues, he started to depart from it. Willie Dixon was inspired by Muddy's distinction in his new musical direction. Dixon says, "There was quite a few people around singin' the blues, but most of 'em singin' all sad blues. Muddy was givin' his a little pep, and ever since I noticed him givin' his blues this kinda pep feelin', I began tryin' to think of things in a peppier form."[18]

The reasons that Dixon felt Muddy's music was "peppier" are possibly (1) the growth in size of the ensemble and equalizing the musical roles of all the players involved—that is, the lead player and the sidemen have almost equal contribution in making music; (2) his introduction of different beat patterns from the traditional walking-bass pattern; and (3) his experimentation with timbre in association with the use of the amplifier.

Muddy used different ensembles for recordings and live performances. For recordings, Leonard Chess who wanted to maintain the commercially successful formula was reluctant to change Muddy's small ensemble, which usually consisted of one electric guitar supported by a standup bass. But outside the studio Muddy played with his band: Jimmy Rogers on electric guitar and Little Walter on amplified harmonica. This trio started even before Muddy's successful records on Aristocrat. By 1949, drummer Leroy Foster (Baby Face Leroy) also joined Muddy's band.

Their recordings, two versions of "Rollin' and Tumblin'" (released by Little Walter and Baby Face Leroy from Parkway Records in 1950) show that they were a loud band for the times. Their musical interaction was no longer that of a lead player supported by others. This was a competitive interaction among musicians. The "Delta National Anthem," previously recorded by a number of Delta blues musicians,[19] was performed with a frenzied city flavor.

Leonard Chess allowed Muddy to bring more musicians into his sessions, and with the extended combo, Muddy started to explore his musical potential and dynamism. One highly noticeable musical exploration was his introduction of different beat patterns. Dixon remembers,

> When you go to changin' beats in music, you change the whole style. . . .
> Muddy was able to change these various styles of music because he was always

lookin' for something unique, and I learned very early that when you're able to create something that's good and different also, you don't have very much trouble sellin' it.[20]

Chronologically such a tendency first appeared in "Evans Shuffle," recorded on October 23, 1950. As the title indicates, this composition has a busy shuffle pattern. The same shuffle pattern also appears in "Stuff You Gotta Watch" (December 29, 1951) and "She's All Right" (January 9, 1953).

A different beat pattern is also seen in "Baby Please Don't Go" (May 4, 1953), which has a series of triplets in a fast tempo in 4/4. "Mad Love" (aka "I Want You to Love Me," September 24, 1953) has a stop-time riff—short melodic-rhythmic figure with a moment of silence—with a strong accent on the first beat played by all the band members (now including pianist Otis Spann). In terms of the beat pattern, "Mad Love" was a test piece for the forthcoming "Hoochie Coochie Man."

There is another musical factor that possibly made Muddy's music "peppier" than others: that is, his exploration of timbre with amplification. It is noticeable that "Still a Fool" and "She Moves Me" (July 11, 1951) have a clearly different sound quality from that of his previous records. Muddy's biographer Robert Gordon describes the heavily distorted guitar sound in "Still a Fool" as "evoking an over-the-top madness."[21] Gordon also says, "This is the beginning of urban blues. This is when the electric guitar is no longer playing amplified Delta blues."[22]

Dixon sensed that the effect of amplification required different processes in both songwriting and arrangement than those for acoustic blues or amplified Delta blues. Even when he was with the Big Three Trio (also using an amplified guitar), Dixon did not like to put his songs into the regular twelve-bar/a-a-b mold. The additional influence of Muddy's musical style pushed Dixon to write songs with an even longer scheme—that is, a sixteen- or twenty-four-bar system, or inserting an eight-bar middle (bridge) section between two verses with a twelve-bar form. Dixon explains this change in an interview with *Living Blues*:

> *Interviewer:* Basically the main transition was, you took the country blues— we'll say Mississippi—and you just put it into an amplifier.
>
> *Dixon:* Yeah, practically the same thing. But naturally putting it into an amplifier you'd have to sing it different and then the instruments could hold a longer chord—longer notes—and this gave it a completely different arrangement.
>
> . . . What happened, the world was trying to hold the blues at one basic thing as a 12-bar music. And by holding it at a 12-bar music, it only meant that you

would be putting another verse to the same music all the time. . . . And so what I would do then is make a 24-bar system out of it. Maybe make it part of the introduction, and then go into the song. By doing that then they began to call this a different style of music and everybody jumped in on it.[23]

There were other elements of Muddy that Dixon could not overlook, although this is not a musical feature. Muddy was known for his elegant appearance. Butch Dixon says: "Muddy was a well-dressed guy. Muddy was a shirt and tie and suit kinda guy. . . . You can't make Muddy from a pair of jeans and shoes that don't shine. So 'Hoochie Coochie Man' sort of describes Muddy from a baby up to his present life."[24]

On top of that, Muddy's sex appeal was what attracted many female fans—important record buyers in the blues market and major customers in gigs. Marshall Chess observes, "It was sex. If you have ever seen Muddy then, the effect he had on women. Because blues, you know, has always been a women's market."[25]

Recognizing these factors listed above, Dixon strongly felt that Muddy needed a song that could project him as a more powerful figure. Shirli Dixon explains why her father offered Muddy "Hoochie Coochie Man":

He often told us that he had heard Muddy. And he felt Muddy had more to offer. . . . So when he was putting a song together, this was in his mind. "This guy has a lot of energy. He has the right voice to deliver it." Muddy reminded my dad of a preacher, actually, in his vocal style . . . like a Baptist preacher is what he told me. He said . . . "He's a good looking man and dresses well, and he has the ability to attract the audience in this manner with this boastful . . . manly kind of character that the song had to offer. . ." And he decided . . . "I'm gonna offer him this song."[26]

Sometime in 1953, Dixon visited Muddy Waters at the Club Zanzibar where he was performing. During the intermission, Dixon took Muddy to the bathroom and taught him the words and riff of "Hoochie Coochie Man." Dixon remembers,

We fooled around with "Hoochie Coochie Man" there in the washroom for 15 or 20 minutes. Muddy said, "I'm going to do this song first so I don't forget it." He went right up on stage that first night and taught the band the little riff I showed him. He did it first shot and, sure enough, the people went wild over it. He was doing that song until the day he died.[27]

Dixon composed "Hoochie Coochie Man" when he was with the Big Three Trio. He remembers, "I had sung 'Hoochie Coochie Man' out there where we used to go out and meet him [Muddy] and play on the South Side when I had the Big Three Trio."[28] This statement is an indication that Dixon did not write "Hoochie Coochie Man" particularly for Muddy. Shirli Dixon gives this account: "I don't know if he wrote it for him, but I think when he wrote it, he wanted somebody like Muddy. He wanted somebody looked like him and felt the blues like he did, and that could deliver that type of message, because they had the whole look, total package."[29]

As previously mentioned, the stop-time riff of "Hoochie Coochie Man" is closely related to the riff of "Mad Love." This song was a successful test piece for Muddy and Dixon; it was ranked sixth in the jukebox category and ninth in sales on the *Billboard* R&B charts on November 21, 1952.[30] Of equal importance, the association of the riff with his expression of manhood and sexual prowess—as the subtitle of this song "I Want You to Love Me" indicates—became a trademark for his audience.

After Muddy learned "Hoochie Coochie Man" at the Club Zanzibar, he and the band members spent some time polishing it.[31] They recorded it on January 7, 1954. This was the first time Dixon played bass for Muddy's recording.

Musically and culturally, "Hoochie Coochie Man" is a significant composition. This composition demonstrates Dixon's important writing techniques: extracting the maximum musical power from the minimum amount of musical means. This composition gave a strong boost to Muddy's performing persona that Dixon developed from the tradition of postbellum black badman tales. Dixon cast Muddy as a hero supported by members of a particular community. Dixon also gave Muddy a role of healer, similar to an important role of black preacher.

The term *hoochie coochie* or *hoochie coochie man* (also spelled *hootchy-kootchy* or *hootchie-coochie*) means (1) a sexually suggestive dance;[32] (2) a sexually attractive person;[33] and (3) a practitioner of hoodoo.[34] As seen in the following text of the song as recorded, this song is the statement or self-narrative of a man who brags about his machismo as aided by hoodoo power.[35]

[Verse 1]
The gypsy woman tol' my mother,
Before I was born,
I [supposedly "You"] got a boy child's comin',[36]
He gonna be a son of a gun,
He gonna make pretty womens,
Jump and shout,
Then the world wanna know,
What this all about.

[Hook]
But you know I'm here,
Everybody knows I'm here,
Well, you know the Hoochie Coochie Man,
Everybody knows I'm here.

[Verse 2]
I got a black cat bone,
I got a mojo too,
I got the John the Conqueror root,
I'm gonna mess with you,
I'm gonna make you girls,
Lead me by my hand,
Then the world'll know,
I'm the Hoochie Coochie Man.

[Hook repeated]

[Verse 3]
On the seven hour,
On the seven day,
On the seven month,
The seven doctor say,
"He were born for good luck,
And that you'll see,"
I've got seven hundred dollars,
And don't you mess with me.

[Hook repeated]

As discussed previously, the technique of electric amplification inspired Dixon to use a new musical structure. Each verse has sixteen measures.[37] The first half of the sixteen measures is a stop-time riff, which is repeated seven times on the same chord. Then, this section is followed by an eight-measure walking-bass pattern, which functions as a hook (see figures 5.1a and 5.1b).

The stop-time riff fits the opening of the drama about the theme: overpowering manhood. The repetition of this riff effectively arouses the expectation of drama and heightens tension by degrees. Dixon previously used the similar riff for "Money Tree Blues" and its derivative "Cool Kind Woman." This riff was not Dixon's invention, but opening a song with this characteristic rhythm pattern and extending it for a long duration was a novel idea. The device is simple, but this is an illustration of the fact that the simplest thing can be the most powerful.

Figure 5.1a.

During the stop-time section ("The gypsy woman tol' my mother . . ."), the vocal melodies remain in the low register without wide melodic movements. This section is similar to the phrases that Muddy uses often; as previously quoted from Dixon, "you learn a lot of the phrases that they do and things that they like in their singing." Similar melodies are found in "Rolling Stone" ("Sho' 'nuff, he just now left . . ."). This section is also analogous to a section of Big Three Trio's "Money Tree Blues" ("A little money tree, it ain't out in the wood . . .").

In the walking-bass section ("And you know I'm here . . ."), the melody starts to soar up to a higher register. On the recording, it is noticeable that

Figure 5.1b.

Muddy is required to use the high part of his vocal register at full volume. The contrast between the verse and the hook gives us a feeling that compressed energy is given off, and then the level of the energy has reached the point of a "red zone."

The most novel characteristic of "Hoochie Coochie Man" is that Dixon connects urbanized musical sounds with a rustic symbol that is based on Southern black mythology. Dixon explains,

> For years people have been thinking about the likes of voodoo and hoodoo. Folks had all kinds of fictitious names related to that type of lore. When I was a kid gypsies came up and down the road in covered wagons. The gypsies could

always find something good to say that would capture people's interest. Poor folks were looking for anything that sounded good like, "Hey, I see your wife is pregnant. I know she is going to have a beautiful boy. Women gonna love him all over the world. I wanna tell you about the boy—I wanna tell you about anything." It could be true or it could not.[38]

Dixon belongs to the generation of African Americans who were familiar with antebellum and postbellum black folktales about Br'er Rabbit, John (aka High John or High John the Conqueror) and the Old Master, and (of course) "Signifying Monkey." When Dixon created the character Hoochie Coochie Man, who is sexy and commanding at the same time, he apparently got ideas from the tradition of secular heroes of African American balladry—black badmen, such as Stagolee and John Henry.

As folklorist Roger D. Abrahams notes, one of the most salient characteristics of black badman is his being "a perpetual adolescent (while the trickster character such as Signifying Monkey is a perpetual child)."[39] Abrahams also writes, "Where guile and banter are the weapons of the trickster, arrogance and disdain serve the badman. He does not aim to be a god but rather to be the eternal man in revolt, the devil. He is the epitome of virility, of manliness on display."[40] For instance, the depiction of the character Hoochie Coochie Man is not simply as a good, popular lady's man but as a boastful "superbad" figure—almost like a godfather of rappers.

The first verse implies that the Hoochie Coochie Man is a badman archetype. For example, the line "The gypsy woman told my mother, / Before I was born" is similar to the opening of one version of the ballad "Stagolee": "Gypsy told Stack's mother, told her like a friend, your double-jinted baby, won't come to no good end."[41] The next lines "He gonna make pretty womens, / Jump and shout" are also similar to one of the openings about John Henry in the sense that both characters are magnificent in sex: "When John Henry was a baby, / You could hold him in the palm of your hand. / But when he got nineteen years old, / He could stand that pussy like a man."[42]

The lines in the second verse "I got black cat bone . . ." show that Hoochie Coochie Man is a conjurer aided by hoodoo power, which is one of the main components of the black badman. Dixon explains,

All through the history of mankind, there have been people who were supposed to be able to tell the future before it came to pass. People always felt it would be great to be one of these people: "This guy is a hoodoo man, this lady is a witch, this other guy's a hoochie coochie man, she's some kind of voodoo person."[43]

African American folklore researcher John W. Roberts explains that the power to foresee the future is traditionally an important trait in the African American community:

> In the black community, both during and after slavery, conjurers were envisioned as individuals whose characteristic behaviors maintained behavioral patterns which protected the values of harmony and community. The worldview which supported the practice of conjuration (the belief that individual misfortune was caused by ill-will or ill-action of one individual toward another, usually through the agency of magic) made the conjurer's use of supernatural trickery socially if not morally justifiable retaliatory actions against a member of the community.[44]

While Dixon and Muddy did not personally believe in hoodoo,[45] they knew that references to this black folk belief were important, because Muddy's audiences, most of whom had down-home Southern roots, could relate to it. Presenting what the audience wants to hear is a required talent for a commercial songwriter. Muddy once said, "When you're writing them songs that are coming from down that way, you can't leave out somethin' about that mojo thing. Because this is what black people really believed in at that time."[46]

While the second verse is applied to Hoochie Coochie Man's conjurer element, the third verse—"On the seventh day . . ."—is about his trickster nature, which is another component of black outlaws. This verse, which contains Dixon's characteristic listing of similar words with an emphasis on the number seven, is about the mythical birth of this character, who was born with superpowers directed against an external threat, according to Roberts' theory.[47] While the ability of the conjurer (black cat bone, mojo, and John the Conqueror root) can be purchased, the ability of the trickster in "Hoochie Coochie Man" was built in when he was born.

As observed, Willie Dixon's creation of Muddy Waters' performing persona was in the tradition of the heroes of African American subculture. But considering the importance and function of storytelling as an educational tool in African and African American culture (as in other black badman ballads), the song "Hoochie Coochie Man" can function as a secular parable to tell people how to act to maintain the welfare of the community, and, paradoxically, how not to act to avoid disrupting the well-being of the community. For instance, while the conjurer Hoochie Coochie Man is a powerful communal hero, he can be an extraordinary figure in both positive and negative senses. As the beginning of the first verse suggests, this figure is portrayed as "a son of a gun," the meaning of which contains love, hate, contempt, and surprise.[48] These mixed feelings toward him are very similar to the phenomenon that rappers are not necessarily respected figures in our society because they can be egotistical and obnoxious. As sung in the beginning of the second verse, "I'm gonna make you girls, lead me by my hand," his use of hoodoo magic is for his self-interest rather than for the harmony of the community. This trait is traditionally considered the moral evil.[49]

Thus, the African American historical-cultural context of "Hoochie Coochie Man" just presented shows that this song is more than the expression of machismo and lust as interpreted by many. In the community that knows how this story functions, this song actually includes wisdom as an important element of the blues.

There is another important function in this song. Dixon knew that bragging about oneself psychologically functioned as an autosuggestion that would bring a person to a different spiritual level. He felt the need to write a song about a boastful person, and he hoped that this song would become a means for the audience to heighten their spirit. He mentions, "The average person wants to brag about themselves because it makes that individual feel big. These songs make people want to feel like that because they feel like that at heart, anyway. They just haven't said it so you say it for them."[50] Muddy is given a role of psychological healer, an important role of blues artists in their performing contexts, as discussed in chapter 1.

"Hoochie Coochie Man" shows Dixon's talent as a producer as well as a songwriter. Two takes of this song—the master and alternate take—reveal that Dixon carefully worked on the rhythmic nuances with other band members. In the alternate take, there are some moments where the band members are not together. Sometimes Elgin Evans' drumming is a little rushed, and as a result, Muddy's vocal is behind. Especially in the stop-time sections, Little Walter starts the pickup a little earlier than other members.

While there is a flaw in the lyrics (as seen in the previous transcription, Muddy sings "I got a boy child's comin'," though it should be "You got a boy child's comin'"), the most noticeable characteristic of the master take is its tight ensemble. This take clearly starts with Evans' snare drum on the third beat of a measure. More importantly, every member of the band plays the pickup of the riff perfectly together and ends it in the same way. During the stop-time section, this ensemble is carefully maintained, and the band members completely get rid of rhythmic blurring. Because of the steadiness, the master take (two minutes and fifty-three seconds) is six seconds longer than the alternate take (two minutes and forty-seven seconds), even though both are in the same tempo.[51]

"Hoochie Coochie Man" got a positive sales report from *Billboard*: "We're so happy with Muddy Waters on CHESS 1560, doing 'Hoochy Coochy Man' [*sic*], that we can't help mentioning it again for a top spot. Action gets better everyday."[52] Within a week after its release, four thousand copies were sold,[53] and it reached third position in the jukebox category and eighth among best sellers on the *Billboard* R&B charts on March 13, 1954.[54] This was the highest ranking for Muddy's career.

For the April 13, 1954, session, Muddy recorded two Dixon numbers: "Just Make Love to Me" (better known today as "I Just Want to Make Love to You") and "Oh Yeah!"

"I Just Want to Make Love to You" is a boldly expressed sexual desire on the surface:

> [Verse 1] (A1)
> I don't want you to be no slave,
> I don't want you to work all day,
> I don't want you to be true,
> I just want to make love to you.
>
> [Verse 2] (A2)
> I don't want you to wash my clothes,
> I don't want you to keep our home,
> I don't want your money, too,
> I just want to make love to you, love to you, love to you. . .
>
> [Harmonica solo]
>
> [Bridge] (B)
> I can tell by the way you switch and walk,
> I can see by the way you baby talk,
> I can know by the way you treat your man,
> That I could love you baby 'til the crying shame.
>
> [Verse 3] (A3)
> I don't want you to cook my bread,
> I don't want you to make my bed,
> I done want you to, because I'm sad and blue,
> I just want to make love to you, love to you, love to you . . .

The structure of the song is unusual compared with traditional blues songs. A three-measure introduction is followed by an eight-measure verse section (A1). The verse section is repeated (A2), but this time it is twelve measures long because of four extra measures of the refrain ("love to you, love to you"). After the second verse, there is a harmonica solo for eleven measures, and this section is followed by an eight-bar bridge section (B: "I can tell by the way you switch and walk . . ."). Then the verse with the refrain is repeated (A3). Therefore, the structure of the whole song is similar to an A-A-B-A pop-song form, although in a pop-song form, each section is usually symmetrical.

The band plays different forms of the riff for the introduction and verses. For the intro and the first verse, a piano is followed by a guitar with a bass in the form of a call and response, in which the harmonica sustains a tremolo. During the second and third verses, all of the band members except the drummer play the stop-time riff together while the drummer plays the quarter beat pulse with his high-hat. This stop-time riff with an accent on the first beat is similar to the riff of "Hoochie Coochie Man."

Compared with the power of "Hoochie Coochie Man," "I Just Want to Make Love to You" has a more restrained feeling and is filled with a sensual atmosphere. One of the musical elements that creates this feeling is Little Walter's harmonica performance. He skillfully alternates tension and release in a suggestive way.

One of the artistic goals of "I Just Want to Make Love to You" for Dixon was similar to that of "Hoochie Coochie Man" in that it allowed Muddy to speak for listeners who could gain confidence by bragging about themselves, and the song could serve as a vehicle for the thoughts and emotions of listeners. Dixon explains,

> Like the song, "I Just Wanna Make Love to You," a lot of times people say this in their minds or think it. You don't have to say it but everybody knows that's the way you feel anyway because that's how the other fella feels. You know how you feel so you figure the other fella feels the same way because his life is just like yours.[55]

"I Just Want to Make Love to You" is a challenge to authority by overturning social norms that are enforced by conservative Anglo American Christian ethos. The song is about the importance of love, and this cannot be separated from bodily expressions of love in African American culture, as explained earlier. In the verses, Dixon lists the broad terms of household chores: "be (no) slave," "work all day," "wash my clothes," cook my bread," and "make my bed." The punch line tells that the importance of love surpasses these chores. At one level he shows that love even overcomes financial desire ("I don't want your money, too") and the social norm of fidelity ("I don't want you to be true").

On a deeper level, "(not) being true" reflects Dixon's cynical observation of the world. On this level, what he means by "being true" is not confined to the prevalent social norm of fidelity, but describes the arbitrary code of value itself, with which one can be judged by others. Dixon says, "My message is a translation of our real life today in the world. We salving [sic], working all day, in a world that does not recognize 'being true,' so my main goal is 'to love.' The world has become a place where nobody has time to enjoy the natural beauty of life."[56]

What Dixon embeds in this song is his idea that "in the world that does not recognize being true," there is no point to being "true." The natural beauty of love surpasses all sorts of values, and this is the truth. As opposed to conventional interpretations, "I Just Want to Make Love to You" is didactic, and here Muddy preaches Dixon's wisdom.

"I Just Want to Make Love to You" was released in May of 1954, and it was a successful follow-up to "Hoochie Coochie Man." On June 5, the song was ranked at the fourth position both in sales and jukeboxes on the *Billboard* R&B charts.[57]

The flip side of this record, "Oh Yeah!" is basically a traditional twelve-bar with an a-a-b blues form (hook) and a quatrain refrain text form (verses) in a fast-medium tempo. This recording captures one of the traits of Muddy's band, a confrontational interaction among musicians, especially Little Walter's harmonica and Muddy's vocal. The song is about a man's reprimand to his faithless girlfriend, and the aggressive performance musically depicts the chaotic and upset feelings of the man.

For a follow-up record to "I Just Want to Make Love to You" coupled with "Oh Yeah!" Dixon provided "I'm Ready" and "I Don't Know Why." Muddy's band (including Dixon) recorded these songs on September 1, 1954.[58]

The inspiration for "I'm Ready" occurred when Willie Foster, harmonica player for Muddy's tour band, visited Muddy's house to leave for a concert tour together. As the story goes, when Foster knocked on the door, Dixon, who was visiting Muddy, answered it because Muddy was busy shaving. From the bathroom, he asked Foster, "Are You Ready?" and then Foster said, "Ready as anybody can be." Muddy remembers, "[I said,] 'Willie, are you thinking about what I'm thinking about? Let's make a song out of it.' . . . It took [Dixon] three days, I think, to finish it out."[59] This comment shows that Dixon composed "I'm Ready" particularly for Muddy, although as discussed earlier, Dixon did not usually write songs with specific artists in his mind.

The general theme of the song is toughness:

> [Hook]
> I'm ready, ready as anybody can be,
> I'm ready, ready as anybody can be,
> I'm ready for you, I hope you ready for me.
>
> [Verse 1]
> I got an ax-handle pistol on a graveyard frame,
> That shoot tombstone bullets wearin' balls and chains,
> I'm drinkin' TNT, I'm smokin' dynamite,
> I hope some screwball start a fight.
>
> [Hook]
> 'Cause I'm ready, ready as anybody can be,
> I'm ready for you, I hope you ready for me.
>
> [Verse 2]
> All you pretty little chicks with your curly hair,
> I know you feel like I ain't nowhere,
> But stop what you're doin' baby, come over here,
> I'll prove to you baby that I ain't no square.
>
> [Hook repeated]
>
> [Harmonica solo]
>
> [Verse 3]
> I been drinkin' gin like never before,
> I feel so good I want you to know,
> One more drink, I wish you would,
> It takes a whole lot of lovin' to make me feel good.
>
> [Hook repeated]

This is another example of Dixon's use of extended blues form. The hook in a twelve-bar/a-a-b pattern is followed by the six-line verse. This section is a combination of a quatrain refrain form and the last two lines of an a-a-b form; eight measures are assigned to the first four lines, and another eight measures to the last two lines. In the first four lines of the verse, the vocal melodies are built over one chord with a stop-time riff, in which the first two notes are strongly accentuated by snare and bass drum. These accents emphasize the defiant attitude of the lyrics. From the hook section, the rhythmic pattern is in a walking-bass. Changing the rhythmic pattern with two kinds of riffs effectively corresponds to the structure of words.

Dixon explains the wisdom in this composition—the courage to face unfavorable situations:

> Being ready in a lot of cases means you have to be ready for whatever the situation is. If people come with evil minds and they are ready to do you some damage, you better be ready to do them some damage to protect yourself. I'm ready for you and I hope you're ready for me. Don't start no rootin' and tootin' and there won't be no cuttin' and shootin'. Being ready for all of life, puts you in a position to enjoy life.[60]

This wisdom seems to be derived from Dixon's personality; he was an ex-fighter, and his mental strength is shown in his refusal to go to war in 1942.

Dixon interweaves such empirical philosophy with the singer's persona in this composition. The boastful attitude in the first verse ("I got an ax-handle pistol . . .") and the confidence in his sexual prowess in the second verse ("All you pretty little chicks . . .") correspond to Muddy's previous hits "Hoochie Coochie Man" and "I Just Want to Make Love to You." In addition, the main theme of the song and Dixon's explanation fit the characteristics of the black badman, an embodiment of toughness and a defiant attitude.

The character in this song, however, is not perfectly strong, as shown by the words in the second verse: "I know you feel like I ain't nowhere" and "I'll prove to you baby that I ain't no square." These expressions seem to result from Dixon's consideration of Muddy's age at this point; he was forty years old. While this verse is on the surface level about sexual ability, it also illustrates a proverb: "A man is not necessarily what he appears to be." This theme will be explored in other Dixon compositions: "Young Fashioned Ways" for Muddy and "You Can't Judge a Book by Its Cover" for Bo Diddley.

On October 23, 1954, "I'm Ready" was ranked fourth in the jukebox category and fifth in sales on the *Billboard* R&B charts.[61] Dixon's compositions for Muddy became top-five hits in the national charts three times in a row.

Similar to two previous Dixon-Muddy collaborations, "I'm Ready" is not just a hit record but also teaches important life lessons. Dixon intended his songs to bring listeners to a different philosophical place. He says: "Oh, it's definitely my intention every time I write a song that it will make somebody feel good. It would bring back memories or make higher hopes or something of the kind."[62]

Compared to "I'm Ready," "I Don't Know Why" is not very inspiring. In addition to the mediocre lyrics, this composition turned out to be Little Walter's showcase. The recording features thirty-six measures of Walter's superb harmonica solo that overshadows Muddy's vocal.

Muddy Waters' following recording session was held on February 3, 1955. Three compositions that Dixon offered to Muddy—"This Pain," "Young Fashioned Ways," and "I Want to Be Loved"—are quite different from one another: melodrama, blues, and pop song. Dixon, who observed Muddy as "the kind of person you can give any kind of lyric . . . what you call a quick study,"[63] possibly wanted to explore Muddy's ability as a singer who could express different subjects. In addition, Dixon might have felt that the musical and text patterns that he utilized for the three past hits had run their courses. He says, "People don't want to hear the same thing all the time. They want to hear something that's good but different and people will accept it."[64]

According to the discography,[65] the first song they cut for this session was a melodrama, "This Pain." This song shares similar characteristics with "My Love Will Never Die," another melodrama that Dixon composed for the Big Three Trio. "This Pain" begins with a dramatic introduction. While the drummer is rolling the floor tom, the harmonica and bass play minor chords, which sound like the opening of Grieg's Piano Concerto. Then Muddy comes in and sings about a heartache. Throughout the song, he tries to express heartache with constricted vibrato.

> [A1]
> Oh, oh, this pain deep down in my heart,
> Oh it pain[s], baby, head the part,
> Everything you do,
> Still in love with you,
> Please ease my broken heart of this pain.
>
> [B]
> All night long I can't sleep for thinking,
> All day long my poor heart is aching,
> The tears on my pillow they have soaked clear through,
> This pain in my heart is only for you.
>
> [A2]
> Oh, this pain, help me, if you please,
> Oh it pain[s], beg on bended knee,
> Prayin' to the Heaven above,
> To bring me back my love,
> Ease my broken heart of this pain.

This extremely sentimental song is obviously irrelevant to Muddy's fervent image that had been shaped by Dixon's songs. In fact, this recording not only was the sole unreleased Dixon-Muddy collaboration during this period but also was not known until almost thirty years later when it was included in *The Complete Recordings of Muddy Waters*. Very possibly Dixon learned an important lesson from this mistake. Except for this particular song, Dixon never provided any artists with such irrelevant songs. Once his songs became successful and associated with the images of singers, he stuck with the songs that explored the same images. To expand his melodramatic compositions, Dixon had to wait until he worked with Lowell Fulson, another artist from Chess Records, and Otis Rush from Cobra Records.

The next cut was "Young Fashioned Ways." The musical and lyrical contents of "Young Fashioned Ways" are somewhat similar to those of "I'm Ready." As in "I'm Ready," "Young Fashioned Ways" is a shuffle blues, and it is in a twelve-bar/a-a-b blues form with a traditional harmonic progression, while "I'm Ready" utilizes an extended blues form.

Also similar to "I'm Ready," "Young Fashioned Ways" is about aging; the wisdom in this song is that a man can prove that he is not what he appears to be, and getting old means knowing better:

> [Verse 1]
> I may be getting old, but I've got young fashioned ways,
> I may be getting old, but I've got young fashioned ways,
> But I'm gonna love a good woman for the rest of my natural days.
>
> [Verse 2]
> If my hair turns gray, I know you think the way I feel,
> If my hair turns gray, I know you think the way I feel,
> And maybe snow upon the mountain, gonna fall on that hill.
>
> [Harmonica solo]
>
> [Verse 3]
> I may be getting old, but I've got young fashioned ways,
> I may be getting old, but I've got young fashioned ways,
> I don't worry about no young one that ain't no wanna take my place.
>
> [Harmonica solo]
>
> [Verse 4]
> A young horse is fast, an old horse knows what's going on,
> A young horse is fast, an old horse knows what's going on,
> A young horse may win a race, but an old horse stay out so long.

Dixon's philosophy of aging and musings regarding human ambiguities are combined with Muddy's macho character. Interestingly, the character in this song is not as strong as that in "Hoochie Coochie Man." Instead of "making pretty women jump and shout," the character in "Young Fashioned Ways" is determined to stick with one woman. More clearly than "I'm Ready," "Young Fashioned Ways" makes Muddy Waters considerate rather than just bold. By singing Dixon's didactic song, Muddy is acting like a preacher. Now he is more experienced, and has more endurance.

"Young Fashioned Ways" was released as the flip side of "Mannish Boy"[66] in July 1955 and reached the fifth position in the jukebox category and ninth in sales on the *Billboard* R&B chart on July 30.[67]

The third Dixon song that Muddy recorded in this session was "I Want to Be Loved." This was probably considered the best cut of the day, because it was released as an A side in April of 1955, only two months after the session. The recording shows Dixon's songwriting, arranging, and production ability, as well as the ability of Muddy's recording band.

The lyrics of "I Want to Be Loved" are based on the traditional pop songs rather than blues or ballad. The song is about a man's feelings toward a woman who treats him coldly. The musical form Dixon uses here is a crossover between pop and blues; it is in an A-A-B-A/thirty-two-bar pop-song form, while the harmonica solo after the third A section is in a twelve-bar pattern:

[Verse 1] (A1)
The spark in your eye sets my soul on fire,
Your voice is like an angel above,
The touch of your hand drive me insane,
But baby, I wants to be loved.

[Verse 2] (A2)
I'm crazy 'bout every little thing you do,
I cherish the way you hug,
Your kisses so sweet, honey, they can't be beat,
But baby, I wants to be loved.

[Bridge] (B)
Every time I ask you for a date,
You don't come at all, or you might little late [you're mighty late],
I ask you to dance a little spin,
You said wait a minute daddy, here come my friend.

[Verse 3] (A3)
I love the way you walk, when you pass me by,
Even when you tryin' to snub,
You kiss me, honey, when you give me the eye,
But baby, I wants to be loved.

[Harmonica solo]

[Bridge and Verse 3 repeated]

The recording shows a remarkable characteristic of Dixon-related Chess Records sounds. The musical interaction between Muddy's vocal and Walter's harmonica is well balanced in volume, and the musical foreground (vocal and harmonica) and background (rhythm section) are carefully laid out. Dixon says that the way he blends instruments comes from his experiences in a spiritual quartet group:

> The sound we got that people began to talk about as the Chess sound was based on the idea of harmony. . . . By me being involved with quartet harmony singing, I would stop and hum the tune that the instrument would be playing. Being able to whistle two tunes at the same time in harmony, I could do the sounds that gave the two instruments this particular blend. People branded that as the Chess sound.[68]

In this particular song, Walter's harmonica phrase, which is a five-note descending riff (C, B-flat, F, F-sharp, G), creates a quasi-contrapuntal relationship with the ascending phrase based on a walking-bass pattern (C, E, F, F-sharp, G) played by the guitar and bass.[69] Upon this semicounterpoint with narrow conjunct motions, Muddy's vocal melodies with large intervals are built (see figure 5.2).

It sounds like this arrangement was inspired by Mabel Scott's "Mr. Fine" (1953). The similar arrangement is also found in Dixon's composition for Jimmy Witherspoon's "When the Lights Go Out" (discussed later in this chapter).

The early take of "I Want to Be Loved" shows that the original choices of notes for the riff and rhythms are slightly different from those in the master take.[70] For the master, Walter switched from a diatonic marine band harmonica to a chromatic one. Throughout the song, the sidemen steadily back up Muddy, especially Fred Below's drum, stressing the backbeat and brisk triplets for the turnaround, and Otis Spann's skillful piano, which engages Walter's stripped-down harmonica in a game of call and response. At the fourth line of the verse, while the instruments stop, only Muddy shouts, "But baby," and then he sings the last line "I wants to be loved" at a subdued volume. The melodies in this section consist only of high and low tonic notes with a few neighboring tones. This is a clever way to build melodies on a simple riff and to avoid a monotonous feeling.

For the session on November 3, 1955, Dixon gave Muddy one composition: "I Got to Find My Baby."[71] This is a shuffle blues in a straightforward twelve-bar/a-a-b blues form. The lyrics do not have the depth at which Dixon usually excelled. The quality of the performance is also a little monotonous.

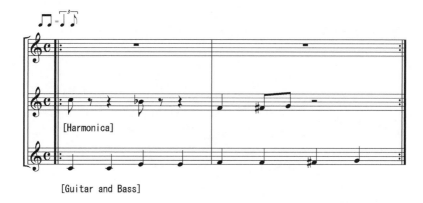

Figure 5.2.

A better result is found in the June 1956 recording "Don't Go No Further," another Willie Dixon classic. This was Muddy's last top-ten hit record until 1958. It was ranked at ninth in the jukebox category and twelfth in sales on the *Billboard* R&B charts on September 8, 1956.

This song has Dixon's favorite listing of similar objects, and this part is followed by a very catchy refrain. The song is basically about a man who is asking a woman to return to him, but it includes a bit of wisdom, "everyone for his own trade." Here providing a didactic song, Dixon casts Muddy as a preacher:

[Verse 1]
You need meat, go to the market,
You need bread, try the bakery,
You need love, don't go no farther,
Just come on home to me.

[Hook]
I got to love somebody,
I got to love somebody,
I got to love somebody,
Somebody's gon' love me.

[Verse 2]
You need grits, go to the grocers,
You need fish, go to the sea,
You need love, look for me, baby,
And just come on home to me.

[Hook repeated]

Roll over, roll over!

[Harmonica solo]

[Verse 3]
You need money, go to the bank, dear,
You need honey, look for the bees,
You need love, don't go no farther,
Just come on home to me.

[Hook repeated]

The music is in a medium-tempo shuffle. Muddy's vocal melodies sound like a succession of swift upward scoops from low to high register, and the brief chord stroking on guitar deftly creates a call-and-response effect.

This is another good example of Dixon's arranging skills. One of the most important features is that the music includes an incomplete measure. While such musical tricks had been used by many Delta bluesmen, this was still an unusual arrangement for a blues composition. The tight quality of the recording implies that these musicians, even though they were very skilled, spent a long time in the studio. In the fourth line, "Just come on home to me," the band stops, and only Muddy's vocal ("I got to") is heard. This measure has only two quarter notes, which function as a pickup for the next measure. The band changes the accompaniment pattern from a series of simple riffs, mainly by the guitar, to a walking-bass pattern. The band again stops the accompaniment for the last line of the verse "somebody's gon' love me" and plays the turnaround together. These rhythmic tricks sound very exiting (see figure 5.3).

Figure 5.3.

In his vocal, Muddy also sounds excited. After the second verse, he shouts at Little Walter, "roll over, roll over," and his harmonica powerfully respond to Muddy. This is one of the best of Dixon-Muddy recordings.

Muddy Waters and his recording band returned to the studio on December 1, 1956. The Dixon composition that Muddy cut for this session was "I Live the Life I Love, I Love the Life I Live."[72]

This song has a philosophical theme; each person has his or her own way to live without being forced into a way of life by others. This is Dixon's version of "Ain't Nobody's Business If I Do":

[Verse 1] (A1)
See you watching me like a hawk,
I don't mind the way you talk,
But if you touch me somethin' got to give,
I live the life I love and I love the life I live.

[Verse 2] (A2)
So if you see me and think I'm wrong,
Don't worry 'bout me just let me alone,
My sweet life ain't nothing but a thrill,
I live the life I love and I love the life I live.

[Verse 3] (A3)
My diamond ring and my money too,
Tomorrow night, it may belong to you,
These girls move me at their will,
I live the life I love and I love the life I live.

[Harmonica solo]

[Bridge] (B)
I may bet a thousand on a bet this time,
One minute later I can't cover your dime,
Tomorrow night I could be over the hill,
I just want you to know, baby, the way I feel.

[Verse 4] (A4)
Oh you rockin' when you pass me by,
Don't talk about me 'cause I could be high,
Please forgive me, if you will,
I live the life I love and I love the life I live.

Dixon explains the philosophy he includes in this composition:

Gamblers would always say it. Drinkers would always say it. Street woman would always say it: "Don't tell me anything—I live the life I love." When people look to condemn certain lifestyles, the best response is "I live my life and you live yours, I live the life I love." Everybody, whatever they are doing—whether it's spiritual things or earthly matters—they feel like they're living the life they love.[73]

Dixon discusses a lifestyle in which each person has a right to make a decision. But the verses (and types of people that Dixon lists in the previous quotation) suggest that this song means more than a decision making. When Muddy assertively sings the punch line "I live the life I love, and I love the life I live," with a break for the band's accompaniment, he makes listeners feel that one must take responsibility in making a decision in life. In addition, the third verse ("My diamond ring and my money too, tomorrow night, it may belong to you") and the bridge ("I may bet a thousand on a bet this time, one minute later I can't cover your dime") show that it is possible that happiness and unhappiness can be divided by a fine line in the way you live.

In this song, Muddy Waters is still cast as a badman whose "sweet life ain't nothing but a thrill," and he is a gambler, as shown above. Nevertheless, the character he plays in "I Live the Life I Love" is a more matured wise man, as if he knows that almost every badman character has a tragic ending as a result of his lifestyle. It is evident that this character here takes a philosophical view, and his pessimism is the direct antithesis to the egoistic, reckless attitude of "Hoochie Coochie Man." In this sense, he is no longer acting like a "pure" badman. Here again, Muddy preaches Dixon's sermon.

The music of "I Live the Life I Love, I Love the Life I Live" is in a medium-slow tempo. It does not have the energetic feeling heard in "Hoochie Coochie Man" and "I'm Ready." Rather, it has subdued atmosphere, which fits its more profound theme about life.

Each verse is basically in an eight-measure blues scheme, but similar to "Don't Go No Further," "I Live the Life I Love" has an incomplete measure. In the verse sections, while the first three lines have two measures each, the last line has one measure and two quarter notes, although for the last verse in the recording, the accompaniment is not on the right beat, so that the band needs to have two extra quarter beats before starting the ending phrase.

This mistake might have been left in the master take intentionally. Throughout the recordings I discuss in this book, there are some sections in which band members make mistakes, vocalists mispronounce words, or words are not clearly heard. While Dixon has a high standard as a producer, as seen in the two takes of "Hoochie Coochie Man," some of the master takes show that his standard does not necessarily mean cutting a so-called perfect take. Rather than making a perfect record, he pays more attention to the feel of recordings. Dixon says, "If it was what you considered a perfect record, it never sold. But if it had a good feeling and good time, even when some of the words couldn't be understand, it would be better to go with that than one that's so perfect the people don't enjoy it."[74]

The vocal melodies sound like a sequence of the quick descending melodies of field hollers. Muddy's vocal performance is convincing in conveying the philosophy of this song. He controls the dynamics that go with the ups and downs of melodies well. His vocal performance in this song is analogous to that of a charismatic black preacher.

"I Love the Life I Live, I Live the Life I Love" is the last Willie Dixon composition that Muddy recorded before Dixon moved to Cobra Records in 1956. Their work from 1958 to 1969 will be discussed in chapter 7.

Little Walter

Following "Third Degree" by Eddie Boyd, the second Chess artist to record Willie Dixon's compositions was harmonica player/vocalist Little Walter. From 1953 to 1956, he recorded six Dixon compositions, including one of his best-selling singles, "My Babe." Therefore, the Dixon-Walter collaborations would logically be discussed after Boyd, but there are two reasons to examine Dixon's output for Walter after Muddy Waters. First, most of Dixon compositions for Walter were recorded after "Hoochie Coochie Man." More importantly, the style of Dixon compositions for Walter sharply contrasts with the Dixon songs for Muddy. Walter was fifteen years younger than Muddy, and their generational difference is clearly reflected in their different musical directions and Dixon's compositions for them. Walter's music often has a faster tempo than Muddy's, and he recorded flashy instrumentals more than anybody else on Chess Records. Walter's records were marketed to younger audiences who were likely to listen to rock 'n' roll records as well.

Shirli Dixon mentions what Willie Dixon thought of Little Walter as an artist:

> I think my dad thought of Walter . . . see a song like "Mellow Down Easy" and "My Babe," those are traditional tunes that had to be covered by a musician that could deliver it to both modern day audiences and traditionalists. I think that modern day audiences, he felt Walter had a special knack with. . . . In his mind, Walter was probably the crossover blues but also . . . that both the audiences could appreciate it.[75]

While Muddy Waters and Little Walter are different types of artists, there are songs in which Walter communicates wisdom as the most important element of the blues. In addition, while a song appears to be a pure love song with no twist, there are sometimes elements showing a character in the song bragging about himself or his girlfriend. It is here that Dixon aims at delivering a meaningful idea about life, and the device of autosuggestion through bragging about oneself—as evident in "Hoochie Coochie Man" and "I Just Want to Make Love to You"—is also seen in the songs for Walter. In essence, the ultimate goal of Dixon's songs is the same, even though what Dixon supplied for Little Walter differs from what he supplied for Muddy Waters.

On the other hand, Walter's performing persona is very different from Muddy's commanding persona that Dixon created in association with the characters of postbellum black badman tales and ballads. The main character in Dixon songs for Walter is an ideal boyfriend who is truthful to his girl-friend: a "one-woman guy" or "nice guy."[76] He brags about his girlfriend, and when she leaves him, he begs her to return to him. These songs never exaggerate expressions of sexual prowess, and there is no theme of challenging a social norm or archetype of resistance. From "My Babe" to "Who," Dixon's last composition for Walter before Dixon left Chess, this persona is consistent, while after returning from Cobra, Dixon gave Walter a different kind of persona with songs (these songs will be discussed in chapter 7).

Shirli Dixon describes Little Walter's position in the recording business and his appearance: "He was new on the business. He wasn't a very large man but was an average-sized man, and always dressed well, polite . . . more like kidlike. I feel like identifying him this way, because he was not as structured or rough as some of the others."[77]

The words that describe Walter's character, such as *polite* and *kidlike*, may contradict some readers' impressions about him, because Walter is known for his reckless lifestyle. He was famous for his bad temper, and he even shot his own foot by accident, which made him crippled. Walter became alcoholic, and in 1968, he died from a fight at the age of thirty-seven. Walter's bandmate guitarist Luther Tucker once said, "That cat was wild . . . loved to smoke grass, drink whiskey, chance [*sic*: supposedly "chase"] women, fight. . . . And he beat women, too. If a woman give him some lip, he'd fatten it up for her. And they'd just love it . . . it was amazing; they liked what he was doing."[78]

However, these episodes from Little Walter's real life could not be elements to create a marketable performing persona, just as Michael Jackson's records in the 1970s and 1980s cannot be associated with his private history. Walter's performing persona was more of a fictitious character created for commercial purposes. Although a performing persona is more or less fictitious, it is more so in the case of Walter. Jim O'Neal talks about the gap between Walter's real and fictitious character:

> On one hand Walter's treatment of women is hard to reconcile with a "nice
> guy" persona in the songs. But giving the appearance of being a nice, faithful,
> desirable man may have been part of the appeal he (and Dixon) were trying

to project—even if it was a lie or a ruse. He was also a young and popular recording artist, more so than middle-aged bluesman like Muddy and Wolf. Remember that a big portion (maybe the biggest portion) of the blues record buying audience was black women, so these songs are designed to appeal to them. They wouldn't have appreciated him singing "I'm going to bust your lip and chase other women!"[79]

In addition, Walter's self-abusive nature did not come to light at the beginning of his career. Muddy recollects, "When I met him, he wasn't drinking nothing but Pepsi Cola. Just a kid."[80]

Little Walter (Marion Walter Jacobs) was born on May 1, 1930, in Marksville, Louisiana. Walter became interested in harmonica at the age of eight when he heard John Lee "Sonny Boy" Williamson.[81] By the age of eleven or twelve, Walter's harmonica techniques became good enough to support himself financially. He left Louisiana for Helena, Arkansas, where he hung out with important musicians for developing his career, including harmonica player Sonny Boy Williamson (Rice Miller) and two of his future bandmates, guitarists Jimmy Rogers and Robert Jr. Lockwood.

Soon Walter moved to Memphis. Here he encountered another main influence, Big Walter Horton. Little Walter's biographers point out that the significant experience for Little Walter in Memphis was that he acquired a taste for being the focus of attention.[82] He was a show-off, and he liked to brag about himself, which later became an important element in Dixon's creation of his performing persona.

Around 1944, Walter headed for Chicago after hearing about Maxwell Street on the South Side, where numerous musicians were playing in a flea market. During this time, Walter changed his playing style. He started using an amplifier. His experimentation with the amp later resulted in harmonica sounds known as the "Mississippi saxophone." In addition, his performance became fast, busy, and nonstop after he was influenced by jump blues and swing jazz saxophonists. Especially Louis Jordan was Walter's favorite.[83]

In 1947, Walter made his first commercial recordings: "Ora Nelle Blues" and "Just Keep Loving Her" for Ora Nelle Records.[84] Later in that year, Jimmy Rogers introduced Walter to Muddy Waters. Through their public performances, Walter gained different kinds of fans than those for Muddy. Walter's biographers write, "Clearly Walter's place among the elite of the Chicago blues scene was becoming undeniable, and he was starting to develop his own following, with younger women as attracted to him as their older sisters were to the smoldering sexuality that the more mature Muddy Waters exuded."[85]

As previously discussed, Muddy's band, including Walter, recorded "Rollin' and Tumblin'" for Parkway Records. This record was a catalyst for Leonard Chess to bring Walter into Muddy's recording sessions. On May 12, 1952, Walter had his first session as a leader. The snappy instrumental "Juke" was released from Chess' subsidiary, the Checker label, under Little Walter and the Night Cats (Muddy Waters and Jimmy Rogers on guitars, and Elgin Evans on drums). On September 6, "Juke" reached number one in both the sales and jukebox categories of the Billboard R&B charts.[86] Walter became one of the top artists of the company.

Subsequently, Walter quit Muddy's band. He had an eye on the band called the Four Aces (aka the Aces): Junior Wells on harmonica, Louis and Dave Myers on guitars, and Fred Below on drums. They were younger than Muddy's band, and they were good at up-tempo tunes. Walter and Wells swapped their positions; Walter became a harmonica player for the Aces and renamed the band the Jukes, and Wells now played for Muddy's band, although Walter still played for Muddy's recording sessions.

Little Walter recorded his first Willie Dixon composition, "Too Late," on July 23, 1953. This song may be the same song that the Big Three Trio recorded for their last OKeh session in 1952, though it was unreleased:

> [Verse 1] (A1)
> Too late, too late, too late,
> I'm tired of your deceivin' and I can't stand your creepin', I'm gone,
> I'm tired of your deceivin' and I can't stand your creepin', I'm gone.
>
> [Verse 2] (A2)
> Too late, too late, too late,
> Tired of all the fussin' and I can't stand your cussin', I'm gone,
> Tired of all the fussin' and I can't stand the cussin', I'm gone.
>
> [Bridge] (B)
> Gee, you know I love you,
> I don't know just why,
> Thought the whole world of you,
> But today I say bye-bye, bye-bye.
>
> [Verse 3] (A3)
> Too late, too late, too late,
> Can't stand your cookin' and you ain't good-lookin', I'm gone,
> Can't stand your cookin' and you ain't good-lookin', I'm gone.
>
> [Harmonica solo]
>
> [Bridge repeated]

[Verse 4] (A4)
Too late, too late, too late,
Can't stand your beatin' and I know you been cheatin', I'm gone,
Can't stand your beatin' and I know you been cheatin', I'm gone,
Can't stand your beatin' and I know you been cheatin', I'm gone.

Dixon often does not depend on a straightforward twelve-bar/a-a-b scheme, and "Too Late" is another example. This song is organized in a modified A-A-B-A pop-song form; the A section has twelve measures each, and the B section has eight measures.

The busy shuffle groove is the most noticeable trait in "Too Late." For arrangement, Dixon, Walter, and other band members referred to Walter's instrumental composition from the previous session "Off the Wall." They have a similar tempo and feel, which are also heard in Walter's main influence, Louis Jordan's "Choo-Choo Ch'boogie" (1946).

The similarity between "Choo-Choo Ch'boogie" and "Too Late" is not only the feel of music. The descending melody line for the introduction and for the first line of the vocal part of "Too Late" is analogous to the opening of "Choo-Choo Ch'boogie" (see figures 5.4 and 5.5).

Figure 5.4.

Figure 5.5.

Walter's talent is that he creates the flashy atmosphere just with his harmonica, while Jordan's song has at least two saxophones.

The phrase "Tired of all the fussin' and I can't stand your cussin', I'm gone" also sounds similar to Jimmy Forrest's "Night Train" (1951), which was taken from Duke Ellington's "Happy-Go-Lucky Local" (1946).

The words are about bitterness toward a woman who is not faithful to a man. Dixon lists similar words to describe a woman's attitude: *deceivin'*, *creepin'*, *fussin'*, *cussin'*, *beatin'*, and *cheatin'*. Then he uses this rhyming to make a sarcastic comment: "I can't stand your cookin', and you ain't good-lookin', I'm gone." A variety of words with a consistent meaning describe one particular feeling—hatred.

"Too Late" was shelved until the spring of 1955, because there were other impressive cuts from this session—"Blues with a Feeling" and "You're So Fine." After "Too Late," Dixon did not provide any songs with similar words for Walter.

Little Walter's following session was held on February 22, 1954. For this occasion, he recorded "Oh Baby." This song is credited to Dixon and Walter, but it is actually a reworking of "You're Gonna Miss Me When I'm Gone" by Tampa Red and Big Maceo in 1942. As the title indicates, the song contains the sentiment of a man who loses his girlfriend. Although this is not purely a Dixon-Walter song, the words capture an integral part of Walter's persona. This character is clearly different from a tough guy or womanizer like Muddy Waters. "Oh Baby" reached the eighth position in the jukebox category of the *Billboard* R&B charts on May 1, 1954.

For the session on July 1, 1954, Dixon offered Walter "My Babe," but this time was only a run-through. Walter tried this song again a half a year later. The details of the rehearsal take will be discussed with the master take later in this chapter.

Prior to the completion of "My Babe," Walter recorded "Mellow Down Easy," another Dixon composition, on October 5, 1954. This song is a blues on the Latin beat ("striptease beat" or "jungle beat;" see figure 5.6).[87]

As Walter's biographers write, the introductory part appears to be based on Louis Prima's composition and Benny Goodman's popular song "Sing, Sing, Sing" (1938), while the vocal melodies could be drawn from a children's tune, "Old McDonald."[88]

The lyrics are organized in a quatrain refrain text form. The words and rhythmic pattern of this tune closely stay together:

[Verse 1]
You jump, jump, here,
You jump, jump, there,

You jump, jump, jump, everywhere,
Then you mellow down easy.

[Hook]
Mellow down easy,
You mellow down easy when you really wanna blow your top.

[Verse 2]
You shake, shake, here,
You shake, shake, there,
You shake, shake, shake, everywhere,
Then you mellow down easy.

[Hook repeated]

[Harmonica solo]

[Verse 3]
You wiggle, wiggle, here,
You wiggle, wiggle, there,
You wiggle, wiggle, wiggle, everywhere,
Then you mellow down easy.

[Hook repeated]

Figure 5.6.

The musical structure of this composition is unusual. Following the eight-bar introduction, there is a first verse for ten and a half measures, during which time a chord stays in the tonic, and the melody lines sound like children's game songs. Probably unintentionally, every time Walter sings around the end of the verse, the structure is slightly different. Harmonica solos are inserted after the second and third verses. The solo part is in a twelve-bar blues scheme with a walking-bass pattern.

Dixon explains the wisdom he included in "Mellow Down Easy":

You know, people do a lot of traveling—getting around everywhere. They'll jump there. They make love here and they make love there. And they think they're raising hell, but you're capable of getting into anything you jump in so many places. Mellow down easy when you really want to enjoy yourself. You get the best results when you stay in one spot for a while.[89]

It is interesting that Dixon chose Walter as a deliverer of this didactic message to the audience. To the listener who knows of Walter's "fire-eater" nature, this song sounds like an anger-management course in modern terms. With an infectious beat and childlike melodies, Dixon tries to grab the listener's attention, and at the same time he teaches an important life lesson through Walter. As he did to Muddy Waters, Dixon casts Walter as a secular preacher.

This recording is another example of Dixon's role as a producer. The released take has some inconsistencies in structure, but the bouncy feeling vastly outweighs its occasional mistakes. In addition, during the first solo and before the second solo, Dixon shouts "go" (or "blow") to let Walter know about the change of form from Latin beat to walking bass, because apparently Walter and possibly other musicians are confused.

Shirli Dixon confirmed that her father was the one who had to give signals to Walter during sessions: "In the sessions, you can hear that my dad really working on him [Walter] for coming in on time with the harmonica. There's a couple of times he's actually having to say to him 'now,' or 'this time go' or 'blow the horn' or 'blow your harmonica.'"[90] Musicians often have difficulty keeping track of musical structure, especially when the music is over one chord for a long duration of time. Furthermore, in the studio it is not unusual for players to have difficulty hearing other players. There had to be someone like Dixon who could indicate important points of structure.

Chess Records engineer Malcolm Chisholm says that Dixon had the knack for working with musicians even though they could be unruly like Little Walter:

Will was absolute magic in dealing with other musicians. Will could handle us on any level and he prefers to handle things by being persuasive and doing his wonderful Buddha act. Will is interested in it coming out right and the people he works with. He's a genuinely nice man and he deals extremely well with musicians, even obstreperous musicians. I've never run across anybody who liked Little Walter but Will could deal with him.[91]

Shirli Dixon says that her father had a good relationship with Walter:

He liked Little Walter. He really did. . . . He was really a sweet man, and . . . he was in our house a lot. He was always visiting. So I know that my dad really appreciated and enjoyed him as a person . . . certainly appreciated his talent. He liked his music, thought him as a great musician. . . . A lot of musicians would come and make session plans, but he just kind of was there. He kind of hung around bringing candies and stuff.

I don't think my dad had any real issues with him, because of course he was his producer in his mind. He was his writer. They had more of musicianship, brotherhood kind of relationship. He never spoke ill of him. . . . I think, on a basis of professionalism and on friendship, he probably didn't have any real adverse experiences.[92]

On January 25, 1955, Walter and the band, including Dixon, completed "My Babe."

[Verse 1]
My baby don't stand no cheatin', my babe,
Oh yeah, she don't stand no cheatin', my babe,
Oh yeah, she don't stand no cheatin',
She don't stand none of that midnight creepin',
My babe, true little baby, my babe.

[Verse 2]
My babe I know she love me, my babe,
Oh yes I know she love me, my babe,
Oh yes I know she love me,
She don't do nothin' but kiss and hug me,
My babe, true little baby, my babe.

[Harmonica solo]

[Verse 3]
My baby don't stand no cheatin', my babe,
Oh no, she don't stand no cheatin', my babe,
Oh no, she don't stand no cheatin',
Everything she do she do so pleasin',
My babe, true little baby, my babe.

[Verse 4]
My baby don't stand no foolin', my babe,
Oh yeah, she don't stand no foolin', my babe,
Oh yeah, she don't stand no foolin',
When she's hot there ain't no coolin'
My babe, true little baby, my babe.

[Tag]
(True little baby,) she's my baby,
(True little baby,) she's my baby,
(True little baby,) she's my baby.

Dixon had a strong feeling that he could not give this song to anyone but Little Walter. Dixon remembers, "I felt Little Walter had the feeling of this 'My Babe' song. He was the type of fellow who wanted to brag about some chicks, somebody he loved, something he was doing or getting away with. He fought it for two long years and I wasn't going to give the song to nobody but him."[93] Shirli Dixon adds a comment on artists' initial refusal of her father's compositions:

> Most of the artists refused to sing Dixon songs at first. Almost all of them, except for Muddy. Muddy was always willing to participate. When the artists refused to work, just like most things, he would say, "That's because they don't understand." He never took an angry position. There's always . . . their need for more of understanding.[94]

Dixon certainly captured Walter's nature as a show-off, and the lyrics of "My Babe" also demonstrate that the way Walter brags about his "babe" is essentially different from the boastful attitude of Muddy, who brags about his maleness.

A possible test piece that convinced Dixon that Walter could be the best deliverer of "My Babe" was Walter's own composition "You're So Fine," which reached the second position in the jukebox category of the *Billboard* R&B charts on January 2, 1954.[95] Both songs share similar content: bragging about a girlfriend and staying true to her—being the "nice guy."[96]

While it has been said that gospel singer Rosetta Tharpe's 1939 recording "This Train" was the melodic source for "My Babe," older folk songs such as "Froggie Went a Courtin'" could be another source. Whatever the sources are, more importantly, "My Babe" shows that Dixon tried to deliver wisdom through Walter, even though this song looks like a simple love song with a catchy melody. Marie Dixon explains that this song is about honesty, one of the facts of life:

> The function of the blues was understood very early in life. They were able to sing about their life, their families, and the stories they were told. It wasn't so much about sex [itself]. It wasn't about getting drunk [itself]. Like today, it's all about sex. I mean for the things I hear from the radio today and from the CDs my grandkids're listening to, they should be arrested for that.
>
> This is why Willie thought [what] the peoples need to do is to listen to the words . . . instead of getting into other people's life. Like Willie wrote the song "My Babe." No one wish to be cheated in no form, fashion, or way. Whether it's about moneys, or they don't want you to make love to another woman or to another man. You just don't want to be cheated. You want the fair life. This is what "My Babe" stood for. . . . It's a song about what people don't put up with, can't tolerate.[97]

"My Babe" is also about one of the basic human needs, the idea of ownership. It is a truth that a human needs something about which he or she can assertively say, "This is mine"; everyone needs something to brag about. When individuals are deprived of their possessions, identities, or any kind of needs, eventually their very existence will be endangered, which was what many African Americans had historically experienced. Dixon says,

> Well, if it wasn't "My Babe" it was someone else's babe. There's always a desire to feel that we have something of our own occasionally that we can brag about. Most of the time when someone thinks you're bragging about them they feel good. You say for example—"boy, that's my baby, I love that woman," or one of those kind of phrases—those are phrases that keep living. There's a human need to hear some of these phrases once in a while. If you get to a place where you can't hear them and can't be around them, and never have these kind of things in your mind, it'll kill you dead.[98]

In this way "My Babe" perfectly fits Dixon's artistic goal. He hopes that catchy rhythms will be a catalyst for listeners' attention to words that contain wisdom:

> When I write a song, I hope that people like it well enough to dance to it. Because most of the time if people dance to something—ten to one—they learn something about the words of it that gives them a certain education they wouldn't learn otherwise. They learn because they like it. But they don't have to be listening directly to the words. As you know, rhythm is the thing. Every-

thing moves to rhythm. Everything that's under the sun, that crawls, flies, or swims likes music.[99]

The run-through of "My Babe" on July 1, 1954, shows that the musicians (including Dixon) tried to put the music together in either of the following two ways. Walter's biographers write, "The version here has droning, one-chord, Howlin' Wolf 'Smokestack Lightning'–like arrangement."[100] However, at the beginning of the fourth line—"She don't stand none of that midnight creepin'"—which is supposedly the eleventh measure (because Walter is inconsistent with the meter, the measure number is approximate), there is a rhythmic break, and here it sounds as if there is a chord shift from the tonic to the subdominant. Second, considering this chord shift, while Walter's vocal melodies are basically taken from Rosetta Tharpe's record, it is possible that the musicians might not be able to comprehend how they should change chords during a verse. Otherwise, it might take awhile to figure out the particular chord progression I-V-I-IV-I, which is an irregular harmonic progression in Western tonal theory and is also unusual compared to the regular blues chord progression.

Regarding their second try on January 25, 1955, Walter's biographers present an interesting assumption; Dixon might have gotten an idea for an arrangement from the preceding session on the same day:

> The session files tell an interesting story. If the master numbers are to be believed, Dixon took part in a gospel session with pianist Reverend Ballinger immediately preceding Walter's recordings that day. One of the two tracks cut was "This Train," the gospel standard that is the direct source for Dixon's chorus, rhythm, and melody for "My Babe."[101]

Two of the most noticeable musical characteristics of Ballinger's "This Train" are a very fast eight-beat pattern (120 BPM [beats per minute]) and vocal melodies containing many ad libs based on Tharpe's original. On the other hand, Walter's master take is in a medium tempo (80 BPM), which is somewhat faster than that of the rehearsal take (72 BPM), and his vocal melodies sound closer to Tharpe's. Dixon possibly learned an appropriate harmonic progression from Ballinger's version, but the differences between his and Walter's versions suggest that Walter's master take more likely developed from his early run-through.

With a brisk tempo and catchier atmosphere, the master take of "My Babe" is better for dancing than the awkward early take. The recording starts with Fred Below's pickup on the snare drum, and it is followed by a jazzy riff with

Robert Jr. Lockwood's chord stroking over Dixon's walking bass.[102] Walter's vocal sounds clear and confident. Melody lines go up from low to middle and then to the high register on each line of the lyrics. The melodic motion goes along with the heightened expression of a man who is proud of his girlfriend, and when the emotion reaches its high point, the music provides a punch line with a rhythmic break: "She don't stand none of that midnight creepin'." This song is a good example of a perfect marriage of words and music.

The two rounds of Walter's harmonica solo are not overly powerful but are very melodious, as though one could whistle his solo part. The last refrain of the chorus is sung by Lockwood and Dixon, which creates a charming call-and-response effect with Walter's vocal.

Chess Records' staff members had strong confidence in Walter's new record. The following is from a sales report with Phil Chess' comment: "Speaking of Chess boys, they're out with several hit potentials again. Of the brand new Little Walter release 'My Babe,' all Phil will say is 'Just watch it!'"[103] The advertisement on the *Billboard* says, "A Sure Hit! Checker #811 'My Babe' by Little Walter."[104]

"My Babe" was released in February 1955. On March 12, it was ranked number one in all categories on the *Billboard* R&B charts—jukeboxes, sales, and airplay—and the song stayed there for five weeks.[105] In addition, this song was ranked at the 106th position on the pop chart.[106] With this nationwide hit, Little Walter was even booked on Alan Freed's package show. For Dixon, "My Babe" was his first number-one hit as a songwriter.

"Nice guy" became the most important song subject of Little Walter's post–"My Babe" repertoire—as seen in "Little Girl," "Can't Stop Loving You," "Hate to See You Go," "One More Chance with You," "Nobody but You," "Temperature," and "Everybody Needs Somebody," as well as two Dixon compositions, "Crazy for My Baby" and "Who."

In "Crazy for My Baby" (recorded on July 14, 1955), Walter again brags about his girlfriend. This song could have been a successful follow-up for "My Babe," but it was not released until six years after the recording date, possibly because during the second round of Walter's solo, a microphone captures somebody having a conversation. Dixon recorded his own version in November 1955, which was only four months after this session.

"Who" (recorded in December 1955) is a slow twelve-bar blues with a somewhat reserved atmosphere. Along with the more laid-back feeling of this song, Walter's harmonica solo is more relaxed than usual. The song is about a bad rumor without foundation, and again it is derivative of the "one-woman guy" persona:

[Verse 1]
Who told you that I was foolin' around,
Who told you that I was goin' to town,
Whoever told you baby, better get outta town.

[Verse 2]
Who told you that I was cheatin' last night,
Who told you that I ain't doin' what was right,
Whoever told you baby, better get outta sight.

[Harmonica solo]

[Verse 3]
People always talkin' about something they don't know,
They like to stir up trouble, 'cause they want to see a show,
Who told you that I was foolin' around,
Whoever told you baby, better get out of town.

[Verse 4]
Some folks just stay happy that other feelin' as bad,
They get the biggest kick, when someone is feelin' bad,
Who told you that I was cheatin' last night,
Whoever told you baby, better get outta town.

One ear-catching characteristic is that Dixon finds different verbs in a progressive tense: *foolin'*, *goin'*, *cheatin'*, *(ain't) doin'*, and *talkin'*. Dixon's favorite compositional technique adds spice to a simple topic. He also inserts his wisdom gleaned from observing human behavior: "People always talkin' about something they don't know, they like to stir up trouble, 'cause they want to see a show."

"Who," coupled with "It Ain't Right," was released at the beginning of March 1956. On March 31, this song was ranked at the seventh position in the jukebox category and thirteenth in sales on the *Billboard* R&B charts.[107] This was Walter's second to last top-ten hit record.

In chapter 7, I will discuss six other Dixon compositions for Little Walter in which Dixon gives the singer a completely different performing persona.

Willie Dixon's Own Chess Recordings

From 1954 to 1957, Willie Dixon as a featured artist recorded fourteen songs including "Wang Dang Doodle," "Walking the Blues," and "29 Ways." In 1962, after he returned from Cobra, he recorded as a member of the Lucky Three Trio (other members were pianist Lafayette Leake and drummer Clifton James).[108]

Dixon's records on Chess—released from its subsidiary Checker label—are similar to those of the Big Three Trio in terms of their variety in musical styles: Tin Pan Alley–like pop songs, storytelling ballads, twelve-bar blues combined with Latin beat patterns, and another type of blues that can be labeled "talking blues."

The song subjects are largely categorized as humorous songs or love songs. It seems that Dixon thought of his own performing persona as that of a more urbanized artist—a friendly, humorous person, large in size, or more succinctly "a fat but good-natured fellow"—someone like Fats Domino. While Dixon was good at writing songs that manifested menacing power like "Hoochie Coochie Man," he did not see himself as an appropriate deliverer of that sort of song.

Although Dixon's reputation as a composer heightens expectations that his own recording output consisted of many famous songs, most of the songs discussed in this section are not well known. Nearly half of his records remained under wraps until they were included in the compilations released in the 1980s and 1990s. Seven out of the fourteen compositions discussed here are still not available in CD format.

According to Dixon, one reason so many cuts remained unreleased is that the company was uneager to promote his records.[109] It is very possible that Dixon's performing style as a solo artist with soft bass vocal and a standup bass was not highly appealing to the Chess brothers, although they definitely needed his talent as a songwriter and producer.[110] Realistically, however, Dixon did not have enough materials in quality and quantity for his own recordings; obviously his main work was to provide artists with potential hit songs. The discography shows that he tended to record fewer songs per session: there were some sessions for which he cut only one or two songs, although most artists would usually cut four or five.[111] Furthermore, there was often a long interval between sessions that he led. To be fair, Dixon was a little too busy to make his own records.

Dixon's first Chess session as a vocalist was held on February 17, 1954. This session was not solely for Dixon but for the vocal group the El Rays, which later became the Dells. Dixon takes a lead vocal for "Wang Dang Doodle" and "So Long."

"Wang Dang Doodle" is one of the Willie Dixon classics, but his own recording was not known until 1995. When this song was recorded for the first time, it was documented as "Whing Ding All Night."[112] While the versions by Koko Taylor and Howlin' Wolf both have three verses, Dixon's own recording has two verses:

[Verse 1]
Tell Automatic Slim,
To tell Razor Totin' Jim,
To tell Butcher Knife Totin' Nannie,
To tell Fast Talking Fanny,
We gonna pitch a ball, down to the union [region?] hall,
We gonna romp and tromp till midnight,
We gonna fuss and fight till daylight,
We gonna pitch a wang dang doodle all night long.

[Hook]
All night long, all night long,
All night long, all night long,
We gonna pitch a wang dang doodle all night long.

[Verse 2]
Tell Cooter-Crawlin' Red,
To tell Abyssinian Ned,
To tell Ol' Ice Pick Pete,
To tell everybody he meet,
Tonight we ain't got no rest, we pitch a ball and throw a mess,
We gonna break down all of the windows,
We gonna tear down all the doors,
We gonna pitch a wang dang doodle all night long.

[Hook repeated]

Go!

(Spoken)
In New Orleans hit 'em with a dip of snuff.

The inspiration for this song—nicknames and a wild party—came from Dixon's early life in Vicksburg:

Well, you take in the Southern states—and practically all over the world—there have always been people that have nicknames. . . . And so, anyway, where I came from in the South, all of these names are pretty well true. If you went in certain parts of the city it was Fanny, or Mose, or John, or Fast-talking Fanny, or something. And I began to think about that. When I was a kid . . . a fellow called Walter Barnes, he had a good band and he was out of Vicksburg, Miss. Everybody knew him and the guys'd say, "Hey, man, we gonna have a ball tonight, y' know. They gonna pitch a wingding." That's what they used to call having a ball—pitching a wingding. And they would tell, "Hey, you tell so-and-so to tell so-and-so." Well, it wasn't in rhyme like this, but I put it in rhyme in order to make it a song. And so I wanted Automatic Slim—you know those guys used to think he was a great guy cause [sic] he carried a big automatic on his side—and Razor Toting Jim, that ole guy carried razors and all like that. All these characters are actually nicknamed that. And that's the way I wrote "Wang Dang Doodle."[113]

The theme of "Wang Dang Doodle" had a long tradition. A description of threatening characters having good times at the dance party had been used for toasts, folk songs, and bluesy pop songs; some of the recordings include "Rules and Regulations 'Razor Jim'" by Edith Wilson (1922), "Down at the Razor Ball" by Sara Martin (1925), and "Razor Ball" by Blind Sammie (Blind Willie McTell) (1930).[114] Some of the names that Dixon lists in his song were already in these recordings; for example, Automatic Slim was one of the characters in Martin's, and Razor (Totin') Jim was the main character of Wilson's.[115]

In addition, the variant of the expression "Wang Dang Doodle" is also observed in the sermon (or toast) of the mid-nineteenth century, "Where the Lion Roareth and the Wang-doodle Mourneth." The version by William P. Brannan, transcribed sometime between 1830 and 1860, is a description of New Orleans' underground scene. The transcription includes the following:

Now, "whar the lion roareth and the wang-doodle mourneth for his first born" . . . ah! This part of my tex [sic], my beseeching brethering, is not to be taken as it says. It don't mean the howling wilderness, whar John the Hard-Shell Baptist fed on locusts and wild asses, but it means, my brethering, the city of New Y'Orleans, the mother of harlots and hard lots, whar . . . gamblers, thieves and pickpockets goes skitting about the streets like weasels in a barnyard; whar honest men are scarcer than hen's teeth; and whar a strange woman once took your beluved teacher and bamboozled him out of two hundred and twenty seven dollars in the twinkling of a sheep's tail; but she *can't* do it again! Hallelujah-ah! "For they shall gnaw a file, and flee unto the mountains of Hepsidam, whar the lion roareth and the wang-doodle mourneth for his first-born"—ah![116]

The meaning of the expression and the list of nicknames explain why this song about threatening characters was later offered to a singer who had a dangerous nickname, Howlin' Wolf, and another wild singer, Koko Taylor.

The structure of the music is similar to Dixon's other ballad-style compositions, "Signifying Monkey," "Tell That Woman," and "Hoochie Coochie Man." During the verse and the hook, there are no chord changes, which count thirty-two more measures total (a twenty-measure verse plus a twelve-measure refrain).

The musical elements of "Wang Dang Doodle" help to build a mad partylike atmosphere. The song has a hard-driving feel with a fast walking-bass pattern. Almost throughout the recording, the piano player randomly alternates different beat patterns using the higher keys to express the frantic feelings of a party. In the very catchy refrain "All night long, all night long," the call and response between Dixon's vocal and high-pitched shouts by the El Rays sounds ecstatic.

"So Long" from the same session was another unreleased recording until 1995, while Dixon later gave this song to Muddy Waters' sideman Jimmy Rogers (discussed later this chapter). This song is based on an eight-bar structure in a minor chord. The song is just about saying good-bye to a girlfriend: "So long, so long, I hope I'll see you again, / If you can't be my baby, I really want you to be my friend." The wordless, low-pitched vocal harmony by the El Rays and the instruments that quietly accompany the lead vocal help to create a melancholic feel.

Dixon recorded "If You're Mine" and "Alone" in May 1955; more than a year had passed since his first session as a leader in February 1954, although he constantly provided songs for his label mates and played bass for their sessions. "If You're Mine" was released as the flip side of "Walking the Blues," while "Alone" was not released until the late 1980s.[117]

"If You're Mine" is a brisk eight-beat song in a lively tempo. The vocal melody consists of some very short phrases primarily based on two pitches (D and G). On these chopped phrases, the words of a love call are humorously sung: "I love, you love, that's all I think of, / Baby, I'll be your lover, if you're mine, if you're mine."

The drummer's emphasis on the backbeat and the saxophone player's car-horn-like sound effects create an exciting feel. But the saxophone solos sound very awkward because they are too short; without this flaw, the song would have been a good rock 'n' roll recording.

"Alone" is a banal lost love song in the Tin Pan Alley style. The words such as *rendezvous* and *romancing* are very anachronistic. Apparently the recording did not meet the standard to be released officially at that time.

The next session was held sometime in July 1955, two months after the previous session. "Walking the Blues" was the only output on this day. This is not Dixon's composition but a reworking of Champion Jack Dupree's 1955 hit written by Dupree and Teddy McRae; not only the words but also the overall arrangement were taken from Dupree's recording. Dixon copyrighted this song under his name, but it appears that he shared the copyright with Dupree and McRae.[118]

"Walking the Blues" is in the "talking blues" style; that is, Dixon's non-melodic monologue is accompanied by his own bass, Lafayette Leake's piano, and Fred Below's foot tapping (these are also characteristics of Dupree's recording). The recording starts with the sound of footsteps in a medium walking pace. After eight footsteps, Leake plays the introduction based on the twelve-bar blues form. After the first round, Dixon begins his monologue. The lines are a description of a man walking a long way home, which is a metaphor of the long process needed to achieve goals. Dixon preaches wisdom that is applicable to various situations in real life:

[Verse 1]
Man, slow down,
We'll get there,
Take your time,
Don't walk so fast,
Stay on the road.

[Verse 2]
I don't blame people,
For singing "Walking the Blues,"
Walking the blues,
Walking the blues,
'Cause, Man, this is it.

[Verse 3]
Man, I think I'll relax,
[Exhale], that's the way to relax,
Now watch this.

[Verse 4]
Boy, is it hot today?
All you got to do is put one foot in front of the other,
And keep on walkin'.

[Verse 5]
Walking the blues,
[Exhale], that's what I call gliding home,
I hope my old lady is home when I get there.

[Verse 6]
All this walkin',
I don't mean my mother-in-law,

I mean my wife,
My mother-in-law, she's always there,
So we'll just keep on walking anyway.

On August 13, 1955, "Walking the Blues," coupled with "If You're Mine," was released as Dixon's solo debut. The record was advertised in print with Chuck Berry's debut single "Maybellene" and the Flamingos' "I Want to Love You."[119] Dixon was marketed in the pop music field. On September 10, "Walking the Blues" was ranked at the seventh position in the jukebox category on the *Billboard* R&B charts.[120]

The follow-up session to "Walking the Blues" was held sometime in November 1955. The commercial success of the last single brought Dixon back to the studio within a half a year. This session was so productive that Dixon cut four sides: "Youth to You," "Crazy for My Baby," "I Am the Lover Man," and "This Pain in My Heart."

The first cut, "Youth to You," has been unreleased to this date, though Dixon later rerecorded it with Memphis Slim for Prestige Records in 1959 (as discussed in chapter 7, this song is a parody of "I Just Want to Make Love to You"). The next cut was "Crazy for My Baby," which Dixon originally offered to Little Walter after "My Babe." As stated earlier, Walter's recording was unreleased. Dixon made his own version and released it as his own single.

Compared with Walter's version, Dixon's sounds more like straight rhythm and blues. While both versions have strong accents on the first quarter beat and the second eighth note of the second quarter beat, in Dixon's version these are treated just as accents rather than as the stop-time riff with a syncopation in Walter's version. For a background, Dixon's bass constantly plays a walking bass in a fast-medium tempo. In addition, the sounds of saxophone and acoustic piano give an R&B flavor in Dixon's version that contrasts with the sounds of amplified harmonica and distorted electric guitar of Walter's version.

The third cut for this session was "I'm the Lover Man," which became the B side of "Crazy for My Baby."[121] Similar to "So Long," "I'm the Lover Man" is in a minor key with a medium tempo. The music sounds melancholy due to its tempo, choice of key, and subdued dynamics. During this period, Dixon did not offer compositions in the minor mode to anybody but himself, except for "This Pain" presented to Muddy. Dixon started to write more songs in the minor after he moved to Cobra Records.

The vocal melody is built on the recurring bass line B-A-G-F-sharp (it sounds similar to Ray Charles' "Hit the Road Jack"). Dixon sings the lines with his soft bass voice, as if he is trying to offer consolation to a girl who has been mistreated:

[Verse 1]
You pretty little girl, don't have to cry no more,
A lover man is here and rarin' to go,
Dry your tears and you can wear a smile,
And I am gonna have you, honey child.

[Verse 2]
If your man don't study stuff the stuff,
His luck goes and times get tough,
You need somebody to hold your hand,
Remember me I'm the lover man.

[Hook]
I'm the lover man, I am the lover man,
I am the lover man, I'm the lover man,
Call me if you need me, I'll make you understand.

[Verse 3]
If you cry, baby, in the middle of the night,
Call me up if things ain't right,
You know you tried and done your best,
I'll come along and do the rest.

[Verse 4]
I'm big and strong and handsome too,
Nothin' in the world that I can't do,
I catch your heart and hold your hand,
And make you know I'm the lover man.

[Hook repeated]

The fourth verse, "I'm big and strong and handsome too, / Nothin' in the world that I can't do," sounds as if Dixon is arrogantly singing about himself.

The fourth and last song that Dixon recorded was "This Pain in My Heart."[122] This song was one of the earliest compositions he wrote in Vicksburg.[123] If this recording retains his original ideas, this composition by young Dixon shows an obvious influence of African American music. The vocal melodies are constructed from a combination of a pentatonic and blue-note scale. When he arranged this song, Dixon added other black musical elements: call-and-response phrases by saxophone and bass in the introduction and a slow walking-bass pattern throughout verses.

While there are some interesting features to look at from an analytical and cultural point of view, "This Pain in My Heart" did not seem to impress the Chess brothers. This song was left on the shelf for about six months until it was released as the flip side of "29 Ways."

Sometime in 1955, Dixon rerecorded the Big Three Trio's "Violent Love." This recording was unreleased until it was included in the box set collection of his compositions, *Willie Dixon: The Chess Box*, released in 1988. He remembers that this session was the bait with which the label executives tried to motivate him to work for the company. Dixon says, "The only reason we recorded it ['Violent Love'] with Chess back then was that Chess was trying to hook me to get me to stay there and help 'em with the other artists."[124] His impression reflects the fact that this was the only song that was recorded in this session, and it was not even given a session file number.

The new version of "Violent Love" starts with Dixon's count, which the producer of the box set might have left intentionally. While the new version features a saxophone, the basic characteristics of the recording, such as verses, tempo, and harmonic progressions, are the same as the original version.

Because of the lack of accurate documentation, the recording data attached to the box set states that "Violent Love" was recorded "either in 1951 or 1955 by The Big Three Trio."[125] However, this rerecorded version could not have been made in 1951. The sound quality of the Chess version is obviously different from that of the Big Three Trio records. In addition, no other Big Three Trio recordings included a saxophone.

Dixon did not have recording sessions for himself during the first half of 1956. More than half a year after the previous session, he recorded "29 Ways (to Get to My Baby's Door)" on July 27, 1956. This song was taken from the repertoire of the Big Three Trio.[126] According to the discography, the Moonglows' session was held immediately before Dixon's.[127] Dixon asked the Moonglows to perform the backup vocal parts when they gave the recording room over to him.

The song "29 Ways" is one of those that gives full scope to Dixon's ability as a songwriter and arranger. The most noticeable characteristic is a busy Latin beat pattern played by the drummer, Al Duncan. As Dixon's cobiographer Don Snowden writes, for the background of "29 Ways," Dixon recycled the beat pattern that he used for "Mellow Down Easy."[128] For the middle ground, the pianist Lafayette Leake doubles the rhythmic pattern of the drums in a higher range but distant from the microphone, which makes it sound like a toy piano. Then, Dixon adds a minimum amount of bass line. The simplicity is more outstanding in each verse; the players play only the first beat during this section—the simplest way to play the stop-time riff. This plain formation effectively emphasizes the humor in Dixon's vocal style and words. Dixon lists different ways to make it to his baby's door:

[Hook]
I got 29 ways to make it to my baby's door
(to my lovely baby's door),[129]
I got 29 ways to make it to my baby's door
(to my lovely baby's door),
If she need me bad, I can find about two or three more
(one, two, many more).

[Verse 1]
One through the basement,
Two down the hall,
When the going get tough,
I got a hole in the wall.

[Hook]
I got 29 ways [just] to make it to my baby's door
(to my lovely baby's door),
If she need me bad, I can find about two or three more
(one, two, many more).

The musical structure of this song is basically a twelve-bar blues form; the hook is in an a-a-b pattern, and the verses are in a quatrain refrain and its variant. While the first verse is twelve bars, the second and the third verses each have an additional four bars, on which Dixon lists more "ways to make it to my baby's door."

[Verse 2]
I can come through the chimney like Santa Claus,
Go through the window, and that ain't all,
A lot of good ways, I don't want you to know,
I even got a hole in the bathroom floor.

[Hook repeated]

[Saxophone solo]

[Verse 3]
I got a way through the closet behind her clothes,
A way through the attic that no one know,
A master key to fit any lock,
A hidden door behind grandfather's clock.

[Hook repeated]

[Tag]
(To my lovely baby's door) Oh
(To my lovely baby's door) Oh, baby
(To my lovely baby's door)
(To my lovely baby's door)
(To my lovely baby's door)
(One, two, many more).

The record of "29 Ways" with "This Pain in My Heart" was released on December 1, 1956, approximately four months after the recording session. This was an unusual interval between a session and a release date. Usually a record would be put out within a month or two from the session date, if the label owners felt that the track was strong enough. In fact Dixon started to work for Cobra Records around the summer of 1956, and by December of that year, he had already become a main staff member at Cobra. Although "29 Ways" has an ear-catching quality, it was not listed in the *Billboard* R&B charts.

Dixon's last session as a vocalist is dated in April 1957.[130] However, this date is dubious, because by the end of 1956, he moved to Cobra. He did not offer any songs to Chess artists until 1958, although he occasionally participated in Chess sessions as a bass player. For this doubtful date session, Dixon recorded three compositions: "Firey Love," "All the Time," and "Jelly Jam" ("Jelly Jam" was unavailable to me). All of these tracks were unreleased until much later.

"Firey Love" is a rhythm and blues song with a gospel flavor. This is another minor mode song. Dixon later offered this song to Jesse Fortune in 1963 with a new title "God's Gift to Man." There is a good variety in the words describing the qualities of love, God's gift:

[Verse 1]
The purest love, the surest love is the love that you can't hide,
The greatest love, the truest love is the love that's on your side,
The only love that one can love, don't have to wonder why.

[Hook]
There is but one and only love,
It sets his soul on fire,
Set his soul on fire,
Touch his soul on fire.

[Verse 2]
The sweetest love, the finest love is the love you can express,
The loveliest love, the kindest love is the love that loves you best,
All these in love you love, I know the reason why.

[Hook]
But love this, love that one can love,
It sets his soul on fire,
It sets his soul on fire.

[Vamp]
Oh, I want you to be my love,
Oh, I want you to be my love.

[Verse 3]
The oldest love, the boldest love is the love that just won't die,
The latest love, the staidest love is the love that do not hide,
If you say your love is true, and you don't sometimes cry.

[Hook]
Remember lovin' love that all,
Till it sets your soul on fire,
Till it sets your soul on fire.

Although this is an attractive composition, the recording has some flaws. The saxophone riff is a little monotonous. There is an abrupt insert "Oh, I want you to be my love" after the second hook. In the same section, there is a moment when Dixon mistakenly comes in late. In addition, the playback speed of the recording sounds inaccurate.

Another cut from this session, "All the Time," which is a love song in a pop-song form, is a remake of "Baby" by Shirley and Lee with Dave Bartholomew and Orchestra in 1952.

After Dixon returned to Chess, sometime in 1962 he had a recording session with the Lucky Three Trio and cut two songs, "Back Home in Indiana" (composed by Sam Levine) and instrumental "Wrinkles" (credited to Lafayette Leake).

"Wrinkles" features Leake's fabulous blues piano. Throughout the recording, Dixon modestly backs up Leake by combining different walking-bass patterns in different ranges with phrases containing many triplets, eighth notes, and slap-bass techniques. Near the end of the recording, Dixon takes a solo. The transcription in figure 5.7 shows Dixon's aptitude for crafting clever phrases:

Figure 5.7.

The quality of compositions discussed above varies from some of the best Willie Dixon compositions to really banal works. Shirli Dixon critically comments on her father's own records:

> "Walking the Blues" he had a pretty good success. "Violent Love" like all the others, he knew [that he] represented sort of a different spin on politically correct issues, if you will. So being the kind of a man he was, and seeing the life as we saw without smoky-colored glasses, he knew that some of his materials would not be promoted well. He would not always be accepted by the label or even by the general public. But he felt that if he was speaking to life's real issues, there would be some chances.[131]

It is true that Dixon felt his records were not promoted well, but it is also true that some of the love songs that he recorded did not show his forte as a songwriter. These songs reflected the musical trends of the times, but even at the point he recorded them, they were no longer appealing. They did not have any quality that could distinguish them from hundreds of other songs, compared to other outstanding works.

Jimmy Witherspoon

Vocalist Jimmy Witherspoon (1923–1997) was one of the most popular rhythm and blues singers in the nation with "Ain't Nobody's Business, Parts 1 & 2" (Supreme, 1949). While he mainly recorded for companies on the West Coast, he recorded for several companies in the Midwest, including Chess Records.

The relationship between Chess Records and Witherspoon existed for a short period of time. From 1954 to 1956, he had four recording sessions, all of which Willie Dixon participated in as a bassist.[132] Witherspoon recorded three Dixon compositions for his first Chess session on June 10, 1954: "When the Lights Go Out," "Live So Easy," and "Big Daddy (I Can Make You Love Me)." "When the Lights Go Out" was a territorial hit in Chicago.[133]

In "When the Lights Go Out," Dixon requires Witherspoon to use a wide vocal range. His vocal performance is filled with a melodic rise and fall. He musically expresses his excited feeling about the girl:

> [Verse 1] (A1)
> I love to look in my baby's face,
> I love to feel that silk and lace,
> And when she kiss, she nearly makes me shout,
> Great God all mighty when the lights go out!
>
> [Verse 2] (A2)
> I love to see her walking down the street,
> She always dresses so nice and neat,
> You never know what it's all about,
> Great God all mighty when the lights go out!
>
> [Bridge] (B)
> You can use your imagination,
> You still be far behind,
> There's nothing in creation,
> Like that girl that gal of mine.
>
> [Saxophone solo]
>
> [Verse 3] (A3)
> I love to hold her when she talks the talk,
> I love to watch when she walks the walk,
> And if I pet her when she's tryin' to part,
> Great God all mighty when the lights go out!
>
> [Tag]
> Great God all mighty when the lights go out.

The arrangement and the production of the last line of the verse are very effective. At the beginning of the line, the band has a rhythmic break, and at this moment Witherspoon probably steps back from the microphone in order to add echo to his voice. These effects make this line sound like a loud congratulatory exclamation; it is more so when Witherspoon hits a high B for the last repetition of this line.

Including "When the Lights Go Out," all the Dixon-Witherspoon collaborations suggest that Dixon always prepared recording material that he could offer to Muddy Waters. Obviously, Muddy was one of the top priorities both for Dixon and the company. Some parts of the lyrics for Witherspoon and the arrangement of these songs are highly related to Muddy's records, while they are arranged to fit Witherspoon's style. For example, the specific musical scheme and the production devices of "When the Lights Go Out" became a model for "I Want to Be Loved," which Dixon provided for Muddy about a year after this Witherspoon session.[134] As well as the A-A-B-A musical structure, these two songs share a similar lyrical theme and atmosphere: an attractive woman and a man's excited feeling for her.

In addition, the rhythmic break and the echo sound in the punch line are identical. The analogy between these two compositions shows that Dixon tended to connect a particular song theme with similar musical and production devices. On the other hand, beyond these similarities, Muddy's distinctive vocal style and Little Walter's harmonica sound make the composition for Muddy more bluesy than Witherspoon's song.

Another Dixon song for this session, "Live So Easy," is a slow twelve-bar blues with a quatrain refrain form. Dixon catalogues the names of creatures to make a point that people's lifestyle should be as easy as that of creatures living happily in any given place. This list of the creatures is similar to Dixon's composition for Eddie Boyd, "Rattin' and Runnin' Around":

[Verse 1]
If fish can love in the water,
Worms can love underground,
Rats can love in a garbage can,
Baby, don't you turn me down.

[Hook]
'Cause we can live so easy, yes, live so easy,
We could live so easy, finding out the art of love.

[Verse 2]
Now snakes can love in the green grass,
Birds can love in the trees,
Moles can make love in muddy holes,
I know you can love with me.

[Hook repeated]

[Verse 3]
Well I ain't got no money,
But I got lots of wits,
And when you think I am starving,
I am coming right back again.

[Hook repeated]

[Verse 4]
Dogs can love in the alley,
Sharks can love in the sea,
Horse can love in the corral,
Baby, come along with me.

[Hook repeated]

There are some similarities between "Live So Easy" and "I Just Want to Make Love to You," which was recorded by Muddy about two months before the Witherspoon session. Both songs have sexually suggestive themes. Along with the similar theme, the tempo for both compositions is a slow one. In addition, both songs have analogous introductory melodies; in "Live So Easy," the saxophone plays a descending melody based on a pentatonic scale, while in "I Just Want to Make Love to You," piano and bass play a similar motive. Dixon recycled some of the musical features of "I Just Want to Make Love to You" (figure 5.8) for "Live So Easy" (figure 5.9).

Figure 5.8.

Figure 5.9.

The last cut for this session was "Big Daddy (I Can Make You Love Me)."

[Verse 1]
Been drinkin' muddy water like a catfish in a stream,
I've been drinkin' muddy water like a catfish in a stream,
I've been loving a pretty woman ever since I was sixteen.

[Verse 2]
I'll have you screamin' and hollerin', talkin' all in your sleep,
I'll have you screamin' and hollerin', talkin' all in your sleep,
I'll make you tell the world big daddy can't be beat.

[Saxophone solo]

[Verse 3]
I'm no hard worker, I can play a long long time,
Yeah, I ain't no hard worker, I can play a long long time,
If I don't drive you crazy, I'll tantalize your mind.

[Verse 4]
I make you do like a turtle drag it all in the sand,
I make you do like a turtle drag it all in the sand,
I'll make you love muddy water drag it off by land.

Because of the sexual overtones of the text and the line that includes words "muddy water," this song could have been given to Muddy, but the arrangement style is different from Muddy's style. This Witherspoon recording shows the strong influence of Big Joe Turner's hit songs around 1953 and 1954, such as "Honey Hush" and "Shake Rattle and Roll."

Similar to "Shake Rattle and Roll," "Big Daddy" has a fast shuffle tempo (although Turner's song has a strong backbeat, while Witherspoon's drummer plays only a shuffle pattern). The introductory phrases of the piano played by the right hand sound very similar. In addition, both tunes feature wind instruments, although Turner's horn section consists of trombone and tenor and baritone saxophones, whereas Witherspoon has only one tenor saxophone.

These three Dixon compositions for Jimmy Witherspoon show both similarities to and differences from the songs for Muddy Waters. While there are musical factors that could be exchanged from Witherspoon's to Muddy's songs or vice versa, the arrangement and the production styles are planned to fit the featured vocalist's characteristics.

Lowell Fulson

Lowell Fulson (1921–1999), famous for "Three O'Clock Blues" (Downtown, 1948) and "Everyday I Have the Blues" (Swing Time, 1950), had twelve sessions with Chess Records from 1954 to 1963. He released fifteen singles from the Checker label, including "Reconsider Baby" (1954). He also recorded two Willie Dixon compositions: "Do Me Right" and "Tollin' Bells."

Whereas most of Fulson's records on Chess were made in Dallas or Los Angeles (he did not like to record with unfamiliar musicians so he sent master tapes to Chess), the two Dixon compositions were recorded in Chicago. On January 13, 1955, Fulson recorded "Do Me Right." This is a simple twelve-bar/a-a-b blues in a brisk walking tempo. The musicians are Fulson himself; at least two of his regulars, Eddie Chamblee (tenor sax) and Earl Brown (alto sax);[135] and three Chess regulars, Dixon (bass), Otis Spann (piano), and Fred Below (drums). This recording features Fulson's guitar solo with his characteristic sounds sans vibrato.

On February 9, 1956, Fulson recorded "Tollin' Bells." Dixon participated in this session as a bassist and producer. This song is an experimental mixture of melodrama with a twelve-bar/a-a-b pattern.

> [Verse 1]
> Well, the big bell is tollin', trouble (been) here an' gone,
> Well, the big bell is tollin', trouble (been) here an' gone,
> It done took my baby, left me all alone.
>
> [Verse 2]
> Well my head hangs so heavy, when the sun start sinkin' low,
> Well my head hangs so heavy, when the sun start sinkin' low,
> It put my soul on a-wonder, which way did my baby go?
>
> [Verse 3]
> Well, I heard loud singin', saw slow marchin'
> I heard deep moanin' and (there was no laughin'),
> It brought tears from my eyes, keep on streamin' down,
> I keep cryin' for my baby, I know she can't be found.

Dixon was probably inspired by Fulson's slow blues song "Lonely Hours," but distinctive features of "Tollin' Bells" are a rhythmic configuration that simulates a funeral march and the sound of a funeral bell through the crush of a major chord by the horns and a minor chord by the piano played simultaneously (see figure 5.10).

Dixon explains this musical experiment:

> I wrote "Tollin' Bells" for Lowell Fulson and the idea was like in New Orleans, when they'd have a funeral, guys would be marching for the funeral with the church bells tolling. The idea was to make these horns blend in a minor tone,

with the minor against the major. I was using the horns to play two parts of a minor chord and the piano playing the other. The idea was to do something with a different harmony blend but a good blend.[136]

The master take was numbered nineteen, but Fulson's album *Hung Down Head*, released in 1970, includes takes one through six.[137] These outtakes show that Dixon had a basic idea of an arrangement: a very slow tempo (it takes more than three minutes to sing all the verses; therefore, there is no room for a guitar solo), a one-pitch horn riff (only a dotted half note followed by a quarter rest), and dissonant textures by the piano and horns. The funeral-march rhythms by bass, piano, and drums were added sometime after take six.

Figure 5.10.

Dixon required high pitches for Fulson's vocal range; the opening note is a high E, and the vocal melody sometimes reaches a high B. The outtakes show that Fulson is frustrated by this range. After take one, Fulson says, "Hold it, Baby," and (probably) Dixon gives an instruction to Fulson and to the horn section (unintelligible). Then Fulson abrasively responds, "Well, I'm going to concentrate on this singin'. I'm gonna put somethin' in there after that. . . . We'll see if we can scream it for you."[138] It is on take six that Fulson and the band finally go through the song from the beginning to the end.

In the master, the tempo is somewhat slower than in the previous takes, and the piano, bass, and drums play the funeral-march riff from the introduction. In the intro, the first beat of the first measure is slightly loose, but from the following measure on, the band expresses the sound of the bell and the funereal atmosphere very well. For vocal melodies, Fulson uses a high range from the beginning; even at the first line ("The big bell is tollin'"), he hits a high B, while in previous takes he saved this pitch for the second line. He alternates line by line, his crooner style in a lower range and the shout style in a higher range, conveying the painful feelings of the song.

"Tollin' Bells" was a nightmare for Fulson. He never recorded again at Chess studio. He remembers,

> We tried some things, but I couldn't do that. Willie Dixon, those songs, I couldn't sing it. Not the way he wanted them. Tolling Bells, I hate that thing. Oh Boy, I hate that with a passion. . . . And for the key raise that he wanted to do, that threw me too far away from baritone, and you go to screaming instead of singing. I am not a screamer. I do good to stay in the range of talking. 'Cause I am not one of them good singers, them boys with the old pretty voices and stuff. You got to do what you can with what you got to do with it. You don't try to be something that you're not. It's not a bad song. I'm singing it in the wrong key so I can get way up there and get preacher type thing singing.[139]

However, the master take does not sound as bad as Fulson thought. On top of the funeral-march-like accompaniment, Fulson's vocal performance expresses agony in the lyrics. It is almost impossible to know how uncomfortable he was with the choice of key without reading the episodes he describes and hearing outtakes.

As opposed to Fulson's impression, Dixon's musical experiment, the amalgamation of the blues and melodrama with an unusual rhythm pattern, was successful. This song shows a segment of Dixon's wide variety of compositional style and arrangement technique. He later used the style of melodrama for an important composition for Howlin' Wolf, "Tail Dragger" (see chapter 7).

Willie Mabon

Pianist/vocalist Willie Mabon (1925–1985) was a versatile entertainer known for the sourly humorous songs "I Don't Know" and "I'm Mad." On June 1, 1955, he recorded a Willie Dixon composition, "The Seventh Son." According to Dixon, Mabon was the one who asked Dixon for a song.[140]

Dixon's decision in giving this song to Mabon reflected the label owner's marketing plan. Mabon says, "They [Chess brothers] wanted to make a Muddy Waters player out of me, you know, that type of playin'. That warn't my style. Chess wanted to do that. That warn't my style."[141] In fact, Muddy could have sung "The Seventh Son" as a sequel to "Hoochie Coochie Man." There are some similarities between these songs. Similar to the songs that Dixon offered to Jimmy Witherspoon, this is another example that suggests Dixon always prepared songs for Muddy.

The theme of "The Seventh Son" is drawn from the down-home Southern tradition of the conjurer, which is indicated by his ability to foresee the future:

[Verse 1]
Now everybody's cryin' about the seventh son,
In the whole round world there is only one.

[Hook]
I'm the one,
Well I'm the one,
I'm the one, I'm the one,
The one they call the seventh son.

[Verse 2]
Now I can tell your future before it come to pass,
I can do things for you that makes your heart feel glad,
I can look in the sky and then predict the rain,
I can tell when the woman's got another man.

[Hook repeated]

[Verse 3]
I can hold you close and squeeze you tight,
I can make you cry for me both day and night,
I can heal the sick and raise the dead,
And I can make your little girl talk all out of your head.

[Hook repeated]

[Saxophone solo]

[Verse 4]
Now I can talk these words that sound so sweet,
And make your lovin' heart even skip a beat,
I can take you baby and hold you in my arms,
And make the flesh quiver on your lovely palms.

[Hook repeated]

The ability of Seventh Son as a conjurer evidently parallels that of another conjurer, Hoochie Coochie Man, who uses a black cat bone, mojo, and John the Conqueror root. Dixon also borrows the song's theme from his own biography; he was born as the seventh of fourteen children. "Hoochie Coochie Man" also has the usage of the symbolical number seven: "On the seventh hour, on the seventh day . . ."

Just as Hoochie Coochie Man can "make pretty women jump and shout," the Seventh Son is a lover man: "Now I can talk these words that sound so sweet, / And make your lovin' heart even skip a beat."

Secularized religious elements of "The Seventh Son" are seen in the line "I can heal the sick and raise the dead, and I can make your little girl talk all out of your head." He is a healer—an important role of a preacher—as well as a lady's man. Therefore, "The Seventh Son" could have fit perfectly with Muddy's persona.

Compared to Muddy's vocal, Mabon's vocal sounds light, and he expresses the powers of the Seventh Son in a comical way. Obviously Mabon's "The Seventh Son" does not sound like the song of a tough conjurer that is associated with black badman heroes. As an urbane artist, Mabon has a more polished rhythm and blues musical style.

The music of "The Seventh Son" is basically in a twelve-bar blues form, but as is usual for Dixon, this is a quatrain refrain text form. Dixon lists the Seventh Son's abilities with a stop-time riff over a tonic chord. While the use of stop-time for this composition is associated with Dixon's compositions for Muddy, this musical figure and overall arrangement style seem to derive from Mabon's previous hits "I Don't Know" and "I'm Mad," and the introductory phrase that is played by three horns is based on his previous hit "Poison Ivy."

Although today "The Seventh Son" is known as one of the Dixon classics for the versions by Johnny Rivers and Mose Allison, this was not a hit for Mabon. By 1962 he left Chess after continuous financial troubles with the label owners.[142] Although Mabon recorded other Dixon songs when he was on Chess, these recordings are unreleased to date.[143] But in 1963, he recorded two Dixon songs, "Just Got Some" and "I'm the Fixer," for USA Records. These songs will be discussed in chapter 7.

Bo Diddley

Next to Chuck Berry, Bo Diddley was the second most popular of Chess Records' rock 'n' roll and rhythm and blues division artists, although his musical style was more like a crossover between blues and rock 'n' roll. Bo recorded three Willie Dixon compositions: "Pretty Thing," "Diddy Wah Diddy," and "You Can't Judge a Book by Its Cover."

Bo Diddley was born as Ellas Otha Bates (Ellas McDaniel) on December 30, 1928, in McComb, Mississippi, and died in Archer, Florida, on June 2, 2008. When he was a child, he moved to Chicago.[144] Although he first took violin lessons, he switched to the guitar. When he was in his teens, he formed a band with his friends.[145] Dixon remembers that he saw Bo's group performing in the streets.[146]

When Bo was nineteen (1947), his band got their first club gig at the 708 Club on the South Side of Chicago.[147] Around this time, he acquired a loud amplification system,[148] and he also added a maraca player, Jerome Green, to his group. Both additions contributed to what later became Bo's trademark sound. In 1954, Bo and Green formed a new band with Billy Boy Arnold (harmonica), James Bradford (bass), and Clifton James (drums).[149] In 1955, Bo brought his demo "I'm a Man" to Vee-Jay Records, but it was turned down. He then took it to Chess Records.[150] His debut single "I'm a Man" coupled with "Bo Diddley" on the Checker label was a number-one hit in the jukebox category on the *Billboard* R&B charts.[151]

The songs that Dixon provided for Bo clearly fit his performing persona, which was a mixture of Bo's own and Muddy Waters' characteristics. Bo states in his biography, "Muddy has been some of my inspiration, 'cause I wanted to be so much like him, but I couldn't even begin to think about bein' the man he is in the blues bag. Muddy is the greatest!"[152]

"Hoochie Coochie Man" is an obvious source for "I'm a Man." The lyrics are about a macho guy coming of age, and its rhythmic configuration is a succession of stop-time riffs over one chord. One aspect of Bo's public image is like "Hoochie Coochie Man"—that is, an offshoot of postbellum secular black outlaw heroes.

From this matrix Bo also developed a playful figure, as heard on the flip side of his debut "Bo Diddley." This song is based on the lullaby "Hush, Little Baby":[153]

[Verse 1]
Bo Diddley bought his babe a diamond ring,
If that diamond ring don't shine,

> He gonna take it to a private eye,
> If that private eye can't see,
> He'd better not take the ring from me.

There are several different stories about the origin of Bo's stage name. Billy Boy Arnold remembers,

> Leonard Chess had never heard the words "Bo Diddley" and he said, "Well I don't know—what does that mean? Is that some kind of discriminating word for Black people?" He said, "I won't put that on there, they wouldn't buy it." He [washtub player named Arnold] said, "No, 'Bo Diddley' don't mean that. 'Bo Diddley' is just a comical word of a guy, maybe bow-legged guy, a comical-looking guy, Bo Diddley, y' know." He said, "We'll call you Bo Diddley" and that's how he got the name.[154]

Bo himself explains the meaning of his pseudonym: "I got it when I was a kid goin' to grammar school, an' I've been tryin' to find out ever since why the heck they called me that. . . . I can't tell you exactly what it means, but it kinda means 'bad boy'—mischievous, you know."[155]

Bo's performing persona primarily consists of his mischievous "bad boy" nature and his comical nature rolled into one. Thus, his personality can be compared to today's rap artists. Then, too, his "mischievous guy" persona is linked with black roots, as the line from the song "Bo Diddley" shows: "Mojo come to my house, black cat bone, / Take my baby away from home."

These words that Muddy could have sung are connected with Bo's particular musical style, which derives from African music by way of the Caribbean Islands and Latin America: mambo, rumba, cha-cha, and calypso. In this way, Bo Diddley's performing persona is musically realized by an assimilation of foreign beat configurations on his guitar—often accentuated by maracas—with down-home black expressions in the text.[156]

While Bo Diddley and Little Walter belonged to the same generation (Walter was two years younger than Bo), they developed antithetical personae. As discussed previously, Walter's persona is not related to the characters of black badman tales and ballads. Unlike Bo's texts, Walter's lyrics are rarely based on African American expressions or clichés. What interested Dixon was the amalgamation of new and old that he saw in Bo: trendy and distinctive beat and traditional down-home expressions.

"Pretty Thing" (recorded on July 14, 1955) is an evident product of Dixon following the musical and text style of the song "Bo Diddley." This song is an innocent marriage proposal:

[Verse 1]
You purty [pretty] thing,
Let me buy you wedding ring,
Let me hear the choir sing,
Oh you purty [pretty] thing.

[Verse 2]
You purty [pretty] thing,
Let me walk you down the aisle,
Darlin' wear a lover's smile,
Oh you purty [pretty] thing.

[Guitar solo]

[Harmonica solo]

[Verse 3]
Let me kiss you gentle,
Squeeze and hold you tight,
Let me give you all my love,
The rest of my life.

[Verse 4]
You purty [pretty] thing,
Let me hold you by my side,
And become my blushing bride,
You purty [pretty] thing.

[Verse 5]
Purty [pretty] thing,
Let me dedicate my life,
You will always be my wife,
Oh you purty [pretty] thing.

[Ending Guitar and Harmonica solo]

Bo sings a very simple melody—basically made out of three pitches, B, A, and G, and their derivatives—in a call-and-response form with harmonica (see figure 5.11).

His vocal melody is accentuated by the hypnotic beat created by his own guitar. Dixon explains this is the heart in this composition: "I knew Bo had a very good rhythmic style and this gave him the thing to emphasize. When you hear a guy come up with a beat like 'Boom da boom da boom, da boom boom,' right out of nowhere, it's going to attract your attention."[157]

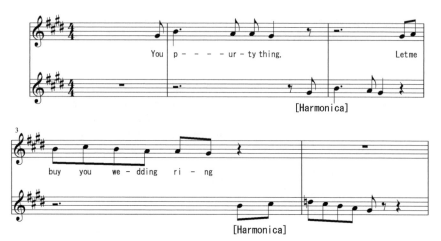

Figure 5.11.

In relation to the characteristic beat, Dixon found that the most appropriate lyrical material for Bo was something that derives from black culture. Shirli Dixon says,

> One of the things that daddy recognized in him [Bo] was he had a more unique method of offering his music. So writing songs like "Pretty Thing" or "You Can't Judge a Book," and again some of these being clichés from the African American culture. So he felt Bo could be the best deliver of those, because he had more rock style of delivering his materials. More direct on the beats, and strict rock formation of the material.[158]

"Pretty Thing" was Bo's second top-five hit. It was ranked at the fourth position in the jukebox category on the *Billboard* R&B charts on January 7, 1956.[159]

In his biography, Bo recalls that Dixon was whispering words in Bo's ear during the session as well as suggesting that he was responsible for a part of the composition: "Willie Dixon wrote 'Pretty Thing.' I remember Willie standin' over me, whisperin' the lyrics in my ear before I got to the next line! (Laughs.) He was nice enough to give me part of the tune. It should be on the credits: 'McDaniel & Dixon.'"[160]

Bo Diddley's following session was held on November 10, 1955. For this occasion, Dixon co-composed "Diddy Wah Diddy" with Bo. Similar to "Signifying Monkey," "Hoochie Coochie Man," and "Wang Dang Doodle," "Diddy Wah Diddy" is based on black folklore. According to Zora Neal Hurston, Diddy Wah Diddy is the largest and best known of the Negro mythical places. Its geography is that it is "way off somewhere." It is reached by a road that curves so much that a mule pulling a wagon-load of fodder can eat off the back of the wagon as he goes. It is a place of no work and no worry for man and beast. A very restful place where even the curbstones are good sitting-chairs. The food is even already cooked. If a traveller [sic] gets hungry all he needs to do is to sit down on the curbstone and wait and soon he will hear something hollering, "Eat me! Eat me! Eat me!" and a big baked chicken will come along with a knife and fork stuck in its sides. . . . It is said "Everybody would live in Diddy-Wah-Diddy if it wasn't so hard to find and so hard to get to after you even know the way."[161]

The Dixon-Diddley composition is about a man's longing for a girl in this fantasy land:

> [Vamp 1]
> Diddy wah,
> Diddy wah.
>
> [Verse 1]
> I got a gal down in Diddy-Wah-Diddy,
> Ain't no town and it ain't no city,
> She love a man 'til it's a pity,
> Crazy for my gal in Diddy-Wah-Diddy.
>
> [Vamp 1 repeated]
>
> [Verse 2]
> This is the girl sweet as she can be,
> And I know she in love with me,
> Lovin' me, she's so pretty,
> But she live way down in Diddy-Wah-Diddy.
>
> [Vamp 1 repeated]
>
> [Vamp 2]
> Ain't no town and it ain't no city,
> Lord, how they love in Diddy-Wah-Diddy.
>
> [Vamp 1 repeated]
>
> [Verse 3]
> She kiss me all the time,
> She gonna drive me out of my mind,
> Everything she say [she's ready?],
> Headin' right back to Diddy-Wah-Diddy.
>
> [Vamp 2 repeated] [162]

Bo's bent-note playing in the introduction and the Moonglows' chorus give a comical taste to the performance.

Another Dixon composition that Bo recorded was "You Can't Judge a Book by Its Cover." This song was recorded on January 24 or 26, 1962, after Dixon's return from Cobra. This didactic song is built around a famous proverb and a catalogue of similar phrases:

[Verse 1]
You can't judge an apple by lookin' at a tree,
You can't judge honey by lookin' at the bee,
You can't judge a daughter by lookin' at the mother,
You can't judge a book by lookin' at the cover.

[Hook]
Oh can't you see,
Oh you misjudge me,
I look like a farmer, but I'm a lover,
Can't judge a book by lookin' at the cover.

[Vamp]
Ah, oh,
(Spoken)
Oh come on in closer baby,
Hear what else I gotta say,
You got your radio turned down too low,
Turn it up!
Oh!

[Verse 2]
You can't judge sugar by lookin' at the cane,
You can't judge a woman by lookin' at her man,
You can't judge a sister by lookin' at her brother,
You can't judge a book by lookin' at the cover.

[Hook repeated]

(Spoken)
Ah, how am I doin', baby?

[Verse 3]
You can't judge a fish by lookin' in the pond,
You can't judge right from lookin' at the wrong,
You can't judge one by lookin' at the other,
You can't judge a book by lookin' at the cover.

[Hook repeated]

[Ending guitar solo]

Dixon explains,

If you put a picture of Superman on the cover of the Bible, you might think you're getting a comic book. The cover hides a lot of things—this is what people judge folks by a lot of times—by what they look like on the outside. And you can't actually judge anything by the cover—no individual, no part of life.[163]

Butch Dixon relates the story behind this song:

People thought that Bo had a square guitar, and he was a different type of person. My dad told Bo one day in the studio. He said, "If you take a farmer out from a farm, put a guy like him in town and walk down on the street, could you tell a farmer from a lover?" He said, "No, I don't wanna." "People judge you by the cover," then he say, "judging the book by the cover here." He says, "No way to tell what you are until you do what you do." Bo loved that aspect and jumped on it.[164]

The interest of this recording is in its unpredictability; funny-looking Bo Diddley delivers a fundamental message. Willie Dixon's technique in this song is as if it was tailored to Bo's public image, assimilating universal wisdom and the most fashionable beat of the time. Clearly, Dixon casts Bo as a preacher in the secular context.

While Bo Diddley is usually valued as a rhythm guitar player, this track shows his unique vocal style. He freely uses various vocal techniques: glissandi in a wide range, howling, changing dynamics and tone quality, alternating melodic and non-melodic singing.

On August 25, 1962, "You Can't Judge a Book by Its Cover" peaked at the twenty-first position on the *Billboard* R&B charts.[165] It was also ranked at the forty-eighth position on the *Billboard* pop single charts.[166] This is one of a few Dixon songs that made a pop chart.

Bo Diddley told his biographer about Willie Dixon's influence, "Willie was a great influence on me, an' he helped me a lot in the studio an' stuff. He was *always* there. He was like a father, you know."[167]

Jimmy Rogers

Jimmy Rogers (1924–1997) recorded about thirty sides as a vocalist/guitarist for Chess Records from 1950 to 1959, while he was Muddy Waters' sideman. Rogers had a medium-sized hit "Walking by Myself" in 1956. For a follow-up session for this hit, he recorded two Willie Dixon compositions, "I Can't Believe" and "One Kiss," on December 1, 1956.

Rogers explains why he did not record many Dixon compositions: "I knew Dixon, of course, he played on some of my records, but I never could see doing his type of material, nothing wrong with them but it seemed as if my own songs just suited me better. So I went on with my own songs."[168]

Rogers was probably thinking of Dixon's compositions for Muddy. Compared with Muddy, Rogers has a more urbane performing style: "My own style developed from Big Bill Broonzy and guys like that—Lonnie Johnson, Tampa [Red]. I like the style and tone that Big Maceo carried in that group."[169] Rogers' songs are rather about simple love or lost love. He usually uses a walking-bass pattern with a traditional blues harmonic progression instead of a succession of short riffs over one chord, which is Muddy's favorite recipe. Dixon's compositions for Rogers follow his style.

"I Can't Believe" is about the alienating attitude of a girlfriend. Rogers' smooth and light vocal style fits the content of this Tin Pan Alley–style song. Big Walter Horton's harmonica, which mainly plays chords in a controlled way, adds a bluesy feeling to the song, while (probably) Jody Williams' guitar complements Rogers' somewhat jazzy vocal sounds.

Another cut, "One Kiss," is a reworking of Dixon's own recording "So Long" in 1954. While the basic structure of the two versions is the same (each verse is eight measures, but the order of verses is different), there are significant differences between them. Dixon's version is a very moody rhythm and blues in a minor key, featuring his soothing bass vocal and reserved solos by tenor saxophone and guitar. On the other hand, Rogers' version is in a major key with a medium walking-blues tempo, and the sound of the guitar is more in the foreground. This arrangement sounds reminiscent of Rogers' "Walking by Myself." In general, this recording is not impressive compared with other Rogers recordings—this is also true of "I Can't Believe"—and it does not surpass the unique characteristics of Dixon's version.

Although Jimmy Rogers made records for Chess until 1959, during the 1960s he retired for a while, because he was disillusioned by the music business. He could never be a top artist of the label like his bandmates Muddy and Little Walter. Looking back at his Chess days, Rogers complained about studio operations and the common practices regarding songwriter credits:

> If you worked out a good arrangement on a song, you'd get into the studio and [producer] Leonard Chess would change it, [Willie] Dixon was producing a lot of his stuff and he'd put in an extra verse, saying that made him the writer of the song. All the years we recorded—Muddy, myself, [Howlin'] Wolf—would always have that studio problem.[170]

Rogers' complaint about Dixon was true, as my studies show some in-stances, although taking credit by changing lyrics was a common practice for a number of blues songwriters.

For about five years, Rogers ran a cab company and a store business, but Sunnyland Slim and Dixon included Rogers in the American Folk Blues Festival in Europe in 1972 and 1983. Rogers played as a recording and per-forming artist until his death in 1997.

This chapter shows Dixon's distinctiveness in providing songs and in his musical and text form. Dixon never confined himself to a twelve-bar/a-a-b blues mold. This tendency was already apparent in his compositions for the Big Three Trio. The different musical structures that he used included eight-bar ("So Long"), sixteen-bar ("Hoochie Coochie Man"), twenty-bar ("My Babe"), and thirty-two-bar ("Wang Dang Doodle"). In addition, the combination of blues with a pop-song form—a blues composition with a bridge section, as seen in "I Just Want to Make Love to You" and "I Love the Life I Live, I Live the Life I Love"—is one of Dixon's most characteristic musical ingredients. A main reason why Dixon preferred a quatrain refrain text form is that, as seen in "29 Ways," he could freely extend the musical form, especially when he used a list of similar words or concepts in the lyrics. His flexible and thoughtful use of forms demonstrates his gift as a composer.

Ultimately, all of the characteristics of Dixon's compositions discussed in this chapter are devices to deliver wisdom, the most important aspect of the blues. In African American cultural context and according to Dixon's inten-tion, songs such as "Hoochie Coochie Man," "I Just Want to Make Love to You," and "My Babe" have far deeper meanings than mere expressions of machismo or fond talk. In fact many songs in this chapter have didactic contents and deliver Dixon's sermons.

Notes

1. Robert Palmer says, "His [Dixon's] real gift, when writing songs for Muddy Waters and later on for Howlin' Wolf, was to take the kind of persona projected by the artist in question, and intensify it, make it almost in a sense larger than life." *Bluesland: A Portrait in American Music* [VHS] (New York: BMG Video, 72333–80087–3, 1993).

2. Willie Dixon, with Don Snowden, *I Am the Blues: The Willie Dixon Story* (New York: Da Capo Press, 1989), 88.

3. Ibid., 150.

4. Joel Whitburn, *Top R&B Singles, 1942–1999* (Menomonee Falls, WI: Record Research, 2000), 471. If Muddy Waters' chart success is narrowed only to top-five hits, three out of four songs are composed by Dixon.

5. Muddy Waters, *The Best of Muddy Waters* (Chicago: Chess Records, Chess LP-1427, 1957; Universal City, CA: MCA/Chess, CHD 51268, 1987).

6. Whitburn, *Top R&B Singles, 1942–1999*, 268.

7. Mike Leadbitter and Neil Slaven, *Blues Records, 1943–1970: A Selective Discography*, vol. 1, A to K (London: Record Information Services, 1987), 133.

8. Whitburn, *Top R&B Singles, 1942–1999*, 42.

9. Dixon, *I Am the Blues*, 86. Dixon says, "I had been trying to do patterns like I was using with Chess before, when I worked for Lester Melrose, but I didn't have enough authority with Melrose. When I got a chance to do it with Chess, I could clue the guys, like on that 'Third Degree' I did with Eddie Boyd."

10. Whitburn, *Top R&B Singles, 1942–1999*, 52.

11. Bob Corritore, Bill Ferris, and Jim O'Neal, "Willie Dixon (Part 1)," *Living Blues*, no. 81 (July/August 1988): 25.

12. Jon Michael Spencer explains "bad luck": "Blues singers often referred to the cultural evil of racial discrimination and poverty (evils of helplessness, depravity, and separation) by using the code word 'bad luck'—that linguistic minstrel mask that deceptively implied mere superstition. The 'bad luck' faced by blacks of this era was essentially the continued legacy of slavery." Spencer, *Blues and Evil* (Knoxville: University of Tennessee Press, 1993), 89.

13. Dixon, *I Am the Blues*, 86.

14. Shirli Dixon, interview by the author, September 23, 2002.

15. John W. Work, Lewis Wade Jones, and Samuel C. Adams, Jr., *Lost Delta Found: Rediscovering the Fisk University–Library of Congress Coahoma County Study, 1941–1942*, ed. Robert Gordon and Bruce Nemerov (Nashville: Vanderbilt University Press, 2005), 8.

16. *Sweet Home Chicago: Story of Chess Records* [VHS], notes by Tadashi Igarashi (Tokyo: Videoarts Music, Imagica Media, VAVZ-2129, 1993).

17. Peter Guralnick, *Feel Like Going Home: Portraits in Blues and Rock 'n' Roll* (New York: Outerbridge & Dienstfrey, 1971; repr., New York: Harper & Row, 1989), 65. Citations are to the Harper & Row edition.

18. Robert Palmer, *Deep Blues* (New York: Viking Press, 1981; repr., New York: Penguin Books, 1982), 166. Citations are to the Penguin Books edition.

19. Barry Lee Pearson and Bill McCulloch, *Robert Johnson: Lost and Found* (Urbana: University of Illinois Press, 2003), 75.

20. Palmer, *Deep Blues*, 168.

21. Robert Gordon, *Can't Be Satisfied: The Life and Times of Muddy Waters* (Boston: Little Brown, 2002), 112.

22. Terry Gross, "Interview with Robert Gordon," *Fresh Air Audio*, October 3, 2002, retrieved from the National Public Radio website, www.npr.org/features/feature.php?wfld=1329547 (accessed October 5, 2002).

23. Bob Corritore, Bill Ferris, and Jim O'Neal, "Willie Dixon (Part 2)," *Living Blues*, no. 82 (September/October 1988): 24.

24. Butch Dixon, interview by the author, September 23, 2003.

25. Guralnick, *Feel Like Going Home*, 71.

26. Shirli Dixon, interview by the author, September 23, 2002.

27. Dixon, *I Am the Blues*, 85.

28. Ibid.

29. Shirli Dixon, interview by the author, September 23, 2002.

30. Whitburn, *Top R&B Singles, 1942–1999*, 471.

31. Dixon, *I Am the Blues*, 85.

32. Tom Dalzell and Terry Victor, eds., *A New Partridge Dictionary of Slang and Unconventional English*, vol. 1, A–I (New York: Routledge, Taylor and Francis Group, 2006), 1022.

33. Ibid., 1028.

34. Jonathon Green, ed., *Cassell's Dictionary of Slang*, 2nd. ed. (London: Cassell, 1998; repr., 1999), 328. In the source, it is written "practitioner of voodoo," but as explained in note 35, hoodoo and voodoo are often mistaken for one another, and this is the case here.

35. Although hoodoo and voodoo are often mistaken for one another (some believe that the terms may have a common etymology), hoodoo is not simply the detritus of the voodoo religion. For instance, hoodoo is not a religion in America. It is spiritual and magical in nature, but it does not have an established theology, clergy, laity, or order of liturgical services. Hoodoo shows some links to the practices and beliefs of African, European, and Native American folk magical-religious culture. "Hoodoo," Wikipedia: The Free Encyclopedia, en.wikipedia.org/wiki/Hoodoo_%28folk_magic%29 (accessed May 26, 2007). David Evans, "A Review for Mitsutoshi Inaba's Manuscript," June 10, 2008, p. 5.

36. This transcription is based on the master take that is included in Muddy Waters, *Hoochie Coochie Man: The Complete Chess Masters*, vol. 2, *1952–1958* (Santa Monica: Geffen/Hip-O Select/Chess, B0002758–02, 2004). In an alternate take (included in this album), he sings, "You got a boy child's comin'."

37. Regarding the musical and lyrical characteristics of "Hoochie Coochie Man," Benjamin Filene writes, "Within the genre of 'blues,' Dixon realized, he had immense latitude. He began to break away from the traditional twelve-bar blues style, writing songs that drew on commercial pop forms." Filene, *Romancing the Folk: Public Memory & American Roots Music* (Chapel Hill: University of North Carolina Press, 2000), 99. As observed in chapter 3, however, Dixon broke away from the traditional twelve-bar blues style even before "Hoochie Coochie Man." When Dixon writes songs with an influence of pop tunes, he usually follows the Tin Pan Alley compositional and lyrical pattern, as seen in "Violent Love" and "Practicing the Art of Love" for the Big Three Trio. In terms of the musical structure, "Hoochie Coochie Man" can be characterized as "a 12-bar refrain type blues extended to 16 bars by doubling the first four bars" (Evans, "A Review for Mitsutoshi Inaba's Manuscript," 5) or a hybrid of

ballad-style composition—the first repetitive part is similar to the musical device of "Signifying Monkey" and "Tell That Woman" for the Big Three Trio—and a blues composition with a walking-bass pattern for the refrain part.

38. Willie Dixon, *Willie Dixon: The Master Blues Composer* (Milwaukee: Hal Leonard, 1992), 152.

39. Roger D. Abrahams, *Deep Down in the Jungle: Negro Narrative Folklore from the Streets of Philadelphia* (Hatboro, PA: Folklore Associates, 1964), 65. Abrahams also says, as opposed to the black badman characters, "trickster, protagonist heroes existed in a permissive, childlike, neuter world, completely divorced from sexual conflict." Ibid., 69. From this, it is reasonably assumed that Hoochie Coochie Man is more like a badman than a trickster, and he is not just sexually but physically tough just like other badman characters, even though it is not directly sung so in verses.

40. Ibid., 66.

41. John W. Roberts, *From Trickster to Badman: The Black Folk Hero in Slavery and Freedom* (Philadelphia: University of Pennsylvania Press, 1989), 201.

42. Abrahams, *Down Deep in the Jungle*, 75.

43. Dixon, *I Am the Blues*, 84.

44. Roberts, *From Trickster to Badman*, 200.

45. See Dixon, *I Am the Blues*, 84–85, and Palmer, *Deep Blues*, 97.

46. Palmer, *Deep Blues*, 97.

47. Roberts writes that the actions of conjurers are depicted as dangerous actions with respect to the well-being of the black community, whereas tricksters' actions are focused against an external (white) threat: "The actions of conjurers served as a model of behavior for dealing with subversive actions directed primarily against other members of the black community, whereas tricksters had offered a model of subversive and manipulative behavior for dealing with the powers of the masters—an external threat to the well-being of the black community." Roberts, *From Trickster to Badman*, 200.

48. The following is a definition for "son of a gun": "1. a despicable person, usually a male; 2. old buddy; 3. exclamation." Richard A. Spears, *NTC's Dictionary of American Slang and Colloquial Expressions*, 3rd ed. (Lincolnwood, Chicago: NTC Publishing Group, 2000), 389. In another dictionary, Spears writes, "1. a soldier's bastard. This literal interpretation is no longer extant; 2. a pal, a fellow, a chum. A mild avoidance for SON OF A BITCH; 3. an oath from 'I'll be a son of a gun!'" Richard A. Spears, *Slang and Euphemism* (New York: Jonathan David Publishers, 1981), 367.

49. Roberts, *From Trickster to Badman*, 28.

50. Dixon, *I Am the Blues*, 85.

51. In addition, the master take balances each instrument better than the alternate take, although this is attributable to the engineer. It is possible that band members changed their positions in the studio to cut a more balanced take, and they might have been told to be careful of their distance to the microphones.

52. "Rhythm and Blues Tattler," *Billboard*, February 20, 1954, 42. Galen Gart, ed., *First Pressings: The History of Rhythm & Blues*, vol. 4, 1954 (Milford, NH: Big Nickel, 1992), 20.

53. Ibid., 21.

54. Whitburn, *Top R&B Singles, 1942–1999*, 471.

55. Dixon, *I Am the Blues*, 85.

56. Margo G. Crawford, "Willie Dixon Embodies 'Spirit of the Blues,'" *Chicago Defender*, March 4, 1978, 5.

57. Whitburn, *Top R&B Singles, 1942–1999*, 471.

58. For this recording, Muddy Waters performs only the vocal lines, without playing the guitar.

59. Sandra B. Tooze, *Muddy Waters: The Mojo Man* (Toronto: ECW Press, 1997), 125.

60. Dixon, *Willie Dixon*, 117.

61. Whitburn, *Top R&B Singles, 1942–1999*, 471.

62. Corritore, Ferris, and O'Neal, "Willie Dixon (Part 2)," 24.

63. Guralnick, *Feel Like Going Home*, 161–62.

64. Dixon, *I Am the Blues*, 149.

65. Les Fancourt, *Chess Blues/R&B Discography* (Faversham, Kent, England: L. Fancourt, 1983; repr., 1989), 41.

66. "Mannish Boy" is adopted from "I'm a Man" by Bo Diddley, which is the reworking of "Hoochie Coochie Man." While Dixon's new song tries to explore Muddy's new, more grown-up image, the A side of the single is still truthful to his old naughty persona.

67. Whitburn, *Top R&B Singles, 1942–1999*, 471.

68. Dixon, *I Am the Blues*, 96.

69. These two instruments do not create a theoretically perfect counterpoint, because while the first two notes on each instrument are contrapuntal, the last three notes move in a parallel motion.

70. The early take of "I Want to Be Loved" is included in Muddy Waters, *Hoochie Coochie Man: The Complete Chess Masters*, vol. 2.

71. Muddy Waters' February 1955 session was followed by the one on May 24 of this year. For this session, he recorded only "Mannish Boy." Dixon's "I Got to Find My Baby" has nothing to do with a song of the same title recorded by Little Walter on May 22, 1954.

72. In addition to the Dixon composition, Muddy recorded "Rock Me," "Look What You've Done," and "Got My Mojo Working" for this session.

73. Dixon, *Willie Dixon*, 116.

74. Dixon, *I Am the Blues*, 151.

75. Shirli Dixon, interview by the author, September 23, 2002.

76. Blues researcher Les Fancourt uses the term "no messing guy" to describe Walter's persona. Les Fancourt, "Liner Notes," *The Chess Years, 1952–1963*, recorded by Little Walter (London: Charly Records, CD RED BOX 5, 1992), 20. I use the term "one-woman guy" because Fancourt's term is somewhat confusing.

77. Shirli Dixon, interview by the author, September 23, 2002.

78. Fancourt, "Liner Notes," 18.

79. Jim O'Neal, e-mail correspondence with the author, June 2, 2005.

80. Guralnick, *Feel Like Going Home*, 75.

81. Paul Oliver, *Conversation with the Blues*, 2nd ed. (Cambridge: Cambridge University Press, 1997), 155.

82. Tony Glover, Scott Dirks, and Ward Gaines, *Blues with a Feeling: The Little Walter Story* (New York: Routledge, 2002), 24.

83. Ibid., 35.

84. Little Walter's debut record "Just Keep Loving Her" is about man's faithfulness to his girlfriend, as the title of the song indicates. Even in this earliest recording, Walter tended to establish one of his performing personae as a nice guy or one-woman guy. Most of the songs that Dixon later provided for Walter correspond to this model. While Walter's performing style in this recording is generally similar to that of Sonny Boy Williamson I, it also shows different influences; this is a fast boogie tune, and a series of energetic driving riffs inspired by jump blues and swing jazz is giving his playing a distinctive characteristic.

85. Glover, Dirks, and Gaines, *Blues with a Feeling*, 62.

86. Whitburn, *Top R&B Singles, 1942–1999*, 268.

87. "Striptease beat" ("jungle beat") is a beat pattern that exaggerates tom-tom drums and is associated with African-derived beat. This beat pattern is heard in the opening of "Sing, Sing, Sing."

88. Glover, Dirks, and Gaines, *Blues with a Feeling*, 223. Evans, "A Review for Mitsutoshi Inaba's Manuscript," 7.

89. Dixon, *Willie Dixon*, 183.

90. Shirli Dixon, interview by the author, September 23, 2002.

91. Dixon, *I Am the Blues*, 151. Billy Branch, who was a harmonica player in Dixon's band in the 1980s, also says,

> Throughout the time I knew Willie and I played in his band, he was basically the same guy. You never saw him losing his temper. . . . He's always steady. He didn't curse a lot. Yeah, I mean, he did cursing, just *bullshit* or something, but he wasn't a big curser, like most of us musicians.

Billy Branch, interview by the author, September 27, 2002.

92. Shirli Dixon, interview by the author, September 23, 2002.

93. Dixon, *I Am the Blues*, 88.

94. Shirli Dixon, interview by the author, September 23, 2002.

95. Whitburn, *Top R&B Singles, 1942–1999*, 268.

96. A similar song subject with a similar musical style (brisk shuffle) is also found in "You'd Better Watch Yourself," which was ranked at the eighth position of the *Billboard* R&B charts in the jukebox category on September 18, 1954.

97. Marie Dixon, interview by the author, September 25, 2004.

98. Dixon, *Willie Dixon*, 188.

99. Worth Long, "The Wisdom of the Blues—Defining Blues as the True Facts of Life: An Interview with Willie Dixon," *African American Review* 29, no. 2 (Summer 1995): 211.

100. Glover, Dirks, and Gaines, *Blues with a Feeling*, 127.

101. Ibid., 141.

102. Robert Jr. Lockwood overdubbed an additional guitar to the original track of "My Babe"; he doubles the bass line with his guitar. He recollects,

> Now on *My Babe*, I played the melody and the bass. We had to overdub because we couldn't find [Luther] Tucker that day. I don't know where in the hell Tucker was. I played the session by myself . . . me, Willie Dixon, and Below. Dixon was playin' bass, but you couldn't hardly hear what he was doin'—that happened all the time. The Fender bass was in, but they didn't want to use it.

Larry Hoffman, "Robert Lockwood, Jr. Interview," *Living Blues*, no. 121 (June 1995): 26.

103. Galen Gart, ed., *First Pressings: The History of Rhythm & Blues*, vol. 5, *1955* (Milford, NH: Big Nickel, 1990), 21.

104. Ibid., 23.

105. Whitburn, *Top R&B Singles, 1942–1999*, 268.

106. Fancourt, "Liner Notes," 16.

107. Whitburn, *Top R&B Singles, 1942–1999*, 268.

108. Lucky Three Trio's instrumental number "Wrinkles," which features Dixon's bass solo, is discussed in this section because the group did not make many recordings. Dixon's recordings for the Prestige label in the 1960s are discussed in chapter 7.

109. Dixon, *I Am the Blues*, 83.

110. Evans, "A Review for Mitsutoshi Inaba's Manuscript," 7.

111. Fancourt, *Chess Blues/R&B Discography*, 7.

112. Michael Ruppli, *The Chess Labels: A Discography*. 2 vols. (Westport, CT: Greenwood Press, 1988), 1:28.

113. Corritore, Ferris, and O'Neal, "Willie Dixon (Part 2)," 24.

114. Paul Oliver, *Songsters and Saints: Vocal Traditions on Race Records* (Cambridge: Cambridge University Press, 1984), 48–55. Paul Oliver, "Lookin' for the Bully: An Enquiry into a Song and Its Story," in *Nobody Knows Where the Blues Come From: Lyrics and History*, ed. Robert Springer, 108–25 (Jackson, MS: University Press of Mississippi, 2006).

115. Oliver, "Lookin' for the Bully," 115–17.

116. Benjamin Albert Botkin, ed., *A Treasury of Southern Folklore: Stories, Ballads, and Folkways of the People of the South*, introduction by Benjamin Albert Botkin (New York: Crown, 1949; repr., New York: Bonanza Books, 1980), 113–14. Citations are to the Bonanza Books edition.

117. "If You're Mine" and "Alone" are not included in any of Dixon's CDs or Chess' compilations.

118. See William Jack Dupree and Teddy McRae, "Walking the Blues," BMI Repertoire, repertoire.bmi.com/title.asp?blnWriter=True&blnPublisher=True&blnArtist=True&keyID=1602107&ShowNbr=0&ShowSeqNbr=0&querytype=WorkID (accessed October 11, 2004); and Willie Dixon, "Walkin' the Blues," BMI Repertoire, repertoire.bmi.com/title.asp?blnWriter=True&blnPublisher=True&blnArtist=True&

page=1&keyid=1602106&ShowNbr=0&ShowSeqNbr=0&querytype=WorkID (accessed October 11, 2004).

119. The advertisement says, "2 GREAT RECORDS BREAKIN' WIDE OPEN IN POP FIELD" [the word *pop* is circled], CHUCK BERRY Singing MAYBELLINE [*sic*] CHESS 1640; WILLIE DIXON, WALKING THE BLUES, CHECKER 822; another BIG one off to a flying start, THE FLAMINGOS, I WANT TO LOVE YOU/ PLEASE COME BACK HOME." Gart, *First Pressings*, 5:91. The advertisement has portraits of Berry and Dixon.

120. Whitburn, *Top R&B Singles, 1942–1999*, 115.

121. "I Am the Lover Man" is not available in CD format.

122. "This Pain in My Heart" is different from "This Pain," a composition Dixon offered to Muddy Waters in 1955.

123. Dixon, *I Am the Blues*, 83.

124. Ibid.

125. Don Snowden, "Liner Notes," *The Chess Box*, recorded by Willie Dixon (Universal City, CA: Chess/MCA, 1988), 10.

126. Dixon, *I Am the Blues*, 83.

127. Ruppli, *The Chess Labels*, 1:54.

128. Snowden, "Liner Notes," 6.

129. The words in the parenthesis are sung by the Moonglows in a call-and-response form.

130. Ruppli, *The Chess Labels*, 1:67; Fancourt, *Chess Blues/R&B Discography*, 7.

131. Shirli Dixon, interview by the author, September 23, 2002.

132. Chess also bought the master tape that Witherspoon recorded in Kansas City (presumably) in 1959. This tape includes "Everything but You," which is credited to Dixon. However, this composition does not sound like Dixon's song. The recording shows that the song has many jazzy chords, which he does not usually use, although he might be responsible for the lyrics.

133. "When the Lights Go Out" was ranked fifth among R&B Territorial Best Sellers, Chicago, in *Billboard*, August 28, 1954, 78; and October 9, 1954, 61.

134. Muddy Waters' "I Want to Be Loved" was recorded on February 5, 1955.

135. There is another unknown baritone sax player.

136. Dixon, *I Am the Blues*, 87.

137. Lowell Fulson, *Hung Down Head*, notes by Noboru Wada, Don Snowden, and unknown writer (Tokyo: Chess/MCA Victor, MVCM 22011, 1994). The description of the session scene is taken from this CD.

138. Fulson, *Hung Down Head*.

139. Mary Katherine Aldin and Mark Humphrey, "Lowell Fulson," *Living Blues*, no. 115 (May/June 1994): 25. Aldin probably had a chance to listen to the rest of the outtakes, and she writes that the session became filled with a contentious atmosphere: "The song's LP release on *Hung Down Head* showed the essential lack of sympathy between Lowell and Leonard Chess; the two traded increasingly profane invectives between studio to control room as take after take fell apart. After that

experience, all of Lowell's remaining Chess sides were cut in Los Angeles." Mary Katherin Aldin, "Liner Notes," *The Complete Chess Maters*, recorded by Lowell Fulson (Tokyo: Chess/MCA Victor, MVCE 30011–2, 1998), 5.

140. Dixon, *I Am the Blues*, 87.

141. Robert Springer, "Willie Mabon Interview," *Blues Unlimited*, no. 143 (Autumn/Winter 1982): 28.

142. Jim O'Neal and Amy van Singel, *The Voices of the Blues: Classic Interviews from* Living Blues *Magazine* (New York, London: Routledge, 2002), 264.

143. Dixon, *I Am the Blues*, 86.

144. Information on Bo Diddley is confusing because of his lack of accuracy and/or the lack of accuracy of interviewers and writers. According to Bo's own statement for his biography *Bo Diddley: Living Legend*, he moved to Chicago with his mother, but Bo himself wrote that he moved there with his mother's first cousin in the liner notes for *Chess Box*. George R. White, *Bo Diddley: Living Legend* (Surrey, England: Castle Communications, 1995), 19; Bo Diddley and Robert Palmer, "Liner Notes," *Chess Box*, recorded by Bo Diddley (Universal City, CA: Chess/MCA, CHD2–19502, 1990), 3.

145. White, *Bo Diddley*, 25–27.

146. Dixon, *I Am the Blues*, 92.

147. White, *Bo Diddley*, 34.

148. Ibid., 41.

149. Ibid., 47.

150. Ibid., 50.

151. Whitburn, *Top R&B Singles, 1942–1999*, 112.

152. White, *Bo Diddley*, 32.

153. "Hush Little Baby" includes the line "Hush little baby don't say a thing, papa's gonna buy you a diamond ring."

154. Mike Rowe and Bill Greensmith, "'I Was Really Dedicated,' an Interview with Billy Boy Arnold, Part 3: 'Whatever I Did It Was Me and I'm Proud of It,'" *Blues Unlimited*, no. 128 (1978): 21.

155. White, *Bo Diddley*, 55. One might assume that Bo's pseudonym is related to a musical instrument diddley bow, but Bo himself denies it: "The other day, I read that there was a instrument in the South, in the old days, called a 'diddley bow': somethin' with one string on it, an' played with a bow. I said: 'Oh yeah? Uh-huh!', but I don't guess I'll ever find out who invented it.'" Ibid., 56.

156. Bo Diddley's album covers also show his performing persona. His early 1960 *Have Guitar Will Travel* (Checker LP 2974, 1960) in which he rides a moped with his trademarked rectangular-shaped guitar creates a naughty, playful atmosphere, while his late 1960 *Bo Diddley Is a Gunslinger* (Checker LP 2977, 1960) reflects the roots of his outlaw persona.

157. Dixon, *I Am the Blues*, 92.

158. Shirli Dixon, interview by the author, September 24, 2002.

159. Whitburn, *Top R&B Singles, 1942–1999*, 112.

160. White, Bo Diddley, 82–83.

161. Botkin, A Treasury of Southern Folklore, 479. The origin of this folklore derives from the Itty Titty, the teale of Cockaigne of the English mummer's play or British folk drama. John Minton, "Cockaigne to Diddy Wah Diddy: Fabulous Geographies and Geographic Fabulations," Folklore 102 (1991): 39–47.

162. Blind Blake recorded "Diddie Wa Diddie" numbers one and two (1929 and 1930), but except for the expression "Diddy-Wah-Diddy," Dixon's composition has nothing to do with Blake's recordings.

163. Dixon, Willie Dixon, 241.

164. Butch Dixon, interview by the author, September 23, 2003. Dixon also discusses how he gave this song to Diddley. Dixon, I Am the Blues, 149.

165. Whitburn, Top R&B Singles, 1942–1999, 112.

166. Joel Whitburn, Top Pop Singles, 1955–1996: Chart Data Compiled from Billboard's Pop Singles Charts, 1955–1996 (Menomonee Falls, WI: Record Research, 1997), 167.

167. White, Bo Diddley, 83.

168. Rogers is quoted in Mary Katherine Aldin, "Liner Notes," The Complete Chess Recordings, recorded by Jimmy Rogers (Universal City, CA: Chess/MCA, CHD2–9372, 1997), 5.

169. John Anthony Brisbin, "Jimmy Rogers," in Rollin' and Tumblin': The Postwar Blues Guitarists, ed. Jas Obrecht (San Francisco: Miller Freeman Books, 2000), 148.

170. Dave Hoekstra, "Jimmy Rogers Gets in His Licks," Chicago Sun-Times, June 15, 1990, 62.

CHAPTER SIX

~

The Cobra Records Period
(1956–1958)

In the summer of 1956, Willie Dixon became a staff member for Cobra Records, a newly established company on the West Side of Chicago. Specifically when he moved from Chess to Cobra is unclear, but from the second half of 1956 to the end of that year, Chess artists recorded a total of only four songs by Dixon, and from the beginning of 1957 to the summer of 1958, no Dixon songs were recorded by Chess artists.[1]

Dixon needed a better income source. He and his girlfriend then, Elenora Franklin, had seven children by the mid-1950s. Around the same period, Dixon met Marie Booker (b. 1937), whom he married in 1956. Their first child, Patricia Ann, was born in 1957. Marie talks about how she met Willie Dixon:

> I had seen him in 1955 at the night club on 47th Street, and the club was named 708 Club. At that time, he was with the combo—I believe they were still using the name Big Three—then in 1956, I worked at a drugstore, and he came in one Sunday night. And he introduced himself. I knew his family, but I didn't know him. And the only thing I remembered who he was when he said the Big Three that I had listened to in my early days. So from there, we became friends, started to date, and then we got married. He was a very nice guy to the day he passed away. You couldn't find anyone nicer than Willie Dixon.[2]

Cobra Records existed only from 1956 to 1958. The founder was Eli Toscano, whose biographical information is not well known. He originally owned a TV repair shop on Roosevelt Street on the West Side where he also sold records. In 1955, he and his partner, Joe Brown, started Abco Records, which on a sporadic schedule had released several singles by 1956. In that summer, after departing from Brown, Toscano with a new business partner, Howard Bedno, reorganized the company as Cobra Records. In the launch of the label, they involved Dixon. Toscano promised Dixon 50 percent of business share because Dixon was responsible for important aspects of the company.[3] As he had done for Chess Records, Dixon worked as a talent scout, songwriter, producer, and bassist. He was also a booking agent for the artists on the label. Guitarist/vocalist Otis Rush says, "Willie was helping with everything."[4]

Cobra could not produce many nationwide hits, but that was not the reason the company closed so soon. Toscano was a chronic gambler, and he apparently embezzled the company's money. Because Dixon was not paid his share, in the summer of 1958, he started to reestablish a business relationship with Chess by providing songs for Muddy Waters. By the beginning of 1959, Dixon completely split from Toscano.

Hoping to clear his debts, Toscano borrowed some money from Chess and sold his publishing company, Armel Music, to Vee-Jay Records, but one day in 1959, he died in a fishing accident in the Fox River, west of Chicago. As the rumor goes, gang members sank him for gambling debts.

The main artists on Cobra Records were guitarists Otis Rush, Magic Sam, and Buddy Guy (Buddy will be discussed in the next chapter, because most of his output with Dixon occurred in his second Chess period). Their style became known as West Side blues. Dixon helped them start their professional careers with this label. Shirli Dixon talks about her father's relationship with them:

> He thought of them as a next generation, a little bit more guitar, a little more attitude. He really loved Otis Rush. And Magic Sam . . . he thought was fantastic. He felt Buddy Guy had something to offer, but the Chess family didn't want him at that time. They were really looking for a traditional blues sound, and Buddy was a little bit more innovative and creative in his playing. I don't think my dad was ever involved with musicians that he wouldn't believe, couldn't produce well, or he couldn't bring out the best of them.[5]

These guitarists had some common characteristics that set them apart from the past generations. They were all born in the mid-1930s (approximately twenty years younger than Dixon and Muddy). They spent most of their adolescence in a more urbanized environment, although all of them were born in the rural South. The influential musicians for them were mainly postwar electric blues artists, including Muddy Waters, Howlin' Wolf, John Lee Hooker, and B. B. King, while they were not directly influenced by down-home acoustic bluesmen.

Among them, B. B. King was the most influential. Blues historian Mike Rowe writes, "The West Siders had taken King's style to heart, made the guitar more prominent, and with R&B (rhythm and blues) band with sax instead of brass set the blues on the road to the '60s."[6] B. B. King grew up listening to the jazz-oriented guitar virtuosi Lonnie Johnson, Django Reinhardt, Charlie Christian, and T-Bone Walker. Similar to King and his precursors, the West Siders' flamboyant guitar solos were highlights of recordings and public performances. Their vocal style was passionate as well, using shouts, growls, and alternations of natural and head voice.

King's text style was another important influence for the new generation. He usually sang of more universal themes, typically blue feelings, such as "Woke Up This Morning, My Baby's Gone"; he still does today. On the other hand, his songs did not contain references to Southern folkloric themes such as mojo and John the Conqueror root. Muddy Waters once said the difference between his and B. B. King's blues: "He only sings urban blues, a little higher class of blues than me, but he's strictly singin' some good deep blues."[7]

More importantly, King is not a kind of bluesman with a performing persona of commanding cultural rebel with sexual prowess, which derives from the characters of black badman tales and is the basis of Muddy's persona. Similar to King, none of the West Siders, at least originally, had a performing persona comparable to Muddy's.

Such artistic trends certainly influenced Willie Dixon's compositions. The most artistically successful area of his compositions was the expression of an aching heart disease. While he still wrote songs around proverbial wisdom and didactic contents, these songs were not his main focus during this period. In addition, he did not write songs with which he could develop a character with fortitude like "Hoochie Coochie Man."

Otis Rush

Otis Rush's "I Can't Quit You Baby," coupled with "Sit Down Baby," written and produced by Willie Dixon, was Cobra Records' debut release. Dixon contributed to Otis' hit records, but their different views of artistic direction caused a conflict between them. While one of the main topics here is Dixon's production ability, another is the difference between the musical perspective that Dixon saw in Otis' style and the artistic direction that Otis himself wanted to pursue.

Otis Rush was born on April 29, 1934, in Philadelphia, Mississippi, but moved to Chicago in 1949. After his sister took him to Club Zanzibar where Muddy Waters was playing, Otis dreamed of becoming a musician.[8] Otis developed his guitar style based on guitarists who used string-bending techniques, not from Muddy and other slide guitar players. Otis says, "When I started to listen to T-Bone Walker, and B. B., you might say (Little) Milton, Albert King, I sorta started listenin' to it then, sort of sounded a little different from Muddy, and I chose this style, just to try to go this route, you know."[9]

Otis sat in with different artists at nightclubs. One day when he was playing with the Aces (Little Walters' band), he caught Willie Dixon's attention. Dixon originally wanted Otis to sign for Chess Records:

> I had done tried to get Otis with Chess Company. Man, they always figured that Otis was too close to Muddy. They couldn't see themselves selling Otis Rush and Muddy. But Otis didn't have no style like Muddy's at all. But they figured it was all blues, y' know. So when I got over there, Eli started to talking his trash and going on. . . . And he needed some artists, so I called up Otis.[10]

One summer day in 1956,[11] Otis Rush, who was twenty-one years old, had his first recording session. Dixon remembers what inspired him to provide "I Can't Quit You Baby" for Otis Rush:

> Otis was involved with a young lady called Freddie, and she left him. She'd gone to St. Louis and when I came up to his house he was sitting up there and all blue and lonesome and I decided to talk about it and he said, "Oh man, don't talk about it." Well, I could see that he regretted whatever it was going on between them. And I said "Yeah—you look like you're in the mood for a real Blues [sic] song now." After I thought about it I came back the next night to rehearse him. I asked him—"Have you just hollered to let your hair down? It's like being out in a field hollering and screaming to get it all off your chest." I started telling him about this song.[12]

"I Can't Quit You Baby" is a twelve-bar/a-a-b blues in a slow tempo. The song subject is the consequences of adultery and the feeling that a man cannot give up a relationship:

> [Verse 1]
> Well, I can't quit you babe, but I got to put you down for a while,
> Well, you know, I can't quit you babe, but I got to put you down for a while,
> Well, you messed up my happy home baby, made me mistreat my only chil'.

[Verse 2]
Yes, you know I love you, babe, my love for you I could never hide,
Oh, you know, I love you, my love for you I could never hide,
Yes, you know, I love you, babe, well, you're just my heart desire.

[Verse 3]
Well, I'm so tired, I could cry, I could just lay down and die,
Oh, I'm so tired, I could cry, ooh, I could just lay down and die,
Yes, you know you the onliest one darling, ooh, you know you my heart desire.

[Verse 4]
When you hear me moaning and groaning, babe, you know it hurt me way down inside,
Oh, when you hear me moaning and groaning, babe, oh, you know it hurt me way down inside,
Oh, when you hear me holler, baby, ooh, you know you're my desire.

Similar in topic to "I Can't Quit You Baby," Dixon also wrote "You Shook Me" for Muddy Waters, in which he sings of regret at an adulterous affair and its effect on his family (see the Muddy Waters section in the following chapter). However, "I Can't Quit You Baby" clearly sounds different from Muddy's commanding performance. On the most audible level, the difference between Muddy and Otis is their voice qualities. Otis sounds mellower than Muddy. Butch Dixon explains,

My dad thought Otis Rush had the silky sounds . . . better sound of voice than Muddy, because it's more pleasing to ear for women. And Muddy's songs traditionally fit more men, because "Hoochie Coochie Man" was a man thing. . . . But "I Can't Quit You Baby" really sold to women. . . . He had the real smooth, if you have been in the time, they called it olive oil voice.[13]

The different feelings in the music of Otis and Muddy are also related to their different performing personae. Otis' urbane image was successfully explored by a song with an expression of agony over a relationship. Dixon's experiment with Muddy's sentimental aspect through "This Pain" (1955) resulted in the sole example of their collaboration that was unissued, but it worked for a singer of the new generation.

Otis remembers the recording process of "I Can't Quit You Baby": "Willie would just hum the sound, he never played anything, you know. He would try to give me some phrases how the song go and I pretty much did it on my own, the way it sounded. The way I sang the song and the way I played my guitar is what I wanted to play."[14] Otis' passionate vocal melody with alternations of natural voice, falsetto, shouts, and growls, is his singing style indeed.

Especially in the second verse ("Yes, you know, I love you, baby, my love for you, I'll never hide."), the change of vocal ranges and dynamics expresses a wide range of human feelings.

However, the opening phrase with a long sustained note on a high pitch, which sounds like the beginning of field hollers, was Dixon's idea. He says, "I explained IF [sic] you could make a holler like, 'Wo, I can't quit you baby. Just let it out of your heart.' So we practiced it quite a bit, and then went into the studio."[15] "But he [Otis] didn't like the idea of holding the first note like 'Oooooo (sings) I can't quit ya baby.' He didn't like that at all. But he finally got involved."[16]

There are two outtakes of "I Can't Quit You Baby." These recordings and Dixon's statements reveal how he directed Otis and other musicians. The ensemble consists of two electric guitars, piano, harmonica, alto saxophone, bass, and drums. Otis plays the lead, and he inserts complementary phrases between vocal phrases. The second guitar, Wayne Bennett, basically plays chords throughout the song. Because Bennett occasionally adds fills that respond to vocal phrases, the two guitars sometimes function as double lead and create a rough counterpoint. On top of that, the pianist, Lafayette Leake, plays high-pitched trill-like figures. The combination of Dixon's bass on strong beats and Al Duncan's drums on the backbeats creates a slow, driving feeling. Harmonica (Big Walter Horton) and sax (Red Holloway) add thickness to the ensemble.

The first take is a run-through. Otis' vocal is weak, and his guitar phrases sound as if he plays whatever comes to his mind. As a result, the two guitars are merely clashing. Some other instruments are hardly heard. Dixon possibly told the musicians to play quietly, or they played tentatively in the process of putting the music together.

The second take shows that the arrangement is almost developed. The instruments are clearly heard, although they are still playing in a reserved way. But the interaction among two guitars and harmonica still sounds disorganized.

Dixon remembers he gave a direction to the band:

Otis made two or three starts on it and I told the engineer to cut the lights down real low and everybody was quiet. "Otis you just get in your own mood—just like you're in the field." He went through it two or three different times and I told the band, "You guys just be quiet." When Otis hits the right chord and hollers, 'Oh, I can't quit you baby.' Then you guys just fall in . . ." Everything was so quiet in there and Otis came back and hollered, "Oh, I can't quit you baby." I didn't have to tell the guys. They fell right in because they felt it.[17]

For the official release, a four-measure introduction is deleted; therefore, the record directly starts from Otis' cry. The guitar interaction is noteworthy. Bennett's smooth, mellow phrases in the style of T-Bone Walker blend with Otis' stuttering single-note phrases.

The staff members and musicians felt this would be an instant hit. Dixon and Toscano immediately brought a test press to local disc jockey Big Bill Hill.[18] *Billboard* gave a very positive report: "Cobra Records has come up with a 'left-fielder' that seems headed for the top. 'I Can't Quit You Baby' by 21-year-old Otis Rush was the top seller at All-State Distribs [*sic*] last week, reports Paul Glass. 'The switchboard lit up like a Christmas tree the first time I played it,' claims Big Bill Hill, WOPA."[19] On October 13, 1956, "I Can't Quit You Baby" was ranked at the seventh position in the jukebox category and ninth in sales.[20] For Otis Rush and company, this was the most commercially successful record. And this was Dixon's first hit in a simple twelve-bar/a-a-b blues form.

The flip side "Sit Down Baby" is a pop song with a bouncy riff by the saxophone and the harmonica. This song reflects Dixon's compositional style that he learned with the Big Three Trio.[21] As the title suggests, his message in this song is to sit down and relax.

After this song, however, Dixon did not give Otis any songs with didactic contents, although around this period, Dixon offered Muddy "Don't Go No Further" and "I Love the Life I Live, I Live the Life I Love."

In the following session (fall of 1956), Otis recorded two Dixon compositions: blues-melodrama "My Love Will Never Die" and pop song "Violent Love," both of which the Big Three Trio premiered in 1951.

The original version of "My Love Will Never Die" featured Dixon's speechlike singing. The demo recording shows that he is performing it in the same style when introducing Otis. While the original version was unconventional, the new version was still unique for a blues recording in the mid-1950s in terms of the choice of key. Dixon explains,

> I got the opportunity to do more songs in the minor key over at Cobra. A lot of people didn't understand minor keys being kind of a soulful sound. Everybody could sing and play straight harmony but knowing a 3rd chord [third of the chord], which made it a minor, a lot of people just couldn't adjust themselves. When you got to tell them about lowering the 3rd chord, they didn't know what the hell you was talking about.
>
> Otis Rush liked minor keys once he got involved in it. It wasn't tough to convince him after he heard the sound.[22]

In addition to the minor mode, Dixon's new arrangement also makes this blues unique. He utilizes a clear rhythmic motive by emphasizing the recurring riff and an accent on the strong beats played by two horns, bass, and drums (see figure 6.1). This arrangement is similar to another melodramatic composition "Tollin' Bells" for Lowell Fulson, in which Dixon used a funeral-march rhythm pattern. In both examples, these rhythmic characteristics give a theatrical effect.

Figure 6.1.

Otis' vocal performance for this recording is very soulful. For the opening vocal melody, he again uses the hollering. Dixon remembers the effect of the hollering in this tune at one public performance:

> We had an introduction with that band that could bust the heart of a grizzly bear. I would get hold of Otis and get him all wound up. He was young and anxious to get out there, so the band would play, we'd bring Otis on and bring it down quieter than a mouse until he started [to sing "My Love Will Never Die"]. That cat would come out there and get to screamin' and hollerin', those folks would be crying and raising hell.[23]

Otis implies that he changed the original words here and there: "Willie Dixon wrote the tune 'My Love Will Never Die.' I had somethin' to do with it. See, he has a way of writing. But I don't like it, you know, I try to twist it around."[24] But table 6.1 shows that Otis did not change words drastically, except that he sings only two verses, while Dixon's demo has three of them.

The flip side of "My Love Will Never Die" is "Violent Love." This song sounds similar to Paul Whiteman's "It's Only a Paper Moon." Blues historian Mark Humphrey critically writes of Dixon's artistic sense, which led him to

Table 6.1. "My Love Will Never Die": Dixon's Demo Take and Rush's Master Take

Dixon's Demo Take	Rush's Master Take
[Melodic] Oh, my love will never die, You have done me wrong for a long, long time But all you've done, I never changed my mind, But please, baby love me, please honey try, My love for you will never die.	[Verse 1] Well, my love will never die, You done me wrong for a long, long time And all you've done, I never changed my mind, But please, honey love me, oh please honey try, My love for you will never die. [Saxophone solo]
I tried to forget you in many lands, I kissed pretty girls and I held queen's hands, But the fire keep on burnin' oooh like [unintelligible], My love for you will never die,	
[Spoken] My love has found a home, Deep down in your heart, And God knows it will never, never die,	
[Melodic] When the flower was growed where I lay at rest, Please pull the blossoms and hold to your breast, You know that's my love, burnin' out inside, My love for you will never die, My love will never die.	[Verse 2] When the flowers, the flowers grow where I lay at rest, Please pull the blossoms, then hold to your breast, Then you know, that's my love burstin' out inside, My love for you will never die.

offer this kind of song to Otis: "'Violent Love' is structurally a 1920s Tin Pan Alley song (Dixon even has Rush 'makin' whoopee') with cornball horns and lyrics that seem jauntily to endorse date rape,"[25] although Dixon meant no more than "burning love." However, it is a fact that Otis felt discomfort with some of the songs Dixon chose. He made an elliptic remark about Dixon's musical directions:

Living Blues: Did he [Dixon] force tunes on you that you didn't feel comfortable with?

Rush: Well, it has been done, yeah. I don't even want to go into all that, 'cause I don't even know some of the tunes I cut, myself.[26]

There are some possible reasons for their disagreement in the musical direction. As stated in the section of Dixon's own Chess recordings (in chapter 5), some of his bluesy pop songs would sound anachronistic even for the standard of the day, and "Violent Love" could be one of them. Shirli Dixon also testifies her father felt that Otis Rush's musical style was not necessarily centered in the blues:

My dad loved Otis and had a great deal of respect for him for a number of reasons, but he thought of him in the same capacity as Sam Cooke. He always felt that . . . he offered the same vocal structure, a smooth, crooner type of singer, more on the R&B side, as opposed to straight blues. He thought him as rhythm and blues kinda, or Memphis soul sounding type of musician.[27]

The next session was held in early 1957. Dixon brought "Groanin' the Blues" and "If You Were Mine." Around this time the friction between Dixon and Otis became obvious. Otis remembers, "Then he [Dixon] had this 'Groanin' the Blues' and 'Jump Sister Bessie'—I said, 'Man, this is some horse-shit all over!' I didn't know whether to scratch my watch or wind my head by now. I said, 'I can do better than this.' So I started writin' my own material."[28]

"Groanin' the Blues" is a twelve-bar blues in a very slow tempo. It is a heavy blues in which Otis cries out about a woman who is leaving for another man:

[Verse 1]
Oh, I'm so tired of moaning, trying to groan away the blues,
Oh, I'm so tired of moaning, oh, trying to groan away the blues,
Oh, I keep weeping and crying, ah, every time I think of you.

[Verse 2]
Oh, I'd rather die from starvation, perish out in the desert sun,
Oh, I would rather die from starvation, ooh, perish out in the desert sun,
Yes, than to think some other man holding you in his arm.

[Verse 3]
Oh, my heart gets so heavy, yes I shake all in my bones,
Oh, my heart gets so heavy, yes I shake all in my bones,
Yes, I can't have murder, oh, but I'm forced to weep and moan.

Although he calls this song "horseshit," this is a good blues record that shows Otis Rush is an extraordinary performer. He depicts the pathos of the text with his emotionally charged vocal and guitar techniques. The very beginning of the introduction, where Otis plays with only one string on the guitar and then punctuates this section by a very quiet chord stroke, creates a high-tension atmosphere. This part is followed by a slow blues phrase in a very solid timbre. During the whole song, there is no moment in which his expression is pretentious. Along with his vocal, Little Walter's harmonica adds responses like sobs.

In contrast to "Groanin' the Blues," "If You Were Mine" is a lighthearted pop song in a medium walking-blues tempo. This is a reworking of another Dixon composition, "For You and Only You," which he offered to a female vocalist Gloria Irving, as discussed later in this chapter. This is Otis' first Cobra recording that features his guitar solo. He shows acute bending vibrato techniques in the solo section.

"Jump Sister Bessie," more "horseshit," was recorded in mid-1957.[29] This is a reworking of "Shout, Sister, Shout" by the Lucky Millinder Orchestra, featuring Sister Rosetta Tharpe, in 1941. Dixon's marcato slap bass and Little Walter's harmonica add a lively bouncy feeling, while Otis' vocal does not sound very enthusiastic indeed.

By the following session in late 1957, Otis learned songwriting. He brought his own song, "Three Times a Fool," while he still recorded Dixon's "She's a Good 'Un."[30] This was an important session for Otis in establishing his musical style that he absorbed from B. B. King's style. Both songs are twelve-bar blues in a medium walking tempo. From this session onward, Otis did not include a harmonica, while a saxophone became more prominent. He made a larger space for his guitar playing in introductions and solos.

Otis Rush maintained this compositional and arrangement style for the rest of the Cobra period. Within this scheme he developed variations: for example, slow blues ("Checking on My Baby" and "Double Trouble"), which also derived from "I Can't Quit You Baby" and "My Love Will Never Die"; medium-tempo blues with a Latin beat ("All Your Love"); and up-tempo blues with a shuffle beat ("Keep on Loving Me Baby" and "My Baby Is Good 'Un").

When Dixon returned to Chess Records, Otis followed Dixon. Around this time Otis' career started to waver. At Chess Records he was not given priority as an artist.[31] Otis had two sessions in 1960, and these two were his only sessions for Chess. In January, he recorded his masterpiece "So Many Roads, So Many Trains," but it was not promoted. For the September 29 session, Dixon offered "You Know My Love" and "I Can't Stop" to Rush. "I Can't Stop" is a remake of "I Can't Quit You Baby" with different lyrics. "You Know My Love" is also a variation of "My Love Will Never Die." As opposed to Otis' own compositions, these records do not have enough space for Otis to play the guitar.

Blues historian Neil Slaven bitterly writes about the relationship between Willie Dixon and Otis Rush: "Otis was a reluctant Dixon protégé. Because of his [Dixon's] position, young musicians courted his favor and in return he'd try to get them on record. . . . From the beginning, Otis found the yoke uncomfortable."[32] It is true that as a novice artist, Otis had to depend on Dixon, who was an important person in the recording industry. While Otis made some negative comments about their different musical views, he also knew that Dixon was trying to help him. When he was asked about the cold treatment in the recording industry, he said that Dixon was an exception: "They got a nice record out and they jammin', you know, but nobody helped me. It's just once . . . Well, Willie Dixon helped me out a little bit here . . . Big Willie Dixon."[33] Dixon's influence on Otis Rush cannot be overstated. Otis' signature singing style developed from the opening of "I Can't Quit You Baby," and his blues compositions in a minor key, including "All Your Love," are clearly offshoots of Dixon's "My Love Will Never Die." These songs are two of the most important in Otis Rush's repertoire to this day.

Harold Burrage

Vocalist/pianist Harold Burrage (1931–1966) was an important figure in the development of the "hard-soul style" in Chicago, represented by Otis Clay and Tyrone Davis. Music writer Robert Pruter comments, "A recording artist from 1950 on, he [Burrage] saw Chicago through its transition from a blues and r&b center to a major soul center during the 1960s, helping to shape the hard-soul style."[34]

Burrage joined Cobra Records in 1956. His Cobra period was the time when he was finding his own style. Compared with his hard-soul style that he established later, his early style is lighter. His vocal at this point sounds smooth and does not much depend on shouts and melisma. He does not pronounce words with slurring.

Burrage's debut on Cobra—"One More Dance" with "You Eat Too Much"—set his commercial direction: one romantic side coupled with a humorous R&B. Three Dixon compositions "Messed Up," "I Don't Care Who Knows," and "Satisfied" for Burrage's second Cobra session in 1957 reflect this strategy.

"Messed Up" is an R&B song with a silly text. The vocal melody sounds like the chants used in army boot-camp training. The lyrics tell of different stories of failure:

[Verse 1]
You're the cutest little baby that I ever seen,
You look like a queen that's in my dream,

A gal like you I'd love to trust,
But if I kiss you, I'm-a all messed up.

[Hook]
Messed up, got me a wife,
Messed up, may have to fight,
Messed up, you're so nice,
Messed up baby for the rest of my life.

[Verse 2]
I went to the tracks with whole a lotta loot,
Bet all the nag that I knew it come true,
Because I waitin' for a week to collect my bet,
That old nag ain't comin' yet.

[Hook]
Messed up, lost my bread,
Messed up, nag full of lead,
Messed up, money's gone,
Messed up, 'cause I need car fare at home.

[Hook]
Messed up, messed up, baby,
Messed up, don't need "maybe,"
Messed up, you're so fine,
Messed up, 'cause I'm losin' my mind.

[Saxophone solo]

[Verse]
Jumping like a rabbit, everything I see,
My best friends aren't down on me,
Show me a woman that a man can trust,
I need a friend, 'cause I'm all messed up.

[Hook]
Messed up, what must I do?
Messed up, mistreatin' you,
Messed up, feelin' bad,
The worst old feelin' I ever had,
Messed up.

A humorous story is told over a long duration of the same chord, and a catchy hook follows. This is Dixon's ballad-style songwriting as seen in "Signifying Monkey," "Hoochie Coochie Man," and "Wang Dang Doodle."

"I Don't Care Who Knows" is a pop song with a typical arrangement style for R&B songs; short horn riffs are inserted between vocal phrases. Dixon lists creatures and their habitats as a comparison to the tight relationship between a man and a woman:

[Verse 1] (A1)
Like a catfish loves the water,
Like a horn cow loves corn,
Like bees, they loves the honey,
Like a po' dog loves a bone.

[Verse 2] (A2)
Like a bo weevil loves cotton,
Like the dark cloud loves the rain,
Like a good man loves his woman,
Like a good gal loves a man.

[Hook]
I love my baby, I love my baby,
I love my baby, and I don't care who knows.

[Bridge] (B)
I may be a little bit jealous,
You know the reason why,
If I don't love my baby,
I declare to the Maker and I hope to die.

[Verse 3] (A3)
Like a baby loves his candy,
Like a prospector loves his gold,
Like a hound dog loves a rabbit,
Like a gopher loves his hole.

[Hook repeated]

[Saxophone solo]

[Bridge repeated]

[Verse 4] (A4)
Like baby loves his candy,
Like a prospector loves his gold,
Like a hound dog loves a rabbit,
Like a gopher loves his hole.

[Hook repeated]

The comparison in the habits of creatures and humans is also seen in "Rattin' and Runnin' Around" that Dixon provided for Eddie Boyd in 1953 and "Live So Easy" for Jimmy Witherspoon in 1954 (both are discussed in chapter 5). Dixon later offered this song to Koko Taylor in 1968.

Two outtakes of "I Don't Care Who Knows" show that this song was originally recorded in F major, while the master take was released in F-sharp major. The heightened playback speed adds artificial excitement to Burrage's vocal.

Another Dixon composition, "Satisfied," is a romantic slow song. The recording features Burrage's high, exciting tenor. When he repeats "try, try, try" on a high pitch, he sounds like Jackie Wilson. Burrage recorded another bluesy pop song by Dixon, "I Cry for You," in 1958.

The recording starts with "field holler" moaning in a falsetto, which derived from label mate Otis Rush's "I Can't Quit You Baby."

These two slow ballads are not as strong as Dixon's blues masterpieces. When he wrote songs influenced more by pop love songs and less by blues, they tended to be merely average in quality.

After Cobra closed down, Burrage recorded for Vee-Jay Records temporarily, and in 1962 he signed with One-derful Records, where he found his hard-soul style. "Got to Find a Way" (1965) was a big hit in Chicago, but on November 25, 1966, he died suddenly from a heart attack. He was only thirty-five years old.

Magic Sam

During his thirty-two-year life, Magic Sam's Cobra Records era marked his earliest growth period as an artist. His ten Cobra sides include three Willie Dixon compositions: "All Night Long," "Easy Baby," and "21 Days in Jail."

Magic Sam was born as Samuel Maghett in Grenada, Mississippi, on February 14, 1937. In 1950, he moved to Chicago. Sam inherited guitar techniques for single-note soloing and string bending from Lowell Fulson and B. B. King in particular.[35] Sam combined these techniques with his own style: fingerpicking, which he learned from country and rockabilly guitar players; playing lead and chords at the same time (usually performed by two guitarists or one guitarist with a horn section or a piano); and adding a tremolo effect to the tone quality.

In 1957, Sam and his bandmate Mack Thompson made a demo recording of "All Your Love." After Chess Records turned it down, they brought it to Cobra. Soon after Sam made a contract, he had his first session under Willie Dixon's supervision. Around this time Sam was known as "Good Rockin' Sam," but because there were other artists who already used "Good Rockin'," he accepted Thompson's suggestion for a different pseudonym, "Magic Sam," which was created from his real name, Samuel Maghett.

Mike Rowe writes about Magic Sam's stylistic limitations: "As a creator Sam was very limited and he constantly returned to the theme on record, using it with slight variations for the slow blues side of each of his Cobra records, *Everything Gonna Be Alright* (5021), *All Night Long* (5025), and *Easy Baby* (5029)."[36]

Sam's Cobra recordings basically consist of three sources: the slow blues category (in addition to the three songs that Rowe lists, "All Your Love" and "Love Me This Way"); the fast rock 'n' roll/rockabilly category ("Love Me with a Feeling" and "21 Days in Jail"); and the boogie category ("Look Watcha Done" and "All My Whole Life"). The composition of the same sources largely shares the same musical traits, such as tempo, theme, and guitar and vocal phrases.

Dixon evidently obeyed Sam's tendency, but he used it as Sam's musical trademark:

> It seemed like Sam had just trained himself to that particular style and couldn't move easy. This is why I used that particular style with him and it turned out to be pretty good because you could always tell him, even from his introduction to the music. I would try to wrap it up with other instruments around him but he always stuck out in the same manner.[37]

The two slow blues compositions that Dixon offered to Sam derived from Sam's slow blues basis. Dixon's "All Night Long" and Sam's "All Your Love" sound too much alike; they both have a slow tempo, a series of triplets in 4/4 as basic beat, the same key (C), a twelve-bar/a-a-b structure, vocal melody lines, and a reverberated sound quality. Figures 6.2 and 6.3 show that in the opening melodies, the vowel sounds which Sam draws out on a high pitch are identical, while this opening phrase could be inspired by Otis Rush's "I Can't Quit You Baby."

Figure 6.2.

Figure 6.3.

Regardless of the similarity, Dixon uses a different wording pattern with more syllables for the second verse. This solution somehow avoids monotony:

[Verse 1]
All night long, baby, all night long,
All night long, baby, all night long,
Squeeze me darling, hold me in your arms.

[Verse 2]
Hold me close and squeeze me tight,
And love me baby both day and night,
Call my name, press your lips to mine,
Thrill me darling, thrill me one more time.

[Guitar solo]

[Verse 3]
Call my name, press your lips to mine,
Call my name, press your lips to mine,
Thrill me darling, thrill me one more time.

[Tag]
Just one more time,
Oh, yeah, yeah, yeah,
One more time.

One of the characteristics of this recording is its arrangement. There is a lot of room for Sam's guitar, contrasting with Otis Rush's early recordings. Dixon talks about Sam's distinction in his guitar style, especially in the harmonic progressions: "Magic Sam had a different guitar sound. Where most of the guys were playing the straight 12-bar blues thing, he was doing it to a 12-bar pattern to a certain extent but the harmonies that he carried with the chords was a different thing altogether."[38] What Dixon refers to is the minor chords that Sam inserts in the regular blues harmonic pattern. Dixon, as a producer, felt Sam's unique guitar was an important component to place in the foreground along with his vocal.

Another slow blues composition, "Easy Baby," is reminiscent of "All Your Love"; thus, it is also similar to "All Night Long."

The song "21 Days in Jail" is credited to Dixon and Lucious Porter Weaver.[39] The outtake of this recording shows that Dixon hums the opening phrase and says "singing it tight" to Sam. As explained, this song follows Sam's rock 'n' roll/rockabilly pattern. He produces crisp, syncopated arpeggio figures by fingerpicking, which is heard in many records on Sun Records in the mid-1950s.

From the point of view of cultural expression, this is an interesting recording. The song is about a man in jail waiting for a letter from his girlfriend:

[Hook]
21 days of torture, 21 nights of fear,
21 days in jail, and nobody seems to care,
21 days of torture, 21 nights of fear,
21 days in jail, and nobody seems to care.

[Verse 1]
I've been waiting for your letter, a gentle word or two,
When I get your letter, baby, I don't care what they do,

[Hook]
21 days of torture, 21 nights of fear,
21 days in jail, and nobody seems to care.

[Guitar solo]

[Verse 2]
Well, I finally got your letter, baby, you did what I wanted you to do,
Now you know it won't be long before I'll be home with you,

[Hook repeated]

[Tag]
Nobody seems to care,
Nobody seems to care. . . .

In spite of the expressions "torture" and "fear," this recording sounds like a happy song rather than an expression of low-down feelings in a traditional sense. As heard, for example, in Bukka White's "Parchman Farm Blues" (1940) and Son House's "Mississippi County Farm Blues" (1930), jail was a common experience often caused by racism in former generations. Whether a singer actually spent time in jail or not, he or she understood what it was like to be in jail and had an ability to share this painful feeling with audiences; in many ways, music making was closely related to the social stance of artists and their audiences.

Jail in Sam's recording, on the other hand, is nothing more than a song subject. Unusual for Dixon (though it is not known to what extent he was responsible for the composition), this recording lacks the connection between words and mood.

Betty Everett

Betty Everett, known for her "It's in His Kiss (The Shoop Shoop Song)" on Vee-Jay Records in 1964, was one of the first female artists to whom Dixon offered his compositions (the other was Gloria Irving, as discussed later in this chapter). As was the case for other artists on the label, her Cobra period marked the beginning of her career.

Betty Everett was born on November 23, 1939, in Greenwood, Mississippi, and served as a vocalist in her church before moving to the West Side of Chicago when she was eighteen. Magic Sam scouted her for Cobra Records at his public performance venue.[40] In two sessions in 1957 and 1958, she recorded six songs, including two Dixon compositions: a pop song, "My Love," and a blues song, "Killer Diller."

Everett was a teen idol and was marketed for a young male audience. "My Love" is about appreciating a boyfriend. This is in a minor key, reflecting Dixon's musical preferences during this period. After a bouncy introduction, which sounds like an introduction to "I'm Ready," Everett sings the opening phrase with her sweet, youthful soprano. The most noticeable characteristic is the cute attitude that she projects through the way she uses the break in her voice.

While the persona in "My Love" has a cute attitude, the girl in "Killer Diller" is a brat. This song is about a young girl's longing for an attractive man living in the South:

> [Verse 1]
> I got a man away down South,
> He ain't southern lookin', but he sure do knock me out.
>
> [Hook]
> He's a killer diller, yes, he's a killer diller,
> Yes, he's a killer diller, but he satisfies my soul.
>
> [Verse 2]
> He may not know his ABC,
> But he got everything, that a good gal need,
>
> [Hook repeated]
>
> [Piano solo]
>
> [Verse 3]
> He may not worry from sun 'til sun,
> You can bet your life, we have lots of fun.
>
> [Hook repeated]
>
> [Tag]
> Mmm, he's a killer diller, mmm.

Dixon realized a simple but vigorous arrangement would express the wild attitude of a precocious girl. The verse is sung over a stop-time riff, which is strongly punctuated by the horns. The hook part is in a walking-bass pattern, in which the rhythm section creates an uplifting feel. Then, Everett's tense vocals express the wildness of the girl in the song. For an eighteen-year-old girl, Everett sounds sexy and tough, and her performance is very soulful.

"Killer Diller" is one of the few examples in which Dixon included Southern imagery in the compositions he gave to Cobra artists. Compared with other songs with provincial images, such as "Hoochie Coochie Man," the man the girl yearns for in "Killer Diller" is somewhat trivialized by the song's title and contents; in spite of a lack of education, "he has everything a good gal need." While the Hoochie Coochie Man is a figure who has everything a good girl needs, the song itself has more than a simple depiction of machismo, and that is what makes that composition interesting. In contrast, there is no equivalent strength in "Killer Diller."

Big Walter "Shakey" Horton

Willie Dixon once said he highly esteemed Big Walter "Shakey" Horton's harmonica techniques: "Big Walter, frankly, was the best harmonica player I ever heard. When he was right, Big Walter could actually play things on the harmonica nobody else could."[41]

Walter Horton was born on April 6, 1917, in Horn Lake, Mississippi, and he grew up in Memphis. He taught himself harmonica as early as the age of five. In the late 1920s he already performed and recorded with the Memphis Jug Band. Dixon remembers that he saw Horton playing on the street corners of Memphis in the 1940s and early 1950s.[42] Also in Memphis he taught Little Walter harmonica techniques, as discussed earlier. Around 1953, Horton moved to Chicago, and then temporarily became a harmonica player for Muddy Waters' band after Junior Wells left the group.

In August 1954, Dixon hired Horton for Tommy Brown's session for States Records. In November of this year, Horton had his own session for States, and Dixon offered "Back Home to Mama." This song is credited to the owner of States Records, Leonard Allen. Dixon could not publish it under his own name because he then had an exclusive contract as a songwriter with Chess Records.[43]

"Back Home to Mama" later became a source for "Bring It on Home," which Dixon presented to Sonny Boy Williamson in 1963. Sonny Boy was another of Horton's student, and these two artists were very much alike in their low-down personalities. These songs have the medium walking blues tempo and the call-and-response structure of the hook section ("Mama"/"Baby" followed by a response phrase played on the harmonica).

Both songs share the same theme, "going home," but "mama" in Horton's song is a real mother—not a girlfriend—and the reason to return home is a having been mistreated:

> [Hook]
> Mama,
> Mama,
> Coming back home to stay.
>
> [Verse]
> Let me tell you mama what these folks done done,
> They wackin' your child from sun to sun,
> I makes a little money to take care of myself,
> The woman I love, she take care of someone else.
>
> [Harmonica solo]
>
> [Hook]
> Mumble [Mama],
> Mumble [Mama],
> I'm coming back home to stay.

This recording shows Horton's techniques of controlling breath and dynamics. However, as a composition, the lyrics appear to be incomplete.

Horton recorded Dixon's "Have a Good Time" for his 1956 Cobra session. This song sounds similar to Louis Jordan's "Let the Good Times Roll." The lyrics are about self-abandonment:

> [Verse 1]
> Get back, little girl, come on roll,
> Don't need nothing but money and gold.
>
> [Hook]
> To have a good time,
> Because you have a good time,
> We gonna have a good time,
> We gonna rock 'n' roll all night long.
>
> [Harmonica solo]
>
> [Verse 2]
> You may preach like Peter, pray like Paul,
> Judgement Day come, that's all, that's all.
>
> [Hook repeated]
>
> [Saxophone solo]

[Verse 3]
I may spend my money, pawn my clothes,
Don't have to worry, 'cause I have a [ball?].

[Hook repeated]

[Harmonica solo]

The structure of the song—use of the stop-time rhythm followed by a walking-bass pattern—is also similar to the midsection of "Let the Good Times Roll."

Horton's vocal is weak. As Dixon implies with his comment "when he was right" (cited at the beginning of this section), Horton was a chronic alcoholic. Because of his furry voice and our knowledge about his alcoholism, this song sounds as if he is justifying his self-destructive lifestyle.

Although Horton was not a good vocalist, he made a marvelous album, *The Soul of Blues Harmonica*, which Willie Dixon produced for Chess' subsidiary Argo label. In one of the cuts recorded on January 24, 1964, "Good Moanin' Blues" (Dixon is credited as the composer), Dixon's wordless, eerie moaning is followed by Horton's superb performance based on slow twelve-bar blues. His expressive techniques of creating vibrato, changing dynamics, and adding various rhythmic nuances prove Dixon's impression about Horton stated earlier.

In 1969 Dixon formed Chicago Blues All-Stars with Johnny Shines (guitar/vocal), Sunnyland Slim (piano), and Clifton James (drums), and Big Walter Horton served as a harmonica player for the group.[44]

Other Artists on Cobra Records

The Clouds were one of hundreds of R&B, doo-wop vocal groups in the 1950s and 1960s. Members were Sherrard Jones, Al Butler, William English, and Bobby Walker.[45] From 1956 through 1968, they released eight singles from various labels, and Dixon's "Rock & Roll Boogie" was their debut single in 1956. This was Cobra's second release after Otis Rush's "I Can't Quit You Baby."

This is not a very attractive record. Too many repetitions of the words—the title phrase "rock 'n' roll boogie"—reduce the quality of the song.

"Fishin' in My Pond," recorded by vocalist/guitarist Lee Jackson, is one of the most humorous Dixon compositions. Jackson was born as Warren George Harding Lee in 1921 in Gill, Arkansas. In the early 1930s, he moved to Chicago. Around the time he worked for a meat-packaging company, he became acquainted with Leonard Chess.[46] Jackson recorded for Chess Records and Vee-Jay Records in the mid-1950s, but these recordings were not released. He made a record debut with Cobra in 1956. Though Jackson could not make his own fame, he played as a sideman for many artists, including J. B. Hutto, Homesick James, Otis Spann, Hound Dog Taylor, and Johnny Shines. He died in Chicago in 1979.

"Fishin' in My Pond" is a twelve-bar blues, but as usual for Dixon, while the opening is in an a-a-b form, the verses are in a quatrain refrain form and its extension. The song is about a man whose fish is stolen from his pond, while one could read these lyrics as a metaphor for illicit sexual activity:

> [Hook]
> Well, somebody fishin', they been fishin' in my pond,
> Oh, somebody fishin', they been fishin' in my pond,
> They're eatin' up all my fish, they must be grindin' up the bones.
>
> [Verse 1]
> Don't mind 'em fishin', rod, reel, or pole,
> Seem like they're catchin' my fish by burnin' up the hole I got.
>
> [Hook]
> Yeah, wee, somebody been fishin' in my pond,
> They're eatin' up all my fish, they might be grindin' up the bones.
>
> [Guitar solo]
>
> [Verse 2]
> Went down to the river, didn't see no tracks,
> I saw they catching little fish, weren't even throwin' 'em back.
>
> [Hook repeated]
>
> [Verse 3]
> Didn't get suspicious, 'til the last day or two,
> I found my next door neighbor was cookin' fish head stew, I got.
>
> [Hook repeated]

Jackson's soaring vocal in the opening effectively expresses frustration, and the way he sings the stop-time sections in a lower range well describes his disappointment at what he witnesses.

The arrangement helps create a humorous mood. The song starts with a strange marchlike introduction played by tenor saxophones in a minor key, and a high-hat cymbal accentuates every downbeat. In the solo part, the guitar and saxophones clash, which sounds as if the ensemble is intentionally disorganized to create an irritating atmosphere. Not many other Dixon songs express such cynical humor as well as this song.

Vocalist Gloria Irving was one of the first female artists to whom Dixon offered a composition, as well as Betty Everett. Irving's biography is not well known, but before she came to Cobra, she was a vocalist with Swinging Sax Kari and Orchestra. Their "Daughter (That's Your Red Wagon)" from States Records in 1954—the answer song for Ruth Brown's "(Mama) He Treats Your Daughter Mean" (1953)—was a popular R&B record. Irving's vocal performance in Dixon's song "For You and Only You" (1957)—presented as the B side for her single "I Need a Man"—actually sounds as if she is imitating Ruth Brown's singing style. The way these singers pronounce words and articulate phrases is very much alike.

A simple love song, "For You and Only You" has identical melodies with another Dixon composition, "If You Were Mine," which was presented to Otis Rush. Also, the arrangement idea for "For You and Only You" was more likely inspired by the arrangement for "Violent Love," another Dixon song presented to Otis. The bouncy introductory phrase by two saxophones has a very similar feel.

Nothing is known about vocalist Charles Clark, except that he premiered "Hidden Charms," which Howlin' Wolf recorded later in 1963. Dixon also used this title for his solo album in 1988. While the song portrays the sexual attraction of a girl, the wisdom here is about an essential quality that is not visible on the surface:

> [Verse 1]
> Lips are sweet, her legs are big,
> Her look can make you dance a jig,
> A touch so soft, and now, a heart so warm,
> What knock me out is, a that hidden charm.
>
> [Verse 2]
> Her kiss is pure, a morning dew,
> A real gone love is frantic too,
> She weak as water, in my arms,
> What move me, baby, is your hidden charms.
>
> [Vamp]
> Woo, wee, what a baby,
> Woo, wee, what a baby,
> When she hold me in her arms,
> It brings out all of her hidden charms.
>
> [Harmonica solo]
>
> [Verse 3]
> A touch so soft, a love so true,
> I think about her, that's all I do,

I [unintelligible], sick and moan
What thrill me, darling, is your hidden charms.

[Tag]
Hidden charms,
Hidden charms. . . .

Dixon explains, "When the hidden charms come out—BOOM—you hardly know each other and you can't even understand each other because you are flying false colors in the first place. And both of you had hidden charms."[47] This theme was a recurring song subject for Dixon's didactic songs—for example, "Young Fashioned Ways" and "You Can't Judge a Book by Its Cover."

Clark's vocal in the original "Hidden Charms" is not powerful and more so for knowing Howlin' Wolf's version. In addition, all-star sidemen Otis Rush and Louis Myers on guitar, Sonny Boy Williamson on harmonica, Harold Burrage on piano, and Dixon on bass sound too relaxed.

While "I Can't Quit You Baby" and "My Love Will Never Die" are great slow blues records, many recordings of Dixon compositions in the Cobra period are not as powerful as those in other periods. There are various reasons for the unsuccessful result. One was definitely a concentration on the business operation of the label for which Dixon could not concentrate on music making. Another was the less attractive quality of Dixon's pop-oriented compositions. And the other is that there was an absence of artists for whom he could provide songs that showed his merits as a songwriter. The ability of the singer is crucial to the artistic and commercial success of songs, whether blues or pop. Most of the Cobra artists were new, just launching and developing their careers as recording artists and therefore not really able to make just any song succeed. In the hands of an experienced and charismatic singer, however, things were different; for example, Howlin' Wolf's "Hidden Charms" is a fabulous recording, as discussed in the following chapter.

Notes

1. See appendix B.
2. Marie Dixon, interview by the author, September 25, 2004. Marie explains the relationship among Willie, Marie herself, and Elenora Franklin:

According to what he told me, their relationship was not good, and when he met me, he was leaving her. The only question I asked him when I met him and started to date him was "Are you married?" because it was total "no no" in my upbringing. You don't deal with a married man. He said no, he was not married. She was a friend. . . . He said he wanted me to be his wife. Again, I still did not ask him a question, "Do you have chidrens?" We were married. He didn't volunteer it, and I didn't ask. . . . I was pregnant with my first kid, when I found out there he had childrens with this lady. And he started to tell me that he was going to take care of both families' childrens, and that he did.

We [Marie and Elenore] didn't really have relationship. We lived far apart. We had nothing in common but I was married to the man she had childrens by. I didn't get between her and her childrens. . . . These childrens always knew where he was. They were always welcome in my home. If she needed him for any reason to discipline childrens . . . , she would always feel free to call my home. No misunderstanding. My upbringing was if a man has childrens, he should be a father. If he has five hundred childrens, he should be a father of those childrens.

Ibid.

3. Willie Dixon, with Don Snowden, *I Am the Blues: The Willie Dixon Story* (New York: Da Capo Press, 1989), 111.

4. Otis Rush, quoted in Diana Haig and Don Snowden, comp., "Liner Notes," *The Cobra Records Story* (New York: Capricorn/Warner Brothers, 9 42012–2, 1993), 9.

5. Shirli Dixon, interview by the author, September 23, 2002.

6. Mike Rowe, *Chicago Blues: The City and the Music* [originally entitled *Chicago Breakdown*] (London: Eddison Press, 1973; repr., New York: Da Capo Press, 1975), 177. Citations are to the Da Capo Press edition.

7. *Chicago Blues* [DVD], produced and directed by Haley Cokliss (Tokyo: P-Vine Records, BMG Fun House, PVBP-953, 2003; original produced in London: IRIT Film Production, 1970). In *Urban Blues* by Charles Keil, the term *urban bluesmen* indicates blues performers who have broader, nationwide popularity, compared with "city bluesmen," who mainly perform for audiences in particular African American communities. B. B. King and Bobby Blue Bland are classified as "urban bluesmen," while Chicago blues artists, such as Muddy Waters and Howlin' Wolf, belong to "city bluesmen." Charles Keil, *Urban Blues* (Chicago: University of Chicago Press, 1966; repr., 1970), 164. From Muddy's description about his style and that of B. B. King in this footage, these two terms were accepted terminologies to indicate different styles of electric blues.

8. Jas Obrecht, "Otis Rush," in *Rollin' and Tumblin': The Postwar Blues Guitarists*, ed. Jas Obrecht (San Francisco: Miller Freeman Books, 2000), 226.

9. Jim O'Neal, Amy O'Neal, and Dick Shurman, "Interview: Otis Rush," *Living Blues*, no. 28 (July/August 1976), 20.

10. Bob Corritore, Bill Ferris, and Jim O'Neal, "Willie Dixon (Part 2)," *Living Blues*, no. 82 (September/October 1988): 22. The thought that Otis was similar to Muddy is due to the fact that Otis often played Muddy's songs for public performances to make a living. Obrecht, "Otis Rush," 236.

11. None of detailed recording dates of Cobra sessions are known, because Toscano did not keep information. But such a sloppy business practice made many outtake recordings available.

12. Willie Dixon, *Willie Dixon: The Master Blues Composer* (Milwaukee: Hal Leonard, 1992), 80.

13. Butch Dixon, interview by the author, September 23, 2003.

14. Debra DeSalvo, "Otis Rush: Still Can't Quit You Baby," *Blues Revue*, no. 21 (February/March 1996): 27.

15. Dixon, *Willie Dixon*, 80.

16. Corritore, Ferris, and O'Neal, "Willie Dixon (Part 2)," 22.

17. Dixon, *Willie Dixon*, 80.

18. Ibid. Corritore, Ferris, and O'Neal, "Willie Dixon (Part 2)," 22.

19. Galen Gart, ed., *First Pressings: The History of Rhythm & Blues*, vol. 6, 1956 (Milford, NH: Big Nickel, 1990), 107–108.

20. Joel Whitburn, *Top R&B Singles, 1942–1995* (Menomonee Falls, WI: Record Research, 1996), 385.

21. This song is credited to Dixon and Howard Bedno, who worked for Cobra Records, but Bedno claims, "Dixon put my name as a writer on several songs that he wrote which were released on Cobra." Howard Bedno, quoted in Haig and Snowden, "Liner Notes," 8.

22. Dixon, *I Am the Blues*, 110.

23. Ibid.

24. O'Neal, O'Neal, and Shurman, "Interview," 15. Otis continues, "He gets the credit for it. But if he gave me a type of song that I think somethin' should be changed, then I just go ahead and change it. Sometime maybe it's the whole song, almost the entire song." Ibid.

25. Mark A. Humphrey, "Bright Lights, Big City," in *Nothing but the Blues: The Music and the Musicians*, ed. Lawrence Cohn (New York, London, Paris: Abbeville Press, 1993), 200–201. Humphrey continues, "Having Otis record 'Violent Love' made as much sense as offering 'Smokestack Lightnin'' to Bing Crosby."

26. O'Neal, O'Neal, and Shurman, "Interview," 15.

27. Shirli Dixon, interview by the author, September 23, 2002.

28. Obrecht, "Otis Rush," 241. Dixon offered "Jump Sister Bessie" for his next session in mid-1957.

29. In the same session, Otis Rush recorded "Love That Woman," for which he credits himself as composer, although he says, "That's the one I hate. That was Willie Dixon's idea." O'Neal, O'Neal, and Shurman, "Interview," 15.

30. "She's a Good 'Un" is not credited to Dixon but to John Eskridge and Arthur White. However, Dixon claims he was partly responsible for this composition:

Arthur White was a friend of mine. In fact Arthur came up with the idea of "She's a Good One"—"She's a Good 'Un." I just put the thing in his name because Arthur couldn't put nothin' together no way. Arthur never wrote nothin' in his life, of no kind. I put the whole thing together.

O'Neal, O'Neal, and Shurman, "Interview," 16.

31. Otis recollects his Chess years: "I wasn't their favorite artist. Chess was like, whoever got the hit, that's his artist. You had a hit record, that's the man he pushed. You record, and hope for the best." Roy Greenberg, "Otis Rush Interview," *Cadence* 5 (December 1979): 10.

32. Neil Slaven, "Liner Notes," *The Essential Otis Rush: The Classic Cobra Recordings 1956–1958* (Universal City, CA: Fuel 2000 Records/Universal Music, 2000), 6.

33. Obrecht, "Otis Rush," 226.

34. Robert Pruter, *Chicago Soul* (Urbana: University of Illinois Press, 1991), 216. Pruter defines "hard soul" as

> vocal music that relied on a raw delivery and made heavy use of melisma (bending of notes) and screaming. Vocals were often shouted rather than smoothly delivered. Hard soul drew more heavily on blues and gospel than did its soft-soul counterpart, and as with blues, hard soul tended to appeal to a largely adult audience and black working-class constituency.

Ibid., 18.

35. Steve Franz, "Magic Rocker: The Life and Music of Magic Sam," *Living Blues*, no. 125 (January/February 1996): 35.

36. Rowe, *Chicago Blues*, 179.

37. Dixon, *I Am the Blues*, 109.

38. Ibid.

39. I could not find any information about Weaver, except he was the composer of "You Sure Can't Do," recorded by Buddy Guy.

40. Pruter, *Chicago Soul*, 37.

41. Corritore, Ferris, and O'Neal, "Willie Dixon (Part 2)," 28.

42. Dixon, *I Am the Blues*, 97.

43. Ibid.

44. Dixon previously used Chicago Blues All-Stars in the early 1960s for his public performances featuring Buddy Guy, Otis Rush, and others.

45. Hitoshi Koide, "Liner Notes," *The Complete Cobra Singles* (Tokyo: P-Vine Records, PCD-18528/31, 2008), 11.

46. Pruter, *Chicago Soul*, 113.

47. Dixon, *Willie Dixon*, 62.

CHAPTER SEVEN

~

The Second Chess Records Period (1958–1971)

In early 1959, Willie Dixon returned to Chess Records. Around the time when Cobra Records became stranded, Dixon ran into Phil Chess. Phil showed Chess' new studio at 2120 South Michigan Avenue to Dixon. Phil promised Dixon a raise in salary if he returned to the company.[1]

During the 1960s, Dixon's artistry as a composer reached another peak. His collaboration with Howlin' Wolf created Chicago blues classics, including "Back Door Man," "I Ain't Superstitious," "Spoonful," and "The Red Rooster." The new version of "Wang Dang Doodle" by Koko Taylor, produced by Dixon, was one of the biggest blues hit records in the 1960s.

The technological advancements affected the way Dixon wrote songs as well as the way artists made records. Chess' new studio had a multitrack recording system.[2] Around 1960 or 1961, Leonard Chess brought in an ex-engineer of King Records in Cincinnati, Ron Malo, who produced James Brown's early hits. Malo improved studio operations by placing soundproofing materials and a separated vocal booth in the room.[3] This equipment helped some vocalists who had difficulty remembering words (especially Howlin' Wolf and Little Walter). The new system allowed them to overdub their vocal parts. Now Dixon did not need to concern himself about the length of lyrics.

On the other hand, Dixon's involvement with Chess decreased. His instrument acoustic bass was replaced with electric bass in most recording sessions, although he was usually present in the studio as a supervisor especially when artists were recording his songs. His role as a house songwriter was also reducing. While twelve Dixon compositions were recorded in 1963, after 1964 no more than seven songs were recorded each year. In 1969 the only newly recorded Dixon composition was "I Am the Blues" by Muddy Waters.

One of the reasons for Dixon's reduced involvement is that he did not have an exclusive contract with Chess, at least not in his mind. He states, "I had an agreement with Chess for songwriting . . . but it wasn't a properly drawn up contract."[4] Dixon expanded his work outside Chess' territory.

There is another reason for Dixon's reduced involvement with Chess. By the early 1960s, blues was no longer the main commercial focus for Chess, although it was a "steady baseline."[5] Since Chuck Berry's "Maybellene" in 1955, rock 'n' roll records were always an important priority. In the same year, Chess launched Argo label to release jazz records by artists such as Ahmad Jamal and Ramsey Lewis (Dixon played bass for jazz organist Sam Lazar's album *Space Flight* in 1960).

In addition, the most popular black contemporary musical style in the early 1960s was soul, even for Chess Records. After Etta James' pop chart hits—"All I Could Do Was Cry" and "Trust in Me" in 1960—Chess explored soul artists such as Fontella Bass and Billy Stewart. These artists were not in Dixon's territory. Also, contemporary blues performing style—that is, B. B. King–type of blues—became influential on Chess artists like Little Milton. Jim O'Neal writes that from 1960 to 1969, the Chess company produced twenty-one hit singles by Etta James and fourteen by Little Milton, while Muddy Waters, Howlin' Wolf, Little Walter, and Sonny Boy Williamson combined had only two R&B (rhythm and blues) hits total.[6]

Still Chess Records made efforts to sell blues records, especially to white audiences. In the early 1960s, many of college students got to know the blues as a kind of folk music. Pre–World War I down-home bluesmen, including Son House, Mississippi John Hurt, and Skip James, were rediscovered by researchers, record collectors, and music fans. They played at festivals and at colleges and also shared bills with contemporary bluesmen. Chess jumped on the folk music craze and made *Muddy Waters, Folk Singer* in 1963 (including Dixon's "My Captain"). Subsequently, the label released a series of *The Real Folk Blues* by Muddy Waters, Howlin' Wolf, Sonny Boy Williamson, and John Lee Hooker, the materials of which were taken from their previously released electric blues records.

In the second half of the 1960s, when "supersessions" became popular, Chess made *Super Blues* (Bo Diddley, Muddy, and Walter, 1967) and *The Super Blues Band* (Muddy, Wolf, and Bo, 1968). Marshall Chess, who by then had become a staff member, produced psychedelic records by Muddy and Wolf, respectively, in 1968: *Electric Mud* and *This Is Howlin' Wolf's New Album*. The company also made the albums in which representative blues artists, who were presented as fathers of rock, played with young white musicians: *Fathers and Sons* (Muddy, Otis Spann, Mike Bloomfield, Paul Butterfield, Donald "Duck" Dunn, Sam Lay, and Buddy Miles; Dixon was credited as an advisor), and a series of *London Sessions* (Muddy, Wolf, Bo, and Chuck Berry).

On the other hand, there were signs of demise. Sonny Boy Williamson returned to his old base Arkansas in 1965, and he died there soon after his return. Little Walter also died from a fistfight in 1968. From 1966, Dixon's work at Chess Records was almost exclusively for Koko Taylor. Shirli Dixon talks of her father's activity in the end of the 1960s:

> He had a hope like any ventures that you begin. . . . Daddy just started working with new emerging talents at that point, any other artists that wanted to be a part of the blues. And he felt that was his real job for almost his entire life. There's always some act or talent.[7]

In 1969, Chess brothers sold Chess Records to General Recorded Tape (GRT Corporation). "That was heartbreaking for him because he really helped that company, and when it gets sold . . . you don't know what the future holds at that point,"[8] says Shirli Dixon. In October of that year, Leonard Chess died. Phil and Marshall stayed with GRT for a while, but both left in 1971. GRT's record division was almost bankrupt.

Even after Chess was sold to GRT, Dixon stayed with the company, though he said to Peter Guralnick, "I'm fixin' to get the hell out of here."[9] Dixon's last work for Chess was producing Jimmy Reeves Jr.'s album *Born to Love Me* in 1970 and writing songs and producing for Koko Taylor's second album, *Basic Soul* in 1971.

Dixon observed and experienced the era of significant sociopolitical change in the 1960s. He wrote compositions that were inspired by the civil rights movement. These songs, however, do not occupy a large part of his song catalogue. The small number of political songs is primarily due to the policy of the record company and radio stations; in general, they were not willing to put out records with political contents.[10]

Although Dixon did not write many political songs, he supervised J. B. Lenoir's albums *Alabama Blues* (1965) and *Down in Mississippi* (1966) in which Lenoir sang of racial violence, riots, and the Vietnam War. These records were released only in Europe at that time. Horst Lippmann, the co-producer of these records, says,

> I made arrangements that J. B. Lenoir finally should get his chance—without any limitation—to sing and play what ever [sic] comes through his mind, whatever he might think was and is wrong in the United states [sic] toward Black People. Since I had to leave before the recording date, I asked Willie Dixon to take over supervision and have no fear that J. B. Lenoir records everything he wants to record regardless if this would cause problems in the United States in the year of 1965.[11]

Lenoir's recordings are some of the few blues records that refer to the civil rights movement. In fact, there are only scattered recordings in which blues artists directly sing of racism.[12] As Jim O'Neal writes, "The politics of the blues world was never cut and dried."[13] There were always some political implications in the blues as musical activity and poetic expression—the blues itself emerged more or less as a product of the tension of racial conflicts—and in the relationship between musicians and entrepreneurs such as record company owners, club owners, and promoters. As shown by the episode of Lenoir's records, record companies wanted to avoid possible controversies. Dixon understood that his political ideas would not be welcome.

One of the reasons the Chess brothers sold the company was "increasing difficulty for white people to own a company geared to black consumers."[14] Nadine Cohodas writes, "Jessie Jackson was pressuring Chess, just as he was pressuring other companies that did business in the black community, to hire more blacks in senior positions."[15]

But Leonard Chess actually collaborated with the civil rights movement by becoming a member of the Chicago Urban League and the National Association for the Advancement of Colored People. He supported Martin Luther King Jr. by making donations.[16] Dixon also contributed to the movement. He performed for the Poor People's March on Washington in 1968 with Muddy Waters, Little Walter, and Otis Spann.[17] However, Dixon could not agree with Dr. King's nonviolent policy:

> I started thinking about that—ain't no way I'm going out there to look at somebody to jump on me and hit me and I don't knock the hell out of 'em back. I told 'em there's no use in me going out there and ruining your thing. I'll go back home because I can't tolerate that.[18]

Shirli Dixon talks about her father's view of Dr. King:

> He said that under normal circumstances naturally where there was a conflict, you would want to resolve without any difficulty, if it's possible. But because of his experience with the Europeans and the early Americans, he knew that it was almost impossible to solve the matters between people of color and those of non-color without some form of response. So while he applauded Dr. King for his commitment, and he certainly held high regard for his desire, he didn't believe that he could accomplish his goal without showing some form of strife when it was required.
>
> Ultimately, one of the biggest things he said was that they're gonna take his life, because they don't have respect for what he's doing and they know that he will not challenge them in any capacity other than for self-examination, which he thought should have come anyway as part of being a decent human being that you would self-exam and morally look at yourself, your own moral meter should kick in at some point.[19]

The following section explores Dixon's compositions for the Chess artists from the late 1950s to the early 1970s when the company closed down. This section is followed by his work outside Chess Records, including the American Folk Blues Festival, Dixon and Memphis Slim, and his compositions for the non-Chess artists.

Compositions for Chess Artists, 1950s to Early 1970s

Muddy Waters

Until 1956, Muddy usually had three recording sessions a year, but from 1957, he only had two a year. Along with reduced recordings sessions, his use of Dixon's songs became sporadic.

In August of 1958, Dixon started to reactivate the relationship with Chess by offering Muddy "Close to You." This is a sixteen-bar blues with a quatrain refrain text form in a medium walking blues tempo. The song is about seducing a woman, a theme still faithful to Muddy's womanizer character. Dixon lists different metaphors to express how to get close to "you":

[Verse 1]
I want to get close to your baby, ha ha, as white on rice, ah ha,
Close to you babe, a ha, as cold is to ice, a ha,
Close to you baby, a ha, as the hair on you head, a ha,
Close to you baby, you better believe what I said.

[Hook]
I want to get close to you baby,
Oh, let me get close to you,
I want to get so close to this little girl, 'til she, ha,
Don't know what to say or do.

[Verse 2]
I want to get close to you baby, a ha, at the sight of your eye, a ha,
Close to you babe, a ha, heat is to fire, a ha,
Close to you baby, ha ha, as a egg is to hen, ah,
Close to you baby, ha ha, as Siamese twins,

[Hook repeated]

[Vamp]
Closer and closer, baby, ah,
Closer and closer, baby, ah,
Closer and closer, baby, ah,
Closer and closer, baby, ah,
I want to get so close to this woman, 'til, she ah ha don't know what to say or do.

[Guitar solo]

[Verse 3]
I want to get close to you baby, a ha ha, as I can get,
Close to you baby, ah, as water is wet,
Close to you baby, ah ha, as fire to smoke,
Close to you baby, ha ha, as pig to poke.

[Hook repeated]

Muddy's vocal sounds very confident. He inserts the vocalization "ha" between almost all the phrases, which resembles vocalization characteristic of African American chanted sermons.

The vamp section (repetitions of "Closer and closer, baby") shows Dixon's characteristic writing style in this period; he frequently utilized a very simplified section with repetitions of a very short text. In this particular case it is in the vamp, but in some other songs, an extremely stripped-down hook is placed as the high point of a composition. This writing style will be detailed later in this chapter.

On October 20, 1958, "Close to You" was ranked at the ninth position on *Billboard*'s R&B charts.[20] This was Muddy's first hit in two years, since Dixon's "Don't Go No Further" (September 1956), and it was Muddy's last single hit.

For the June 7, 1960, session, Muddy recorded two Dixon songs, "Tiger in Your Tank" and "I Got My Brand on You." "Tiger in Your Tank" is an

energetic, up-tempo song. It is in a busy eight-beat pattern, similar to label
mate Chuck Berry's rock 'n' roll songs. The lyrics were inspired by the 1959
Esso gasoline campaign slogan that started in Chicago: "Put a Tiger in Your
Tank."[21] The analogy between sexual prowess and the potential of a vehicle is
traditional in blues songs from early on: for example, Bessie Smith's "You've
Been a Good Old Wagon" (1925) and Blind Willie McTell's "Broken Down
Engine Blues" (1931). In the case of Dixon's song, an engine is equated with
a woman's attraction, which is boosted by the Esso additive—"Tiger," which
is equated with a man's sexual ability:

> [Verse 1] (A1)
> I like the way you look and I love your little car,
> [I] try to console you, you know it don't go very far,
> I talk to you, baby, your mind's all a blank,
> I wanna put a Tiger in your tank.
>
> [Verse 2] (A2)
> Everything you do, you know, you knocks me out,
> I want to feel good while you can jump and shout,
> I have no money, you know, in the bank,
> I wanna put a Tiger in your tank.

A sixteen-measure verse on a tonic chord is followed by an eight-measure
bridge section that starts with a subdominant and ends with a dominant
chord. This is another example of amalgamating a blues with an A-A-B-A
pop-song form, observed in "I Just Want to Make Love to You":

> [Bridge] (B)
> I can raise your hood, I can clean your coil,
> Check your transmission, then even the oil,
> I don't care what the people think,
> I wanna put a Tiger, y'know, in your tank.
>
> [Verse 3] (A3)
> Your motor's a puffin', an' a missin', too,
> One thing left for you to do,
> You give it a push and the car won't crank,
> I wanna put a Tiger in your tank.
>
> [Guitar solo]
>
> [Tag]
> I wanna put a Tiger in your tank,
> I wanna put a Tiger in your tank . . .

Francis Clay's drumming creates the speedy atmosphere. Muddy's vocal sounds like that of a naughty boy. He takes a slide guitar solo, but while it is supposed to be a twelve-bar solo, he only plays eleven bars. Regardless of a flaw, this is an exciting record.

"I Got My Brand on You" is about a man's proprietary attitude toward a woman; the theme developed from Muddy's womanizer persona. While this song reflects Dixon's typical writing style—a twelve-bar blues with a quatrain refrain text form—the opening section shows Dixon's distinctive writing style of this period. Here Dixon attempts a hypnotic effect through persistent repetitions of the title phrase "I got my brand on you":

[Hook]
I got my brand on you,
I got my brand on you,
I got my brand on you,
I got my brand on you,
There ain't nothin' you can do, honey,
I got my brand on you.

[Verse 1]
Oh you may go away and leave me girl, I declare you can't stay,
You gonna come runnin' back to me some lonesome day.

[Hook]
I got my brand on you,
I got my brand on you,
There ain't nothin' you can do, darlin',
I got my brand on you.

[Harmonica solo]

[Verse 2]
Oh I'm puttin' my brand you know baby on no certain part,
But whenever I kiss you I stab it in your heart [sic].

[Hook repeated with slightly different wording]

[Verse 3]
Oh I got you like a fish baby, you know, hangin' on my line,
I can reel you in, most anytime.

[Hook repeated with slightly different wording]

In spite of too many repetitions, it sounds like the magical spell that can hold a woman, and it brings out Muddy's persona that developed from

"Hoochie Coochie Man"—a conjurer, an important component of black badman heroes.

On June 27, 1962, Muddy overdubbed the vocal part for "You Shook Me" to the instrumental track "Blue Guitar" by Earl Hooker (recorded on May 3, 1961, for Age Records). The music is in a slow twelve-bar blues style, which features Hooker's marvelous slide guitar performance. Dixon and J. B. Lenoir wrote the words that are based on Muddy's early record "Mad Love" (1953).

While "Mad Love" is about the uncontrollable sexual desire, "You Shook Me" shows the consequence of what is sung in "Mad Love":

[Verse 1]
You know you shook me, baby, you shook me all night long,
You know you shook me, baby, you shook me all night long,
Oh, you kept on shakin' me darlin',
Oh, you messed up my happy home.

[Verse 2]
You know you moves me, baby, just like a hurricane,
You know you moves me, baby, just like a hurricane,
Oh, you know you moves me darlin' just like earthquake move the land.

[Verse 3]
Oh sometime I wonder what my poor wife and child gon' do,
Oh sometime I wonder what my poor wife and child's gon' do,
Yeah, you know, you made me mistreat them, darlin,'
    whoa, I'm madly in love with you.

[Tag]
You know you shook me, baby, you shook me all night long,
Mmm. . . .

The third verse starts with the line "Oh, sometime I wonder what my poor wife and child gon' do." Instead of giving Muddy simply the role of a macho figure, Dixon exhibits that this womanizer's action now leads to the destruction of a family, the core of the community. While Dixon describes erotic pleasure as an essential part of human spirit—as seen in "I Just Want to Make Love to You"—he also stresses that one must take responsibility for his or her behavior. "'You Shook Me' can bring many ideas to mind. It all depends on how you feel about being shook all night long and with the way you're being shook. . . . 'Roll me, roll me, roll me like a wagon wheel.' Rolling is a good thing, it all depends on who's rolling you,"[22] says Dixon.

The lyrics of "You Shook Me" are related to one of the beliefs conveyed in many blues songs: you "reap what you sow."[23] As often observed, Dixon's words in this song function as a sermon in the secular context. The way Muddy exaggerates words such as *shook*, *move*, and *wonder*, emphatically expresses a feeling of being torn between reason and emotion. His expression never possesses the smoothness that Otis Rush expresses in "I Can't Quit You Baby," which is also about adultery and its result.

On October 12, 1962, Muddy again overdubbed vocal parts to Earl Hooker's instrumental tracks.[24] Dixon wrote words for one of them, "You Need Love." As the title implies, the lyrics are about the necessity of love:[25]

[Verse 1]
You've got yearnin' and I got burnin',
Baby you look so, ho, sweet and cunnin',
Baby way down inside, woman you need love,
Woman you need love,
You've got to have some love,
I'm gon' give you some love.
I know you need love,
Just gotta have love,
Gotta have some love,
You make me feel so good,
You make me feel all right,
You make me feel so good,
You make me feel all right,
You make me so good,
You make me feel all right,
She's so nice, she's so nice,
She's so nice, she's so nice,
She's so nice, she's so nice,
She's so nice, she's so nice.

[Verse 2]
You are frettin', and I am pettin'
A lot of good things, ho, you ain't getting,
Baby, way down inside, woman, you need love,
I know you need love,
You gotta have some love.

[Organ solo]

[Verse 3]
I ain't foolin' you need schoolin',
Baby you know you need coolin',

> Woman, way down inside, woman you need love,
> You gotta have some love,
> Mmm . . .
> She gotta have some love,
> Mmm . . .
> She gotta have some love.

The vocal melody derives from Muddy's early records "Rolling Stone" (1950), "Still a Fool" (1951), and "She's All Right" (1953). As in "Rolling Stone," the music is built on one chord (E minor) and a repetitive riff, but in a much faster tempo this time. Muddy's reciting in the second half of the first verse ("You make me feel so good") is a haunting call of love.

Marie Dixon feels that this is one of the songs that Dixon wrote particularly for her:

> I felt that was more close to me that he wrote is "You Need Love." If you listen to those words, I feel that. "You're frettin', I'm pettin', you need love" . . . that would be more soothing to me, more fitting to me that he wrote. And he had a way of speaking to you through his songs. And I feel that that may have been the one. I've always said that that was the one he sort of built the story around me.[26]

"You Need Love" was later recorded by Led Zeppelin as "Whole Lotta Love" (1969).[27] In 1985 Dixon filed a lawsuit, because his name was not credited as a composer, which means that he did not get a copyright share. Shirli Dixon, who brought this matter to her father's attention, says,

> I ultimately learned . . . about the "Whole Lotta Love," because I was typing those songs, and he taught me to write music. So I immediately could recognize one of his songs. He taught me the lyric structure and he taught me the music. So, you know, it became obvious to me after a while I listened and listened.
>
> I was at girlfriend's house, and the song came on the radio. And I said, "You know what? That's my dad's song." And she says, "The song is probably as old as you are (I was thirteen, then), and let's see I've got the album," she said, "If they've got your dad's name on it . . ." She said to me, "Well, they've got another song on here that your dad wrote, 'I Can't Quit You Baby,'" but that's ["Whole Lotta Love"] not his song. I said, "Oh, yes it is." And she said, "Have you ever heard him singing it?" I said, "No, I haven't, but he taught me how to write. And I see a similar pattern, either he wrote it or it's twained [sic], and that's why."[28]

Although "Whole Lotta Love" was one of the heavy rotation discs in radio stations, Dixon's action took place sixteen years after its release; that is even five years after Led Zeppelin disbanded in 1980. Shirli explains why:

> We didn't have a record player. We didn't have a radio, not in a car, not in a house. We had a television. He did not want to cross his writing style with any-one's. . . . Plus, my dad was very angry at the way the blues was being treated. He said, "Why would I help, support, and endorse these radio stations? They don't even play my songs, and they don't even have a format for blues music. So I'm not buying a radio." We got a brand new car, [with] no radio. Kids screamed and cried. My sisters and brothers were like "Please get a radio this time." And when he got one, we couldn't play it except for the news radio.[29]

She continues to discuss the issue of Led Zeppelin:

> Ultimately even when I borrowed my girlfriend's record . . . , and I talked to him about it, he said, "Oh, it's an oversight . . . these guys wouldn't do that." And he had me look into the files and check the royalty statements. He said, "I'll turn it over to this guy . . . to look into," who at that time never did any-thing . . . of this nature.
> And it took him about two years to actually bring the allegation. In his mind, these were his children. This was all part of his extended family. Every musician that he had ever worked with, touched or shared his blues with was a part of his extended family, and he could not accept that this was intentional. . . . He thought, "If I bring it to their attention, they will straighten it out." That's what he believed. He had a genuine sense of decency about them, al-though he didn't know them.
> I think what hurt him more was the fact that I had developed this relation-ship with young rock musicians. . . . I call them and go to see them, have them call him, put the two of them together. . . . And he thought of that as the generation for him sort of passing a torch not only to young rockers but young blues artists and others, anybody he worked with.[30]

Although it is a fact that Led Zeppelin lifted a Dixon composition, from the point of view of the history of the blues, this matter is not that simple. As seen in many blues compositions, including some of Dixon's compositions I discuss in this book—for example, "If the Sea Was Whiskey," "My Babe," "Walking the Blues," "Jump Sister Bessie," and "The Red Rooster" (which is discussed in the Howlin' Wolf section)—it was a traditional practice that a composer recycled words or melodies that had been created by another, even after copyrighting songs became enshrined into law.[31]

"You Need Love" (figure 7.1)—the origin of "Whole Lotta Love"—is not an exception. The vocal melody is traced back to Robert Petway's "Cat Fish Blues" (figure 7.4) (1941) by way of Muddy's "Rolling Stone" (figure 7.2) and "Still a Fool" (figure 7.3). The basic melody may be considered traditional (there is no evidence that Petway was the original composer), while the lyrics are most likely Dixon's original, as shown by the characteristic list of words in gerund form: *yearnin'*, *burnin'*, *cunnin'*, *frettin'*, *pettin'*, *gettin'*, *schoolin'*, and *coolin'*.[32]

Figure 7.1.

Figure 7.2.

Well now there's a two there's two tra - in run -

nin', well ain't not one, ho, going my wa - y.

Figure 7.3.

When I f - - - ind, a lot cat fish, ma - ma,

I say soon deep down in the blu-e se-a,

How little down now sweet ma-ma, say now, send out ho -

pe her from me, send out ho - pe her from me send out hope

Figure 7.4.

In 2004, Robert Plant discussed this allegation; the band members thought that they were following the traditional practice of blues songwriting:

We had an idea throughout the time in the band that we were in a part of some kind of flow that began either with chain gang music of Mississippi Parchman Farm, Dockery's Plantation, down on with the medicine shows of the 19th century, Joe Turner, you know, "C. C. Rider." The whole idea of the origin of these songs was quite translucent and almost eternal. And there were many times, throughout all musicians' lives, that you say "Okay, this piece of music, that's come from here, and it goes back to there, and it goes, it dodges right back through to the very earliest time." And our impression was that all this music was kind of translucent and moved on down through time. And with the power of Jimmy Page's guitar riff, and the actual "Wanna whole lotta love" vocal line, which became the chorus, and the psychedelic centerpiece, the melody was the lift, my responsibility, but it was only a part of the entire effect. . . . I just thought it was a part of the game. I know that might sound naïve and irresponsible.[33]

In 1987, two years after Dixon filed a lawsuit, both parties agreed to an out-of-court settlement. Dixon is now credited as the writer, while the creative contributions of the Led Zeppelin members are also acknowledged—that is, "Whole Lotta Love" by Page, Plant, Jones, Bonham, and Dixon.

Around the end of the 1950s, Chess Records started to make Muddy Waters' albums: *Sings Big Bill Broonzy* (1959) and *At Newport 1960*. Another album, *Folk Singer* (1963), was an attempt to attract folk music fans. Dixon offered "My Captain" for this album.

For the recording session, instead of playing with the regular electric band, Muddy returned to his early performing style, "unplugged." The musicians are Muddy and Buddy Guy on acoustic guitars, Dixon on bass, and Clifton James on drums—the instrumentation for "My Captain" is just two guitars.

"My Captain" is a twelve-bar/a-a-b blues, and it describes the harsh working situation on a plantation:

[Verse 1]
Oh captain, captain, hmm, ooo, my captain so mean,
Oh captain, captain, hmm, ooo, my captain so mean,
Ah, ain't feed me nothing, oh yeah, but soya bean.[34]

[Verse 2]
Oh the cook's alright, oh yeah, but the captain so mean,
Hey, the cook's alright, oh yeah, but the captain so mean, I mean so mean,
Ah, don't let me drive nothing, but just a old beat up wagon team.

[Verse 3]
Yey, I worked all night, oh yeah boys, and I worked all day, ah, um, so sad, so sad,
Yey, I worked all night, oh yeah boys, and I worked all day,
Ah, I couldn't find my mule, oh yeah, fella'd show nowhere.

[Guitar solo]

[Verse 4]
Yey, my wheel mule is crippled, hum, you know, my lead mule is blind,
Yey, my wheel mule is crippled, hum, yes boys, my lead mule is blind,
Now I ain't gonna buy my baby no more stockings, oh yeah boys, soon [seem?]
    behind, mmm.

[Tag]
Seem behind,
Hum, people seem behind.

As a professional songwriter, Dixon fulfilled the requirement for the album concept. He chose an appropriate song subject and imagery that many white audiences assumed was likely to be sung in typical old-time country blues songs.

Muddy's vocal consists of reciting the words melodically more than actually singing them. He freely extends phrases with moans, hums, and repetitions of words rather than following the fixed twelve-bar form, and Buddy Guy skillfully adds another guitar part that responses to Muddy's voice.

Muddy returned to perform with his electric band for the April 9, 1964, session. Dixon played bass, but this was his last participation as a sideman for Muddy's recordings. For this session, Muddy recorded two didactic songs: his own "You Can't Lose What You Ain't Never Had" and Dixon's "The Same Thing." Dixon utilized a popular fashion of the time and connected the philosophical theme: the fundamental cause for any kind of conflict.

[Verse 1]
Why do men go crazy when a woman wear her dress so tight?
Why do men go crazy when a woman wear her dress so tight?
Must be the same old things that makes a tomcat fight all night.

[Verse 2]
Why do all these men try to run a big legged women down?
Why do all these men try to run a big legged women down?
Must be the same old thing that makes a bulldog hug a hound.

[Vamp]
Oh that same old thing,
Oh that same old thing,
Tell me who is to blame,
The whole world fightin' about the same thing.

[Verse 3]
What make you feel so good when your baby get her evening gown?
What make you feel so good when your baby get her evening gown?
Must be the same old thing that made a preacher lay his Bible down.

[Tag]
Oh that same thing. . . .

Muddy is cast as a preacher again. Dixon's succinct wording for this allegory tells us one of "the facts of life." He explains: "Life, love, peace, happiness, everybody's fighting about 'The Same Thing.' Most of the time when you see animals fighting it's over some sex or love affair. When you see people fighting they are usually fighting because of greed or evil."[35]

The music is in a slow-medium tempo. The lyrical structure in the verse is an a-a-b form, in a question-and-answer format. Here Dixon slightly deviates from the traditional twelve-bar blues form. The first two lines are on a tonic chord, and the chord shift occurs from the third line described as V-IV-I.

The arrangement is restrained but powerful. Muddy's slide guitar introduction has a startling effect. He creates a controlled vocal performance, and when he sings the third line of the verse (answer), in a sultry way he expresses the disappointment at human nature. Otis Spann's piano phrases complementing Muddy's vocal create an atmosphere similar to the response of a congregation to a preacher. Dixon, drummer S. P. Leary, and support guitarist James "Peewee" Madison play very simply. The overall performance is one of Muddy's best in this period.

Muddy's second session in 1964 was held in October, and he recorded Dixon's "My John the Conqueror Root." This is an awkward reworking of "Hoochie Coochie Man" and "Back Door Man" for Howlin' Wolf.

After the October 1964 session, Muddy did not record a Dixon composition until 1967, when he had a session for the album *They Call Me Muddy Waters*.[36] One of the tracks is Dixon's up-tempo number "When the Eagle Flies." The song is about payday, which is loosely associated with T-Bone Walker's "Call It Stormy Monday." For the hook, Dixon humorously makes a parody out of a gospel song cliché—"let the [Your] light [shine] on me"—and he connects it to one of the most mundane matters.

In 1969, Muddy Waters recorded "I Am the Blues" for his album *After the Rain*, which was the second attempt of his controversial psychedelic album, *Electric Mud* (1968).[37] This is the last Willie Dixon composition that Muddy recorded (Dixon was not involved in the album production itself).

This song is one of the few Dixon compositions with political content. Dixon gives the word *blues* various meanings, but the song shows that one of them is the historical ill-treatment of African Americans:

> [Hook]
> I am, I am the blues,
> I am, oh, I am the blues,
> And all the world know I've been mistreated,
> And the whole world know I've been misused.
>
> [Verse 1]
> I am the moans of suffering womens,
> I am the groan of dying mens,

I am the last one to start,
But I'm the first one to begin [supposedly "end"].

[Hook repeated]

[Verse 2]
Ah, I am the beacon of peoples,
Who play and die,
I am the last one who's hired,
I am the first one fired.

[Hook repeated]

[Guitar solo]

[Verse 3]
I am a man of generation,
Of poverty of starvation,
I am the underdog, friends,
Yes, of the United Nations.

[Hook repeated]

[Tag]
I am,
Oh, friends, I am the blues,
I am, friends, friends, I am the blues,
Yeah, the world know I've been mistreated, boys,
The whole round world know that I've been misused.

The song is in a medium-slow tempo. In the hook, Muddy's moaning vocal melody is built on a simple five-note riff played by an electric guitar with a distortion effect. This riff sounds like Dixon's idea for his characteristic writing style with a short repetitive phrase (see figure 7.5).

The accompaniment for the verse is almost exclusively made out of root notes without noisy gimmicks. The reciting vocal imitates that of a preacher expressing anger. Although the production of *After the Rain* sounds still somewhat overproduced, the amalgamation of the old and new in Dixon's composition is well presented in a modern rock sound with traditional songwriting.

"I Am the Blues" is the unhappiest Dixon composition in the sense that it never earned proper appreciation, only because it was included in Muddy's psychedelic record. Along with album *After the Rain*, this song is rarely heard.[38] However, it still speaks to listeners, and it certainly captures the time when it was made.

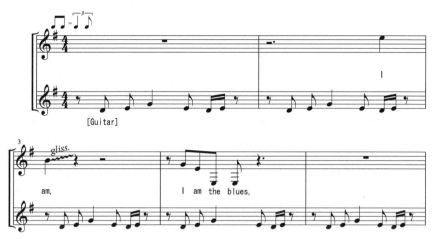

Figure 7.5.

From "Hoochie Coochie Man" to "I Am the Blues," Dixon's compositions for Muddy were created with a coherent thought. Dixon almost always cast Muddy as a sexy womanizer with a boastful attitude, a powerful outlaw with the ability of conjurer and trickster, and a preacher in the secular context. All of these elements were rolled into one and formed Muddy's characteristic public image, and Dixon's compositions serve as the background that makes Muddy sound good.

The relationship between Muddy and Dixon once became strained because of the trouble over Dixon's share as a songwriter, especially when rock artists covered a significant number of Dixon-Muddy songs.[39] Besides this problem, they generally had a good friendship even after Chess Records folded, and they belonged to the same management, which Muddy introduced to Dixon. According to Butch Dixon, they hung out together quite often. Butch stresses how important his father's songs were for Muddy:

> My dad liked Muddy a lot. He talked with Muddy quite a bit. He toured with Muddy quite a bit. . . . He and Muddy were great friends. They could sit down anytime. When the Stones were coming to town, he and Muddy would always hang out with the Stones, because the Stones were influenced by Muddy's singing, but they were more influenced by my dad's writing. So no matter how good Muddy was as a singer, the words wouldn't have been made.[40]

Little Walter

As discussed in chapter 5, Dixon's idea of Little Walter's performing persona was as a healthy young person who could be the most favorable boyfriend. In the songs that Dixon offered to Walter from 1959 to 1963, Dixon initially followed this idea, but later he changed it from simply a nice guy to a dirty old man and a person with cynicism.

On February 2, 1959, soon after Dixon returned to Chess Records, he regained the composer-singer relationship with Walter by presenting "My Baby Is Sweeter" and "Crazy Mixed Up World." As the title indicates, "My Baby Is Sweeter" is clearly a derivative of "My Babe" and "Crazy for My Baby" in 1955. This is an odd recording. Walter, who does not understand the structure, picks up his solo before the music has a perfect cadence. According to Freddie Robinson (the guitarist of Walter's band), Dixon pushed his musical idea onto the musicians, although Walter and his band had already worked on the arrangement based on Little Willie John's "Country Girl."[41]

"Crazy Mixed Up World" has better integrity. The words and the vigorous beat fit a young audience's musical taste, though Walter was too old to call himself a "kid" at this point—he was twenty-eight then:

[Verse 1]
Well I'm a crazy mixed up kid,
And I love to dance like this,
Well I love to rock 'n' roll,
Because it satisfy my soul,
Well I love to jump and shout,
Hey, it really knock me out,
You give me music with a beat,
It'll knock me off my feet,
I don't care what you heard,
This is a crazy mixed up world.

[Hook]
Crazy mixed up world,
Crazy mixed up world,
Crazy mixed up world,
I'm in a crazy mixed up world.

[Harmonica solo]

[Verse 2]
When I loosen up down inside,
Feets begin to glide,
My heart go pump, pump, pump,
The music make me jump, jump, jump,
I can't control myself no more,
The music got me on the floor,

Well I'm crazy, ain't you heard,
I'm in a crazy mixed up world.

[Hook repeated]

For the second verse "My heart go pump, pump, pump, / The music make me jump, jump, jump," Dixon recycled a portion of their early collaboration "Mellow Down Easy"—"You jump, jump, here, / you jump, jump there."

Walter's solo part sounds weak because of non-amplification and reduced space for soloing. Previously Walter usually had two rounds of solo (even when he accompanied Muddy); in this song, his solo is only one chorus.

Walter's biographers write of his vocal quality, "There's a touch of bitterness in his voice,"[42] and they found irony in the line "I'm in a crazy mixed up world."[43] By this time, Walter had become an alcoholic, and he had a gun accident. The bitter quality in his voice is not just "a touch." Compared with "My Babe," for example, there is clearly no gloss in his voice.

Walter's persona in "I Don't Play" and "As Long As I Have You" (this is another odd recording that shows he was unsure about the structure), recorded in December 1960, is also created on the basis of the "one-woman guy." In "I Don't Play," however, he is described not as a kid but as an adult as the third verse shows. The song is a confession from him to his young girlfriend.

[Verse 1]
Better listen to me, hear what I say,
Don't you hurt my hand, baby squeeze it this way,
Baby, I don't play, 'cause I'll be your man one day.

[Verse 2]
Don't you be no fool, try to stay in school,
When you play with me, I may forget those rules,
Baby, I don't play, I'll be your man one day.

[Harmonica solo 1]

[Verse 3]
Baby, you're so young, and I'm too old,
I know this can't be love, what'll be my goal,
Baby, I don't play, 'cause I'll be your man one day.

[Harmonica solo 2]

[Verse 4]
Hate to see you like this, baby you're so fine,
A pretty girl like you, make me change my mind,
Baby, I don't play, 'cause I'll be your man one day.

The song is in a twelve-bar form with a quatrain refrain lyric structure. According to Walter's biographers, the arrangement of this song, which was a mixture of a Latin beat and hard-driving eight-beat pattern, derived from Roscoe Gordon's "Just a Little Bit."[44] Walter's voice sounds husky, which suits a new element of his persona: adulthood. His harmonica solo and his vocal sound very confident.

Little Walter did not have any recording sessions in 1961 and 1962. He returned to the studio on February 5, 1963. For this session, he recorded two Dixon compositions: "I'm a Business Man" and "Dead Presidents."[45] These two songs represent a turning point in developing Walter's persona.

The most striking characteristic of "I'm a Business Man" is its suggestive lyrics. Walter is no longer a healthy "one-woman guy":

> [Hook]
> I'm a business man,
> I'm a business man,
> I'm a business man,
> I'm a business man,
> I love good business, baby, I give you all I can.
>
> [Verse 1]
> If your business is bad and you need a lift,
> Catch me early in the morning on my midnight shift.
>
> [Hook]
> I'm a business man,
> I'm a business man,
> 'Cause I love good business, baby, I give you all I can.
>
> [Verse 2]
> It ain't never too early, it ain't never too late,
> To come to me, mama, get your business straight,
>
> [Hook repeated]
>
> [Harmonica solo]
>
> [Verse 3]
> I don't need no sign, baby, hanging on my door,
> If you needs good business, just let me know.
>
> [Hook]
>
> [Ending solo]

APPLICATION BLANK
American Federation of Musicians
Local No #208

I, the undersigned, desire to become a member of **MUSICIAN'S PROTECTIVE UNION LOCAL 208**

under Article................of the Constitution and By-Laws, and I do hereby promise and agree that if elected to membership I will faithfully and at all times support, conform to and be bound by the Constitution, By-Laws, Rules, Regulations, Resolutions and Price List of said **MUSICIAN'S PROTECTIVE UNION LOCAL 208**
................, and of the American Federation of Musicians, as the same now exist and as they may be added to, altered, amended or repealed, at any time during which I may in future be a member, and I furthermore agree to forfeit my membership in this Local if it shall be proven that I have answered untruthfully any question contained in this application, and furthermore agree to forfeit all fees paid to the Local or American Federation of Musicians, as the case may be.

1. Name?.... **Willie Dixon**
   (Professional Name)
2. When and where born?.... **July 1st, 1915**
   .... **Vicksburg Miss**
3. Where do you reside?.... **Chicago Ill**
4. How long have you resided there?.... **8 yrs**
5. Where did you reside before entering this jurisdiction?....
   .... **Vicksburg Miss**
6. Why did you fail to apply for membership there?....
   .... **not playing music**
7. What instrument or instruments do you play?.... **Bass**
8. Are you a citizen of the United States?.... **yes**
   (Citizens of Dominion of Canada will so state)
   Final papers issued:
   When?.... ✱✱✱ Where?.... ✱✱✱ Number?.... ✱✱✱
9. If "No" to Question No. 8, have you legally declared yourself to become a citizen of the United States?.... ✱✱✱ First papers issued:
   When?.... ✱✱✱ Where?.... ✱✱✱ Number?.... ✱✱✱
10. Are you at present a member of any Musicians' Protective Organization in the United States or Canada?.... **no**
11. Name it?.... ✱✱✱
12. Have you ever been a member of any Musicians' Protective Organization in the United States or Canada, and if so, name it?....
    .... **yes**
13. Have you ever made application for and been refused membership by a Local of the American Federation of Musicians, and if so, for what cause?.... **no**
14. Have you ever been suspended, erased or expelled from a Musicians' Protective Organization in the United States or Canada?.... **yes**
15. When and where?.... **Local 208   1942**

This application for Local membership will not be accepted from any prospective member until a complete answer on said blank has been made to No. 8 and/or No. 9 (this relating to citizenship status in the United States or Canada).

16. For what cause?.... **non-payment of dues**
17. Have you ever rendered service at a place or with an organization on the National Unfair List?.... **no**
18. If so, where and with whom?.... ✱✱✱
19. Have you ever rendered service at a place on the Forbidden Territory List of the American Federation of Musicians?.... **no**
20. If so, where?.... ✱✱✱
21. Do you work at any other trade or vocation?.... **no**
22. If so, name it?.... ✱✱✱
23. Is there a Union of that trade or vocation in this jurisdiction?.... ✱✱✱
24. Are you a member of the Union of that trade or vocation in this jurisdiction?.... ✱✱✱
25. Have you ever been suspended, erased or expelled from any Union affiliated with the American Federation of Labor or any other Labor Union?.... **yes**
26. If so, for what cause?.... **non-payment of dues**
27. Have you been imported into this country by an agent, musical director, or employer?.... **no**
28. Have you played any professional engagements during the time you were not a member of the Federation, and if so, where and with whom?.... **no**
29. Have you been persuaded to come here under promise of engagements? If so, state who made such promises, and the conditions under which you were induced to come here?.... **no**

30. Signature.... *Willie Dixon*
    Social Security Number.... **321-05-1771**
    Residence.... **4837 Prairie Ave**
    Telephone Number.... **Liv 3518**
    Recommended by.... *Wm Dover*

BOND

The undersigned does hereby pledge himself as Surety for................
a minor, until he has reached his majority, who promises to faithfully support the Constitution, By-Laws and Price List of the
.... and the provisions as enumerated in the above application, and that in case of any violation of the same, the undersigned will be responsible for all such charges brought, or fines imposed against said person.

(Signed)................, Surety

This application was made on.... **AUG 3 1 1944**
Signed by.... *Wm Everett Samuel*
Secretary, Local No #208 of CHICAGO, ILL.

44 Printed in U. S. A.

(left margin, handwritten, rotated): AUG 31 1944 RECORDED M.B. in full ... join fee of 50. = in full of

Dixon's Musicians' Union application form. This reapplication was a result of his suspended membership. *Courtesy of Blues Archive of Chicago Public Library.*

Musician's union dues card from May 31, 1941. Around this time Dixon was a member of the Five Breezes. *Courtesy of Blues Archive of Chicago Public Library.*

Dixon with unknown guitarist, circa late 1940s or early 1950s.
Photographer unknown; courtesy of Mary Katherine Aldin.

Dixon at the American Folk Blues Festival in France, circa mid-1960s. *Photographer unknown; courtesy of Mary Katherine Aldin.*

Dixon at the recording session for the *Folk Singer* album by Muddy Waters in September 1963. Guitarist is Buddy Guy. *Photo by Don Bronstein. Collection from Jim O'Neal, BluEsoterica Archives.*

TAIL DRAGGER

(1)

When the mighty Wolf
Make a midnight Creep
The Hunters they Can't find him
Stealing Chicks everywhere he go
Dragging his tail behind him

2
He a Tail dragger
Wiping out his tracks
Its the Cute little Chicks — (The Innersonlonly)
The Big Bad Wolf do like

(3)

When little Bo Peep
had lost his sheep
No Body els Could find them
The Big Bad Wolf had ran them down
Dragging his tail behind them

Im a tail Dragger
"   "   "   "
"   "   "   "
I wipe out my tracks

Original handwritten lyric sheet of "Tail Dragger." The recording of this song by Howlin' Wolf shows that Dixon reworked words and changed the order of verses. Details are found in the Howlin' Wolf section of chapter 7. *Courtesy of Willie Dixon's Blues Heaven Foundation.*

Handwritten lyric sheet for "You Need to Be Loved." The discussion about "You Need Love" is found in the Muddy Waters section of chapter 7. *Courtesy of Willie Dixon's Blues Heaven Foundation.*

Chess Records publicity photo of Dixon and Koko Taylor, circa 1964–1965. *Photographer unknown; courtesy of Mary Katherine Aldin.*

Dixon at a Toronto studio for the 1966 CBC-TV "Festival" series. *Courtesy of Mary Katherine Aldin.*

Dixon at the photo session for the album *I Am the Blues* (Columbia Records) in the summer of 1969. *Photo by Peter Amft.*

With Chicago Allstars (Johnny Shines, guitar; Big Walter Horton, harmonica) at Grant Park Blu
Festival, 1969. *Photo by Amy van Singel; courtesy of Jim O'Neal.*

Dixon in the control room of Ter-Mar Studio in 1971 for Koko Taylor's album *Basic Soul*. The engineer is Gary Star. *Photo by Amy van Singel; courtesy of Jim O'Neal.*

Dixon at Steve Wisner's session at Dixon's studio, March 29, 1975. Dixon voluntarily helped with the production and is shown here arguing with musicians. *Photo by Jim O'Neal.*

Flyer of concert at the Jubilee Auditorium in Sherwood Park, Alberta, Canada, circa early 1970s. *Courtesy of Mary Katherine Aldin.*

Dixon with Shirli Dixon and Mick Jagger, Chicago July 9, 1978. *Photo by D. Shigley; courtesy of Scott Shigley.*

Dixon with Chicago Allstars (Freddie Dixon, bass; John Primer, guitar; Billy Branch, harmonica) i
Mexico City, 1979. *Photo by Jim O'Neal.*

Dixon in Mexico City, 1979. *Photo by Jim O'Neal.*

Dixon in Mexico City, 1979. *Photo by Jim O'Neal.*

Publicity photo from Rosebud Agency, circa early 1980s. *Courtesy of Mary Katherine Aldin.*

Dixon with James Cotton and Snooky Pryor at the Chicago Blues Festival, 1984. *Photo by Jim O'Nea*

Dr. John, Stevie Ray Vaughan, Irma Thomas, Willie Dixon, and John Mayall, 1988. *Photo by Mary Katherine Aldin.*

Dixon at home with his wife, Marie, 1987. *Photo by Mary Katherine Aldin.*

Dixon with his grandson Keith, 1989. *Photo by Mary Katherine Aldin.*

Dixon on Mary Katherine Aldin's radio show with Champion Jack Dupree, circa 1990–1991. *Photo by Mary Katherine Aldin.*

Dixon with B. B. King and John Lee Hooker, 1991. *Photo by Mary Katherine Aldin.*

Labels for several Dixon records. *"Crazy for My Baby"* and *"AIDS to the Grave"* record photos by the author; *"29 Ways," "Signifying Monkey,"* and *"Walking the Blues"* record photos by Jim O'Neal.

Poster used for Dixon's funeral procession, January 1992. *Courtesy of Blues Archive of Chicago Public Library.*

The music is in a walking-bass pattern in a medium tempo, which sounds a bit lazy. The opening hook (repetitions of a phrase "I'm a business man") has sixteen measures, which shows Dixon's simplified writing style in this period.

Little Walter's voice lacks the youthful energy that he used to have. According to his biographers, Walter sounds like his label mate, Sonny Boy Williamson.[46] The lack of enthusiasm in his voice makes the song sound like an expression of a dirty old man, which indeed overlaps Sonny Boy's image.

In "Dead Presidents," Dixon casts Walter in the role of a sarcastic observer of the real world, where everybody is obsessed with money. As for the inspiration for this song, Dixon says, "'Dead Presidents' was done during the time they had that payola thing going [in the music industry]."[47] Listing various types of currency, he explains how each one works:

[Hook]
Them dead president[s],
Them dead presidents,
Well, I ain't broke but I'm bad bent,
Everybody loves them dead president[s].

[Verse 1]
A little bit of Lincoln can't park the car,
Washington, he can't go too far,
Jefferson is good, he played the track,
If you think you're gonna bring some big bet back.

[Hook repeated]

[Verse 2]
Hamilton on a ten can get you straight,
But Jackson on a twenty is really great,
And if you're talkin' about a poor man's friend,
Grant will get you out of whatever you're in.

[Hook repeated]

[Harmonica solo]

[Verse 3]
A hundred dollar Franklin is really sweet,
Five hundred McKinley is the one for me,
If I get a Cleveland, I'm really set,
A thousand dollar Cleveland is hard to get.

[Hook repeated]

[Ending solo]

The arrangement style is unusual for Walter's recordings. Many instruments were brought in: a baritone sax, acoustic piano, electric organ, electric guitar, electric bass, and drums, as well as Walter's harmonica (again non-amplified) and vocal. The musicians seem to have worked on a tight arrangement, as heard in the call and response by his voice and an organ with a saxophone and a car-horn-like stop-time in the hook.

Walter's parts sound overdubbed. This might have been due to his successive low-quality recordings and difficulty in remembering Dixon's lengthy lyrics. Walter's rough and bitter vocal quality contributes to expressing the sarcastic contents of the lyrics. His harmonica solo is strong and succinctly organized.

After "I'm a Business Man" and "Dead Presidents," Little Walter did not have a recording session until February 1966, which became his last session as a leader. No recordings from this session were issued in his lifetime (Dixon compositions were not recorded for his last session).

The chronological study of Dixon-Walter collaboration shows that Dixon's strategy for creating Walter's image was coherently conceived. But just as Muddy's persona changed slightly as he got older, Walter's age was at least one of the factors behind the transformation of his persona; that is, youth could no longer be a part of his image. The Dixon songs for the grown-up Walter were now based on a sort of dirty old man. This was a drastic change. More importantly, Walter is given a new role as a social critic with the last Dixon song for him, "Dead Presidents." Even though this is a new performing persona for Walter, he is still cast as a blues preacher communicating the facts of life.

Howlin' Wolf

Providing songs for Howlin' Wolf was the most important project for Willie Dixon in the early 1960s. Wolf recorded an impressive total of seventeen Dixon songs from 1959 to 1963. Some of these songs not only became Wolf's representative recordings but also are at the heart of Dixon's song catalogue as well as Chicago blues classics. Of equal importance, these compositions helped Wolf intensify his performing persona.

Howlin' Wolf's performing persona is more complex than that of Muddy Waters. Some of the Dixon songs for Wolf, such as "Back Door Man" and "Tail Dragger," portray him as a more directly dangerous guy than Muddy, but at the same time these songs show that Wolf is a tragic and humorous character as well. A certain sadness that is expressed in his early recordings, such as "Moanin' at Midnight" and "Smokestack Lightnin'," is an extension of his ferocious side. On the other hand, his feral aspect can be developed into a facetious character, as heard in "Rockin' Daddy." In this song Wolf plays the role of a sexy lover.

Such a complex performing persona is hinted in his stage name and trademark action. As Wolf himself once said, his grandfather nicknamed him "Wolf" after the wolf character of the Little Red Riding Hood tale. It happened when he was three years old, because he was always in devilment.[48] And his trademark wolf imitation in his performance came from what he had learned from Jimmie Rodgers, the Singing Brakeman.[49] While this wolf character has a brutal nature, he can be a kind man. He also has a comical aspect. At the same time, his humorous nature is inseparable from his tragic side. Furthermore, this tale has a didactic purpose; his tragic ending is a consequence of his audacious behavior. Dixon's compositions for Wolf always fit somewhere in these characteristics implied by his stage name and performing style.

There are important similarities between Dixon's compositions for Muddy and Wolf beyond their differences. As the character Hoochie Coochie Man developed from the elements of postbellum badman heroes of African American balladry, Wolf's persona that is realized in Dixon songs also grew out of the same badman matrix. For instance, similar to Muddy's role in "Hoochie Coochie Man," Wolf is cast as a conjurer—an important component of badman heroes—in "Evil," the first Dixon song Wolf recorded. A role Wolf plays in other Dixon compositions, "Back Door Man" and "Tail Dragger," fits Roger D. Abraham's characterization of the badman: "a perpetual adolescent" filled with "arrogance and disdain"; "the eternal man in revolt"; and "the epitome of virility of manliness on display."[50] Of equal importance, the Dixon songs that explore Wolf's boastful and menacing attitude work like "Hoochie Coochie Man"; that is, bragging about oneself psychologically functions as an autosuggestion that inspires the one doing the boasting with a heightened spirit. In addition, Dixon casts at least one side of Wolf's persona in the role of a blues preacher by providing didactic songs. Therefore, Dixon's casting of Muddy and Wolf is ultimately the same type of blues performer.

Born Chester Arthur Burnett on June 10, 1910, in White Station, Mississippi, Howlin' Wolf grew up in the midst of the Delta blues culture. While helping to farm, he met one of his idols, Charley Patton. Patton's low, cracking vocal style and his clownlike performing style were certainly passed on to Wolf.

In 1933, the Burnett family moved to Arkansas, where Wolf met another of his main influences, Sonny Boy Williamson (Rice Miller), who was married for a while to Wolf's sister. Sonny Boy taught Wolf harmonica, and they occasionally teamed up for street performances. Other musicians who Wolf played with during his early semiprofessional period include Robert Johnson, Son House, and Willie Brown. Wolf also met his future band members, guitarists Willie Lee Johnson and Hubert Sumlin, around this time.

As soon as Wolf was discharged from military service (1941–1943), he focused on public performance. In 1948, he formed his band, the House Rockers, and started a radio show on KWEM in West Memphis, Arkansas. His show caught the attention of Sam Phillips, the owner of Memphis Recording Service. In 1951, Wolf made a recording contract with Phillips. He leased some of Wolf's masters to Chess Records and others to RPM Records. In 1952, Chess bought Wolf's exclusive contract. Subsequently, Wolf moved his base to Chicago.

Howlin' Wolf is known for his powerful one-of-a-kind performing style, which saxophonist Eddie Shaw, who has played with both Muddy and Wolf, describes thus: "Muddy never had the energy Wolf had, not even at his peak. Muddy would rock the house pretty good, but Wolf was the most exciting blues player I've ever seen."[51] Sam Phillips once said of his impression of Wolf, "When I heard him, I said, 'This is for me. This is where the soul of man never dies.'"[52] With his low, loud, and thick voice given off from a huge body—reportedly he was six feet three inches tall and weighed 270 pounds—Wolf howled, moaned, growled, and shouted. He liked to wear overalls rather than a tuxedo onstage, which contrasted with Muddy's sharp outfits. He spent a good part of his show walking around, crawling around, and rolling on the stage.[53] He had a chilling smile and often rolled his eyes while he was playing. Sometimes he even licked his guitar neck.

Shirli Dixon remembers Wolf personally and as an artist. She finds a similarity between him and today's rappers. She also says what impressed her father was Wolf's voice:

Howlin' Wolf was a very strong character, kind of a bad boy of blues. . . . He would be a rap artist today. I know him as a performer, and I know him as an individual. He was a very gentle, kind man on a personal basis, but because he was such a large . . . figure, most people were somewhat intimidated by him. Then it coupled with this huge voice that comes from a tradition of blues music. . . .

My dad happened to think that he had one of the most original sounding voices as related to blues music, and more so of the raw, rough, field style of vocal style, as opposed to Muddy, who was more of a singer. Wolf would be what you would call a very raw talent. But if you listen lyrically, you hear a lot of soul in his voice, very natural soul sound that comes from this real rough, strong, bass voice.[54]

Howlin' Wolf had his first Chess session in March 1954, for which Dixon played bass. For his next session on May 25, he recorded Dixon's "Evil."

> [Verse 1]
> If you're a long way from home, can't sleep at night,
> Grab your telephone, something just ain't right.
>
> [Hook]
> That's evil, evil is goin' on wrong,
> I am warnin' ya, brother, you better watch your happy home.
>
> [Verse 2]
> Well, a long way from home and can't sleep at all,
> You know another mule is kickin' in your stall.
>
> [Hook repeated]
>
> [Harmonica solo]
>
> [Verse 3]
> Well, if ya call her on the telephone, and she answered awful slow,
> Grab the first thing smokin', if you have to hobo.
>
> [Hook repeated]
>
> [Harmonica/piano solo]
>
> [Verse 4]
> If you made it to your house, knock on the front door,
> Run 'round to the back, you'll catch him, just before he go.
>
> [Hook repeated]

In this song Dixon required Wolf to alternate two voices. The voice for the first two lines of the verse is less throaty, which is unusual for Wolf. The voice for the hook is thicker and more confident. The former is a narrator who explains bad signs, and the latter is the conjurer who foresees the infidelity and gives a warning. Dixon says that Wolf's voice fit this song of the conjurer: "This song worked for Howlin' Wolf because of his type of voice and the way he pronounced words. There's a particular song for every voice. You just have to get out of the voice what's in it."[55]

The arrangement derived from Dixon's compositions for Muddy. Similar to "Hoochie Coochie Man," this song has a one-measure introduction with a stop-time rhythm followed by a verse, in which this rhythmic configuration on the tonic chord is carried on until the beginning of the hook. The form is basically a twelve-bar blues, but as usual for Dixon, the lyrics follow a quatrain refrain form.

Billboard gave "Evil" a positive sales report: "Gathering momentum slowly in the Middle Western and Southern territories, where he has always had a good following, Howling Wolf stands a good chance to break out into a national market on this one."[56]

After "Evil" of 1954, Wolf did not record any Dixon compositions until his return from Cobra in 1959. This was quite unusual for the composer-singer partnerships of Dixon and Chess artists; it was more so because Wolf was one of the top blues artists of the label. This interruption occurred primarily because of the antagonistic relationship between them. Dixon remembers,

> Most of the guys tried to cooperate in the recording studio because they wanted to record but Howlin' Wolf was pretty rough to deal with. It required a lot of diplomacy working with him. He always felt everything was going the wrong direction and he'd try all kinds of angles. His band knew he was a rugged customer.[57]

Shirli Dixon gives more details:

> Wolf became a problem when Muddy became successful with a lot of those Willie Dixon songs. . . . My dad and Wolf in particular had very adverse ideas. Wolf had limited amount of musical understanding in terms of structure, while he had the most soulful blues voice that has existed. . . . And he was also challenged with formal education. And he was a person that sometimes indulged with alcohol. My dad did not. And that brought up a number of complications. . . . And Wolf was a very large man, and he was accustomed to being very forceful with musicians. And my dad was accustomed to "no one disrespect him in that way"—sort of like his father. And so they exchanged this difficulty.[58]

Dixon talks about one of his difficult experiences with Wolf: "Sometimes you'd sing a song with that guy [Wolf], man—that's what I think messed up my voice. I had a good voice for a while there, but singin' songs to him over and over again, until we finally got a tape recorder."[59]

Another possible reason for their discontinued partnership was that at least up to the end of the 1950s, Dixon did not know how to compose songs that fit Wolf. Shirli Dixon says that her father did not comprehend the meaning of "Smokestack Lightnin'," one of the most representative songs that Wolf recorded in 1956 (Dixon played bass for this recording):

> I remember my dad bringing home a song, "Smokestack Lightnin'." In the middle of the night with a pizza, I should have been in bed, but of course he got me up and my brothers and sisters. What he wanted us to do was to listen to this song . . . probably at one in the morning. . . . And he asked, "What do you guys think of this song? Tell me what it means." We could make no sense of it. I had never seen a smokestack on a train going to the moonlight. So I wouldn't have a clue, and I didn't. But I liked the musical role. But he didn't. He kept saying, "I don't get it. I don't get it."[60]

This episode happened sometime in the late 1960s or later, because Shirli Dixon was born in 1963. Thus, this song remained mysterious to Willie Dixon for more than a decade. Actually "Smokestack Lightnin'" is a surreal song, especially compared to Dixon's songs with clear stories. The song is built around images of a train and a crying man, and it is somewhat similar to field hollers in which some unrelated images are juxtaposed.

As discussed earlier, Dixon offered songs that could be compared to a musical and/or a lyrical essence gleaned from the artist's previous recordings. The episode remembered by Shirli implies that it took Dixon some time to learn how to develop appropriate songs for Wolf's character.

After Dixon returned to Chess Records, he and Wolf resumed their partnership. According to Dixon, Leonard Chess persuaded Wolf to do so.[61] He agreed grudgingly, saying, "I can do my own songs better, but you see, they won't let me. They'll let Dixon give me songs to do, that's to keep me out of being the writer."[62]

When Dixon proceeded with the collaboration with Wolf, he came up with some practical and diplomatic strategies. First, Dixon gave Wolf concise songs to learn: for example, a composition with one chord in which a hook and a verse alternate, or a composition with a twelve-bar/a-a-b form. On the other hand, a twenty-four-bar/A-A-B-A form was to be avoided for the most part, because this form required more words. "Wolf, you can't give him too many words, because he gets 'em all jumbled up. And if he gets 'em right, he still ain't gonna get the right meaning," explains Dixon. [63]

Setting new words to well-known melodies seemed to be another strategy that Dixon practiced for Wolf. This traditional blues compositional technique of "reworking" facilitated Wolf's learning of new songs.

In terms of diplomacy, when Dixon wanted to give songs to Howlin' Wolf, he intentionally told Wolf, "This is for Muddy." Dixon calls this strategy "backward psychology":

He [Howlin' Wolf] came in with his things and every once in a while he'd mention the fact, "Hey, man, you wrote that for Muddy. How come you won't write me one like that?" But when you write one for him he wouldn't like it. And then I got to the place, found out that all I could do was use backward psychology and tell him, "Now here's one I wrote for Muddy, man." "Yeah, man, let me hear it. Yeah, that's the one for me." And so, I'd just let him have it [laughter].[64]

Finally, although this might not have been Dixon's decision, it appears that Wolf was made to concentrate on singing without playing an instrument. The discography shows that from 1960 to 1963, the years in which Wolf intensively recorded Dixon songs, he rarely played instruments. Out of seven sessions during this time, he played the guitar or harmonica in only two sessions—in May and December 1961. Out of sixteen Dixon compositions, Wolf played the guitar (but not harmonica) for only two songs, "Down in the Bottom" and "The Red Rooster."[65]

In addition, in terms of the recording procedure, the introduction of a multitrack recording system allowed not only Wolf but also all the vocalists to record their vocal parts separately. Considering the efficacy of this modern technology, Dixon gave Wolf fairly long lyrics.

The reactivation of Dixon-Wolf collaboration took place for the July 1959 session. Dixon wrote the words of "Howlin' for My Darling" to the music that Wolf, his band, and producer Leonard Chess were putting together. The outtakes indicate that they were originally reworking Big Joe Williams' "Highway 49." However, they changed this plan; they made an instrumental track to which Wolf could overdub his vocal. It seems that Dixon was required to write new lyrics at this point.[66]

The finished take shows that Dixon tries to be concise. He combines his love song clichés, such as "makes the lights go out" and "makes me jump and shout" with the special word for the vocalist "howlin'." In addition, a good portion of the hook consists of vocables, Wolf's famous wolf imitation, "Hoo hoo hoo whoe." This record captures Wolf's humorous side.

For the next session in June 1960, Wolf recorded three Dixon songs: "Wang Dang Doodle," "Back Door Man," and "Spoonful." This is a very important session that shows how Dixon tried to realize Wolf's performing persona with two outlaw songs and one didactic song.

Dixon previously offered "Wang Dang Doodle" to Wolf, but he refused to record it. Dixon says, "The one Wolf hated most of all was 'Wang Dang Doodle.' He hated that. . . . He'd say, 'Man, that's too old-timey, sound like some old levee camp number.'"[67] In spite of his dislike, Wolf recorded a great rockin' version. His gruff vocal is just right to express an ominous feeling of an outlaws' underground party, and Hubert Sumlin's guitar creates an out-of-control atmosphere.

The words and the musical structure on one chord are basically the same as Dixon's own recording in 1954, while Wolf's version has an additional third verse:

> [Verse 3]
> Tell Fats and Washboard Sam,
> That everybody gon' jam,
> Tell Shaky and Boxcar Joe,
> We got sawdust on the floor,
> Tell Peg and Caroline Dye,
> We gonna have a heck of a time,
> When the fish scent fill the air,
> There be snuff juice everywhere,
> We gonna pitch a wang dang doodle all night long.

The next cut was "Back Door Man." The song is about stealing other men's wives and its consequences:

> [Hook]
> I am a back door man,
> I am a back door man,
> Well the men don't know, but the little girls understand.
>
> [Verse 1]
> When everybody's trying to sleep,
> I'm somewhere making my midnight creep,
> Every morning, the rooster crow,
> Something tell me, I got to go.
>
> [Hook repeated]
>
> [Verse 2]
> They take me to the doctor, shot full of holes,
> His nurse cried, please save the soul,

Killed him for murder, first degree,
Judge's wife cried, let the man go free.

[Hook repeated]

[Verse 3]
Stand out there, cop's wife cry, don't take him down,
Brother [supposedly Rather] be deads, six feets in the ground,
When you come home, you can eat pork and bean[s],
I eats mo' chicken any man seen.

[Hook/Tag]
I am [a] back door man,
I am [a] back door man. . .

While the theme of cuckolding is universal, the particular phrase *back door man* was a Southern expression. "When the front door man goes out the front door someone else could come in the back door. And this is the kind of a phrase they use in the South a lot of times. The back door man can get more out of the back than you can in the front," explains Dixon.[68]

Dixon amalgamates this expression *back door man* with the phrase *making a midnight creep*, a habit of wolves. Dixon casts Wolf as a spooky, roaming, and brutal figure.[69] Dixon certainly recognized that Wolf's performing style was a perfect medium to express the theme of the song: "Howlin' Wolf had the type of delivery that could express the concept real well—and then he knew exactly what I was talking about. That's why I think he put so much emphasis in it. He might have had some experience of that type."[70] In addition, this song fits Abraham's list of the characteristics of a black badman, as discussed previously.

Wolf's vocal performance is impeccable. He transforms himself into this ill-fated character. While "Back Door Man" reinforced Wolf's character, of equal importance, this song has two significant effects that emphasize wisdom for listeners, effects that are parallel with those of "Hoochie Coochie Man" for Muddy Waters. First, by hearing the singing of this powerful figure and his braggadocio, a listener can bring himself to a different psychological level. By doing so, he enables himself to conquer difficulties. On the other hand, this song can be a warning device that makes a listener think about his behavior.

The musical structure rests on one chord (E minor, but occasionally the seventh chord, D, appears in the vocal and guitar melodies) in which a hook and verses alternate. While this was Dixon's characteristic writing style, the riff consisting of an alternation of two pitches (G and E) derives from Wolf's songs "Moanin' at Midnight" and its variations, "I Asked for Water" and

"Smokestack Lightnin'." Around this riff, the band, including Dixon on bass, creates a beat that sounds like a wobbling march.

There is a choking feeling when a guitarist punctuates the vocal line "Well the men don't know, but the little girls understand" with a clashing sound in two pitches (B and D), which create a minor seventh chord with the bass line (E and G—see figure 7.6).

Figure 7.6.

The last cut in this session is "Spoonful." Wolf preaches a sermon, how a tiny amount of a thing will be significant for either good or bad:

> [Verse 1]
> It could be a spoonful of diamonds,
> Could be a spoonful of gold,
> Just a little spoon of your precious love satisfy my soul.
>
> [Hook]
> Men lies about a little, [the lead guitar finishes off the line]
> Some of 'em cries about a little,
> Some of 'em dies about a little,
> Everything fight about a spoonful,
> That spoon, that spoon, that spoon.
>
> [Verse 2]
> It could be a spoonful of coffee,
> Could be a spoonful of tea,

Put a little spoon of your precious love,
Good enough for me.

[Hook]
Men lies about that,
Some of 'em dies about that,
Some of 'em cries about that,
But everything fight about a spoonful,
That spoon, that spoon, that.

[Guitar solo]

[Verse 3]
It could be a spoonful of water,
Save from the desert sand,
Put a little spoon of lead from my forty-five,
Save you from another man.

[Hook]
Men lies about that,
Some of 'em cries about that,
Some of 'em dies about that,
Everybody fightin' about a spoonful,
That spoon, that spoon, that.

[Tag]
Woo, fightin' about a spoonful.

Dixon explains,

A "Spoonful" can be about a lot of different things, because it doesn't take a whole a lot of something for a person to enjoy it. The most important things in life come in small amounts. The most important things in life are the things you really don't see—a lot of those you just feel.[71]

Marie Dixon remembers what inspired her husband to write this song:

I remember that particular composition he wrote, and it was about how peoples killed over nothing, you know, ten cents or a dollar. . . . He was also a man who knew the Bible, because his mother instilled it in him and all her children. And he talked about in that particular song—he didn't put in the song—how the multitude of people were fed with five fish in the Bible. . . . This is how he got some of the ideas about "Spoonful."[72]

"Back Door Man" and "Spoonful" are musically related to each other. The characteristic two-note (E and G) thumping riff of "Spoonful" (figure 7.7) has an obvious resemblance to the spooky marchlike riff of "Back Door Man" (figure 7.8), and both songs use a one-chord structure in E minor. The riff of "Spoonful" is also linked to "Moanin' at Midnight," which is Wolf's signature song (figure 7.9).

"Spoonful" represents Dixon's characteristic writing style better than any other songs. This riff is as simple as it gets, but it is haunting, especially at the end of the hook, "That spoon, that spoon, that." On top of this succinct musical device, he sets the good wisdom.

The performance of Wolf and the band in "Spoonful" is noteworthy. Especially the timing of Hubert Sumlin's guitar complementing the vocal phrases sounds like the secular realization of a preacher's sermon punctuated

Figure 7.7.

Figure 7.8.

Figure 7.9.

by the congregation. In fact, some people find a similarity between Wolf's vocal style and that of a preacher. Monroe Burnett, Wolf's cousin, says, "He could get to singin' just like a guy preachin' or singin' spirituals and feel the spirit."[73] Sam Phillips says how persuasive Wolf's voice sounded:

> I think that he had the honest sound and that heartfelt feeling that he gave with that unbelievably different, totally different voice that the young people that I was looking for that didn't have anything they could call their own would have heard this man and said, "Man, he is . . . telling it like it is."[74]

It has been said that Dixon's "Spoonful" is based on two sources: "All I Want Is a Spoonful," by Papa Charlie Jackson (1925), and "A Spoonful Blues," by Charley Patton (1929). However, these songs are not much related to Dixon's song except for the title phrase. Jackson's song is metaphoric expression of sexual desire built around a cooking recipe:

[Verse 1]
I told you once, this makes twice,
That's the last time, don't cha boil them rice,
'Cause all I want, honey baby, just a spoonful, spoonful.

[Verse 2]
You can brown your gravy, fry your steak,
Sweet mama, don't make no mistake,
'Cause all I want, honey baby, just a spoonful, spoonful.

Some phrases in Patton's song imply that his song is about drug addiction:

[Spoken]
I'm about to go to jail about this spoonful.

[Verse 1]
In all a spoon, 'bout that spoon,
The women goin' crazy, every day in their life 'bout a [the instrument finishes off
   the line].

It is possible that Dixon had these songs in mind at the same time as the biblical episode, but his characteristic listing (*diamonds, gold, coffee, tea, water, desert sand,* and *forty-five*) is evidently his original idea, and there is also no melodic similarity between these songs.[75]

On the other hand, the way Wolf drops the end of phrases in the hook ("Men lies about that, / Some of 'em dies about that") is a derivative of Patton's singing style. This appears to be Wolf's interpretation. In the officially printed version of this song in *Willie Dixon: The Master Blues Composer,* all the lines of the hook end with the word *spoonful.*[76]

Most of the songs that Wolf recorded in 1961 were written by Dixon. "Down in the Bottom" and "Little Baby" (recorded in May) are remakes of preexisting songs. In "Down in the Bottom," Dixon set new words to the melodies of "Rollin' and Tumblin'" by Hambone Willie Newbern (1929) and "Lawdy Mama" by Bumble Bee Slim (1935). Dixon's reworking is about an elopement: "Well now, meet me in the bottom, bring me my running shoes./ . . . Well, I'll come out the window, or I won't have time to lose." The animated rhythmic figures in a medium-fast tempo deftly portray a runaway. Dixon casts Wolf as a man trying to take a risk to save a woman from her "bad old man." The song shows a clever combination of Wolf's Delta roots and a facet of his persona: a feral but kind person.

"Little Baby" is a reworking of Dixon's own "My Babe." Similar to the original, this song is about faithfulness to a partner.

> [Hook]
> You'll go and I'll come with you little baby,
> You'll go and I'll come with you little baby,
> You'll go and I'll come with you,
> You bet your life that I won't quit you,
> You'll go and I'll come with you little baby.

Wolf again plays a nice guy who does anything to please a woman. Although Dixon said he could not give Wolf many words, there are more words in this song than its original, "My Babe," especially in the verses where Dixon catalogues places ("court," "jail," "church," and "fair") and actions ("get paid," "bet the horses," and "work hard").

[Verse 1]
You'll go to court,
And I'll come along,
You'll go to jail,
I'll throw your bond,
You got time,
Tell you what I'll do,
I'll stay outside and wait for you.

[Hook repeated]

[Verse 2]
You'll go to church, and I'll go there too,
You'll go to work, I'll tell you what I do,
You'll get paid, I'll hold the money,
I'll be right there to protect you honey.

[Hook repeated]

[Verse 3]
You'll get the fair, and I'll go to show,
You'll bet the horses, and I'll pick up the dough,
You work hard, hurt my pride,
I'll be right there by your side.

[Hook repeated]

[Tag]
Ooh, little baby,
Ooh, little baby.

Wolf returned to the studio a month after the last session. In June of 1961, he recorded two twelve-bar/a-a-b blues songs by Dixon, "Shake for Me" and "The Red Rooster." "Shake for Me" is in a fast eight-beat pattern, and as the title implies, it is a dance song describing a voluptuous woman. The words are somewhat similar to "You Sure Look Good to Me" by the Big Three Trio. This song fits Wolf's fun side: "Sure look good, but it don't mean a thing to me, / . . . I got a hip shaking woman, shake like a willow tree."

This is another outstanding Howlin' Wolf record. Hubert Sumlin talks about Wolf's soulful vocal performance in this recording: "This was a number that really, I said, now, I had it. . . . This is the Wolf. This is the voice, hear the music."[77]

The arrangement style is unique. A drummer (Sam Lay) beats only a cowbell, which creates a very hard-hitting beat, and a pianist (Johnny Jones) hits high-pitched notes in the same rhythm as the cowbell. On the bottom, Dixon's bass gives accents, while on top of these instruments, Sumlin plays sharp chords with his skillful string-bending technique. As well as Wolf's vocal, this is Sumlin's showcase.

"The Red Rooster," better known today as "Little Red Rooster," has didactic parable-like lyrics. Dixon again casts Wolf as a preacher. The wisdom in the song is that the value of the thing is not recognized until it is lost. Dixon explains,

> On a country farm there's always one particular animal that creates a kind of disturbance in the yard and keeps it alive around there. Some have a rooster, some have a horse, a goat or little dog. All it takes is a character that raises hell and attract's everyones [sic] attention. I remember when I was a kid we had a goose and every time somebody came around that goose would begin a chase.
>
> The constant commotion becomes the standard and it kept everyone upset. Then all of a sudden it gets quiet. Suppose somebody had to kill the little red rooster. Then it's so peaceful that no one could rest. Then everybody wants the rooster back.[78]

The theme, "There is no peace in the barnyard after the rooster is gone," was prevalent folk wisdom, but when Dixon composed this song, he seems to have referred to at least two preexisting songs: Charley Patton's "Banty Rooster Blues" (1929) and Memphis Minnie's "If You See My Rooster (Please Run Him Home)" (1936).[79] For instance, Dixon's first and second verses are similar to Patton's second and sixth verses, and the prime concept of the songs is the same as well (see table 7.1).[80]

Dixon's third verse is very similar to the first and the last verses of Memphis Minnie's song (see table 7.2), although, as Josh White sings, "If you see my milk cow, buddy, I say, please drive her home" in his "Milk Cow Blues" (1935), this might be a common vernacular expression, while each narrator or singer can use a different animal to express the same theme.

In addition to the lyrical similarities, the vocal melodies of these recordings are somewhat similar to one another (see figures 7.10 and 7.11).

Table 7.1. Dixon's "The Red Rooster" and Charley Patton's "Banty Rooster Blues"

"The Red Rooster" by Dixon (1961)	"Banty Rooster Blues" by Charley Patton (1929)
[Verse 1]	[Verse 2]
I have a little red rooster, too lazy to crow 'fore day,	What you want with a rooster, he won't crow 'fore day?
I have a little red rooster, too lazy to crow 'fore day,	What you want with a rooster, he won't crow 'fore day?
Keep everything in the barnyard, upset in every way.	What you want with a man, when he won't do nothin' he say?
[Verse 2]	[Verse 6]
Oh, them dogs begin to bark, and hounds begin to howl,	I know my dog anywhere (doggie when) I hear him bark,
Oh, them dogs begin to bark, hounds begin to howl,	I know my dog anywhere (doggie when) I hear him bark,
Oh, watch out strange kin people, little red rooster's on the prowl.	I can tell my rider, if I feel her in the dark.

Table 7.2. Dixon's "The Red Rooster" and Memphis Minnie's "If You See My Rooster"

"The Red Rooster" by Dixon (1961)	"If You See My Rooster" by Memphis Minnie (1936)
[Verse 3]	[Verse 1]
If you see my little red rooster, please drive him on home,	If you see my rooster, please run him on back home,
If you see my little red rooster, please drive him on home,	If you see my rooster, please run him on back home,
There ain't no peace in the barnyard since my little red rooster been gone.	I haven't found no eggs in my basket, eeheee, since my rooster been gone,
	[Verse 5]
	Now, Bob, if you see my rooster, please run him on back home,
	Now, Bob, if you see my rooster, please run him on back home,
	I haven't found no eggs in my basket, eeheee, since my rooster been gone.

The recording features Wolf's slide guitar, which gives a dusty, country feeling to the song, and his hoarse voice, which adds a more countrified flavor and makes the song wistful. His ability to express the feeling of songs when it fits his character is clearly demonstrated here.

For the December 1961 session, Howlin' Wolf recorded three Dixon songs: "You'll Be Mine," "Just Like I Treat You," and "I Ain't Superstitious."[81]

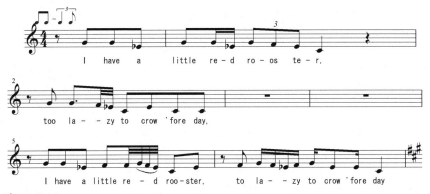

Figure 7.10.

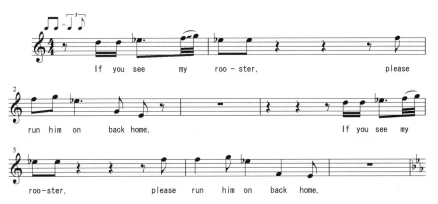

Figure 7.11.

Similar to "Howlin' for My Darlin'" and "Little Baby," "You'll Be Mine" focuses on Wolf's bright side. This is one of the few songs with a pop-song form that Dixon offered to Wolf. But the lyrics have too many repetitions of the phrase from the title "You'll be mine," and its reliance on platitudes made this song mediocre.

"Just Like I Treat You" is also built around Wolf's bright side. Dixon concisely juxtaposes opposite concepts with similar words and includes wisdom, "do onto others as you would wish them to do onto you." While the performance is rhythmic and soulful, the recording has flaws. Around the end of the first guitar solo, Dixon's voice giving the timing to Wolf is audible, and in the ending instrumental section, chattering (probably Dixon's) is heard.

"I Ain't Superstitious" has a better integrity. This song of the Southern superstition describes contradictory human psychology. Wolf is again cast as a preacher, and his vocal perfectly fits the Delta provincialism:

> [Hook]
> Well, I ain't superstitious, black cat just cross my trail,
> Well, I ain't superstitious, oh the black cat just cross my trail,
> Don't sweep me with no broom, I might get put in jail.
>
> [Verse 1]
> When my right hand itches, I gets money for sure,
> When my right hand itches, I gets money for sure,
> But, when my left eye jumps, somebody got to go.
>
> [Hook repeated with slightly different wording]
>
> [Verse 2]
> Well, the dogs are howlin', all over the neighborhood,
> Whoa, the dogs are howlin', all over the neighborhood,
> That is true sign of death, baby, that ain't no good,
>
> [Hook repeated with slightly different wording]

Dixon explains, "You say you ain't superstitious, but when you see a dark cloud rising you say there's gonna be a storm. And sometimes there will, sometimes there won't. Sometimes it rains and sometimes it doesn't. You're superstitious. Everybody's superstitious of something one way or another."[82]

The arrangement is unique. Different from a typical twelve-bar blues, the first two lines are on a tonic chord; the chord changes occur at the third line. The band frequently inserts rhythmic breaks in a walking-bass pattern, which musically expresses the psychology of the narrator of the song, who stops at the sight that he does not usually care about and thinks of it as a bad omen.

On September 26, 1962, Wolf recorded four Dixon songs: "Mama's Baby," "Do the Do," "Tail Dragger," and "Long Green Stuff." The recording format changed from this session in at least two ways. First, a horn section was featured for all the compositions. Wolf recorded with a horn section as early as his Memphis days in 1952, but this was the first time in Chicago.

Second, aided by a multitrack recording system, Wolf's vocal was overdubbed. Along with this system, the songs that Dixon offered to Wolf have longer lyrics, although he still depended on a lot of repetitions.

"Mama's Baby" is about a dance. This song is in a fast eight-beat pattern reflecting the popularity of rock 'n' roll in this period. As well as uninspiring lyrics, this recording displays the futility of efforts to explore the trendy musical style. "Do the Do" is again about a dance, but this record sounds more alluring. The melody of this song derives from Robert Petway's "Catfish Blues," which is also the origin of Muddy Waters' "Rolling Stone," "Still a Fool," and "She's Alright," and Dixon's "You Need Love" for Muddy, the last of which, however, at this point was not yet recorded. The use of Petway's pattern on one chord seems to be Wolf's idea to challenge his rival Muddy. Dixon's own version, recorded live with Memphis Slim in Paris around the same period, November 1962, is in the traditional blues harmonic progression. Wolf's version features striptease beats (jungle beats) in which the use of tom-tom and the flashy passages by the horn section are emphasized. Sumlin's sharp guitar also helps create a fierce atmosphere. Although the performance is exciting, the words lack consistency.

"Long Green Stuff" describes how people are obsessed with money. This was Dixon's favorite theme around this period, as seen in "Dead Presidents" for Little Walter. The song includes too many repetitions in words—especially "I can't get enough of that stuff"—and melody. This recording was unissued until it was included in a compilation album released in England.

The best result in the September 26, 1962, session was "Tail Dragger," a custom-made theme song for Howlin' Wolf.

> [Hook] (A)
> I'm a tail dragger,
> I wipe out my tracks,
> When I get what I want,
> I don't come sneakin' back.
>
> [Verse 1] (B1)
> The Mighty Wolf,
> Makin' a midnight creep,
> The hunters,
> They can't find him,
> Stealin' chicks everywhere he go,
> Then draggin' his tail behind.
>
> [Hook repeated] (A)
>
> [Verse 2] (B2)
> The cooter drags,
> His tail in the sand,

The fish wiggles,
His tail in the water,
When the Mighty Wolf come along,
Draggin' his tail,
He done stole somebody's daughter.

[Hook repeated] (A)

Wolf's biographers Segrest and Hoffman write that this song provided "the perfect soundtrack for the onstage antics of the prowling Wolf."[83] Dixon's ability to amalgamate melodramatic music and blues, observed in "Tollin' Bells" for Lowell Fulson and "My Love Will Never Die" for Otis Rush, is now developed to create a perfect song for the personification of a feral beast.

Dixon wrote long words with an A-B-A-B-A form, in which each section is eight measures, although the first A (hook) accidently became nine measures. Considering the quality of lyrics with no reliance on many repetitions or clichés, he probably spent more time on this song than on the others recorded in this session. In fact, the lyric sheet, which is displayed at the Blues Heaven Foundation, shows that Dixon's early idea was different:[84]

[Verse 1]
When the mighty wolf,
Making a midnight creep,
The hunters they can't find him,
Stealing chicks everywhere he go,
Dragging his tail behind him.

[Verse 2]
He a tail dragger,
Wiping out his tracks,
It's the cute little chicks, (The innocent lamb)
The big bad wolf do like.

[Verse 3]
When little Bo Peep,
Had lost his sheep,
Nobody else could find them,
The Big Bad Wolf had run them down,
Dragging his tail behind them.

At some point of the compositional (and/or recording) process, Dixon rewrote the lyrics. A half of verse 2—this section became the hook—and most of verse 3 were replaced with new words.

In the hook, Wolf brags about how mighty he is. This arrogant attitude is again closely related to the badman characteristics, and it is the same psychological effect that is seen in "Back Door Man" and "Hoochie Coochie Man." Of equal importance, this is a musical portrait of Wolf's tragicomic persona. Knowing the concept of a wolf stealing chicks derives from Little Red Riding Hood, this character's tragic ending is implied even though he brags about his power from the start to finish.

The music is very theatrical. It is in a slow tempo (69 BPM [beats per minute]) like a slow march. In the introduction, immediately after the bassist and saxophonists play a tonic chord, which is embellished with a pianist playing a series of high-pitched notes, Hubert Sumlin's guitar comes in with a very sharp tone and plays a dramatic phrase, as if this is the opening of a show. Then Wolf starts his phrase in a low, sinister tone.

While the hook has functional chord changes, the verse is exclusively on the tonic. Here the drummer hits a backbeat and the bassist plays mostly root notes with a quarter note pulse in a marcato way, which sounds like a heartbeat. Over this unshakable background, the horn section in the middle ground keeps playing a syncopated riff. This riff sounds like music for a mobster movie, and it is also like a shortened version of the riff of "Smokestack Lightnin'." In the foreground, Wolf's vocal interacts with Sumlin's guitar. This relationship is comparable to that of a boss being cheered by his follower.

Two other takes from this session exist besides the master: the one is an outtake that shows Wolf losing his timing and mispronouncing words.[85] The other contains Dixon's guide vocal from which Wolf could learn melodies and words. Possibly Wolf was listening to Dixon's version from headphones while he was singing his part.

Interestingly, Dixon's take shows that his original idea was truly based on the melodramatic style. Dixon starts the opening phrase "I'm a tail dragger" like a spoken phrase, and then he melodically sings the next line, "I wipe out my tracks." One of the important characteristics of melodrama is spoken words that are accompanied by musical passages. In contrast, Wolf sings these phrases melodically from the beginning. Furthermore, Wolf does not necessarily copy Dixon's melodies, while he refers to the rhythmic structure that Dixon sings. Figures 7.12 (Wolf) and 7.13 (Dixon) show how differently they sing the first hook and the first few lines of the verse.

This difference tells us that Dixon's compositional procedures included, to some extent, the singer's interpretation and his or her creativity, while there are other recordings that show singers mostly copying the melodies that Dixon presented. The former case is also seen in the two versions of "Do the Do" as well as the difference between Dixon's briefing version of

Figure 7.12.

Figure 7.13.

"My Love Will Never Die" and the master take by Otis Rush. In contrast, the latter case is seen in other recordings by Wolf, such as a remake of "Wang Dang Doodle," "Little Baby," and "Hidden Charms" (this song is discussed in this chapter).

In addition, in "Tail Dragger," Hubert Sumlin's guitar technique is a very important factor that supports this musical drama. When he recorded the backing track, he was of course not hearing the vocal. While making this take, Sumlin had to assume when and how Wolf would come in and how his complementary phrases would fit the imaginative vocal lines. This is a difficult task, even though the musicians spend hours rehearsing with the vocalist. Ultimately, what gives the composition "Tail Dragger" life is Wolf's vocal and Sumlin's guitar.

In essence, what brought out the potential of Dixon's compositions was the artistry of top-notch musicians and singers. Songs have to be sung, while musicians need good materials to project their musicianship. It is impossible to think that Dixon made a distinction between his work as a composer and as an arranger and a producer. When he started to write a song, his ultimate goal was to cut a master take of the song. In this long process, various internal and external factors were involved. There is a Japanese saying, "When you carve a sculpture of the Buddha, do not forget to inject soul into it"; Dixon's work included extracting the best creativity of singers and musicians to add soul to his compositions.

For the August 14, 1963, session, Wolf recorded three Dixon songs: "Hidden Charms," "Three Hundred Pounds of Joy," and "Built for Comfort." This was the final occasion that Wolf recorded Dixon's new compositions.

None of these songs were intended for Wolf to sing. "Hidden Charms" was premiered by Charles Clark on Cobra Records (1958).[86] And "Three Hundred Pounds of Joy" and "Built for Comfort" "weren't particularly made for Wolf. I think I made both of them for myself at that time but I didn't get a chance to record them," says Dixon.[87] Because Dixon wrote these songs without an assumption that Wolf would sing them, all of them have long lyrics. The humorous texts in these compositions reflect the songwriting techniques that Dixon learned when he was with the Big Three Trio.[88]

While the melodic structures of the two versions of "Hidden Charms" by Clark and Wolf are basically the same, a strutting rhythmic configuration and the bouncy riff by two saxophones in Wolf's version make this song more rhythmic and danceable than the original.

As Segrest and Hoffman write, the highlight in this recording is again the exquisite teamwork of Wolf and Sumlin.[89] The most exciting section is just before the guitar solo. Wolf emphasizes the after-beat when singing, "Woo, wee, what a baby, / . . . when I hold her in my arms, brings out all of your hidden charms," and then he calls out to Sumlin, "Get it!" In response, he plays a very aggressive solo.

"Three Hundred Pounds of Joy," an amusing anthem to obesity, is Dixon's autobiographical song.[90] Dixon says, "You can have as much enjoyment in life as they can and the average person will like someone heavy or fat."[91]

[Verse 1]
Well, all you girls think your days are done,
You don't have to worry, you can have your fun,
Take me, baby, for your little boy,
'Cause it's three hundred pounds of heavenly joy,
Ah-this is it,
This is it,
Look what you get.

[Verse 2]
You been creeping and hiding behind his back,
And you got you a man that you don't like,
Throw that Jack, baby, out your mind,
Follow me, baby, have a real good time,
This is it,
This is it,
Look what you get.

[Verse 3]
Hoy! Hoy! I'm the boy,
I got three hundred pounds of heavenly joy,
I'm so glad that you understand,
I'm three hundred pounds of muscle and man,
Ah-this is it,
This is it,
Look what you get.

While the song describes Dixon's physical appearance, it also fits Wolf's large size and his humorous aspect. The characteristic horn riff, which creates a call and response with the vocal phrase, musically describes the shake of ample flesh. This is a clever arrangement.

"Built for Comfort" is about accepting differences. Dixon says, "Everybody's built a little differently. . . . People are built in different ways—some are built for comfort and some for speed. But whatever, with the two of them you get what you need. It's important that we get to make a choice. It all depends on your priorities."[92]

[Verse 1]
Some folk built like this, some folk built like that,
But the way I'm built, ah, don't you call me fat.

[Hook]
Because I'm built for comfort, I ain't built for speed,
But I got everything all the good girl need.

[Verse 2]
Some folk rip and run, some folk believe in signs,
But if you want me, baby, you gotta take your time.

[Hook repeated]

[Verse 3]
I ain't got no diamond, I ain't got no gold,
But I do have love, it start a fire your soul.

[Hook repeated]

[Ending guitar solo]

The phrases "built like this, built like that," "rip and run, believe in signs," and "no diamond, no gold" reflect Dixon's typical writing style that juxtaposes similar or opposite concepts to make a point.

Here again, Wolf's interpretation gave Dixon's original a new character, recorded with Memphis Slim and others on December 3, 1959, for Prestige Records (see figure 7.14). Wolf's version creates the feel of a swaggering walk, and this rhythmic effect is the soul of this song (see figure 7.15).

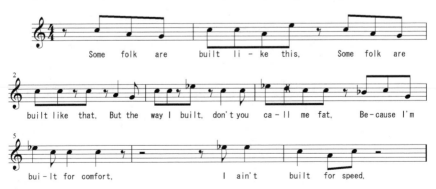

Figure 7.14.

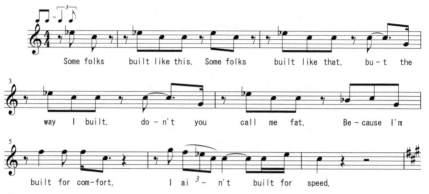

Figure 7.15.

"Three Hundred Pounds of Joy," "Hidden Charms," and "Built for Comfort" fit Wolf's humorous personality, although they were not originally intended for him. As seen in other Dixon compositions, they all have well-thought-out, witty lyrics that display and brag about physical and psychological features, a sense of humor, and wisdom. Dixon's talent is that even when he wrote a song about a fat man, there was more than a description of a physical appearance.

One of the prime characteristics of Willie Dixon's compositions performed by Howlin' Wolf is the opposing natures of the song subjects. Different song themes explore different aspects of this singer, just as the blues is the reflection of life itself with its great variety of experiences. Butch Dixon stresses his father's blues philosophy:

> His idea of the blues was a lot more different than most people's idea of what blues is. He didn't think the blues was always traditional. And the blues is not always traditional, because life is not always traditional. So the blues is as various as life can be. If you can only see life one way, you can always put the blues one way. But if you see life is good, bad, sad, and then different, you can put the blues in those different dimensions.[93]

In the sense that Dixon's blues songs reflect various aspects of life, Howlin' Wolf was an ideal singer. The way Dixon provided songs for Wolf was quite effective, though it is never known if this was Dixon's intention or not, while he of course hoped that his songs would become hits for Wolf. Because Wolf is described as a sinister figure in "Back Door Man" and "Tail Dragger"—that is, as someone who has sinned—he can effectively "preach" to listeners in other important songs with philosophical themes, such as "Spoonful." In other words, when Wolf "talks the talk," he is convincing enough to preach to someone to redeem himself or herself, because he tells us that he actually "walks the walk." In this way Dixon makes a context for Wolf in which he delivers wisdom from the point of view of someone who has sinned. B. B. King, another preacher in the secular context, explains why he respects Wolf: "One of the things I admire about Wolf, though, is he didn't just sing about tragedy. Like all great bluesmen, he sang for the sinners, which meant he sang for everyone."[94] Such a song-providing pattern by Dixon is also observable in his songs for Muddy Waters and Koko Taylor, whose work will be discussed later in the chapter.

It is not known why Wolf stopped recording Dixon songs, while Dixon still played the bass for Wolf's recordings—for example, "Killing Floor" in 1964. But there is evidence that their relationship became strained again. Hubert Sumlin talks about one episode at the American Folk Blues Festival in Europe in 1964: "We was playin' songs that [Dixon] wrote on this tour. He figure on since we playin' the songs he write he wanted money, you know what I mean? Ten per cent. Wolf told 'im, 'Get out of here.' He was mad. You didn't do those things to Wolf."[95] To be fair, however, it was legitimate for Dixon to ask for royalties if Wolf's performance included Dixon's songs, although it is not certain that "ten per cent" is the right number or not. In the late 1960s, when Peter Guralnick was interviewing Wolf, someone mentioned Dixon was in the building, and Wolf replied, "That big fuck," and made a fist.[96]

While they did not like each other, their artistic relationship produced an outstanding artistry in the history of the blues. Willie Dixon gave some of his best compositions to Howlin' Wolf, and Wolf embodied Dixon's songs in their best form. Segrest and Hoffman write of "Tail Dragger," "No one squeezed out more emotion out of a Dixon song than Wolf."[97] Not just of "Tail Dragger" but of all the Dixon compositions, as Dixon's own daughter and I agree:

Author: In spite of their difficult relationship, it sounds to me that Wolf was the best interpreter of your father's songs.

Shirli Dixon: Absolutely, absolutely! That's why it's so weird. Now Wolf's wife, Lilly Burnett, also shared a lot with me. She said Wolf really didn't know how to deal with my dad, because he wasn't easily intimidated like most. She also told me that he wanted to be a sort of daddy's project, like Muddy, Chuck, and some of the others that daddy was assigned to. . . . And Wolf always felt left out.

Now who would've ever thought, this towering, ferocious figure of a human being, who was gentle—Wolf was a wonderful man personality wise—felt somehow ostracized from the Dixon camp, although I don't think there's anyone that could deliver my daddy's material better?[98]

Buddy Guy

Buddy Guy was one of "the new generation" of Chicago blues guitarists along with Otis Rush and Magic Sam.[99] During his Cobra and Chess periods, Buddy recorded seven Dixon compositions as well as eight co-compositions by Buddy himself and Dixon.[100]

The co-compositions with Buddy were largely his responsibilities, while Dixon helped in finishing them up. Since Buddy was a novice artist, when he wrote songs, Dixon found weak parts and modified them. This is the reason that his name is credited as a cowriter. "That's the way things were working. I was a beginner and he had been there so I guess they would say if Willie says this line ain't strong enough, it ain't strong enough. I would say that my material got run through Willie for approval at Chess, yes," remembers Buddy.[101] Therefore, co-compositions with Buddy and Dixon are not included in my discussion.

George "Buddy" Guy was born in Lettsworth, Louisiana, on July 30, 1936. He was strongly influenced by B. B. King's musical style.[102] Another important influence on Buddy was Eddie "Guitar Slim" Jones, who was known for his extreme showmanship: dyeing his hair to match his stage costumes and doing all kinds of acrobatics while playing the guitar. Buddy remembers, "When I saw him . . . I'd made up my mind. I wanted to play like B. B. But act like Guitar Slim."[103]

In 1957, Buddy moved to Chicago with the ambition of becoming a professional musician. When he was wandering hungrily, Muddy Waters saved him by offering sandwiches. Because Buddy recognized that his guitar technique was not yet good enough to compete with others, he focused more on gimmicks like his idol Guitar Slim—for example, playing the guitar with his teeth and walking into the club with his guitar hooked to an amp with a one-hundred-foot cable—he still does it today, though a wireless system makes it much easier.

In 1958, either Magic Sam or Otis Rush introduced Buddy Guy to Eli Toscano of Cobra Records.[104] Subsequently Dixon organized Buddy's debut session. After Buddy made two singles, Cobra folded, and then he moved to Chess Records, to which Dixon returned as well.

As described above, one of the main factors that characterized Buddy Guy's performing style was flamboyance—"crazy" gimmicks. In fact, Dixon, who once managed Buddy's public performances, advised him to develop his showmanship. Dixon remembers, "I used to take [Buddy] over there [to Jewtown] every Sunday morning and tell him, 'Man, put some show into the guitar. Throw it up, catch it.' When he got it going, boy, he turned out all the guys."[105] Buddy's stage action is compared to that of James Brown, says

Butch Dixon: "Buddy's a real hard hitter. Buddy thought he was James Brown . . . Buddy used to slide around, scream, and do James Brown-type moves."[106]

On the other hand, Dixon initially thought that Buddy Guy "sounded too much like B. B. King."[107] Dixon remembers, "When he [Buddy] got his start . . . he didn't go over because that was B. B.'s style."[108] By going through Dixon's compositions for Buddy and their co-compositions, it appears that Dixon, as a producer, had to consider Buddy's stylistic balance. For instance, Buddy usually recorded four songs in each Chess session, and if he prepared a fast-tempo song, Dixon brought a slow blues song, or the other way around. By doing so, Buddy could maintain the musical balance in his repertoire. Practically, songs with different styles were necessary to make single records; if one side was a slow blues, the flip side should be an up-tempo R&B or rock 'n' roll song. Buddy's slow blues songs are usually about blue feelings, and they functioned as an emotional outlet. In contrast, the songs with a fast tempo have more joyous content, such as declarations of love or descriptions of a new dance style. These songs corresponded to his eccentric performing style.

While Buddy Guy's extreme showmanship was his commercial and artistic strength, it was difficult to capture on records. He was unable to get the Chess brothers (and possibly Dixon) to allow his use of sound modifiers to embellish his gimmicks in public performances—for example, a volume pedal, wah-wah pedal, and feedback. Buddy remembers, "Chess Records called it *noise*; they wouldn't let me cut it. They was telling me, 'Who's going to listen to that noise?'"[109] These effects—and his stage actions—tremendously influenced Jimi Hendrix later on (and even the Chess studio production, as heard in Muddy Waters' *Electric Mud* album). Buddy Guy was a little too much ahead of the times.

The first composition that Dixon offered to Buddy was a slow blues, "Sit and Cry (the Blues)" (1958). This song apparently sounds reminiscent of B. B. King's slow blues like "How Blue Can You Get." The basic pulses are a series of triplets on top of 4/4 time in a slow tempo. The text style is a typical description of blue feelings:

> [Verse 1] (A1)
> Oh, there's no one to have fun with,
> Since my baby's love have been done with,
> Oh, I don't know what to do,
> I sit and cry and sing the blues.
>
> [Verse 2] (A2)
> Oh, no one to call my sweet name,
> And my heart is filled with pain,

All I do is think of you,
I sit and cry and sing the blues.

[Vamp] (B)
Blues are in my bloodstream,
Blues are in my home,
Blues are in my soul,
I got the blues all in my bone.

[Verse 3] (A3)
Oh, no one to depend on,
Since my baby love have been gone,
Oh, I don't know what to do,
I sit and cry and sing the blues.

[Guitar solo]

[Verse 3 repeated] (A3)

[Tag]
I sit down and cry and sing the blues. . . .

In addition to the B. B. King influence, there is also a trademark of the Cobra blues. The vocal melody of the opening section sounds similar to Otis Rush's "I Can't Quit You Baby" and Magic Sam's "All Your Love," both of which start with a high-pitched cry coming down to a lower range.

Although this is a simple slow blues song, one of the interesting traits is that Dixon gave a musical variety to the structure. For example, the first two verses have only eight measures; that is, the last four measures of a typical twelve-bar pattern are omitted. While the verse section is in the triplet pattern, the pulses in the middle (vamp) section are strongly accentuated quarter beats. Here Dixon lists the places where "the blues are found": in the "bloodstream," the "home," the "soul," and the "bone."

Dixon remembers that "Sit and Cry (the Blues)" excited the audience in Germany: "Everybody liked it so much they had a riot in one theater over it. Every time I'd sing it, somebody would run amuck. Somebody would start shouting or get excited and create some kind of disturbance."[110] Nevertheless, Buddy's record was not commercially successful, primarily because it was not promoted well. But it remained Buddy's favorite. He rerecorded this song later for Chess Records with a different arrangement.

Buddy Guy had his first Chess session on March 2, 1960. He recorded four songs: "First Time I Met the Blues," by Little Brother Montgomery; "Slop

Around," by Guy, Dixon, and Montgomery; "I Got My Eyes on You," by Guy and Dixon; and "Broken Hearted Blues," by Dixon.

"Broken Hearted Blues" is a slow twelve-bar blues with a content of blue feelings:

[Verse 1]
Runnin' tears on my pillow, ice, ice water, ice water in my baby's veins,
Yeah runnin' tears on my pillow, ice, ice water, ice water in my baby['s] vein[s],
Ah, out of all the good things I've done for you, woman,
  oh, you're gone and left me, 'cause of another man.

[Verse 2]
Now if you happen to see my baby, tell her I've been cryin', tell her I've been cryin'
  on my knees,
Ai, ah, if you ever see my baby, ah, I want you to tell her, tell her I've been cryin'
  on my knees,
Ah, eee, ah, I've been prayin' to my master, please, oh, come back to me.

Mercy baby.

[Guitar solo]

Mercy woman.

[Verse 3]
Yeah, if I had ten million, million, million dollar, woman,
  you know, I give you, I would give up every, every dime,
Yes, if I had ten million, ten million dollar, woman,
  I, I would give up, I would give up, every, every, every dime,
Yes, did you hear me? Call me daddy one more time.

Dixon wrote a very impressive line, "Runnin' tears on my pillow, ice water in my baby's veins." The recording captures Buddy's highly emotional performance. Dixon's possible original melodic idea for the first line is described in figure 7.16.

Then Buddy sings with many embellishments, as shown in figure 7.17. As explained earlier, the quality of the performance is a vital element in extracting the potential of the composition.

Figure 7.16.

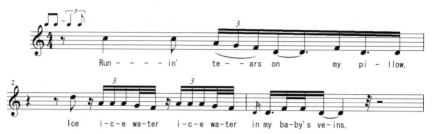

Run - - - - in' te - - ars on my pi - llow.

Ice i-c-e wa-ter i-c-e wa-ter in my ba-by's ve-ins.

Figure 7.17.

For the December 16, 1960, session, Buddy recorded two Dixon compositions: "Let Me Love You Baby" and "I Got a Strange Feeling."[111]

"Let Me Love You Baby" is a call for love. This song remains Buddy's
crowd-pleaser to this day. The inspiration for the lyrics came from "You Sure
Look Good to Me," a hit by Dixon's early group, the Big Three Trio:

[Verse 1]
Well now, oh wee baby, well I declare you sure look fine,
Well now, oh wee baby, I declare you sure look fine,
Well a girl like you make a many man change his mind.

[Verse 2]
Now baby, when you walk, you know, you shake like a willow tree,
Now baby, when you walk, you know, you shakin' like a willow tree,
Well a girl like you would love to make a fool of me.

[Hook]
Let me love you baby,
Let me love you baby,
Whoe, let me love you babe,
Yes, let me love you baby,
Let me love you baby 'til your good love drives me crazy.

[Guitar solo]

[Verse 3]
I give you all I own just for a little bit of your love,
I give you all I own just for about a little bit of your love,
Since I met you baby, that's all I've been living for.

[Hook repeated]

This is a typical twelve-bar/a-a-b blues in a brisk shuffle beat, but the
insertion of a catchy hook—repetitions of a simple line ("Let me love you
baby")—creates a musical excitement. This is Dixon's characteristic compositional style in this period.

A slow blues song, "I Got a Strange Feeling" is built around Southern superstition. Buddy's vibrato-filled vocal style effectively expresses the strange feeling that he is experiencing. This song fits his eccentric character.

There is evidence that Dixon thought he could cast Buddy Guy in the more serious role of blues preacher, a role similar to the one played by mischievous Bo Diddley when he sang the didactic "You Can't Judge a Book by Its Cover." Buddy claims that he was presented with Dixon's "The Same Thing," a blues preaching song recorded by Muddy Waters in 1964. Buddy remembers,

> Muddy cut a tune once called *That Same Thing*. Actually Willie Dixon had given me the song and I had rehearsed it with Willie for six to eight months. I went in on a typical morning. . . . Leonard walked in and he heard us gettin' to record the song. He called Muddy. The next thing I know, Muddy Waters walks into the studio. Leonard said, "This is a Muddy Waters tune." Muddy just looked at me and said, "Don't move, play motherfucker." So I ended up playin' guitar for Muddy Waters on *That Same Thing*. I couldn't go against Muddy Waters because I don't do that. I couldn't even get angry at Muddy.[112]

Dixon's idea of giving Buddy Guy a serious blues preacher role—an authentic role of blues performers—never developed. Instead, Buddy pursued more contemporary blues styles by introducing the influences of jazz, soul, Motown, funk, rock, and pop. For example, when he recorded Dixon's blues song "Hard but It's Fair" for the August 12, 1962, session,[113] he (and probably Dixon) added an overwhelming pop feeling in the arrangement, contrary to the words about the misery of drifting, as the title suggests. The song itself is adequate, but the arrangement style does not fit the song subject. The tempo is fast (150 beats per measure) with a very bouncy beat configuration. The horn section and the female backup chorus sound too flashy and joyous to sing of abject feelings.

On February 8, 1963, Buddy recorded four compositions, of which "American Bandstand" ("American Bandstand Thing") had possible additions by Dixon and organist Billy Emerson, as indicated by the song credit.

On July 26, 1963, when a Chess blues all-star gig was held at the Copa Cabana club on the South Side of Chicago, Buddy live recorded "Don't Know Which Way to Go" by Dixon. This is a typical slow blues song with a conventional a-a-b form and lyrics for the musical style:

[Verse 1]
I think I'm gonna leave this morning, baby, watch you're crying, woman, help you
    now,

Yes, I think I'm leaving this morning, stop you crying, woman, help you now,
Yes, I think the whole time I was with you, woman, everybody don't know you
  wasn't no good no how.

[Verse 2]
You took up a long time comin' baby, ah, sure enough but I know you finally made
  it home,
Yeah, yeah, yeah . . . it was a long time comin', woman, but you, but you, finally
  made it home,
Yes I done realized, I want you to realize, baby, surely you know you done me
  wrong.

[Verse 3]
You built my hope so high, and then you let me down so low,
Ah, I said, I said you built my hope so high, baby (spoken: have mercy), Lord
  knows you let me down so low,
Oh but you got me walking around in circles, baby, woman, I don't know which
  way to go.

[Verse 4]
Just one more chance, let me prove my love to you,
Woo, just one more chance, baby, love me, love me, love me, let me prove my love
  to you,
You're [unintelligible] do a lot of things, baby, one little thing you ask me to.

Though this song does not reflect much of Dixon's writing style, it seems
that he consciously chose a musical style and lyrical content—reminiscent
of a B. B. King–style song—that Buddy could exploit with his passionate performing style. This recording captures one of the best of Buddy Guy's intense
performances on all his Chess sides.

On April 30, 1964, Buddy recorded a banal novelty song about a beauti-
cian, "I Dig Your Wig." This is a co-composition by Guy-Dixon. This was the
only song he recorded for this session.

On the other hand, a recording from the April 1965 session, "Crazy Love
(Crazy Music)," is a masterpiece that humorously captures Buddy's "crazy"
performing persona. The long quatrain refrain lyrics are sung very rapidly, as
in today's rap songs:

[Verse 1]
Well, if you love me baby, this is what you've got to do,
You got to let the world know, that you love me too,
If I'm crazy, you be crazy too,
We gonna have a crazy time just playin' crazy music for you.

[Verse 2]
We gonna have a crazy time, we gonna jump for joy,
You, be my crazy girl, and I'll be your crazy boy,
If I'm crazy, you be crazy too,
We gonna have a crazy time just playin' crazy music for you.

[Short guitar insert]

[Vamp]
Crazy, crazy, crazy,
Crazy, crazy, crazy,
We gonna have a crazy time just playin' crazy music for you.

[Guitar solo]

[Verse 3]
I'll play a crazy box, and I'll get a crazy sound,
I'm gonna play it standin' up, and I'll play it layin' down,
If I'm crazy, you be crazy too,
We gonna have a crazy time just playin' crazy music for you.

[Ending guitar solo]

The music expresses hysteria. While it is in a twelve-bar blues form, it is in a very busy 8/8 time with a hemiola (3+3+2; see figure 7.18)

In the first two lines, most of the melody consists of a persistent repetition of one pitch, G. In contrast to the busyness, a short, more stable passage

Figure 7.18.

occurs in the third line, but the music soon returns to the busy pattern from the fourth line on.

Though Dixon usually did not compose songs with particular artists in mind, "Crazy Music" is an evident exception. Similar to "Tail Dragger" for Howlin' Wolf, this song shows Dixon's ability to tailor songs to the singer. Especially in the third verse, Dixon includes some expressions that specifically describe Buddy Guy's performing style: "crazy box" (meaning guitar), "crazy sound," "standin' up," and "layin' down." In addition, the punch line "We gonna have a crazy time just playin' crazy music for you" is a great statement for Buddy.

This recording features Buddy's tricky guitar solo, which might have been more embellished with sound modifiers in live performance. After the link passage of the horns that is taken from Glenn Miller's "In the Mood," Buddy imitates Chuck Berry's style, using double-stop techniques to make phrases in thirds. Buddy is a versatile guitarist. Dixon had high esteem for Buddy's musicianship:

> Buddy was really a better guitar player than most people estimated. A lot of people can play pretty fair guitar, but they don't have the ideas. Buddy plays anything Muddy could play, only better. After Buddy learned to keep his time together, he was better than all those guys around there. He was better than all of them at Chess. I don't know none that was better than Buddy at Chess.[114]

Buddy recorded two other Dixon songs in this April 1965 session: "Every Girl I See"[115] and "Too Many Ways." "Every Girl I See" is a shallow song. This song is about a man who is perplexed in choosing women: "You look good, and you look good . . . And every girl I see, a-lookin' good to me." Sometime in the early 1980s, Dixon revised this song when he offered it to a local Chicago guitarist/singer Roy Hytower.[116] Another song "Too Many Ways" is a pop song, which is again about choices: "You got too many ways to raisin' sound, / You got too many ways to please your man, / You got too many ways, too many ways for me." This is not an impressive song, either.

For his last session for Chess Records in July 1967, Buddy recorded Dixon's "Goin' Home." The arrangement style of this song has strong influence from the Southern soul sound, shown especially in the interaction between the tenor saxophone and the vocal. In addition, Buddy's solo with its choppy guitar tone sounds very similar to Albert King's style.

The highlight of this session was a rerecording of "Sit and Cry (the Blues)," which Dixon presented for Buddy's first Cobra session. This song was given a new title, "I Cry and Sing the Blues." The basic eight-bar structure of the original is maintained, but this song is now sung in A minor, while the original version is in G major. By changing the mode, heart-wrenching tension is effectively added, while the original version sounds relaxed. Buddy's emotional and soulful vocal style extracts the pathos of the composition. Surprisingly, this recording was unreleased until the 1990s.

Buddy Guy did not make many commercially successful records with Chess Records. Nevertheless, this was an important period for his entire career. His Chess recordings provide a popular repertoire for his live performances to date—for example, "First Time I Met the Blues," "Stone Crazy," "Leave My Girl Alone," and Dixon's "Let Me Love You Baby."

Dixon's contribution to Buddy was to expand his musical territory and to provide him with good material that could inspire some of his best performances, though some other songs are too commercial to withstand the test of time. "Crazy Music" in particular captures Buddy's eccentric performing persona, and it shows Dixon's ability as a professional songwriter.

Sonny Boy Williamson
Shirli Dixon says,

> My dad just believed some of the spirits that came forward from Sonny Boy and actually his own. They were influenced by each other. . . . My dad was just as much a fan of Sonny Boy as Sonny Boy was of my dad. . . . They all had this, if you will, brotherhood.[117]

Sonny Boy Williamson's real name is usually indicated as Rice Miller, but its variants are Alec, Alek, or Alex Miller, and his last name could be Ford—Bob Koester says that Williamson's passport has "Willie Williamson."[118] According to different sources, Sonny Boy's birth date varies from 1897 to 1911, while his tombstone says, "Born March 11, 1905 and Died June 23, 1965."[119] Whatever the birth date, it is agreed that Sonny Boy was born in Glendora, Mississippi.

Miller started to play a harmonica in the early 1920s. By the mid-1930s, he became a traveling musician. His musical partners included Robert Johnson, Robert Nighthawk, Robert Jr. Lockwood, Elmore James, and Chester Burnett (Howlin' Wolf). In 1941, Miller started his radio show *King Biscuit Time* on KFFA in Helena, Arkansas. Max Moore of Interstate Grocery, the owner of the sponsoring company of the show, renamed Miller "Sonny Boy Williamson," following the very popular harmonica player of the time, John Lee "Sonny Boy" Williamson. In 1948, when the "original" Sonny Boy was murdered, Miller then became "the original and only Sonny Boy."[120]

In 1951, he had a recording contract with Trumpet Records, and in 1955, his contract was sold to Chess. For his first Chess session, Muddy Waters' regular recording members (including Muddy himself and Willie Dixon) participated as sidemen.

Dixon talks about Sonny Boy Williamson: "Writing songs, drinking, chasing some chicks—that was his main thing all the time."[121] In fact his nicknames included "the goat" and "foots."[122] He was also known as a "bummer" and a vagabond. Howlin' Wolf's biographers, Segrest and Hoffman, characterize Sonny Boy as "the trickster figure of folklore made flesh—Br'er Rabbit in human form."[123] As opposed to his lazy, dirty old man image, he can be a philosopher and preacher, as he sings of wisdom in some of his compositions, such as "Don't Lose Your Eye" and "Fattening Frogs for Snakes."

Although Dixon could have explored Sonny Boy's unique performing persona, he provided only a few compositions for Sonny Boy. The primary reason is that Sonny Boy was not the type of singer who rehearsed assigned songs beforehand. Marshall Chess says, "What's interesting about him, Sonny Boy, I don't think ever wrote down songs in his life. He just was a spontaneous artist. He'd come in totally unprepared to do a recording, make up the songs, write them in his head, and they would just come out."[124] Actually the style of Dixon-Williamson recordings implies that Sonny Boy recorded Dixon songs only to meet immediate needs—that is, when he did not have enough songs for a session. "That's All I Want" and "Bring It on Home" do not have long texts. "Close to Me" was originally presented to Muddy as "Close to You," and Sonny Boy probably knew this song, because it was a hit in 1958. "Bye Bye Bird," co-composed by Dixon-Williamson, is an instrumental track with just a brief text "Bye bye bird, I'm gone."

"That's All I Want" was recorded on September 8, 1961. This song is in a twelve-bar/a-a-b blues form in a medium walking-blues tempo. The song sounds like a pure love song, but knowing this singer's persona, it is easy to interpret that phrases like "the goat" and "foots" are for seducing a woman. This song does not have a good story or imagination compared with the best of Dixon's songs or Sonny Boy's own as well. In fact, Sonny Boy Williamson was fabulous at supplying great stories spontaneously, such as "One Way Out" and "Nine below Zero," both of which he recorded in the same session.

When Sonny Boy returned to the studio on January 11, 1963, Dixon offered "Bring It on Home."[125] Dixon reworked "Back Home to Mama," a composition he presented to Big Walter Horton in 1954.[126] The new version fits Sonny Boy's vagabond persona:

[Hook]
Baby,
Baby,
Gonna bring it on home to you.

[Verse 1]
I done bought my ticket, I got my load,
Conductor done hollered, "All, aboard,"
Take my seat, rare [way?] way back,
And watch this train move down the track.

[Hook repeated]

[Verse 2]
I think about the good times I once have had,
Soul got happy now, heart got glad,
I think about the way you love me, too,
You can bet your life, I'm comin' home to you.

[Tag]
Gon' get on home,
Gon' bring it on home now,
Gon' bring it on home now,
Gon' bring it on home now,
Gon' bring it on home,
Bring it on home to you.

The imagery of a traveling man in the train in the first verse and the description of his longing for his home in the second verse make an intriguing combination. Especially in the first verse, there is a great sense of rhyming: "load" and "aboard," and "back" and "track." Instead of directly saying, "I am going home," using the expression "bring it on home" is more touching, as Marie Dixon explains,

> Willie was traveling and writing . . . he wrote about everyday life. Let's say you was out on the road. And I wanna bring it on home to you. In other words, I wanna bring myself back home to you . . . my love, my hug. Yeah, these are the things. This is what the song meant. You know, I've been gone away a long time so I'm coming back home to you.[127]

The arrangement is simple but very effective. The background is simply the bass line of the cut-boogie pattern, which an organ, guitar, and bass play in a somewhat lazy way. This bass line musically portrays travel and a train that starts to move slowly. The foreground is, of course, Sonny Boy's vocal and his harmonica interlude. His opening vocal melody "Baby" on one pitch with a slight bend is followed by the imitation of a train whistle by harmonica. From Sonny Boy's vocal, it sounds as if he is personally talking to someone waiting for him.

On April 30, 1964, Sonny Boy recorded "Close to Me." He and/or Dixon changed the words slightly from "I want to get close to you" to "I want you to get close to me." But what changed was not just a portion of lyrics. The comparison of the first few lines of Muddy's original (figure 7.19) and Sonny Boy's interpretation (figure 7.20) shows how freely Sonny Boy re-creates a conversation-like performance.

Figure 7.19.

Figure 7.20.

Compared with Muddy's confident expression in the style of a preacher, exaggerating his manhood, Sonny Boy's performance, with his smoky voice, makes this song sound like the words of "an old goat." Especially when he extends the vowel of the word *close*, he sounds very suggestive.

Although this recording captures Sonny Boy's unique personality, he does not remember the words correctly. For example, he sings, "I want you to so close to me, we look like Chinese twins," though it is supposed to be "Siamese twins," according to Muddy's version.

Sonny Boy Williamson stayed at Chess Records until 1964, but he tried to emigrate to England, where many musicians and fans appreciated his talent. According to what he told Dixon, Sonny Boy was issued citizenship in England.[128] However, for some reason he went back to Arkansas in 1965, and he died there soon after his return. Dixon remembers, "He told me in fun if he come back, he would die. That was the last time I remember Sonny Boy."[129]

Koko Taylor

Willie Dixon's work for Koko Taylor was one of his final projects for Chess Records in the period of its demise. Although Dixon had previous experiences in working with female artists, Betty Everett and Gloria Irving on Cobra Records, Koko Taylor was the first woman with whom Dixon spent a significant amount of time and energy in nurturing her artistry. She recorded twenty-one Dixon compositions. "Wang Dang Doodle" became her signature song. Her Chess sides were released from the Checker label, Chess' subsidiary.

Shirli Dixon talks about her father's relationship with Koko:

He loved her as a sister. He thought she was a great talent, a great spirited woman. And he believed that she had the right mix, formula, performance style to be successful. And he felt that because of the demise of the label during that period, she had not gotten all of what she could've gotten from the blues community.[130]

What Dixon sensed in Koko's vocal quality and performing style was the same artistry that the classic blues women—such as Ma Rainey and Bessie Smith—possessed. Koko was young but a powerful and commanding woman, and more important, she could take on the persona of a priestess of the blues or female blues preacher, as did her predecessors. As a focal point of this book, one of the most important characteristics of blues artists is the ability to deliver a sermon as a preacher in the secular context. Clearly, the role in which Dixon cast Koko followed this tradition. In addition, as my interview with her reveals, she recognizes herself as a healer in her performing context.

Born Cora Walton on September 28, 1928, in Memphis, Koko Taylor grew up listening to blues through Rufus Thomas' radio show on WDIA.[131] When she was eighteen, she and her husband-to-be, Robert "Pops" Taylor, moved to Chicago.

In Chicago, they often visited blues clubs and became acquainted with the performers, including Muddy Waters and Howlin' Wolf. As she built her self-confidence in singing, she sat in with them in their gigs and auditioned for some record companies, including Mercury, King, and Chess, but all of them turned her down. In 1962, however, when she was performing with Wolf at the Pepper's Lounge, Willie Dixon approached her. Koko remembers,

> When I finished and came down, I looked at this big man coming over to me. . . . He said, "Good God, never met a woman sing the blues like you sang the blues tonight." He said, "Who is you? Who is you?" I said, "Who is you?" He said, "I'm Willie Dixon." I said, "Well, I'm Koko Taylor. That's what they call me, but my legal name is Cora Taylor." He said "Well, the reason I'm asking you these questions . . . because we ain't got no women sing the blues like you sing the blues. And that's what the world need today, a woman to sing the blues like you sing the blues."
>
> He said, "I'd like to take you down to the studio right away to meet the producer down there and the owner of Chess Records, and see if he feels the same way I feel about your voice. . . . I guess I was answering too slow for him. My ex-husband said, "Yeah, she would go."
>
> Anyway the next day . . . he took me down to Chess Records. He had me down there singing and had a little band down there waiting for me to sing. And Leonard Chess listened to me sing . . . and before I could get through my song, Leonard said, "Yeah, that's her. That's the one we need," And he said to Willie Dixon, "Get her ready right away." Dixon said, "Okay, you heard that?" I said, "Yeah, I heard it."
>
> In the same night, he had me down in his basement rehearsing those songs. I said, "Good God, has it got to be this fast?" He kept me up till two o'clock in the morning, working on these songs.[132]

In spite of what Koko remembers, her debut song, "Honky Tonk," written and produced by Willie Dixon, was released not from Chess Records but from USA Records in 1963. In the same year, two other recordings—"Which'a Way to Go," written by Dixon, and "What Kind of Man Is This," written by Koko herself—were included in album *Chicago Blues: A Bonanza All Star Blues LP* on Spivey Records, a very small label founded by blues singer Victoria Spivey and jazz historian Len Kunstadt.[133] I asked Koko about different recording contracts and release dates:

> Now USA Records—was it with Victoria Spivey? I didn't know about that . . . I didn't know what the deal was, and I still don't know. But I know I did

a couple of tunes on her label. But I know we was always, every day, we's in Dixon's basement, rehearsing those songs.[134]

The record on USA was not commercially successful, and an album from Spivey had a very limited distribution. In the summer of 1964, Dixon wrote and produced her debut record on Checker label *I Got What It Takes*. She stayed with Chess until the end of the company in 1971.

Today Koko Taylor is known as "Earthshaker" or "Force of Nature," but Dixon was the one who exploited such a persona. As her interview above shows, female blues artists—especially powerful ones—had become a relic of the past by the beginning of the 1960s, though there were few exceptions, such as Big Mama Thornton. Naturally Dixon felt that "the world needs a woman like you." In addition, around this period Chess Records enjoyed the success of Etta James' soul records, and they were looking for other female talents.

Koko Taylor's most distinctive performing style was the use of growls; she characterizes her own voice as "rough, tough, harsh, greedy."[135] In addition, Koko had her own trait that was not typical for a classic blues woman: she was a petite woman. Therefore, the prime components for her performing persona were her small but robust stature and her loud voice with use of growls. Shirli Dixon gives this account:

Koko was not fragile. As opposed to Etta James . . . , my dad thought Koko represented tradition and modernization in one, because she was a very small woman in stature but with this big booming voice. And he always said she had the very perfect voice to be the queen of the blues, which ultimately she became.[136]

In spite of her well-established image, Koko originally did not see herself as such a powerful figure. According to Shirli Dixon, Koko's goal then was to become another Diana Ross:

I think one of the challenges that happened with Koko—of course, was probably resolved with her—my dad told me that Koko wanted to be Diana Ross. . . . "Can you imagine Koko Taylor trying to sing like Diana Ross?" It's funny, because I believe he was so far ahead of most people that often they couldn't even catch up with or keep up with where he was.[137]

Koko initially refused to sing "Wang Dang Doodle" when Dixon offered it to her. She remembers,

I said, "Good God, I should not learn this song. How come I get to sing, talking about all of these bad folks with guns and razor blades and everything? I don't wanna sing this song." [Dixon said,] "How come? You don't know what's good." I said, "I know what's bad. . . . Give it to Etta James." That's what I told him. [Dixon said], "Etta James can't do this like you can do it. You can do a real good job on this song. And I want you to do it." He insisted on that . . . but I tell you I'm glad he insisted on me doing it, because of the best seller I have so far.[138]

This is another episode that demonstrates Dixon's foresight and his ability to draw out the potential of artists, which the artists themselves often could not recognize.

The way Dixon provided songs for Koko Taylor had been an established pattern that is seen in the sets of his songs for Muddy Waters and Howlin' Wolf—that is, a commanding black outlawlike figure who is also a conjurer or trickster sings didactic songs and communicates wisdom. Upon this matrix, the twenty-one Dixon songs for Koko are categorized into the following four types by subject: (1) descriptions of an almighty lady figure; (2) a representative of women making a critical attack on society from a woman's perspective; (3) exploration of a sexy love seeker or so-called red hot mama; and (4) the complaining of a frustrated woman over material or financial shortage. In short, through his compositions, Dixon cast Koko as a powerful spokeswoman and as a feminist provocateur. On the other hand, Dixon never gave her sentimental blues songs that could have explored her fragility and given her a role of blues crier—something like "My man's gone, and I don't know what to do." By thoroughly avoiding such songs, Dixon strengthened Koko's menacing persona.

Of equal importance, Koko recognizes her role as a healer—a prime responsibility of the preacher—in her performing context, the function of which is idiomatic in African American performers, as discussed earlier. She says,

I realized the healing function of my singing when I started doing concerts and things when I was out on the road. And people would come to me. I mean a lot of people . . . would walk up to me and say, "Oh, Koko, you know that song you did, it just meant so much to me. It made me feel so much better . . ." I learned from that.

People would say that my singing was a healer. It was just like a medicine to them. And it is a good feeling to know that you can sing a song, something mean so much to people, do something for people. . . . To me that's healing, because if somebody feel depressed and all down . . . , he can hear the song and uplift him. It can heal this person.[139]

Shirli Dixon, who was also present at this interview, asked Koko, "How has it helped you? How did this music work for you?" She responded,

The same way. Whenever I can do something to help somebody else, it helps me generate what I'm trying to do. And it makes me more powerful, because I say, "Well I can do this, I can do a little bit more." Think about something Dixon would say, "Just keep on pushing. Keep doing it a little bit more." So it helps me, too.[140]

Koko Taylor's debut "Honky Tonk" was recorded on July 23, 1963. This is a humorous description of a woman staying in cheap hotel above a juke joint where a band has been playing loud. Knowing the power of her vocal and the quality of her Chess recordings, this record sounds naively charming, though she occasionally uses her growl.

The outtake from this session shows that Dixon was carefully working on the rhythmic nuances. From the control booth Dixon gives detailed directions to Koko and the band:

Hold it. That was good, too. That was a good start. Let's try it again. (Koko: I'm sorry). We, we, we picked it up a little bit. I wanted to have that [Dixon sings the hook melody] "Honky tonk, bam pa, dum, dum, dum." I want that like that.

And Cliff [drummer Clifton James], I want you to hit with that all four beat: [Dixon sings the bass drum part] "boom, boom, boom, boom" at the bottom. And bongo, you don't have to put [tape was cut].

Now, um, when you change them beats, and Leake [pianist Lafayette Leake] ah, try and keep, watch that timing. I tell you, you're still pickin' it. You still makes your introduction much faster than we settled it down. So if you try and get that introduction now. [Dixon sings the walking-bass pattern] "doom-ba, doom-ba, doom-ba, doom-ba . . ." Let that left hand be right there.[141]

Dixon had full creative control for the production of Koko's recording, and his role as general of the floor was maintained when they started to record for Chess. This was a natural working relationship. Dixon was forty-eight years old then and had been in the music scene for twenty-three years (since 1940), while Koko, who was thirty-four, was just starting her professional career as a recording artist.

Koko remembers it was not easy to work with Dixon:

I had a lot of disagreement. He wasn't the type that just agreed with everything I'd see or I did. . . . I can't think of every detail, but whatever it was, it wasn't like he agreed to because I said it. . . . He stared at me straight up [and said], "Koke, I don't like that. You have to do another take. Where did you get that from? No, no, we got to change that . . ." Then he'd tell me how he wanted it to be done. "Now I told you I wanted it done. I want you to do certain things. Now what about the growl you put in? I want you to put that in there." And sometimes I wouldn't be just ready to put it in there. . . . That's the way he was. He was the man always knew exactly what he wanted, when he wanted, how he wanted. And he didn't take "no" for an answer.[142]

Nevertheless, she also observes that Dixon's direction brought a favorable result:

But I learned it was good. I didn't see it then when he was saying it. But now that is all over, and I did what he say to do . . . trying to please him, to keep him from fussing and trying to do the same thing, because I was tired. But after it was all over . . . I loved it, and I'm glad, because I found that later what he was talking about was right. Then what I was talking about was somehow my fault. That was a big difference![143]

Eight months after the USA session, on March 26, 1964, Koko Taylor and Dixon recorded for Spivey Records. "Which'a Way to Go" is presumably Dixon's composition, but this is a reworking of Blind Lemon Jefferson's "Match Box Blues." Koko's vocal is accompanied by two acoustic guitars by Homesick James and Evans Spencer and a tambourine by Dixon. Although the words and music describing typical blues feelings do not match her powerful image, this recording is no more than a private jam session.

The Spivey session was followed by the first Chess session held on June 30, 1964. Dixon's "I Got What It Takes" is a powerful assertion of an almighty woman and a perfect declaration of the birth of "Force of Nature." Koko turns herself into a female version of a black badman with the ability of a trickster. This song is the equivalent of what "Hoochie Coochie Man" was to Muddy Waters and "Back Door Man" was to Howlin' Wolf. All of these songs manifest the menacing attitudes of the singers and have the effect of autosuggestion for the audience.

Koko's power is superior to that of a man:

[Verse 1]
Yeah, I got what it take, make a good man, a good man deny his name,
Yeah, I got what it take, make a good man, a good man deny his name,
I got the same thing that make a bulldog break, break, break his chain.

She can control the order of nature:

[Verse 2]
Yeah, I got what it take, mate a rabbit with, with, with a pack of hounds,
Yeah, I got what it take, mate a rabbit with, with, with a pack of hounds,
I got that same thing that make a man kick, kick, kick a tiger down.

Furthermore, the sexual allusion makes her an all-powerful figure in the secular context:

[Verse 3]
Yeah, I got what it take, makin' love jelly, jelly, jelly jam,
Yeah, I got what it take, makin' love jelly, jelly, jelly jam,
I got that same thing that make a lion lay, lay, lay down with a lamb.

The music helps create an image that this powerful lady is coming out of the Delta tradition. Not only is the song in a twelve-bar/a-a-b form in a slow blues tempo, but also the harmonica by Big Walter Horton is the main instrument that provides complementary phrases to Koko's vocal and that creates a dusty Southern feeling. This happens right at the opening of the song. Immediately after the bass player plays the syncopated riff with a strong accent on the second beat, Big Walter plays the sustained note, and then Koko yells, "Yeah, I got what it take!"

Koko and Dixon continued rehearsing, and they went back to the studio on January 20, 1965. For this session, she recorded two Dixon compositions, "Don't Mess with the Messer" and "Whatever I Am You Made Me.

"Don't Mess with the Messer" is a fast rock 'n' roll song, but the subject is similar to "I Got What It Takes." Dixon's characteristic catalogue of words shows this woman as a wild card:

[Verse 1] (A1)
I'm gonna cross the crosser (cross 'n' cross),[144]
I'm gonna cheat the cheater (cheat 'n' cheat),
I'm gonna use the user (use 'n' use),
I can beat the beater (beat 'n' beat),
You can't mess with the messer,
'Cause I'm gonna mess with you (I'm gonna mess with you).

[Verse 2] (A2)
I'm gonna catch the catcher (yeah, yeah),
I'm gonna kill the killer (yeah, yeah),

I'm gonna dig the digger (yeah, yeah),
Oh then thrill the thriller (yeah, yeah).
You can't mess with the messer,
'Cause I'm gonna mess with you (I'm gonna mess with you).

[Bridge] (B)
What you doin', you can't get me down,
You're kidding yourself, when you're runnin' around,
I ain't gonna let you drive me to ruin,
I gotta whole lotta energy and money to burn.

[Verse 3] (A3)
I'm gonna fix the fixer (mmm, hmm),
I'm gonna burn the burner (mmm, hmm),
I'm gonna trick the tricker (mmm, hmm),
And then love the lover (mmm, hmm),
You can't mess with the messer,
'Cause I'm gonna mess with you (I'm gonna mess with you).

[Saxophone solo]

[Bridge repeated] (B)

[Verse 3 repeated] (A3)

[Tag]
Ah-don't you mess with the messer (don't you mess with the messer),
Ah-don't you mess with the messer (don't you mess with the messer),
Don't you mess with the messer (don't you mess with the messer),
Ah-don't you mess with the messer (don't you mess with the messer),
You can't mess with the messer,
'Cause I'm gonna mess with you (I'm gonna mess with you).

A medium-tempo blues song "Whatever I Am You Made Me" is strongly related to the performing style of the classic blues women. This song is a woman's criticism against a man who has toyed with her:

[Verse 1] (A1)
I was a innocent child, when you taught me your style,
But the love that you made drove me so wild,
Don't scandalize me, save me,
Whatever I am, you made me,
Whatever I am, you made me.

[Verse 2] (A2)
You know I'm tryin' to hang on because my love's so strong,
But you got me doin' things that I never have done,

Don't criticize me, save me,
Whatever I am, you made me,
Whatever I done, you made me.

[Bridge] (B)
Well I tried to be good as anybody could be,
But you kept on talkin' that talk to me,
And as soon as I failed this, you put me down,
Now you got 'em talkin' 'bout me all over this town.

[Verse 3] (A3)
You know I can't eat a bite, and I can't sleep at night,
Got me doin' things that you know ain't right,
Don't scandalize me, save me,
Whatever I am, you made me,
Whatever I done, you made me.

[Tag]
Whatever I am, you made me,
Whatever I done, you made me. . . .

This song shows a different side of Dixon's artistry as a commercial song-writer. While he could write extremely chauvinistic songs, like "Hoochie Coochie Man," he could explore a woman's perspective on her socially vulnerable existence. Koko's cold and cynical attitude in this recording indicates that she is strong enough to fight back, as there is a dictum, "even a worm will turn."

Koko Taylor's December 7, 1965, session was her pivotal moment. She recorded three Dixon songs—"Wang Dang Doodle," "Blues Heaven," and "(I Got) All You Need."

As explained earlier, "Wang Dang Doodle" originates from a long tradition of tales of threatening black characters' having good times, such as a toast transcribed sometime between 1830 and 1860, "Where the Lion Roareth and the Wang-doodle Mourneth" and Edith Wilson's "Rules and Regulations 'Signed Razor Jim.'"[145] The vocal line in the three versions by Koko, Wolf, and Dixon is basically the same, but the distinction of Koko's version is that the words are sung over a strongly syncopated bass line. Dixon's fresh arrangement effectively amalgamates the old-time story with the new music, and it creates a blues performing style that corresponds to the era of soul music. In addition, what makes this recording special is Koko's voice and especially her growls here and there, which perfectly deliver the song about an outlaw's wild party.

I asked Koko why Dixon was determined to give her this song. Originally she was unsure: "Now I can't tell you what he heard and how it sounded to him."[146] But it seems that what Dixon found in Koko's voice was something that corresponded to Howlin' Wolf's voice: Koko's growl to Wolf's howl, which explains why Dixon gave the same song to these vocalists. In fact, Koko recorded two Dixon songs premiered by Wolf, "Spoonful" and "Evil," for her label at the time of this interview, Alligator Records. Having this fact in mind, I asked her if she recognized the parallel between her voice and that of Wolf. She answered, "Oh yeah. 'Cause Wolf had that [Koko imitates Wolf's howl] 'Wooo,' and I had the special sound, growl, in my voice. So I think that is kind of similar."[147]

Koko's "Wang Dang Doodle" was ranked at the fourth position on the *Billboard* R&B charts, and it stayed in the charts for thirteen weeks.[148] This song publically defined her persona as a powerful wild blues woman.

Another song recorded in the session on December 7, 1965, was "Blues Heaven" by Dixon. This is a tribute to the black popular music artists who had passed away, including Nat Cole, Bessie Smith, Sonny Boy Williamson, and Big Bill Broonzy. Although the subject is intriguing, it is not a very impressive song. It does not sound bluesy, nor does it sound like black music.

The other track from this session, "(I Got) All You Need," has better integration of words and music. The driving feel of the brisk shuffle pattern moves the body, and the movement leads to an appreciation of the words. Dixon lists needs and supplies, and says that this singer can provide everything that is required. This song follows one aspect of Koko's persona, an almighty figure:

[Verse 1]
I got bread for you, when you're hungry, baby,
I got water for you, when you are dry,
I got good times, when you get lonesome,
I got [dues?] for you, when you die.

[Hook]
I got all you need,
I got all you need,
And if you wanna have fun,
Baby please make it to me.

[Verse 2]
I gotta heat for you, when you're cold, baby,
I gotta air condition, when you are warm,

I gotta youth, when you get old, oh baby,
I gotta protection, when you are alone.

[Hook]

[Guitar solo]

[Verse 3]
I got rhythm, when you wanna dance, baby,
I got a towel, if you need some clothes,
I got love for you, when you're lonesome,
I got money, if you are broke.

[Hook repeated twice]

This is another example of good blues writing without using the twelve-bar/a-a-b pattern. It is a sixteen-bar form with a double quatrain refrain text; eight measures are assigned to the first four lines, and the other eight measures are to another four lines. The verse, which is sung solely on a tonic chord, draws listeners' attention, and then a very catchy hook is prepared at the point where the listener's expectation reaches its peak—something that has been observed in "Hoochie Coochie Man."

After 1966, Dixon's work for Chess Records' productions was almost exclusively for Koko Taylor. Because he was concentrating on Koko, Dixon created more complex recordings during this period.

On May 17, 1966, Koko recorded J. B. Lenoir's composition "Good Advice," but this take was unissued, and it was rerecorded about a month later, on June 29 (unavailable to me). In December 1966, Koko and Dixon recorded three songs, including Dixon's "What Came First the Egg or the Hen" and "Love Me."

"What Came First the Egg or the Hen" is another song that provides Dixon's wisdom. "Egg or hen" is a fact of life and an eternal argument not only in natural science but also in human life. Sometimes it is impossible to determine what causes the conflict, because a conflict itself can be a cause, as in the many examples Dixon lists in this song. Here Koko, as well as Dixon himself for the punch line, is a preacher of secular context:

[Hook]
You may be a hater, you may be a lover,
I bet your life one destroys the other,
I don't know how it all began,
Which come first, the egg or the hen?
Now tell me which come first, the egg or the hen?

[Verse 1]
Like fire dry the water, you know, water puts out the fire,
Like a lie destroy the truth, you know, the truth destroy the lie,
Like white cover the black, you know, the black, it covers the white,
Like night cover the day, you know, the day, it covers the night.

[Hook repeated]

[Saxophone solo]

[Verse 2]
Like the bad destroy the good, you know, the good destroy the bad,
Like the glad destroy the mad, you know, the mad destroy the glad,
Like cold destroys the hot, you know, the hot destroy the cold,
Like the old outsmart the young, you know, the young overpower the old.

[Hook repeated]

Dixon gave this song an elaborate arrangement. The music has a fast
tempo (160 beats per measure) with a syncopated beat configuration,
which derives from "Wang Dang Doodle." The pickup starts on the second
eighth note of the second quarter beat of the measure. After the pickup
by a drum, piano, and bass, the saxophone comes in, and all the players
play a passage with a strong accent on the second quarter beat of the first
complete measure (see figure 7.21).

Figure 7.21.

The hook irregularly consists of ten measures and one incomplete measure (two quarter beats). This section has two rhythmic tricks that create musical excitement. After the chord change from the tonic to the subdominant in "I don't know how it all began," the band stops. In the first punch line, "Which come first, the egg or the hen?" only vocals are heard. The repetition of this line lasts two and a half measures, and this section is directly linked to the pickup for the introductory phrase (see figure 7.22).

Figure 7.22.

Koko's performance is very soulful. In the first half of the line, she yells with her growl in a higher range, and she concludes this phrase with her natural voice in a lower range. Because of the fast tempo, the alternation between tension and release happens very quickly, and the song reaches the highly tensioned hook sung by Koko and Dixon.

All of these musical characteristics required a great amount of rehearsal time. Koko remembers the long hours and days that she spent with Dixon in his basement around this period of time:

There's nothing you can learn overnight. We stayed up all night in the basement, rehearsing on one song. I don't mean no a few or both [sic] songs. One song. And it'd take forever, and when I say forever, I don't mean one night. We spent sometimes three months trying, 'cause he was the type that he didn't just take it any way you give it to him. It'd have to be a certain way, a certain sound, and it'd have to be something that he's convinced with that you are doing your best. He'd know if I weren't doing my best. He'd go, "Koke, you can do better than that. I know when you do it right." You know, so I had to get it right.[149]

"What Came First the Egg or the Hen" has everything that is required for popular music: good lyrics, catchy hook, clever arrangement, and a great performance. This is one of the best of the Willie Dixon productions in the 1960s.

"Love Me" is more relaxed than "What Came First." This song is in a medium walking-blues pattern, and it explores Taylor's love hunter persona:

[Verse 1]
This old world is in a mess,
And I'm the victim like all the rest,
I didn't come here just to change a thing,
I come to a good time, man, love a man.

[Hook]
Love me (love me baby),[150]
Love me (don't mean maybe),
Love me (drivin' me crazy),
Love me, baby, love me,
Love me, baby, love me.

[Verse 2]
I love to love from sun to sun,
Late at night and early in the morn',
And when my man say he's all in,
I kiss him twice and start again,

[Hook repeated]

[Saxophone solo]

[Verse 3]
Hold your man, girls, if you can,
But if you hit ma' door, I'm gonna let him in,
For you say the wrong thing, the whole world hush,
But a man in the hand is worth two in the bush.

[Hook repeated]

[Ending saxophone solo]

The main theme of this song is that girls want to have as much fun as men, as if this song more or less reflects the women's movement in the 1960s. Dixon wrote an interesting line for the third verse: "For you say the wrong thing, the whole world hush, / But a man in the hand is worth two in the bush." Here a man is portrayed as a foolish object. The underlying idea of this song is that it is profitable to hold on to a man, rather than going after more uncertain prospects. There is no sense of romanticism in this song. This interpretation is enhanced by the female backup chorus's response in the hook section—"Love me baby!"—a line they sing with extremely sugary voices. This is another song that is written from a woman's point of view and from Dixon's cynicism.

From 1967, the demise of the Chess Records started to affect the Willie Dixon–Koko Taylor production rate. They had only one recording session per year from 1967 to 1972. In 1967, they recorded "Fire" and "Insane Asylum." "Fire" is associated with Taylor's "red hot mama" persona, but this is not a particularly impressive song. It consists of repetitions of overused expressions: "Fire, fire, fire in my baby's heart, and that set my soul on a flame."

The next cut, "Insane Asylum," is a duet by Dixon and Koko. Dixon reworked a famous folk song, "St. James Infirmary," and made it a melodrama.[151] The opening line "I went out to the insane asylum, / And I found my baby out there" obviously derives from the original: "I went down to the St. James Infirmary, / Saw my baby there."

This song is about a girl who has been sent to an insane asylum and her boyfriend who finds her. The descending phrase by the tenor saxophone in the introduction—A-G-E-flat-D-C—sets the mood of an uneasy situation (see figure 7.23).

Figure 7.23.

Then Dixon's strong singing and speech are followed by Koko's elegiac vocal:

[Dixon, non-melodic]
I went out to the insane asylum,

And I found my baby out there,
I said please come back to me darlin',
What in the world are you doin' here?
Then the little girl raised up her head,
Tears was streamin' down from her eyes,
And these are the things that the little girl said.

[Verse 1]
[Sung by Koko, with responses by Dixon]
When your love has ceased to be (Lord, have mercy),
There's no other place for me (mmmm),
If you don't hold me in your arms (oh child, oh child),
I'd rather be here from now on.

[Hook]
[Sung by both]
Some people have the halfway fare,
Without your love I ain't nowhere.

[Verse 2]
[Sung by Koko, with responses by Dixon]
Oh I can't eat and I can't sleep (oh child, oh child),
Lord I can't even live in peace (mmmm),
Please take me baby for your slave (oooh),
And save me from that early grave.

[Hook repeated]

[Dixon, non-melodic]
And then sorrow struck my heart,
Tears began to stream down from my eyes,
The only woman that I ever loved in all my life,
Out here in a place in a condition like this,
And I began to thinkin' about what my mama told me when I was a little boy,
She told me when I couldn't help myself,
To get down on my knees and pray,
Then I fell down on my knees, and these are the words that I said.

[Hook 2]
[Sung by both]
Save me, save me, save me, babe,
Save me, save me, save me, dear,
Whoa, I don't know just how we made it,
But I'm so glad our love is here.

[Tag]
But I'm so glad our love is here,
But I'm so glad our love is here. . . .

Similar to the original "St. James Infirmary," "Insane Asylum" is about a socially vulnerable person, and it forces listeners to speculate on many things, just as the original does. What sent her to the insane asylum? What does the punch line, "Some people have the halfway fare," mean? Although every listener has his or her own interpretation, here again, Dixon casts Koko as a spokeswoman against social disease and injustice. This is a powerful remake of a classic song.

For the October 1968 session, Koko recorded three Dixon songs: "Separate or Integrate," "Yes, It's Good for You," and "I Don't Care Who Knows." "Separate or Integrate" was influenced by the civil rights movement. This song is Dixon's version of "We're a Winner," a number one R&B hit by the Impressions in late 1967. Similar to its counterpart, Dixon's song features anthemlike horns as well as provocative lyrics, but it sounds like an imitation of other hit record.

"Yes, It's Good For You" is about equality between the sexes. Similar to other songs, this was written from a woman's perspective.

Another song from the October 1968 session was a remake of "I Don't Care Who Knows," which Dixon originally offered to Harold Burrage on Cobra Records in 1957. The arrangement for the new version is based on the walking-blues style in a medium tempo, while the original is in a fast jump-blues style. Koko's soulful vocal style makes a modernized version, compared to Burrage's sweet crooner vocal style.

"I Don't Care Who Knows" is a lighthearted song with a list of creatures and their habits, while it still supports Koko's red hot mama persona. Providing this song to her, Dixon started to expand Koko's ability as a singer and explore a different musical direction. The same tendency is seen when he established a pattern in his work with Muddy Waters. After Dixon succeeded in intensifying Muddy's persona with "Hoochie Coochie Man," "I Just Want to Make Love to You," and "I'm Ready," he provided different types of songs. The bluesy pop "I Want to Be Loved," for example, maintained Muddy's public image; giving him the sentimental "This Pain," however, was an obvious mistake.

For the April 23, 1969, session, Koko rerecorded Dixon's single "29 Ways" of 1956.[152] While Dixon's version is sung only with drums and a piano that sounds like a toy piano, hers features a full band, including harmonica, piano, two guitars, drums, and acoustic bass. The list of different ways "to get to my baby's door"—such as "through the basement," "down the hall," "a hole in the wall," "through the chimney," and "through the closet"—fits her "almighty" image.

In 1969, Chess Records compiled Koko's first album, *Koko Taylor*, from her previous singles, including "Wang Dang Doodle," "Don't Mess with the

Messer," and "Whatever I Am You Made Me." As she represented a revival of the classic blues women, the album cover features her portrait in an "art nouveau" style that looks like an old record advertisement and sheet music.

But after the album release, Chess Records was sold to GRT Corporation. Around this time, Koko's recording contract again became unclear. In 1970, Dixon produced her single "A Mighty Love," coupled with "Instant Everything," on Yambo Records, Dixon's own label (unavailable to me). Subsequently, on November 22 and 24, 1971, he produced Koko's second album, *Basic Soul*, for Chess under its new management. This album has five Dixon compositions: "Let Me Love You Baby" (premiered by Buddy Guy); "Bills, Bills and More Bills;" "I Need More and More"; "Um Huh My Baby"; and "Violent Love" (premiered by the Big Three Trio; unavailable to me). This record was their final collaboration.

Different from Buddy Guy's version of "Let Me Love You Baby" with a shuffle pattern, Koko's version has more of a soul music flavor, with its syncopated funk bass that was popular in the early 1970s. With the use of her lower vocal range extensively, she projects her tough and sexy image.

"Bills, Bills and More Bills" is a description of a frustrated woman who gets herself into serious money trouble. Dixon lists various bills that the woman received. It is a humorous song that depicts frustration over bills, but the repetition of the entire hook ("I got bill, bill, bills, more bills") is overdone.

"I Need More and More" shares a similar concept with "Bills, Bills and More Bills" and "Let Me Love You Baby." This song is again about frustration over her narrow living space and overabundant sexual stamina. In the hook, Koko gradually increases volume, which expresses her overwhelming frustration, although her voice could have been turned up in the mix, especially in the verse sections.

In a declaration of love in "Um Huh My Baby," Koko is cast as a sexy red hot mama. The music is more of "back to basics." It is in a fast boogie-woogie pattern, which features Lafayette Leake's gorgeous piano. Taylor's vocal sounds more polished than that of her earlier Chess recordings. She controls her voice well and adds her trademarked growl effectively.

The Willie Dixon–Koko Taylor recordings show that Dixon pushed his songwriting ability further to correspond to the age of soul, while he was using the established techniques, such as listing of similar or opposite things, expanding the blues form, and utilizing melodrama style.

Koko Taylor passed away on June 3, 2009, after complications from surgery for gastrointestinal bleeding. Her last performance was at the Blues Music Awards held in Memphis on May 7, 2009. Until the day she died, Koko sang Dixon's compositions. She never got off a stage without singing "Wang Dang Doodle." Her final album *Old School* (Alligator, 2007) features Dixon's "Young Fashioned Ways" and "Don't Go No Further" (both premiered by Muddy Waters in 1955 and 1956, respectively). She was still playing the same performing persona that was created with Dixon. With her menacing attitude, she spoke for women. More importantly, she was a preacher in a secular context and was a healer in a performing context.

Whenever she was interviewed, she mentioned that Dixon was the most important person in her career. When I interviewed her, she talked about the most important lesson she learned from Dixon:

> He taught me this: "Whatever you do, Koke, if you don't get one thing, don't rush to do one thing and go to the next. Make sure you do that right." You know what I'm saying? In other words, you do fifty things and they ain't no right, don't mean nothing. But one thing right mean more than fifty things done wrong. Do your best on that one thing, and then go to the next thing. That's what I learned from him. Make yourself perfect in everything you do.[153]

Dixon's careful work for Koko Taylor is evidence for this philosophy. His stubborn perfectionism bothered her, but their collaboration was a great achievement in blues history.

Jimmy Reeves Jr.

In 1970, Dixon produced vocalist Jimmy Reeves Jr.'s album *Born to Love Me*. Dixon was a session leader, arranger, and composer for three compositions for the album: "Hoo Doo Blues," "Born to Love Me," and "Don't Let That Music Die." As well as working for Koko Taylor, producing Jimmy Jr.'s album was one of Dixon's final projects for Chess Records.

Jimmy Reeves Jr. never made a household name. Not even highly dedicated blues fans know who he was. Jimmy Reeves Jr. was a Jimmy Reed wannabe. According to the liner notes for *Born to Love Me*, Jimmy Jr. was sixteen years old when Jimmy Reed recorded "High and Lonesome" in 1955, meaning that Jimmy Jr. was born around 1930.[154] Following his idol, Jimmy Jr. became good enough to be a substitute in his idol's shows when Jimmy Reed could not perform.[155]

Six out of eleven cuts from *Born to Love Me* are Jimmy Reed's numbers, including "Honest I Do," "Bright Lights Big City," and "Baby Whatcha Want Me to Do." All the songs of the album were recorded on March 12, 1970. Peter Guralnick happened to be visiting Jimmy Jr.'s session led by Dixon.[156] Guralnick observes that Dixon was producing this record "under auspices that remain obscure."[157] Guralnick also writes, "He [Dixon] was also, it was strongly hinted, taking something of a kickback from the singer himself simply for the privilege of being allowed to record."[158]

As previously quoted from Shirli Dixon, around the end of the 1960s and the beginning of the 1970s, exploring new talents became an important mission for her father, as well as running his own label, Yambo. And, of course, it could bring some financial substance while his work for Chess Records was drastically reducing. In addition to Jimmy Reeves Jr., one of the artists he produced around this time was five-year old Lucky Peterson.[159]

"Hoo Doo Blues" is about hoodoo, the Southern folk belief, as the title indicates. Dixon lists various kinds of magical objects: "black cat bone," "John the Conqueror Root," "world in a jug," "fast rabbit foot," "lucky horseshoe," and even "four leaf clover." This song is in a brisk shuffle beat with a medium tempo, but the band featuring guitarists Matt Murphy and Mighty Joe Young sounds too tight and too crisp to re-create the characteristic laid-back sound of Jimmy Reed's records, while the singer copies his master's loose vocal style well.[160] The album title track "Born to Love Me" is on the beat pattern of Jimmy Reed's "Shame Shame Shame." "Don't Let the Music Die" is Dixon's composition for the Big Three Trio in 1949. Dixon modernized his old song by giving it a fresh arrangement with many syncopated phrases, while he kept the backup chorus associated with the Big Three Trio.

Overall production of the album *Born to Love Me* does not sound like rough and hurried work. The band Dixon organized with his regulars sounds well balanced and steady. However, not even Dixon could do so much for the singer who trained himself to sound like someone else.

Dixon's Work Outside of Chess Records

Willie Dixon's work in his second Chess Records period cannot be confined solely to his work for Chess Records. In particular, his work as a concert organizer for the American Folk Blues Festival from 1962 to 1964 was highly significant in the history of blues and rock. Also, around 1957, when Dixon was a staff member of Cobra Records, he teamed up with vocalist/pianist Memphis Slim. They continued their activity in the 1960s, and their collaborations were issued from non-Chess labels. In addition, as a sideman, Dixon participated in recording sessions for the artists on small labels in Chicago, and he also provided songs for the artists on these labels.

The American Folk Blues Festival

The American Folk Blues Festival (AFBF) developed from the overseas performances of Dixon and Memphis Slim in 1960. An Israeli woman named Aviva was looking for musicians whom she could take to her country, and she scouted Dixon and Slim. They agreed, because they were having a hard time getting their music exposed.[161] Marie Dixon remembers that she was with them talking about going to overseas:

> Both were saying, "Let's go somewhere," because it was not happening here. There was little clubs on the West Side of Chicago. Around the South Side, nothing was really happening. I remember both of them saying, "Well, you know what? We both got a name. So maybe we take our name somewhere and see if we can get more recognition." And that's what they did.[162]

When they were in Israel, Dixon met German TV director and concert promoter Horst Lippmann, who was planning to bring blues musicians to his show *Jazz Gesehn und Gehört*.[163] Dixon provided Lippmann with his Chicago musician network, while Lippmann himself called T-Bone Walker, John Lee Hooker, and Sonny Terry and Brownie McGhee. This program became the basis for the AFBF. These blues package shows featuring various artists with different styles introduced blues to many audiences of European countries.[164]

Bob Koester, who also helped the AFBF in 1964, remembers that Dixon's work as a tour manager was a lucrative business for him.[165] Koester says Dixon made more money than Howlin' Wolf, the most popular headliner:

> I saw the pay book. Now, what other money was being paid, maybe they gave Howlin' Wolf a bunch of money . . . but Dixon made . . . 750 bucks a week, and Wolf was taking 450, 500 . . . I know it's less [than Dixon's]. . . . Dixon was sort of the manager. He was not being paid just for playing bass. He's being paid for his work in rounding up people. I believe he did get commissions from some of the artists. He got commissions from John [Sleepy John Estes] and Hammie [Hammie Nixon], but he probably got commissions from the other Chicago artists on that tour. . . . Willie had a lot of kids to feed.[166]

The AFBF had a strong impact, especially in the British music scene where blues records had been circulated among record collectors, and those who were interested in blues rarely had opportunities to see blues musicians from the United States. When Dixon and Memphis Slim were performing in Piccadilly Square, they let young music fans into the show from the back door of the hall.[167] Also Giorgio Gomelsky, who owned Crawdaddy Club in London and was the English representative of the AFBF, invited young musicians, including the members of the Rolling Stones, to the show. Gomelsky brought Dixon, Slim, Howlin' Wolf, and Sonny Boy Williamson to his house and set the meeting with his club regulars, including Jimmy Page, Eric Clapton, John Mayall, and Brian Jones. Dixon generously let them record his originals, including "Three Hundred Pounds of Joy," "The Red Rooster," and "You Shook Me," which were at that time unreleased.[168] Dixon remembers,

> And these kids, we gotta ready to leave, and we went different places and I put—oh, I had garbage songs that just to put—them on everybody's tape, you know, and tellin' 'em this, "Any time you want to get, put this on the tape," you know, "and play it." Sho' 'nuff, they'd play it. Some years later here they come. Next thing was new guys was comin' to . . . "You remember me? I met you [at] Piccadilly Square, behind the stage. I was a little boy." Yeah, these turned out to be Mick Jagger, some of the Rolling Stones. I couldn't remember myself, but they remembered me.[169]

This way Chess blues became an important musical model for the emerging British blues scene. As well as Muddy, Wolf, Sonny Boy, and others, Dixon was a very influential figure to the British bands, because, as Benjamin Filene explains, "Dixon also helped ease whatever doubts the British bands had about the legitimacy of their efforts to play in the blues idiom."[170] This is the main reason that Dixon's compositions were significant in repertories for the British bands. Many American audiences (and Japanese audiences, including me) got to know the electric blues and Dixon compositions through these British rock records.

Dixon says he appreciated these young, white British musicians popularizing the blues:

> Well, frankly I'm glad they did, because this's the idea in the first place to get blues known to the public. And there's a way of making different changes out of it. It just shows there's a wide variety of the blues. And I'm very glad they did, because nine times out ten they [blues artists] probably wouldn't ever got as popular as they are today. Because through a lot of those rock artists and things like that, I give 'em credit for helping to promote the blues into a position where the world is interested in them today. Nine times out of ten, had it not been for them, it wouldn't happen.[171]

While Dixon was in Europe, his wife, Marie, took care of the house and family. She shares her memories of her husband's touring days:

> When he chose to go to Europe, he came in and sat down with me, and he said that he was going to take his music to overseas, because he didn't see he was

getting the respect that he deserved here in the United States. That did not affect me, because I know, again, as a musician, they just travel. And I felt he was true to me. I never had the fear that he would leave me or abuse me and his childrens. And that was true. He stood firm until the day he died as a true man, as a good father.

And one day I said to him, "Willie, you know, you'll be truly missed if you go to Paris." And he said, "Most women don't say that to man until he's gone ..." I said, "Well, you know, let me be the first one that say you'll be greatly missed in my life, in the life for the world." And, you know, he just laughed. He said, "Oh, my god, I never thought I'd hear this." And that is true [that] most of people speak good of you, once you've gone. I wanted to share that with him during his lifetime.

We were always happy to see him when he's back home. The kids were always happy to have him every day, when he's back home. He always bought us souvenirs. He was a little souvenir buyer. You know, he'd go buy those little gifts and things, and the kids were always looking forward to it. So it was very pleasant. He sent a card from every country. Everywhere there was a phone available, yes, he did call us.[172]

Willie Dixon and Memphis Slim

Dixon and Memphis Slim began their duo around 1957. Their collaborations produced five albums: *Willie's Blues* (Prestige, 1959), *Memphis Slim and Willie Dixon* (Folkways, 1959), *The Blues Every Which Way* (Verve, 1960), *At the Village Gate* with Pete Seeger (Folkways, 1960), and *Live at the Trois Mailetz* (Polydor, 1962). From 1959 to 1970, Dixon recorded thirty-four of his own compositions, and these included songs that he originally offered to artists on Chess and Cobra Records.

As the names of record labels imply, these records were largely marketed for white audiences, especially jazz and folk music listeners. As previously quoted from Marie Dixon, they had difficulty exposing themselves in Chicago clubs—where most of audiences were African Americans. Mike Rowe writes of the characteristics of the compositions that Dixon wrote for his duo with Slim: "Playing for white audiences Willie learned a vast quantity of folk material and included in his act little homespun homilies calculated to please such an audience."[173] Filene also writes, "In effect, he [Dixon] shifted his focus from mass markets to collective memory."[174]

Many new materials that were presented by Dixon and Memphis Slim are typical, pleasant, pop-oriented blues songs, such as "That's My Baby" in *Willie's Blues* (recorded in Englewood Cliffs, New Jersey, on December 3, 1959).[175] While this type of composition, full of love song clichés, is not highly impressive, other songs—"Nervous," "Good Understanding," "Youth to You," and "I Got a Razor"—show good integrity and Dixon's unique sense of humor, message, and social criticism.

"Nervous" is one of the best known of Dixon's solo records for its one-of-a-kind performance. This song is about a man who cannot stop stuttering words because he is very nervous with his girlfriend. As the following transcription shows, Dixon stammeringly sings of this situation:

[Verse 1]
When my b-b-baby call me d-d-daddy, and she c-c-call me real slow-sh,
I a-ask her what she want, and she says "I-I don't kn-know."

[Hook]
I get-a nervous,
M-m-man, I get nervous,
I'm a n-n-nervous m-m-man,
And I t-t-tremble all in my b-b-bones.

[Verse 2]
A-when she she take me in her arms, and she squeeze, squeeze me tight,
Start to sh-shakin' in her voice, and she say, "Ev'ry th-th-thing's alright."

[Hook]

[Guitar solo]

[Verse 3]
Now, a-when when my b-b-baby, k-k-kiss me, f-f-f-feel like-a, l-l-l-lightnin'
    hit my b-b-brains,
My heart b-b-beat like thunder, and she call me's a-baby names.

[Hook repeated]

It is difficult to imagine that any other singer could deliver this song the way Dixon does. His characteristic jocular voice is perfect for the song subject, and he expresses a lack of confidence with various kinds of vocal techniques: stumbling, stuttering, and repeating words; exhaling; and changing tone quality and dynamics.

The music is basically in a twelve-bar form in a slow tempo, but because of the characteristics of the performance, the musicians adjust within the form. Dixon treats the measures up to the third line freely; for example, there are five measures up to the end of the second line of the first verse, although two measures are supposed to be assigned to each line of the six-line text. Such a free treatment of the form helps express the theme of uncertainty and awkwardness in the song.

"Good Understanding" shows another aspect of Dixon's wisdom. Dixon uses simple words that even children can understand to show one of the true "facts of life."

[Verse 1]
Now, when you see two women runnin' hand in hand,
And neither one a-worried about the other one's man.

[Hook]
They got a good understandin',
Yes, a good understandin',
You know a good understandin' can make everything alright.

[Verse 2]
Now, when you see two dogs gnawin' on the same bone,
It ain't no growlin', and a-fightin' goin' on.

[Hook repeated]

[Saxophone solo]

[Verse 3]
Now, when the lamb and the lion can lay side by side,
And rover lick the tomcat in his eye.

[Hook repeated]

[Tag]
Yes, a good understandin' can make everything alright.

Dixon says, "If there was a good understanding, we wouldn't have the humiliation and misunderstanding that we have all over the world. . . . Narrow-minded people a lot of times don't have an understanding with themselves."[176] True facts of life are true anytime and anywhere. The message in this song has been true, and it still is today. The simple and catchy hook is another attraction of this song. Some of today's young blues musicians covered this song: John Primer, Smokin' Joe Kubek, Al Copley (the Fabulous Thunderbirds), and Deborah Coleman. All of them play this song in a brisker boogie tempo than that of Dixon's version.

"Youth to You" is a parody of "I Just Want to Make Love to You." Dixon originally recorded this song for his November 1955 session on Chess. He playfully changes the original and creates a completely opposite meaning, while he keeps the musical device in the original: a stop-time riff repeated over one chord for the verse, followed by a walking-bass pattern for the bridge. The man in the parody is extremely egotistical:

> [Verse 1] (A1)
> You know I want you to wash my clothes,
> I got to have you to keep and hold,
> Yes, I want yo' money, too,
> If I'm gonna give my youth to you,
> Youth to you.
>
> [Verse 2] (A2)
> You know I want you to cook my bread,
> I got to have you to make my bed,
> Yes, I'll tell you what to do,
> If I'm gonna give my youth to you,
> Youth to you.
>
> [Bridge] (B)
> Tell by the way that I walk that walk,
> And you can see by the way that I talk that talk,
> And you can know by the way I hold, ah, out my hand,
> I think you should give me everything.
>
> [Verse 3] (A3)
> I got to have you to treat me right,
> I really need you day and night,
> Yes, I want you to be true,
> If I'm gonna give my youth to you,
> Youth to you.
>
> [Piano solo]
>
> [Bridge repeated] (B)
>
> [Verse 2 repeated] (A2)
>
> [Tag]
> Youth to you, youth to you, youth to you.

This song shows Dixon's dry sense of humor. Knowing that there are many people like the self-centered person in this parody, Dixon's humor can also be taken as a paradoxical message.

Another cut from *Willie's Blues*, "I Got a Razor," is about a man with a razor blade. Similar to "Walking the Blues" that Dixon recorded for Chess in 1955, the music opens up with foot tapping. Then, over a slow walking-bass pattern played by himself and piano comping by Memphis Slim, Dixon speaks the lyrics that are inspired by the folktale "Preacher and the Bear":

Who me?
Man, you know I ain't never lost no fight,
I'm way too fast for that cat.

[Verse 1]
Now look,
If me and a grizzly's havin' a fight,
No, don't you think the fight ain't fair,
You talkin' 'bout helpin' me?
You better help that grizzly bear.

[Hook]
I got a razor, man,
And I got a chib,[177] that's a cinch,
Man, I can split a bolt of lightnin',
Before the lightnin' could move an inch.

[Verse 2]
Now look,
If me and a wildcat is all in a clinch,
You ain't got to worry,
I got him cinched,
Man, I'll tie a couple knots in his tail,
Then I'll pull his teeth and clip his nails.

[Hook repetaed]

[Verse 3]
Now look,
Man, I can toss up a apple,
And then shoot out the core,
Yeah, I can peel it and then slice it,
Before it hit the floor.

[Hook 2]
Man, you know I got a ràzor,
And can't nobody win over me, when I got a razor,
Man, I always got a razor,
And I don't never miss,
You know I got a razor. . . .

Unlike his vocal in "Nervous," Dixon's voice in "I Got a Razor" is full of confidence and very calm, as he is "ready as anybody can be." As a vocalist, he is not as powerful as Muddy or Wolf, but Dixon is a tasteful expressionist.

A premiere recording of "Weak Brain and Narrow Mind" was included in the album *Chicago Blues: A Bonanza All Star LP* on Spivey Records (1963). During the AFBF in 1964, this song was on his set list. Here he casts himself as a blues preacher.[178]

[Verse 1] (A1)
If you got a weak brain and a narrow mind,
World gonna leave you way behind,
Your friend will deceive you, leave you cryin',
Can't keep yours, 'cause you are watchin' mine.

[Verse 2] (A2)
If you got a strong brain and your mind is broad,
You gonna have more friends than a train can hold,
You won't have no trouble or worries at all,
If you got a strong brain and your mind is broad.

[Bridge] (B)
You know the strong overpower the weak,
And the smart overpower the strong,
The clever are the only ones enjoying the world,
While the greedy save all and enjoy none.

[Verse 3] (A3)
If you got a strong brain, mind is smart,
Nothin' in the world is gonna' be too hard,
We gonna keep on goin' before other start,
You got a strong brain and your mind is smart.

When he performed this song, it was still a diamond in the rough. Dixon accompanied himself on an acoustic guitar, which was very rare. He neither rerecorded this song with a band nor gave it to his fellow artists, but his simple performance is very impressive because of its unpolished, personal performing style. Similar to the message in "Good Understanding," Dixon's wisdom in this song still speaks to us today. This is the kind of song that shows the full scope of his ability as a songwriter.

By artistic rather than commercial measures, how successful was Willie Dixon as a recording artist? Songs that explore his humorous side have irreplaceable value, as seen in "29 Ways," "Nervous," and "Walking the Blues" (although this is not his own composition). None of his protégés' personae could have expressed the jesting quality in these songs as well as his "Big Dixon" persona did. These records are some of the gems of Chicago blues.

On the other hand, it seems that Dixon did not produce valuable results as a romanticist, mainly because his love songs sound like hundreds of others. These songs reflect musical trends of times, so they were fated to fade. Some of them were anachronistic even at the time they were released.

Dixon's singing is comparable to that of Ringo Starr. Ringo could never be a top singer of the Beatles, but no other Beatle could add Ringo's brand of lightheartedness to their repertoire. Likewise, as a recording artist, Dixon enhanced the Chess Records and Chicago blues catalogue with a humanity and buoyancy that only he could express.

Dixon's Compositions Recorded by Non-Chess Artists

During the 1960s and in the early 1970s, Dixon participated in many recording sessions that were held outside of Chess Studio. In 1960, Dixon produced the Five Blind Boys of Mississippi's album *Precious Memories* (Duke/Peacock Records). Around 1963, Dixon participated in the sessions for the artists on small independent labels in Chicago, such as Chief, USA, and Supreme.[179] Some important works include "Two-Headed Woman," for Junior Wells; "Too Many Cooks," for Jesse Fortune; and "I'm the Fixer," for Willie Mabon.

Junior Wells (Amos Wells Blackmore) was a powerful Chicago harmonica player. He was born on December 9, 1934, in Memphis and died on January 15, 1998, in Chicago. When he was ten or eleven, he learned harmonica from Junior Parker. Around 1946, he came up to Chicago. As discussed previously, in 1952, when Little Walter left Muddy Waters' band, he and Wells swapped their positions; Wells became Muddy's harmonica player, while Walter became the leader of Wells' group the Aces.

Dixon and Wells had a long-term relationship. Dixon, with Memphis Slim, created an opportunity for Wells' debut session for States Records in 1953.[180] This was one of the earliest recordings for which Dixon worked as a session bassist. In 1957, Wells, who was on Chief Records then, recorded Dixon's "Two-Headed Woman." In 1963, he recorded four other Dixon compositions: "I'll Get You, Too," "One Day," "She's a Sweet One," and "When the Cat's Gone the Mice Play."

As a sideman and producer, Dixon participated in most of Wells' Chief sessions. Dixon sang a backup vocal part for Wells' hit "Little by Little" (1959). The three-part vocal harmony by Dixon, Wells, and Mel London (the owner of Chief Records) sounds very similar to the performing style of the Big Three Trio. Furthermore, the feel of the song is very similar to Big Three Trio's "You Sure Look Good to Me (Wee Wee Baby)." Possibly these are Dixon's inputs.

All the songs listed here are not highly impressive. Dixon originally offered "She's a Sweet One" to Otis Rush, and the others are reworkings of preexisting compositions to which Dixon set new words; for example, "When the Cat's Gone the Mice Play" is based on Wells' "Messin' with the Kid" (1960).

However, looking at "Two-Headed Woman" (1957) leads to an interesting speculation about Dixon's songwriting style from the late 1950s to the end of the 1960s. I suspect that through writing this composition, which was based on Muddy Waters' 1956 recording "Got My Mojo Working" (composed by Preston Foster and recorded with Dixon as bassist), Dixon got the idea to write a different style of hook or vamp.

Similar to "Got My Mojo Working," "Two-Headed Woman" has a reference to hoodoo. Also like the original, the vamp section of "Two-Headed Woman" consists of repetitions of the title phrase. A similar style of this vamp—a simple, singable, catchy line (consisting of no more than six words) repeated for a long duration (one full chorus)—is often seen in Dixon's compositions after 1957: "Jump Sister Bessie," "Close to You," "I Got My Brand on You," "I'm a Business Man," "Let Me Love You Baby," and "Love Me," while the same device appears only in "Money Tree Blues," "Don't Let the Music Die," and "Wang Dang Doodle" before 1957.

My speculation is that Dixon was inspired by "Got My Mojo Working," and that he wrote "Two-Headed Woman" in response. While the initial idea was simply a reworking of Muddy's song, Dixon's song became a prototype for the effective writing of simplified vamps and hooks that are inserted in the songs listed here. Dixon was originally good at writing a catchy hook, but "Two-Headed Woman" was possibly good practice in adding a different characteristic to his compositions.

As heard in Muddy's impressive performance of "Got My Mojo Working" at the Newport Folk Festival in 1960, this musical device is very effective, especially in public performances. Because of the simplicity of the line, an audience can sing along with a singer, or they can participate in a call and response. Furthermore, the singer can extend this section as long as he or she wants, and both singer and audience can send out their energy, creating what is often the highest and the most impressive point in the performance. This kind of musical device also increases commercial success in record sales.

Nearly every artist needs at least one or two songs with the sort of musical device that functions as a crowd-pleaser. Presumably, as a commercial composer, Dixon considered the practical effect of his compositions in the public performances of the artists to whom he gave songs. Two of the greatest examples are "Close to You" for Muddy Waters and "Let Me Love You Baby" for Buddy Guy—this song is Buddy's favorite to this day (see figure 7.24).

Figure 7.24.

Jesse Fortune was a local Chicago vocalist in the 1950s and 1960s. He was born on February 28, 1930, in Macon, Mississippi. In 1963, he made two singles with USA Records. For his debut session on April 26, Dixon offered and produced "Too Many Cooks" and "God's Gift to Man" (originally recorded by Dixon himself as "Firey Love" in 1957).[181]

Among blues fans, Fortune is known for "Too Many Cooks," a song later covered by the Robert Cray Band in 1980. This song is another example of

Dixon's use of a proverb, like "You Can't Judge a Book by Its Cover" and "What Came First the Egg or the Hen." Unlike these songs, however, "Too Many Cooks" is built around a suggestive allusion, though they all speak of true facts of life:

[Hook]
Too many cooks are gonna spoil a stew,
Too many cooks are gonna spoil a stew,
Too many cooks are gonna spoil a stew,
Ain't nobody cooking but me and you.

[Verse 1]
Too many cooks tryin' to get in your kitchen,
The first thing you know, there's something missing,
You got a real good oven, you got a hot flame too,
Oh, let me boil your water while you start a stew.

[Hook repeated]

[Harmonica solo]

[Verse 2]
That stew that you're cookin', it smells so good,
It's got everybody talkin' in the neighborhood,
Your spice is spicy and your sugar so sweet,
Your meat is so tender and your juice is a treat.

[Hook repeated]

[Guitar solo]

[Hook repeated]

[Ending guitar solo]

Many people have the experience that different opinions cause nothing other than confusion. Dixon also explains this song, "Too much of anything in any one spot can be dangerous. Too many folks can't make any one thing alright unless they are working on a project together. When you are dealing with things like cooking or with love affairs, too many opinions can spoil the situation."[182]

The music is in a minor mode (though it changes to a major from the second verse), and the vocal melody sounds like an African American folk song based on a pentatonic scale (see figure 7.25). The rhythmic configuration is that of a rumba in a fast tempo. The joyous, brisk beat and the humorous lyrics are a perfect marriage.

Figure 7.25.

Fortune shows his strong ability as a vocalist in this song. He alternates chest voice and head voice, and skillfully changes volume to express the humor of the song. Besides his vocal, Big Walter Horton's harmonica and Buddy Guy's guitar add musical excitement to this recording.

As discussed in chapter 5, Willie Mabon left Chess Records for USA Records in 1963. Dixon offered two compositions for Mabon: "Just Got Some" and "I'm the Fixer," the latter of which is the best known song in Mabon's post-Chess career.

"Just Got Some," a co-composition with Billy "The Kid" Emerson, re-corded on February 7, 1963, is about drugs. Mabon's sour vocal style makes this song an expression of sardonic humor rather than a praise for drugs. In the late 1950s and early 1960s, Dixon's compositions expressed his cynical observation of the world, as seen in "Dead Presidents" for Little Walter. This is another expression of cynicism. The music is in a medium-fast tempo with a walking-bass style. Mabon's vocal sounds lethargic, and the accompani-ment, including an electric organ (Billy Emerson), also sounds very laid-back. As well as the vocalist, the sidemen express the cynicism of the words well. This is one of Dixon's obscure songs, but it is an example of his choice of song and singer resulting in an ideal marriage.

"I'm the Fixer" was recorded on May 23, 1963. This song is about a person who can turn an unhappy situation into a happy one:

[Hook]
[Sung]

Baby, I'm the fixer,
I am the fixer,
I'm the fixer, pretty baby, I got everything that you need.

[Spoken in rhythm]
[Verse 1]
Now when your man done fail you, and you are down and out,
I'll make you feel so good, you'll want to jump and shout,
I'll bring joy to the girls and-a love to the men,
When you think I'm gone, I'm comin' back again.

[Hook repeated]

[Spoken in rhythm]
[Verse 2]
I'm a heartbreaker, later makes you feel so fine,
Good feelin' incubator, working all the time,
I can do things for you ain't never been done,
Can't you tell the one that I'm the only one.

[Hook repeated]

[Piano solo]

[Spoken in rhythm]
[Verse 3]
(Now listen,)
When your heart is heavy like a chunk of lead,
Feel like your last friend is dead,
You're all mixed up, baby, in a twirl,
Remember me and forget the world,

[Hook repeated]

This song is related to "The Seventh Son," which Dixon offered to Mabon in 1955. Like "The Seventh Son," who can "do things for you that make your heart feel glad" the "Fixer" can fix a love problem or down-and-out feelings. The similarity of the song contents could be the reason that Dixon gave this song to Mabon.

"I'm the Fixer" is similar to "The Seventh Son" for another reason: it seems to be another of Dixon's autobiographical songs. He was actually a fixer for the companies he was affiliated with in many senses. When an artist needed songs, Dixon could always pull out some from his bagful of songs; he could arrange and produce them and had an ability to bring out the best of the singer. The line "I'm a heartbreaker, later makes you feel so fine, / Good feelin' incubator, working all the time" is an exact description of Dixon.

When Dixon gave a song to an artist, he or she might initially refuse to sing it, but often it became the signature song of the artist.

The music of "I'm the Fixer" is in a medium-tempo walking-blues pattern with a very laid-back feeling. The arrangement is catchy. Until the end of the third line of the verse, Mabon narrates the lines with only accents. His listless voice is sarcastic, because his vocal quality does not sound like a powerful fixer but like a lecherous man who is constantly seeking a sex partner.

The artistic quality of Dixon compositions from 1958 to 1971 is more mature for many reasons, compared to his compositions in the first Chess period and the Cobra period. Clearly his compositional techniques were more polished than previously, while still maintaining his basic techniques, such as combining a blues form and a pop-song form and cataloguing words. Musical devices such as a stripped-down section, using an incomplete measure combined with a rhythmic break, creating a hemiola, and using a melodramatic style give his music more variety. As observed, one of the most important of Dixon's strengths as a songwriter was an ability to incorporate different musical styles. Many songs discussed in this chapter are compatible with currently popular music, soul, rock 'n' roll, and funk.

Lyrically, Dixon has broader song themes, including autobiography, feminism, chauvinism, cynicism, and social criticism, in addition to some of the themes that he explored before, such as life lessons, humor, sexuality, love, lost love (blue feelings), and Southern folklore. He also reached an artistic high ground that enabled him to write his most ideal blues, which delivered wisdom as the most important element, and thus his work as a blues preacher/sermon writer of the secular context came to full fruition.

As well as his work as a songwriter, his contribution to the AFBF should be highly regarded considering how influential he was to the British rock scene, which eventually appealed to worldwide audiences.

Notes

1. Willie Dixon, with Don Snowden, I Am the Blues: The Willie Dixon Story (New York: Da Capo Press, 1989), 145.

2. The authors of the Little Walter biography call it "a 12-channel mixing board," but I assume this system is not a twelve-track recording system but a system that had twelve inputs, which allowed overdubbing. The advent of eight-track recording system occurred around 1965, and it was popular from 1965 to late 1970. Tony Glover, Scott Dirks, and Ward Gaines, Blues with a Feeling: The Little Walter Story (New York: Routledge, 2002), 169.

3. Nadine Cohodas, *Spinning Blues into Gold: The Chess Brothers and the Legendary Chess Records* (New York: St. Martin's Press, 2000), 203. Malo remembers, "My first Chess session was with Wolf, and I'm setting up the equipment. You know, the studio at 2120 was an exceptional piece of engineering. It was a room within a room, adjustable walls, state of art microphones, and so on." Mary Katherine Aldin, "Liner Notes," *Chess Blues* [CD] (Universal City, CA: Chess/MCA, CHC4-9340, 1992), 40.

4. Dixon, *I Am the Blues*, 162.

5. Cohodas, *Spinning Blues into Gold*, 162.

6. Jim O'Neal, "I Once Was Lost, but Now I'm Found," in *Nothing but the Blues: The Music and the Musicians*, ed. Lawrence Cohn (New York: Abbeville Press, 1993), 370. David Evans points out two reasons soul music gained its popularity while blues became out of fashion. One is the continuing movement of the black population during the twentieth century from the rural South to America's urban centers, and because of that, blues lost much of their population base. Another reason is that blues no longer expressed the values of most modern blacks. Evans writes, "It is true that blues deal mainly with love problems and other universal subjects, but they tend to offer no solutions to problems and say instead that the world will probably always be as it is and has been." Evans, *Big Road Blues: Tradition and Creativity in Folk Blues* (Berkeley: University of California Press, 1982), 86.

7. Shirli Dixon, interview by the author, September 24, 2002.

8. Ibid.

9. Peter Guralnick, *Feel Like Going Home: Portraits in Blues and Rock 'n' Roll* (New York: Outerbridge & Dienstfrey, 1971; repr., New York: Harper & Row, 1989), 238. Citations are to the Harper & Row edition.

10. Dixon, *I Am the Blues*, 178.

11. O'Neal, "I Once Was Lost," 380.

12. Blues records with evident political contents include Lightnin' Hopkins' "Tim Moore's Firm" (1948) and Big Bill Broonzy's "When Will I Get to Be Called a Man" (1951).

13. O'Neal, "I Once Was Lost," 383.

14. Cohodas, *Spinning Blues into Gold*, 294.

15. Ibid.

16. Ibid., 276.

17. Clyde Woods, *Development Arrested: The Blues and Plantation Power in the Mississippi Delta* (New York: Verso, 1998), 211.

18. Dixon, *I Am the Blues*, 178. Junior Wells gives this account of the march in Chicago: "I would have marched with him [Dr. King] once but he was talkin' that non-violence thing. He asked was I [sic] non-violent. Because me, him, and Willie Dixon and them was talkin'. I said, 'Yeah, I'm non-violent. But I *am* violent if somebody hits me.'" Jim O'Neal, "Junior Wells," *Living Blues*, no. 119 (January/February 1995): 25–26.

19. Shirli Dixon, interview by the author, September 24, 2002.

20. Joel Whitburn, *Top R&B Singles, 1942–1999* (Menomonee Falls, WI: Record Research, 2000), 471.

21. Exxon Mobil Corporation, "Tiger History," www.exxonmobil.com/Corporate/ About/ History/Corp_A_H_Tiger.asp (accessed February 5, 2005).

22. Willie Dixon, *Willie Dixon: The Master Blues Composer* (Milwaukee: Hal Leonard, 1992), 267.

23. Jon Michael Spencer, *Blues and Evil* (Knoxville: University of Tennessee Press, 1993), 76. St. Louis Jimmy Oden's "Going Down Slow" is an example for blues songs with a content of "reap what you sow."

24. The Chess brothers, who followed the formula for "You Shook Me," had Earl Hooker make backing tracks to which Muddy could record vocal parts. These include "You Need Love," "Little Brown Bird," and "Black Angel." Sebastian Danchin, *Earl Hooker: Blues Master* (Jackson: University Press of Mississippi, 2001), 139–40. Dixon was not involved when Hooker was recording these tracks.

25. Dixon's handwritten lyric sheet of "You Need Love" is found in the photo spread in the middle of this book.

26. Marie Dixon, interview by the author, September 25, 2004.

27. Led Zeppelin learned this song not from Muddy's recording but from the Small Faces' "You Need Loving" (1966).

28. Shirli Dixon, interview by the author, September 24, 2002. "I Can't Quit You Baby" is included in *Led Zeppelin* (first album), and "Whole Lotta Love" is included in *Led Zeppelin II*.

29. Shirli Dixon, interview by the author, September 24, 2002.

30. Ibid.

31. David Evans lists thirteen processes to compose traditional blues songs. The list includes "using the record as a frame and filling it with new material," "lifting lyrics from a record and setting them in a new blues," and "recombining stanzas from two or more records." Evans, *Big Road Blues*, 131.

32. The author could not get a permission to include a musical excerpt of "Whole Lotta Love."

33. Terry Gross, "Interview with Former Led Zeppelin Singer Robert Plant," *Fresh Air Audio*, originally aired on August 24, 2004, on the National Public Radio. Retrieved from the National Public Radio website: www.npr.org/templates/story/story .php?storyId=3868283 (accessed August 26, 2004).

34. Similar phrase "My captain's so mean to me" is included in Robert Johnson's "Last Fare Deal Gone Down" (1936).

35. Dixon, *Willie Dixon*, 196.

36. *They Call Me Muddy Waters* was released in 1971, four years after its production. This album won Muddy his first Grammy Award (best ethnic/traditional recording).

37. *Electric Mud* was Muddy's first album that was ranked on the album charts of *Billboard* and *Cash Box*, but it received severe criticism, because the album was extremely aloof from his traditional musical style. The music in this record is decorated by

excessive psychedelic effects, such as noisy guitar sounds with a fuzz box and a wah-wah pedal, overdubbed cat's caterwaul, and a stereo effect rapidly moving from right to left.

38. *After the Rain* was finally reissued in Japan in 2007, though it soon became out of print.

39. Dixon, *I Am the Blues*, 174.

40. Butch Dixon, interview by the author, September 23, 2003.

41. Glover, Dirks, and Gaines, *Blues with a Feeling*, 192.

42. Ibid.

43. Ibid.

44. Ibid., 214. Although the biographers of Little Walter say that the song has "an odd musical mix of rumba and shuffle," it does not sound like shuffle, and it does not sound odd, either, to me.

45. Both songs are credited to Dixon and Billy "The Kid" Emerson, who plays the electric organ for these songs. In the same session, Walter also recorded instrumental "Southern Feeling," and Dixon took a composer credit.

46. Glover, Dirks, and Gaines, *Blues with a Feeling*, 224.

47. Dixon, *I Am the Blues*, 148.

48. John Collis, *The Story of Chess Records* (London: Bloomsbury, 1998), 53–54. Collis transcribed this interview from Howlin' Wolf, *Chess Box*, notes by Chris Morris, Dick Shurman, and Andy McKaie (Universal City, CA: Chess/MCA, CH5–9332, 1991); and/or Howlin' Wolf, *The Complete Recordings, 1951–1969*, notes by Les Fancourt (London: Charly Records, CD RED BOX 7, 1993).

49. Wolf talks about the influence from Jimmie Rodgers in Howlin' Wolf, *In Concert 1970* [DVD] (Cambridge: Rounder Records, Vestapol 13009, 2007).

50. See the section entitled "Muddy Waters" in chapter 5.

51. Robert Palmer, *Deep Blues* (New York: Viking Press, 1981; repr., New York: Penguin Books, 1982), 232. Citations are to the Penguin Books edition.

52. Colin Escott, with Martin Hawkins, *Good Rockin' Tonight: Sun Records and the Birth of Rock 'n' Roll* (New York: St. Martin's Press, 1991), 30.

53. Ed Ward, "Chester Burnett: The Man Who Became the Wolf," in *Bluesland: Portraits of Twelve Major American Blues Masters*, ed. Pete Welding and Toby Byron (New York: Dutton, 1991), 213.

54. Shirli Dixon, interview by the author, September 23, 2002.

55. Dixon, *Willie Dixon*, 30.

56. Galen Gart, ed., *First Pressings: The History of Rhythm & Blues*, vol. 4, 1954 (Milford, NH: Big Nickel, 1992), 97. Initially "Evil" did not make national charts, but when it was reissued in 1969, it was ranked at the forty-third position on the *Billboard* R&B charts on April 12. Whitburn, *Top R&B Singles, 1942–1999*, 197.

57. Dixon, *I Am the Blues*, 146–47.

58. Shirli Dixon, interview by the author, September 23, 2002.

59. Anthony DeCurtis, "Willie Dixon and the Wisdom of the Blues," *Rolling Stone*, no. 548 (March 23, 1989): 113.

60. Shirli Dixon, interview by the author, September 23, 2002.

61. Dixon, *I Am the Blues*, 147.

62. Guralnick, *Feel Like Going Home*, 162.

63. Ibid.

64. Bob Corritore, Bill Ferris, and Jim O'Neal, "Willie Dixon (Part 2)," *Living Blues*, no. 82 (September/October 1988): 21.

65. Les Fancourt, *Chess Blues/R&B Discography* (Faversham, Kent, England: L. Fancourt, 1983), 8; Chris Morris, Dick Shurman, and Andy McKaie, "Liner Notes," *Chess Box*, recorded by Howlin' Wolf (Universal City, CA: Chess/MCA, CH5–9332, 1991), 28–29. See appendix B.

66. "Howlin' for My Darling" is credited to Dixon and Burnett.

67. Dixon, *I Am the Blues*, 88. Consequently, Dixon recorded this song himself on February 17, 1954. See the section entitled "Willie Dixon's Own Chess Recordings" in chapter 5.

68. Dixon, *Willie Dixon*, 11. Marie Dixon also said to me, "'Back Door Man.' We all grew up listening to people say, 'her husband went to work at the front door, and she was dating with so and so down on the street.' That's what the 'Back Door Man' means." Marie Dixon, interview by the author, September 25, 2004.

69. Jon Michael Spencer writes that "making a midnight creep" was originally one of the modern British beliefs, which along with the idea of the devil, was absorbed into black lore during the slavery period. In addition, this idea was inextricably linked with the concept of evil, as Alice Moore sings, "I'm evil, need watching 'cause I might make a midnight creep" in her "Blue Black and Evil Blues" (1935). Spencer, *Blues and Evil*, 22.

70. Dixon, *Willie Dixon*, 11.

71. Ibid., 211.

72. Marie Dixon, interview by the author, September 25, 2004.

73. James Segrest and Mark Hoffman, *Moanin' at Midnight: The Life and Times of Howlin' Wolf* (New York: Pantheon Books, 2004), 59.

74. Ibid., 99–100.

75. Regarding "Spoonful," Dick Shurman writes in the liner notes to Howlin' Wolf, *The Chess Box*, "Dixon and Arc Music took the credit despite the Patton derivation ['A Spoonful Blues']." Morris, Shurman, and McKaie, "Liner Notes," 26. However, the two songs sound different even though they share a similar concept and title. Compared to Patton's four-bar blues with rather complicated chord changes—a chain of dominant chords moving in the circle of fifths, described as II/V(C-sharp)-V/V(F-sharp)-V(B)-I(E)—Dixon's song only has one chord (E minor) throughout the sixteen measures.

76. Dixon, *Willie Dixon*, 209.

77. Segrest and Hoffman, *Moanin' at Midnight*, 185.

78. Dixon, *Willie Dixon*, 176.

79. Segrest and Hoffman write that in addition to Patton's "Banty Rooster Blues," hillbilly singer Cliff Carlisle's "Shanghai Rooster Yodel" (1931) influenced Dixon's composition. Segrest and Hoffman, *Moanin' at Midnight*, 185. But there is no similarity between Carlisle's and Dixon's.

80. Jeff Titon, *Early Downhome Blues: A Musical and Cultural Analysis*, 2nd ed. (Chapel Hill: University of North Carolina Press, 1994), 65.

81. In this session, Wolf also recorded one of the most famous blues preaching songs, "Going Down Slow" by St. Louis Jimmy Oden. In this recording, Dixon and Wolf share vocal parts, although this is not a duet in a true sense. This kind of attempt featuring two voices is exceptional for the Chess recordings, except for duets by Dixon and Koko.

82. Dixon, *Willie Dixon*, 67.

83. Segrest and Hoffman, *Moanin' at Midnight*, 196.

84. The lyric sheet of "Tail Dragger" is found in the photo spread in the middle of this book.

85. In this take, Wolf sings, "I'm a tail dragger, I swipes out my tracks." On the other hand, the reason for his losing the timing was possibly due to the irregularity of the first hook, which has nine measures instead of eight.

86. See the section entitled "Other Artists on Cobra Records" in chapter 6.

87. Dixon, *I Am the Blues*, 149.

88. For this reason, the vocal was overdubbed, which can also be identified from the separation of the vocal part from the instruments in the recordings.

89. Segrest and Hoffman, *Moanin' at Midnight*, 198.

90. See appendix A, "Dixon's Compositional Procedure: Songwriting, Teaching Songs to Featured Artisits, Arrangements, and Production." Marie Dixon remembers when he wrote this song.

91. Dixon, *I Am the Blues*, 148.

92. Dixon, *Willie Dixon*, 27.

93. Butch Dixon, interview by the author, September 23, 2003.

94. Segrest and Hoffman, *Moanin' at Midnight*, xvi.

95. Will Romano, *Incurable Blues: The Troubles & Triumph of Blues Legend Hubert Sumlin* (San Francisco: Backbeat Books, 2005), 76.

96. Guralnick, *Feel Like Going Home*, 165.

97. Segrest and Hoffman, *Moanin' at Midnight*, 120.

98. Shirli Dixon, interview by the author, September 23, 2002.

99. For the definition and characteristics of "the new generation," see the introductory paragraphs of chapter 6.

100. Some of these co-compositions are credited to three composers, such as Guy, Dixon, and Little Brother Montgomery or Billy "The Kid" Emerson.

101. Dixon, *I Am the Blues*, 146.

102. Buddy replies to the question about who his main influences were:

B. B. King always. Well, I like Muddy Waters and Howlin' Wolf, you know, and I always did dig Little Walter and T-Bone Walker and all of 'em, but I still dig B. B. I would put B. B. No. 1, you know, because I just like the style he play, and some of the things he plays just really mess up my mind.

Jim O'Neal and Tim Zorn, "Interview: Buddy Guy," *Living Blues* 1, no. 2 (Summer 1970): 3.

103. Donald E. Wilcock, *Damn Right I've Got the Blues: Buddy Guy and the Blues Roots of Rock-and-Roll* (San Francisco: Woodford Press, 1993), 21.

104. In one source, Buddy says Magic Sam introduced him to Toscano, while in another, he says he was introduced by Rush. Andrew M. Robble, "Buddy Guy: You Got to Play That Thing Like You Was Flyin' a Plane," *Living Blues*, no. 112 (November/December 1993): 13; Wilcock, *Damn Right I've Got the Blues*, 42.

105. Dixon, *I Am the Blues*, 111.

106. Butch Dixon, interview by the author, September 23, 2003.

107. Dixon, *I Am the Blues*, 109.

108. Ibid.

109. Jas Obrecht, "Buddy Guy," in *Rollin' and Tumblin': The Postwar Blues Guitarists*, ed. Jas Obrecht (San Francisco: Miller Freeman Books, 2000), 266.

110. Wilcock, *Damn Right I've Got the Blues*, 44. Dixon's performance was in a minor mode, as it is included in his 1959 solo album *Willie's Blues*.

111. "I Got a Strange Feeling" is a co-composition by Dixon and Al Perkins. Perkins was a singer, DJ, producer, and manager based in Memphis, Chicago, and Detroit. He made several 45s and produced Little Milton's album on MCA.

112. Robble, "Buddy Guy," 15–16.

113. In this session, Buddy rerecorded "I Got a Strange Feeling" under the new title "When My Left Eye Jumps."

114. Wilcock, *Damn Right I've Got the Blues*, 50.

115. This song is a co-composition by Dixon and Michael P. Murphy.

116. Dixon's briefing version to Hytower is included in appendix A.

117. Shirli Dixon, interview by the author, September 23, 2002. In Dixon's autobiography and in the interview for *Living Blues*, he introduces some humorous episodes with Sonny Boy when they were in Europe for the American Folk Blues Festival tour. See Dixon, *I Am the Blues*, 140–41, 153–54; Corritore, Ferris, and O'Neal, "Willie Dixon (Part 2)," 25–28.

118. Bob Koester, interview by the author, September 20, 2004.

119. A possible birth date of Sonny Boy Williamson is discussed in William E. Donoghue, *'Fessor Mojo's "Don't Start Me to Talkin'"* (Seattle: Mojo Visions Productions, 1997), 10–11.

120. Cub Koda, "Sonny Boy Williamson [II]," in AMG *All Music Guide to the Blues: The Experts' Guide to the Best Blues Recordings*, 2nd ed., ed. Michael Erlewine, Vladimir Bogdanov, Chris Woodstra, and Cub Koda (San Francisco: Miller Freeman Books, 1999), 484; Mark A. Humphrey, "Bright Lights, Big City," in *Nothing but the Blues: The Music and the Musicians*, ed. Lawrence Cohn (New York: Abbeville Press, 1993), 191.

121. Mark Humphrey, "Liner Notes," *The Essential Sonny Boy Williamson*, recorded by Sonny Boy Williamson (Universal City, CA: MCA/Chess, CHD2–9343, 1993), 2.

122. Chris Morris and Willie Dixon, "Liner Notes," *The Real Folk Blues*, recorded by Sonny Boy Williamson (Universal City, CA: Chess/MCA Records, CHD-9272, 1987), 5. "Foots" probably derives from "footsie," a slang term that means to waste

time. Jonathan Green, ed., *Cassell's Dictionary of Slang* (London: Cassell, 1998; repr., 1999), 440. It also means "to express affection by using the foot to caress another's foot and ankle, esp. surreptitiously, as under a table." J. E. Lighter, ed., *Random House Historical Dictionary of American Slang*, vol. 1, A–G (New York: Random House, 1994), 799. In another theory, he was called "foots" because of the size of his feet.

123. Segrest and Hoffman, *Moanin' at Midnight*, 40.

124. *Sweet Home Chicago: Story of Chess Records* [VHS]. Dixon also says: "If Sonny Boy Williamson didn't have the right song on one of his sessions, he would make up something that would fit just as good and keep right on playing." Dixon, *I Am the Blues*, 154.

125. For this session, Sonny Boy recorded "Bye Bye Bird," an instrumental that he and Dixon co-composed.

126. See the section entitled "Big Walter 'Shakey' Horton" in chapter 6.

127. Marie Dixon, interview by the author, September 25, 2004.

128. Corritore, Ferris, and O'Neal, "Willie Dixon (Part 2)," 28.

129. Ibid.

130. Shirli Dixon, interview by the author, September 23, 2002.

131. Michael B. Smith, "Koko Taylor," *Goldmine* 27, no. 2 (January 26, 2001): 15.

132. Koko Taylor, interview by the author, September 27, 2002. In one interview in 1972, Taylor said that she auditioned for a Chicago radio deejay and A&R (artist and repertoire) person for several record companies, Big Bill Hill, and he introduced her to Willie Dixon. Taylor says, "I met Big Bill Hill before I met Willie Dixon. He was the first to take me to Willie and asked him if there was anything he could do to help me. So actually been knowing Bill Hill longer than I been knowing Willie." Amy O'Neal, "Koko Taylor," *Living Blues* (Winter 1972): 11.

133. *Chicago Blues: A Bonanza All Star Blues LP* on Spivey Records features Sunnyland Slim, John Henry Barbee, St. Louis Jimmy, and Homesick James, as well as Dixon and Koko—here, her name is spelled "Cocoa Taylor." In addition to two recordings featuring Koko's vocal, there are two recordings by Dixon, "Weak Brain! Narrow Mind!" and "So Long!" (written by Spivey and Albert Luandrew—a different song from Dixon's Chess recording with the same title). Spivey Records was a very low-budget label. Producer Len Kunstadt had a rough-and-ready approach to recording, and the sound quality of the records is as if they recorded for personal use with a cassette tape recorder. They made a small number of copies only for limited fans but released forty albums from 1961 to 1980.

134. Taylor, interview by the author, September 27, 2002. USA Records had nothing to do with Victoria Spivey.

135. Niles Frantz, "Koko Taylor: Forever the Queen of the Blues," *Blues Revue*, no. 38 (June 1988): 18.

136. Shirli Dixon, interview by the author, September 23, 2002.

137. Ibid.

138. Taylor, interview by the author, September 27, 2002.

139. Ibid.

140. Ibid.

141. Willie Dixon, *Working on the Blues*, vol. 2 (Tokyo: P-Vine Records, PCD-2347, 1992).

142. Taylor, interview by the author, September 27, 2002.

143. Ibid.

144. The words in parentheses are sung by a male backup chorus in a call-and-response form with Koko.

145. See the section entitled "Willie Dixon's Own Chess Recordings" in chapter 5.

146. Taylor, interview by the author, September 27, 2002.

147. Ibid.

148. Whitburn, *Top R&B Singles, 1942–1999*, 435. In spite of the phenomenal success, Koko claims that she was unrewarded by the company. She remembers,

> Well, they told me it sold a million copies, but then I owed for the session and I owed for this and that and hey, you know, wasn't nothin' I could do about it and I didn't know the difference. Plus I was just happy to have been able to do recording, so that was the end of that. I accepted happily then I'm still accepting it happily because even though I didn't get any money for it, "Wang Dang Doodle" did give me recognition through a lot of fans.

Larry Hollis and Eddie Ferguson, "Koko Taylor Interview," *Cadence* 10 (May 1984): 19–20.

149. Taylor, interview by the author, September 27, 2002.

150. The words in parentheses are sung by Taylor with a female backup chorus.

151. "St. James Infirmary" is a folk song of anonymous origin, though sometimes it is credited to Joe Primrose—a pseudonym for Irving Mills. Louis Armstrong made it famous in his 1928 recording. Others artists who recorded this song include Cab Calloway, King Oliver, Big Mama Thornton, and Billie Holiday.

152. The lyrics of "29 Ways" can be found in the section "Willie Dixon's Own Chess Recordings" of chapter 5.

153. Taylor, interview by the author, September 27, 2002.

154. Ed Winfield and Hitoshi Koide, "Liner Notes," *Born to Love Me*, recorded by Jimmy Reeves Jr. (Chicago: Checker, LPS-3016, 1970; reissue, Tokyo: Universal Music, UICY-93317, 2007). This record was out of print for a long time, but it was reissued in Japan.

155. Ibid.

156. Other musicians involved were guitarists Mighty Joe Young and Matt Murphy, pianists Sunnyland Slim and Lafayette Leake, harmonica player Big Walter Horton, bassist Sylvester Boines, drummer Morris Jennings, and the backup singers called the Pick-Ups. Les Fancourt and Bob McGrath, *The Blues Discography, 1943–1970* (Canada: Eyeball Productions, 2006), 460.

157. Guralnick, *Feel Like Going Home*, 229.

158. Ibid.

159. See note 7 (p. 282). In his autobiography, Dixon talks about his troublesome relationship with Peterson and his family. Dixon, *I Am the Blues*, 208.

160. Guralnick critically writes about the singer and musicians: "The band sounds too great, too good for the singer, a pale carbon copy of Jimmy Reed whom he sporadically claims to be his father." Guralnick, *Feel Like Going Home*, 231.

161. Dixon, *I Am the Blues*, 119.

162. Marie Dixon, interview by the author, September 25, 2004.

163. Dixon, *I Am the Blues*, 126. At that time, Lippmann believed there were no blues performers left, mainly because Big Bill Broonzy, who had visited Europe previously, introduced himself as the last of the bluesmen. Corritore, Ferris, and O'Neal, "Willie Dixon (Part 2)," 25.

164. Benjamin Filene writes the significance of the AFBF was "the concept of a blues 'package' tour, in which large 'all-star' troupes traveled from city to city." More importantly, the AFBF rosters "included an eclectic mix of down-home and big-city performers," whereas the first phase of the blues revival mostly featured rural, old-fashioned style of blues performers. Filene, *Romancing the Folk: Public Memory & American Roots Music* (Chapel Hill: University of North Carolina Press, 2000), 121.

165. Dixon says one of his duties as a tour manager was preparing legal documents to get passports for the musicians. In the autobiography, he talks about the difficulty getting documents because musicians often did not know the necessary information, such as correct birth dates and places, and legal names of family members. Dixon, *I Am the Blues*, 127.

166. Koester, interview by the author, September 20, 2004. He adds, "There is another story. Willie Dixon would come back from European tour, smuggling Swiss watches in his bass. I don't know if that's true. That's a good story. A cute story." Ibid.

167. Willie Dixon, *I Am the Blues* [DVD] (Huntingdon Cambs, England: CJ Productions and Quantum Leap Group, DRB-1345, 2002).

168. Dixon, *I Am the Blues*, 135.

169. Dixon, *I Am the Blues* [DVD].

170. Filene, *Romancing the Folk*, 123.

171. Dixon, *I Am the Blues* [DVD].

172. Marie Dixon, interview by the author, September 25, 2004.

173. Mike Rowe, *Chicago Blues: The City and the Music* [originally titled *Chicago Breakdown*] (London: Eddison Press, 1973; repr., New York: Da Capo Press, 1975), 172. Citations are to the Da Capo Press edition. Their second album, *Memphis Slim and Willie Dixon*, is a collection of folk materials and old blues songs that were their main repertoire, such as "Stewball," "John Henry," "44 Blues," and "Kansas City."

174. Filene, *Romancing the Folk*, 113.

175. In addition to Dixon and Slim, other musicians included Wally Richardson (guitar), Hal Ashby (tenor sax), and Gus Johnson (drums).

176. Dixon, *Willie Dixon*, 56.

177. Dixon probably means a "shiv" (knife), though he pronounces it "chib."

178. This transcription is based on his performance in Hamburg, Germany, on October 9, 1964, which is included in *American Folk Blues Festival '62 to '65* [CD]. Notes by Bill Dahl (Conshohocken, PA: Evidence, ECD 26100, 1995). See bibliography.

179. See appendix B for details.

180. Jim O'Neal, "Junior Wells," 22.

181. Dixon's version of "God's Gift to Man"—originally titled "Firey Love"—is discussed in the section entitled "Willie Dixon's Own Chess Recordings" in chapter 5.

182. Dixon, *Willie Dixon*, 231.

~

Postscript

Before concluding my work, I will briefly summarize Dixon's work and life in the 1970s and 1980s. Dixon kept performing, writing songs, making records, and occasionally producing other artists' recordings after Chess Records closed down. In 1969, before Dixon ended his relationship with Chess Records, he purchased an old store and made a storefront studio called Blues Factory. This place was also used to give seminars on the blues. He also started his own label, Yambo.

The albums Willie Dixon made in the post–Chess Records period include *Peace* (Yambo, 1972), *Catalyst* (Ovation, 1973, Grammy Award nomination), *What's Happened to My Blues?* (Ovation, 1976), *Mighty Earthquake and Hurricane* (Pausa, 1984), *15 July, 1983 Live! Backstage Access* (Pausa, 1985; Grammy Award nomination), *Hidden Charms* (Bug/Capitol, 1988; Grammy Award winner), and a film soundtrack, *Ginger Ale Afternoon* (1989, Varese Sarabande/MCA Distributing Corp.; Grammy Award nomination).

One of his representative compositions in his post–Chess Records period is "It Don't Make Sense (You Can't Make Peace)" in *Mighty Earthquake and Hurricane*. This song still reflects Dixon's stance of the blues preacher:

> [Verse 1]
> You have made great planes to span the skies,
> You gave sight to the blind with other men's eyes,
> You even made submarines stay submerged for weeks,
> But it don't make sense you can't make peace.

[Verse 2]
You take one man's heart and make another man live,
You even go to the moon and come back thrilled,
Why you can crush any country in a matter of weeks,
But it don't make sense you can't make peace.

[Vamp]
You know it don't make sense (you can't make peace),
You know it don't make sense (you can't make peace),
You know it don't make sense (you can't make peace),
When you can't make peace (you can't make peace).

[Harmonica solo]

[Verse 3]
You can make a transfusion that can save a life,
Why you can change the darkness into broad daylight,
You make the deaf man hear and the dumb man speak,
But it don't make sense you can't make peace.

This is a minor blues in a medium-slow tempo. Dixon's technique of
listing words and concepts is alive and well. According to Dixon, this was
his favorite of all the songs he wrote.[1] As seen in some of the compositions
discussed in chapter 7, Dixon continued to be enthused about social issues,
and this song consolidates his philosophy.

In 1977, Dixon's diabetes took a turn for the worse, and his right leg was
amputated. Shirli Dixon says that this did not affect him at all, although
there was another family accident that caused acceleration of his death:

> He was counseling the other men who had been in amputations, and one man
> said he felt like he had lost his life. My dad said, "You didn't, because you're
> talking. You're making this more than it is. God has you here talking to me."
> And it was so amazing to me . . . nothing really shook him. I saw one incident,
> the loss of my younger brother. I had never seen him crying a tear, even at my
> grandmother's funeral, but the loss of my younger brother, David, who was
> born on his birthday, I think accelerated his death.[2]

In 1977, with an aid of his business manager Scott Cameron, Dixon
retrieved the copyrights of his songs that had belonged to Arc music, the
publisher owned by the Chess brothers and Gene Goodman. In 1982, Dixon
established Blues Heaven Foundation to help musicians retrieve their copyrights, to promote an ongoing blues tradition, and to educate children; in

1997, the foundation was moved to 2120 South Michigan Avenue, Chicago, which had been the Chess Records building. Dixon participated in many blues workshops held at public schools, and he donated many instruments to children.

As previously mentioned, Dixon and Muddy Waters belonged to the same management, and they occasionally performed together. Dixon was featured for many blues festivals, and shared bills with artists such as John Lee Hooker, Jimmy Rogers, and Big Walter Horton. Dixon's 1984 performance with his old friend Leonard "Baby Doo" Caston is now available on DVD, *I Am the Blues*.

In 1983, Dixon and his family moved to California to escape Chicago's severe winters. His move to California resulted in his involvement with the film industry. Besides *Ginger Ale Afternoon*, in 1986 he recorded "Don't Tell Me Nothin'" for the soundtrack of *The Color of Money* (produced by Robbie Robertson), and Dixon produced his old label mate Bo Diddley's "Who Do You Love" on the *La Bamba* soundtrack (1987). Dixon also appeared in the film *Rich Girl* (1990).

In 1987, Dixon recorded a single, "AIDS to the Grave." This record was for the AIDS awareness campaign in California. According to Vernell Jennings of American Music Legends Publishing, who brought this project to Dixon, one thousand copies of this recording were distributed to local schools and relevant ministries.[3] This was Dixon's last recording as a featured artist.

In 1988, MCA Records issued *Willie Dixon: The Chess Box*, a compilation of his representative works performed by Muddy Waters, Little Walter, Howlin' Wolf, Koko Taylor, Dixon himself, and others. In 1989, Dixon published his autobiography, *I Am the Blues*.

Dixon's last recording session was with Bob Weir of the Grateful Dead at Dixon's home studio in early 1992. Dixon's famous saying, "The blues are the roots of all American music," is proven by his career, which started with a Mills Brothers–like vocal harmony group and ended with a session with a member of the Grateful Dead, by way of the Bluebird sound, jump blues, and the postwar electric Chicago blues.

On January 29, 1992, Willie Dixon died in Burbank, California. The immediate cause was acute circulatory collapse, which was due to cardiomyopathy and diabetes mellitus. He was seventy-six years old.

His body was moved to Chicago. The colorful procession (like those seen in New Orleans) was followed by a funeral service, in which three black Baptist ministers and Louis Farrakhan, minister of the Nation of Islam, participated, as well as musicians, friends, family members, and fans. Dixon's death brought the leaders of different religious groups together. The following statements by two religious leaders actually describe the work of Willie Dixon as a preacher in the secular context. Louis Farrakhan said,

> Willie Dixon brought forth what was within. It was a song. It was creative genius. And that song and the creative genius helped Willie Dixon to face the oppression of his life, the pain of being black in a racist society. Without that song we couldn't be here today. Without the music of the gospel that touches our soul, we couldn't walk in this world without comfort. It was the song that comforted us. It is the word that comforts us.[4]

Reverend A. Patterson Jackson talked about Dixon's song as secular hymn: "I could understand the singing of Big Willie, because I said that the blues is the gospel turned inside out, and the other side of the picture, amen."[5]

In 1994, Dixon's achievements were honored with his induction into the "early influence" category of the Rock and Roll Hall of Fame.

The most important motivation for me in this research was to find the missing link between Dixon's definition of the blues, in which wisdom is the most important element, and the actual songs through which he characterized singers. As presented in the introduction, I proposed several questions: How do we reconcile the quest for wisdom with such Dixon creations as "Hoochie Coochie Man"? Also, the song "I Just Want to Make Love to You" is apparently about machismo, but is blatant sexual appetite all that Dixon wanted to express through Muddy's performance? Similarly, what made Dixon decide to give a didactic song like "Spoonful" to Howlin' Wolf, the same man he cast as an ominous figure in "Back Door Man"? Therefore, one of the aims of this work is to reread Dixon's songs through a consideration of what they meant to him and understanding of his people's culture and traditions.

In sum, as demonstrated by Dixon's statements and other evidence presented herein, blues is placed at the opposite end of the spectrum from the gospel music in the philosophical level. One is about an afterlife, and the other is about an existential (realist) idea—that is, life here and now, "the true facts of life"—operating in a secular context. Regardless of their differences, some of the functions of the blues are comparable to a religion. The role of blues singers in their performing context is parallel to that of preachers of organized religion. Similar to charismatic African American preachers, blues singers are lifters, healers, and educators in the communities, and they deliver life lessons, proverbs, parables, wisdom, and a code of life to their audience. This is what blues meant for Willie Dixon.

As a professional songwriter, his work was of course to write hit songs. But more importantly, when he wrote blues songs and gave them to some particular singers, he developed preachers in the secular context and wrote sermons for them to preach. Dixon's theorizing about the blues, his philosophy, and his compositions clearly reflect this paradigm of the blues, whether he was conscious of it or not, besides providing singers with potentially hit songs.

Shirli Dixon summarizes her father's work as follows. She supports my view of his role—a preacher/sermon writer in the secular context:

All of his work, he thought, was message music. In particular, my father believed that the blues represented the life circumstance, and gospel represented afterlife circumstances or the desire for the afterlife circumstance. . . . He wrote some very controversial songs towards the end of his life, "May not be no pie in the sky, when you die." What he meant was "May not be heaven and hell." He thought, they may exist on earth . . . heaven and hell may be how we live day to day.

While he loved and appreciated God, he also recognized that the facts that he saw in life had certain things on a questionable basis. . . . Because he was a realist, as he later grew in his life, he began to voice his concerns about how some of the gospel music or some of the gospel messages may challenge the things that we understood in life.

So, in terms of him being a preacher or scholar or his theory being one that he was offering to the general public, he was, in fact.[6]

Considering the background of traditional black cultural values and the philosophy behind the blues, Willie Dixon was more than a commercial songwriter, and blues singers were more than entertainers. The heart and soul of Dixon compositions cannot be understood until they are interpreted in this paradigm. Shirli Dixon explains that her father's ultimate aim of songwriting was sending messages and providing therapy to his audiences:

My dad used to say to me, "If you have that many people listening to you, then you should be saying something worthwhile." So whether it was Muddy as his messenger, or Wolf as his messenger, or Koko Taylor, you know, or Little Walter, he believed that if somebody was willing to pay attention, you should have something with a real substance to offer. . . . What he told us was blues could be a therapy, because it let you know that you were not alone in your circumstance, that the reality of getting out that issue was near at hand or at least a possibility.[7]

Shirli stresses the idiomatic attitude of bluesmen toward life and how her father's songs work in relation to their attitude. One of the key elements of his music is its psychological function—therapy:

> I used to manage a rap act, Dr. Dre, when he was in his early band, the Wrecking Cru. One of the things that I sought to teach him as well as all the other young artists that were around us, was the difference in blues artists and rap artists is the resolve, the response, and the reaction to your circumstance by a bluesman and blueswoman is to look for a way out.
>
> As a "Hoochie Coochie Man," "I'm good. I'm boastful. I'm great. You can see that, you know. I can do some phenomenal things." A song like "I'm Ready" would be "Hey, I can do anything I need to do, including protect myself if you approach me." And "Back Door Man," "I can do absolutely anything. I'm a man. I'm a real man that's able to conquer any situation that I approach."[8]

As discussed earlier, "Hoochie Coochie Man" establishes the character of the singer—Muddy Waters—and of equal importance, this song functions as a "cheer-up song." The boastful content of the song functions as a psychological boost and gives the audience an uplifting feeling.

At the same time, Shirli Dixon says, another key element in Dixon's compositions is educational—wisdom:

> When I think of writers like Albert King and others as well that were around my dad . . . "Everybody wants to go to heaven, but nobody wants to die. Everybody wants to hear the truth, but everybody will tell a lie."[9] You see, the blues has this wisdom built in it automatically, and it's just a matter of whether you could receive it.
>
> His [Willie Dixon's] songs like "Good Advice," "Keep on going, when you sure you're right . . ." "A barking dog will seldom bite." He explained this to us as kids. He said, "While you hear a dog barking, you are not likely to go up to the gate and walk in the yard." "What's done in the dark will come to the light." Anything you hide eventually will surface. "An eye for eye, and a tooth for tooth." I'll do the same thing you do to me. "Back of the berries, squeeze of the juice." We all know that. "You can't tell a farmer from a lover." He'd say you might put on a set of overalls, or Muddy Waters wore a set of overalls, you wouldn't know he is just a romantic, wonderful person, just like "You can't judge a book by looking at the cover."
>
> So wisdom was a key factor and the deliverance of blues then and now. And what is happening, as it has become diluted, it no longer makes any sense. And sometimes the message is pure love relations. My dad used to say the love of anything will give you the blues. Anything at all will make you, if

you love anything, it will bring on your true feelings. In his mind, true feelings represented the blues.

He just believed in it [the blues] as a communication tool, and certainly as a therapy. He would say, "If I can feel what I feel, there's gotta be more people in the world like me."[10]

In this sense, Dixon's compositions more or less contain wisdom and they are sermons to preach, regardless of who received his songs. But his songs work most effectively when he gives commanding roles to singers, as seen in Muddy Waters, Howlin' Wolf, and Koko Taylor. On one hand, he cast them as black badmanlike figures that can be placed at the opposite end of the spectrum from high moral figures—the preachers of sacred context—but on the other hand, these outlaws deliver wisdom for the real-life situations as preachers in the secular context. In this way, providing Howlin' Wolf with the ominous "Back Door Man" and the didactic "Spoonful" is not contradictory in Dixon's mind.

It is important not to forget that Dixon was a working songwriter who wanted to make hit songs and some money, but the way he wrote songs for a commercial purpose was much more meaningful than making money. He knew his songs could speak for people of his community, and that was his ultimate wish as a songwriter. Dixon summarizes his songwriting philosophy and how to write appealing songs:

> Many people have something that they would like to say to the world and would like the world to know about. But most people never get a chance to say these things. And then, you're going to try to make them see something in a song that individuals can't see for themselves. Like the average man has his own feelings about women or love or whatever—what's in his heart or what's in his mind. All of a sudden, here comes somebody that's singing it outright. You know good and well what he's talking about, and he knows what you're talking about. Then that gives you an inspiration because here's a guy who's saying just what you wanted to say. That's what makes hit songs, things that are common to any individual—and it's not a complicated thing. It makes it easier for life, easy to express, easy to say. Blues songs are facts of life, whether it's our life or somebody else's.[11]

Willie Dixon's work cannot be confined to his work as a composer, arranger, producer, and bass player. Over the course of his life and through his experience, he grew as a blues spokesperson into the embodiment of the blues preacher. As a philosopher and a sermon writer, he had to select suitable artists

with appropriate style to deliver his wisdom as blues preachers. His exploration of the performing persona was inseparable from the act of creating a blues
preacher. And he documented important parts of his culture. As a preacher of
the blues, Dixon wanted to inspire listeners though outstanding singers.

Through Dixon's efforts to embed his culture in several lines of poetry and
sounds of instruments, I have discovered a rich African American tradition.
My discovery went beyond just understanding Willie Dixon's work. His work
is a key in understanding the abundance of his culture. Harmonica player
Billy Branch, who was a member of Dixon's band in the 1980s, said that
Dixon had foreseen that the blues would be a means to discover the richness
of the African-derived tradition:

> I think Willie, above all musicians, and especially from his era, he is the single
> most person that had this vision and understanding of the blues and its rel-
> evance to the world and its historical significance past and future. He had the
> vision. . . . He understood how significant, how powerful, and how big a debt
> of that the world owes to the blues.
>
> Like a lot of guys happen to play music and make the money. But Willie
> realized the political ramifications of the blues. . . . I never forget. This is an
> interesting thing. At one point Willie sent a letter to . . . every member of the
> Congress . . . and stating that there was a conspiracy to keep the blues off the
> radio. And that was a pretty bold and pretty insightful move. Here's the guy,
> certainly not college educated, but very world educated and street educated,
> that was able to surmise that there was a virtual conspiracy to keep the blues
> off the radio. And you say, "Well, why?"[12]

The answer Billy derives from Dixon is linked to the Dixon's fundamental
definition of the blues, which Billy uses as a slogan for his program "Blues
in Schools":

> "Why are we here? To sing and play the blues. What are the blues? The facts
> of life." Well, I got that directly from Willie Dixon. And then it says, "What
> makes the blues so important? They are our history, our culture, and the roots
> of American music."
>
> So Willie said, "If it becomes known my culture is just as great or greater
> than your culture, then what basis do I have to put you down?" So you see the
> connection? In other words, by suppressing the blues, you're suppressing the
> culture, and you're enabling racism. . . . To me, it was just a fantastic correla-
> tion. Who'd have thought that? Who would have thought that by not playing
> the blues, you're enabling racism? Because if you play blues, then you're goin'

back to the roots. And when you go back to the roots, people goin' to start looking into, delving a little bit more in the history. When you delve in history, then you get the true story. . . . If you get in history, you find out that African-derived culture is much much richer and broader than has been widely publicized. . . . He truly was a visionary.[13]

"What did Willie Dixon want to teach us through all those songs he wrote?" I asked Marie Dixon when concluding my interview. She answered, "He wanted you to know the facts of life. And if you understand life, then you will understand the blues."[14]

I think I understand at least some parts of Willie Dixon's blues and his philosophy, although this understanding has taken many years to develop since my first exposure to his music—"Little Red Rooster" on the Rolling Stones' *Love You Live*. This comment by Mick Jagger on Dixon's work actually describes my feelings now: "Rather foolishly I didn't take notice of more of his work."[15]

Notes

1. Willie Dixon, with Don Snowden, *I Am the Blues: The Willie Dixon Story* (New York: Da Capo Press, 1989), 228.
2. Shirli Dixon, interview by the author, September 24, 2002.
3. Jennings wrote,

Willie and I worked together for about 8 years. . . . The AIDS project was done in summer of 1987 in Northridge, California, at Kings Record Studios. Willie's musicians on this project were: Al Duncan (drums), Cash McCall (bass), Freddy Robinson (guitar). I was asked by a staff of doctors to write a song about AIDS to help save the kids. . . . When they heard the ones we had already written, they had a fit. We received a lot of awards. The recording was put into the U.S. Education Data Base and endorsed by the CDC, The Surgeon General, The Mayor, The Governor and a lot of major people. We received write-ups and went on T.V. The Radio DJs decided that people didn't want to hear a song about AIDS, so they refused to play it!

Vernell Jennings, e-mail correspondence with the author, July 11, 2005.
4. Louis Farrakhan is quoted in Jim O'Neal, "Willie Dixon, 1915–1992: A Tribute," *Living Blues*, no. 103 (May/June 1992): 48.
5. Rev. A. Patterson Jackson is quoted in O'Neal, "Willie Dixon," 48.
6. Shirli Dixon, interview by the author, September 24, 2002.
7. Ibid.
8. Ibid.
9. "Everybody Wants to Go to Heaven" is written by Don Nix.

10. Shirli Dixon, interview by the author, September 24, 2002.

11. Worth Long, "The Wisdom of the Blues—Defining Blues as the True Facts of Life: An Interview with Willie Dixon," *African American Review* 29, no. 2 (Summer 1995): 210.

12. Billy Branch, interview by the author, September 27, 2002.

13. Ibid.

14. Marie Dixon, interview by the author, September 25, 2004.

15. Mick Jagger is quoted in *Willie Dixon's Blues Heaven Foundation's Record Row Festival* [concert brochure] (Chicago: Willie Dixon, 2002).

~

Appendix A: Dixon's Compositional Procedure: Songwriting, Teaching Songs to Featured Artists, Arrangements, and Production

Shirli Dixon, Butch Dixon, Marie Dixon, Koko Taylor, and Billy Branch Remember

As discussed in chapter 2, Willie Dixon started to compose songs quite early on. Because he had practiced writing poetry and songs since he was a teenager, he did not choose a special time or place to start the earliest stage of composition. When he was asked when and where he would write songs, he answered,

> Oh no, I don't have no set time. When I get the right idea—it comes to me—I start writing. I always have a book. If I don't have the book and pencil with me I get in my mind and I start thinking about it. Sometimes I'll stop just to think it over and when I get to the house I write on it.[1]

Dixon's daughter Shirli remembers he was writing "all the time, wherever he was able to."[2] Where and on what? "He would take napkins at a restaurant. . . . He wrote a song on the back of the place mat. . . . Or in the car, he would grab a book . . . anything. He always had a pocket full of pens just in case because he said he gets inspirations all the time."[3] Dixon's son Butch adds,

> He could be sitting and hearing something, or watching TV and rocking his little recliner, and then he'd go, "You know what? Gimme a piece of paper. That's ok. Gimme a pen." He had a pen and a paper bag, and he would write

a song. So I think it depends on exactly what he had at that time. He did that song about Hank Aaron broke Babe Ruth's record. He did that "It Don't Make Sense You Can't Make Peace" when the war was on. So I'm sure whatever hit at that moment, he wrote about. It was never like someday he sat and thought out. . . . And next thing is, you know, "Butch, come here, get on the piano. Play just like this and this." We'd go to dig a lead sheet, and before you know it, it would be on record.[4]

According to Butch, the first stage did not take very long for Willie. It was "usually a matter of thirty or forty minutes to put down his first idea, though of course he might change here and there later in a course of recording."[5]

Now, how did the creative inspiration come about? Butch Dixon replies, "Life in general. Life."[6] Dixon's wife, Marie, also asserts, "In writing his songs, he wrote about everyday events—maybe 95 percent of everything that could happen to a person in this world."[7] Willie Dixon once explained his knack to write impressive songs—using an inspiration from life experiences that his audiences could relate to:

Well, you see, I'd begin after a certain length of time to take in a part of life. Whether it was my experiences or other people's experiences and putting it together in words and trying to find the right time to emphasize these facts of life. And I found out by using some of the past it fitted a lot of the people and fits also our hopes for the future. So filling these things up in your mind, and putting the various tunes to 'em, why, it always interested people.[8]

As was the case with many popular music songwriters, when Willie Dixon wrote a song, he would usually write only words. As Butch Dixon says, "For him, it's mostly lyric sheets."[9] Willie did not write specific arrangement ideas or musical instructions such as chords and riffs, and needless to say, he left out a musical notation system as well. Using music sheets to note more concrete musical ideas was Dixon's partner Lafayette Leake's idea, says Butch:

Well, I think, most of the time, Lafayette Leake did all that notation thing. It was his idea. Lafayette Leake put it on paper. My dad wrote words and hummed what he wanted to hear. And Lafayette Leake or later on myself was sitting at the piano . . . and put black dots to 'em.[10]

I had a chance to see two of Dixon's original lyric sheets displayed by the Blues Heaven Foundation: "You Need to Be Loved," later recorded as "You Need Love" by Muddy Waters; and "Tail Dragger," recorded by Howlin' Wolf. On both sheets, all the lyrics are written with a blue ballpoint pen on a page of notebook paper in very neat cursive. The title of the song is written on top of the page, followed by the first verse. After a single space, this is followed by another verse. Although there are some words crossed out in "You Need to Be Loved," both sheets indicate that Dixon wrote words directly from the ideas in his mind—almost without change, if these lyric sheets were typical.

Marie Dixon shared some actual moments of the earliest phase of Dixon's writing. "The Same Thing," which Muddy Waters recorded in 1964, was born from a conversation about popular fashion of the time:

> Lots of times I would see Willie sitting and doing it with a pencil, and then someone would say something, and he'd say, "You know, that's a good title to a song." And he would write that what you said, and he would build around that. Like when he did "The Same Thing," that was during the sixties. And he mentioned how women wore dresses so tight. And they did, well, barely fit in clothes in those days. We all did. And he'd sit down, and he wrote down what'd make a man go crazy when a woman wore a dress so tight.[11]

She also remembers when Dixon was writing "Three Hundred Pounds of Joy," which Howlin' Wolf recorded in 1963:

> He was sittin', and the sun was settin' for the evening. And I said something to him like "Your music is not going anywhere at this time. Maybe you should change your career." And he said, "No, I'm gonna make it with my music. . . ." He was leaning back in the chair, legs crossed . . . and he said, "You know, I think I write me a song." And I said, "About what?" He said, "'Three Hundred Pounds of Heavenly Joy.' That's my size." And that's how he wrote it.[12]

Besides writing a lyric sheet as a start of composition, there were times he used a tape recorder to capture basic musical ideas, when it became a handy and affordable device. Shirli Dixon says, "He was never anyplace without a tape recorder to sing the melody."[13] Then, after establishing the fundamentals, he hired an amanuensis—either a guitar or piano player—to see the more concrete shape of the composition. Shirli Dixon describes,

> And ultimately to play the melody either by piano or guitar, he would need to bring in a guitarist or pianist. There were never any popular musicians, but young ones that he knew. And he would say, "This is what I want." And sometimes he would hum it to him, sometimes he would play it for him, or sometimes he would tell them, "I already started putting this down, and I want you to play like this, and we're gonna make these changes as I like to complete it," or whatever.[14]

306 ⌣ Appendix A

After the first stage of songwriting, the next step was to teach the song to a featured artist. While the songs Dixon wrote for the Big Three Trio were for them to record, his compositions for Chess Records were mainly written with the assumption that artists (usually other than himself) of the company would record them. He rarely anticipated who would sing a song when he wrote it, except in a few cases—for example, "Tail Dragger" for Howlin' Wolf—but his large inventory of varied compositions meant he was always ready to provide a suitable song whenever a vocalist needed something.

There are several ways Dixon taught songs to singers. In the case of "Hoochie Coochie Man," Dixon told Muddy Waters just the words and the riff while they were in the bathroom of the club where Muddy and his band were playing. Bo Diddley remembers when he recorded "Pretty Thing," Dixon was "standin' over me, whisperin' the lyrics in my ear before I got to the next line."[15] In the case of "Tail Dragger," Dixon provided Howlin' Wolf with a guide vocal recording with the same backing track. Butch Dixon says the latter two methods were Dixon's usual ways to demonstrate songs, "because most of the artists didn't have reading skills to pick up things a little quickly. If he can whisper to you right there, you can grasp it . . . or he would sit down to do it over tape. . . . So it's like a class or something you go to study this, and then we get back to it."[16]

In the case of Koko Taylor, Dixon invited her to his house any time he had an idea for her. Shirli Dixon says, "He would call her all the time. She lived like down the street from us. She and her husband would come over, and then he just started working on, saying, 'This is a perfect song for you that I have ever written.'"[17] Koko describes,

> Then he'd give me the words. I'd read the words. Here are the words to sing. Then he would give me a demonstration of how the song was supposed to, you know, flow . . . with the music. Then at that point, I just concentrated and learned the song the way I can. He played that for me, with a demonstration record or something.[18]

Typically artists learned songs by hearing Dixon's humming while hitting something like a newspaper or magazine to keep the beat with his fingers or a pen—no formal instruments required at this point. Shirli Dixon played for me a private tape that captured such a moment.

This tape was made sometime in the 1980s for vocalist/guitarist Roy Hytower to introduce "Every Girl I See Looks Good to Me."[19] First Dixon used the tape as a form of voice mail. Dixon gives general information, and then he gives a brief explanation about the song. Then Dixon starts to hit a pile of paper to show the basic beat and tempo. He sings the introductory melody, which is followed by the hook and verses. After singing, Dixon again provides more information about the song:

This is Willie Dixon. Frankly, to Jack and Jill, Roy Hytower. You know, I wrote quite a few songs for Muddy, and I appreciate the beautiful show that you fellas are doin.' I'm doing everything I possibly can to help promote people to come in there to see you, get you more customers. Of course, I'm telling them also that some of the songs that I actually wrote for Muddy,[20] and Muddy wasn't able to get to [play this song] before he passed, but maybe you will be probably doing some of them. Anyway I talked to you about it while I was in Chicago. And this particular tune, I'll give it to you a idea with my voice. Then I also give you a idea, (uh) with me playin' the harmonica; it [will] give you different ideas about it. So I'm not able to be there to direct you any other way. But this particular tune is called "Every Girl I See Look Good to Me." And you heard me do it, but I know—I hope you got the letter that I sent just yesterday. So anyway, this will give you a idea of how it's written and how it's done as a song. And the musical part of it, you can get the whole band do this part like this. [Dixon starts to hum the introductory melody while keeping a beat by hitting a paper pile as a drum. He tries to make the sound of harmonica by singing "tu tu tu tu tu." He repeats the introductory melody, and then he sings a hook.]

[Hook]
You look good, and you look good,
You look good, baby, you look good,
And every girls I see look good to me.

[Verse 1]
You know the girls I see that don't have feet [?],
They've got so much to cook in the [unintelligible],
What to do, well I can't tell,
All you can [could?] you know you sure look well,
Every girl I see look good to me.

[Dixon speaks, "Now you gonna pick this up, but I mean have that solid beat."]

[Hook]
You look good, and you look good,
You look good, and you look good,
Every girl I see look good to me.

[Dixon speaks, "Now I'm gonna give you the verses, too,"]

[Verse 2]
And the girls I see that are dressed in black,
You know you got just what I like,
And the girls I see that dressed in white,
I love you baby all day and night,
And the girls I see that are dressed in blue,

Baby, I know you know just what to do,
And the girls I see that are dressed in pink,
Are you the sweetest little thing that I ever seen.

[Hook]
Every girl I see look good to me,
Now every girl I see look good to me,
You look good, baby, you look good,
You look good, you look good, baby you look good,
Every girl I see look good to me.

[Verse 3]
Now the girls I see that are dressed in yellow,
Are, you know, you look sure fine and mellow,
And the girls I see that are dressed in red,
I could love you, baby, till [unintelligible] all day.

[Hook]
Every girl I see look good to me,
You look good, baby, you look good, sure enough,
You look good, baby, you look good,
And every girl I see, baby, look good to me.

[Verse 4]
The girls I see that are dressed in brown,
Sure don't look you put me down,
The girls I see that are dressed in pink,
Are you [unintelligible] for one drink.

[Hook]
Every girl I see look good to me,
You look good, baby, you look good,
You look good, baby, you look good,
Every girl I see look good to me.

Well, anyway that's the first idea that's giving you a kinda melody line. You'll probably do it in whatever key you want to, and you can also do a little ad-libbin' because other colors that's involved I got that too, you know. And so, I'll give you—like "the girls I see that's dressed in white, I like to make love to you all night, you know, the girl I see with a flowered dress on, I love you baby from now on, you know, I will sure like to win a happy home." You know, all these, they can be involved. Anyway, this is the way it's wrote here. So anyway, I'm gonna give you now a few ideas in couple of different keys. Now, one of these—a couple of keys is kind of minor keys, and they ain't never been done in this. I'd like you to keep this kind of idea to yourself, because this done in a minor key, it will be a brand new thing. And I want you to kinda keep it—you kinda have this thing done as your own style thing for the future or anytime, you know. And it will make a difference in the sound or whole band. But you're gonna have to learn how to play the minor keys of it with your guitar, or somebody else will play the minor keys. Not it may be—it will be kinda hard on the piano player if he hasn't been playing these, you too. But then I mean, if you do it in major or minor, it's a good thing. But so, anyway, listen to the other sound of it.

[End of the recording]

Although this tape is very short, it provides important information. First, the way Dixon introduced a song to an artist was quite simple. He only needed a pile of paper. Second, when he demonstrated a song, he had completed most of the basic scheme of the song. As seen in the preceding transcription, at the point that Dixon introduced this song he had basically completed the lyrics. He also had some optional verses. In addition to the words, Dixon had ideas about musical features, such as melodies, rhythms, riffs, introduction, and instrumentation. In this particular recording, Dixon clearly said that he prefered a minor to a major key. Third, Dixon allowed Hytower to develop the arrangement with his own style, based on the ideas that Dixon presented.

Next stage is studio work—arranging and producing. When Dixon worked for Chess Records and Cobra Records, he had full responsibility for the arrangements and production when it came to his own compositions. To my question "To what extent do you think Dixon was responsible for arrangements and for producing his own songs?" both Shirli and Butch Dixon briefly replied, "One hundred percent."[21] They both agree that he had clear ideas of how his song should sound "always right from the start."[22] Marie Dixon also says, "He had it already arranged when he got to the studio with an artist."[23] Billy Branch, a harmonica player in Dixon's band in the 1980s, gives more details of his studio experiences with Dixon:

Usually by the time he'd call me and do what he had, he had a general idea pretty much and pretty well formulated it. He had a melody and words. I never remember him writing actual music or the chords. . . .
    Basically he would kind of assign to you what he wanted you to play. . . . Otherwise, if there isn't anything new, he basically want you to reproduce what was already recorded to the degree, that would be note for note. A certain song has a certain arrangement with a harp at certain part or a certain intro. So he'd basically tell you what he wanted you to do. But of course, he didn't tell you what kind of solo to play. . . . I guess he just gave the musicians freedom to create within the context of their musical ability. That's why he was always surrounded with top-notch players around in his band. A lot of creativity comes from musicians themselves.[24]

The musicianship of artists in the recordings of Dixon compositions—such as Koko Taylor's powerful vocal, the teamwork by Howlin' Wolf and Hubert Sumlin, or Muddy Waters and Little Walter—is unarguably irreplaceable. Because of that, musicians think that their performances were major contributions to the arrangement of Dixon's songs, but from Dixon's point of view, squeezing out the abilities of musicians and singers was his work as a producer. How they responded to Dixon's expectation was a crucial factor in bringing a composition to a successful conclusion. Shirli Dixon says,

> Musicians believe that they contributed to an arrangement because it's nobody else couldn't have done the solo . . . and especially blues musicians. Some of them are quite elegant. I remember my dad in the rehearsal, he would say, "Absolutely leave that area open." So generally they would have contributions overall, but what he wanted was ultimately [what would] get on that recording. All the rest of it was just because of the sake of experiment.
>
> For example "Hoochie Coochie Man," Muddy performed that song right before any band member had ever heard it from Daddy's hum to him in the restroom. When they got in the studio, the song was repeated the way Muddy understood it and Daddy understood it. So the musicians would have had to play whatever is that Muddy or Daddy felt they wanted in the song.
>
> But generally, see in the blues, musicians will add little parts. . . . My father had a very unique way of putting musicians together, and he didn't believe one or the other was the solo act. He would tell two musicians soloing together to listen for each other's break, and then to come forward with the strongest performance that you could offer. That's not usual because that creates quite a conflict, and most musicians can't do it. But he demanded it of everybody. He even did it in the live. You know, often he would say, "Both of you, together." Some of the musicians would not cooperate. Then, he would change him out. Pianist Lafayette Leake and Al Duncan, who was a drummer for Chuck Berry and several others, they had quite a knock down. . . . The songs like "29 Ways," they were absolutely perfect in following the arrangement. . . . He was really hard on drummers and keyboard players.[25]

Was Willie Dixon open to other musicians' suggestions in the studio? His family members have different opinions. On one hand, Shirli Dixon observes, "My dad often said, 'Two heads are better than one, and three are better than two,' unless he found the guy to be difficult overall. . . . But if he thought that musician was genuine, like Lafayette Leake, all of his suggestions were welcome."[26] On the other hand, Butch Dixon says, "No way. If he says this is what it's gon' to be, this is what it's gon' to be."[27] Marie Dixon's observation is closer to that of Butch: "I believe he was open [to other musicians' ideas]. Did he accept? I'm not sure. Because he was a giant and he was a self-made man. Very little you could suggest to him."[28]

Generally Willie Dixon was the "floor general when it came to recording his material."[29] As discussed in chapter 7, Koko Taylor remembers she was not given much artistic freedom. It is not difficult to imagine that "my way or no way" kind of studio operation caused conflicts with other musicians. Marie Dixon shares an episode between Dixon and guitarist Cash McCall:

> Now he had a young man—Cash McCall down in Tennessee. He can tell you how Willie would make him so angry. He said, "Willie had this idea of what he wanted you to do with your instrument. But it was impossible to do some of that. Willie thought you could do it, because he heard it in his ear." But he couldn't. Willie would go to the artist and say, "Do it this way, do this, do that. This is what I want to hear." And the artist would get it as close to as he could.[30]

Similar events surely occurred when Dixon worked for Chess Records. Freddie Robinson, guitarist of Little Walter's band, talks about his sour experience of recording "My Baby Is Sweeter" in 1958:

> When Dixon gave us the lyrics in advance, we'd go rehearse and arrange this stuff the way we wanted it to go, then we'd get to the session and Dixon would change it. Walter had a thing going on that, we had patterned it off of Little Willie John's "Country Girl." As soon as Willie Dixon heard it, he was "Oh, no, no, no!" That was the end of that. . . . Dixon would change everything and just throw that whole thing into another dimension. He made it real bad for us, because we had what we thought was hip and up to date. He changed it into something else.[31]

After these stages—sometimes some procedures could be a little bumpy—the final step of Dixon's compositional process was to cut a master take. Branch recalls Dixon wasted no time when it got to this point:

> We just rehearsed and did it. Usually with Willie, I don't remember wasting a lot of time, because when you get into the studio, sometimes it's a long process. But by the time we got into the studio, we had it down, do track a take or two. It wasn't like, sometimes when you are in the studio, you got to go over and over again.
>
> [To make one album], I would think [it took] at the most one or two days. Most blues albums, until recent years, were done in one day. I know our involvement on "Mighty Earthquake and Hurricane," we had background vocals on it. It might have taken some more times, but our involvement was one or

two days. . . . We were that good, and just happen like that. And when you have good chemistry and you have good musicians, and they feel each other, it doesn't take a lot of time.[32]

Such an efficient procedure was what Dixon learned by working for small independent record companies that had limited budgets. But of course, he worked with superb musicians. While Dixon's work had to be practical, the quality of many recordings that he was affiliated with shows that it was certainly effective—just like packaging a fresh meal. The lessons about music making that Dixon learned with Chess musicians and others—the strong musical legacy of Chicago—were certainly passed on to the younger generations of the tradition. Billy Branch, today's top harmonica player, describes what he learned from Dixon: how to control volume, how to play in an ensemble, and how to develop solos, which he applies to his music making to this day:

I really learned how to play with Willie Dixon. I learned about volume levels. I was forced into becoming a good player, because I had to replace Carey Bell on the spot. And it wasn't fun. I was young . . . twenty-something years old, and hot shot, and [had] a thing I got together. And Carey Bell, he quits one night, and Willie said to me, "You got it." I said, "I got what?" He said, "You got it. You want the job, don't you?" I said, "Yeah, I guess." And what happened was when we started touring, I wasn't as good as I thought I was. I wasn't quite ready as I thought. They were asking Carey Bell. Carey Bell was like a backbone of that band at that particular time. He was just phenomenal. And I had to hurry to get my stuff together. I learned ensemble playing. And I learned more from osmosis a lot of times rather than actual direct instruction. It's just, keep it down. That was Willie Dixon's blues also. It's not loud volume playing in a band. . . . When we accompanied Willie's [blues], very much in ensemble, very controlled, round sound. But don't get me wrong. What's in that frame was very powerful, very powerful. . . . I view 130 recordings. And I think the reason I am such a demanding session man was because I learned from Willie. I learned how to listen, and I know how to deliver what's required in a session. I learned that. A lot of musicians, younger guys, they are great musicians, but they don't get, they don't understand about ensemble playing, accompaniment. I learned to make attractive harp playing even if I'm not taking a solo; trying something nice and concise, rhythmic, or I make a horn line, or whatever. I always try to weave them into a tapestry. I learned that from Willie.[33]

Notes

1. Bob Corritore, Bill Ferris, and Jim O'Neal, "Willie Dixon (Part 2)," *Living Blues*, no. 82 (September/October 1988): 24.

2. Shirli Dixon, interview by the author, September 23, 2002.
3. Ibid.
4. Butch Dixon, interview by the author, September 23, 2003. Harmonica player Billy Branch, a member of Dixon's band in the early 1980s, also recalls,

> He was always writing, all the time. He would actually encouraged myself and others like Freddie Dixon [another of Dixon's sons], who was originally in the Sons of Blues, to write, because, you know, where the money is is really in publishing. For example, "Flamin' Mamie," he actually wrote that, I believe, while we were on the road. He would get these ideas, and anybody who's worked with Willie would tell you this. He would call you up in any hour and say, "What are you doing? No matter what you're doing, hey, come on up here. I gotta a new song. Come on and check it out. . . ." It can be a little annoying, because we'd have to drop whatever we are doing, and it can be midnight or something, you know. But that's [what] Willie was doing. A lot of times he would take a piece of notebook paper, then put it on a book, and take a pencil and keep time, like making almost like a snare drum. That's how he'd keep time and hum this out.

Billy Branch, interview by the author, September 27, 2002.
5. Butch Dixon, interview by the author, September 23, 2003.
6. Ibid.
7. Marie Dixon, interview by the author, September 25, 2004.
8. Corritore, Ferris, and O'Neal, "Willie Dixon (Part 2)," 24.
9. Butch Dixon, interview by the author, September 23, 2003.
10. Ibid.
11. Marie Dixon, interview by the author, September 25, 2004. "The Same Thing" is discussed in chapter 7.
12. Ibid. "Three Hundred Pounds of Joy" is discussed in chapter 7.
13. Shirli Dixon, interview by the author, September 23, 2002.
14. Ibid.
15. George R. White, *Bo Diddley: Living Legend* (Surrey, England: Castle Communications, 1995), 82–83.
16. Butch Dixon, interview by the author, September 23, 2003.
17. Shirli Dixon, interview by the author, September 23, 2002.
18. Koko Taylor, interview by the author, September 27, 2002.
19. Blues vocalist/guitarist Roy Hytower was born in 1943 in Coffeyville, Alabama. In 1962, he moved to Chicago and performed at local clubs. In 1968, he made some records, including "Your Good Man Is Going Bad," "Must Be Love," and "You Pleases Me" for the Brainstorm label. In 1969, his "I'm in Your Corner" coupled with "Undertaker" on Mercury's Blues Rock subsidiary became a minor local hit record. Robert Pruter, *Chicago Soul* (Urbana: University of Illinois Press, 1991), 249–50. When Dixon recorded this tape, he had already moved to California. He sent this tape to Hytower in Chicago.
20. "I actually wrote for Muddy" seems to be a misrecollection, because this song was premiered by Buddy Guy in his album *Left My Blues in San Francisco* in

1965. Dixon told Hytower so probably because Hytower portrayed Muddy in a play that was produced in Chicago. "Every Girl I See Looks Good to Me" is discussed in chapter 7. While there are similarities between Dixon's tape and Buddy Guy's version—for example, in the hook ("You look good, and you look good. Every girl I see look / lookin' good to me") and in the basic structure (vocal melodies are built on one chord)—the words in Dixon's tape are newly written, and Dixon tries to imbue this composition with a different idea.

21. Shirli Dixon, interview by the author, September 23, 2002; Butch Dixon, interview by the author, September 23, 2003.

22. Ibid.

23. Marie Dixon, interview by the author, September 25, 2004.

24. Billy Branch, interview by the author, September 27, 2002.

25. Shirli Dixon, interview by the author, September 23, 2002.

26. Ibid.

27. Butch Dixon, interview by the author, September 23, 2003.

28. Marie Dixon, interview by the author, September 25, 2004.

29. Tony Glover, Scott Dirks, and Ward Gaines, *Blues with a Feeling: The Little Walter Story* (New York: Routledge, 2002), 191.

30. Marie Dixon, interview by the author, September 25, 2004.

31. Glover, Dirks, and Gaines, *Blues with a Feeling*, 192.

32. Branch, interview by the author, September 27, 2002.

33. Ibid.

~

Appendix B: Recording Sessions Attended by Willie Dixon and Recording Chronology of Willie Dixon's Compositions

In each table in this appendix, Dixon's compositions are indicated by bold-face type. I only listed premiered recordings of his compositions; therefore, for example, Muddy Waters' *After the Rain* (1969) is listed because "I Am the Blues" is premiered with this album, while his *Electric Mud* (1968), which includes a rerecording of "I Just Want to Make Love to You," is not included. The sessions that Dixon participated in only as a composer and/or producer are noted. As far as I can confirm Dixon's presence in the studio as a producer, I included his name among the personnel, even though his name is not listed in conventional discographies—listed personnel include only musicians who actually performed in recording sessions. However, in many cases Dixon was giving directions to musicians in the studio, even though his name is not documented in session files, such as Howlin' Wolf's "Tail Dragger" session (September 27 and 28, 1962); the recording that includes Dixon's guide vocal track exists.

Typically artists cut multiple songs in one session, but there are many cases in which they change their roles during that single session. For example, for the 1946 Big Three Trio session, Willie Dixon plays bass and takes a lead vocal for "Signifying Monkey," but he only takes backup vocal, along with playing bass, on other tracks. Such role switches are indicated as follows:

Willie Dixon (v/b, lead v-1)
Lonely Roamin'
You Sure Look Good to Me

Signifying Monkey-1
Get up Those Stairs Mademoiselle

For this discography, I have used the sources listed below.

Dixon, Robert M. W., John Godrich, and Howard Rye. *Blues and Gospel Records, 1890–1943*. 4th ed. Oxford: Clarendon Press, 1997.

Dixon, Willie. With Don Snowden. *I Am the Blues: The Willie Dixon Story*. New York: Da Capo Press, 1989.

Fancourt, Les. *Chess Blues: A Discography of the Blues Artists on the Chess Labels, 1947–1975*. Faversham, Kent, England: L. Fancourt, 1983. Reprint, 1989.

———. *Chess Blues/R&B Discography*. Faversham, Kent, England: L. Fancourt, 1983.

———. *Chess Blues/R&B Discography*. Faversham, Kent, England: L. Fancourt, 1983.

Fancourt, Les, and Bob McGrath. *The Blues Discography, 1943–1970*. Canada: Eyeball Productions, 2006.

Glover, Tony, Scott Dirks, and Ward Gaines. *Blues with a Feeling: The Little Walter Story*. New York: Routledge, 2002.

Leadbitter, Mike, Leslie Fancourt, and Paul Pelletier. *Blues Records, 1943–1970: The Bible of the Blues*. Vol. 2, L to Z. London: Record Information Services, 1994.

Leadbitter, Mike, and Neil Slaven. *Blues Records, 1943–1970: A Selective Discography*. Vol. 1, A to K. London: Record Information Services, 1987.

Rothwell, Fred. *Long Distance Information: Chuck Berry's Recorded Legacy*. York, England: Music Mentor Books, 2001.

Ruppli, Michael. *The Chess Labels: A Discography*. 2 vols. Westport, CT: Greenwood Press, 1988.

Segrest, James, and Mark Hoffman. *Moanin' at Midnight: The Life and Times of Howlin' Wolf*. New York: Pantheon Books, 2004.

Tooze, Sandra B. *Muddy Waters: The Mojo Man*. Toronto: ECW Press, 1997.

In addition to these sources, I have consulted various CD booklets and album sleeves (see the bibliography, including the discography contained therein).

Abbreviations Used in This Appendix

Countries		Instruments		Other	
AU	Austria	as	alto saxophone	AFBF	The American Folk Blues Festival
CN	Canada	b	(acoustic) bass	alt.	alternate take
E	England	bgs	bongos	comp.	composition
FR	France	bj	banjo	exc.	except
GER	Germany	bs	baritone saxophone	feat.	featuring
IT	Italy	bv	backup vocal	fem.	female
JP	Japan	d	drums	grp.	group
		eb	electric bass		
Record Labels		fl	flute	inst.	instrumental
Ab	Abco Records (former name of Cobra Records)	g	guitar	poss.	possibly
Ar	Aristocrat Records (former name of Chess Records)	gs	guitars	prob.	probably
At	Artistic Records (subsidiary of Cobra Records)	h	harmonica	prod.	produced
Bb	Bluebird Records (subsidiary of Victor Records)	horns	horn section	tks.	takes
Cb	Cobra Records	k	keyboard	unk.	unkown
Ch	Chess Records	mrcs	maracas	VA	various artists
Ckr	Checker Records (subsidiary of Chess Records)			w.	with
Co	Columbia Records	o	(electric) organ		
LRB	Le Roi Du Blues	p	piano		
OK	OKeh Records (subsidiary of Columbia Records)	perc	percussion		
Vic	Victor Records	sax	saxophone		
VJ	Vee-Jay Records	tamb	tambourine		
		tp	trumpet		
		ts	tenor saxophone		
		v	vocal		
		vl	violin		
		wb	washboard		

The Bumpin' Boys: Eugene Gilmore (v); Leonard Caston (v); Arthur Dixon (v); Willie Dixon (v); Lionel Douglas Turner (v). It is not known if any of the members played instruments.

1938 or 1939	Unk. number of cuts, including **"Beat Her Out Bumpin' Boys"** by Dixon.	Recorded for Decca, prod. Mayo Williams. All unissued.

The Five Breezes: Gene Gilmore (v/p); Leonard Caston (v/g); Willie Dixon (b/v); Joseph Bell (v); Willie Hawthorne (v)

Date	Songs	Matrix	Original Release
11/15/40	**Sweet Louise** (feat. Dixon's speech)	04962-1	Bluebird B 8590
	Minute and Hour Blues	04963-1	B 8590
	Laundry Man (Dixon on lead v)	04964-1	B 8710
	Return, Gal o' Mine	04965-1	B 8614
	What's the Matter with Love	04966-1	B 8679
	My Buddy Blues	04967-1	B 8614
	Just a Jitterbug	04968-1	B 8710
	Swingin' the Blues	04969-1	B 8679

The Four Jumps of Jive: Gene Gilmore (v/p); Bernardo Dennis (g); Ellis Hunter (g); Willie Dixon (v/b)

Date	Songs	Matrix	Original Release
9/12/45	Satchelmouth Baby	101	Mercury 2001
	It's Just the Blues	102	Mercury 2001
	Boo Boo Fine Jelly	103	Mercury 2015
	Streamline	104	Mercury 2015

The Big Three Trio (1946–1952): Leonard Caston (v/p); Bernardo Dennis (v/g); Willie Dixon (v/b, lead v-1)

Date	Songs	Matrix	Original Release	Other Musicians
1946	Lonely Roamin'	UB 2898B	Bullet 274	unk. (d)
	You Sure Look Good to Me	UB 2899B	Bullet 275, Dot 1104	
	Signifying Monkey-1	UB 2900B	Bullet 275,	
	Get up Those Stairs Mademoiselle	UB 2901B	Dot 1104 Bullet 274	
3/11/47	**Signifying Monkey**-1	CCO 4750	Co 37358, 30019	Charles Sanders (d)
	If the Sea Was Whiskey (w. Caston)	CCO 4751	Co 37584, 30055	
	Money Tree Blues-1	CCO 4752		
	Lonely Roamin'	CCO 4753		
9/3/47	After Awhile (We Gonna Drink a Little Whisky)	CCO 4841	Co 37893, 30103	Alphonse Walker (d)
	It Can't Be Done	CCO 4842	Co 38064,	
	No More Sweet Potatoes-1	CCO 4843	30108 Co 38064, 30108	
	Baby, I Can't Go On without You	CCO 4844	Co 37893, 30103	
12/30/47	Reno Blues	CCO 4982	Co 30142	Charles Sanders (d)
	Just Can't Let Her Be	CCO 4983	Co 30144	
	Big Three Boogie [inst.] (w. Caston)	CCO 4984	Co 38125, 30125	
	Since My Baby Been Gone	CCO 4985	Co 30144	
	Evening	CCO 4986	Co 38125, 30125	
	88 Boogie (w. Caston)	CCO 4987	Co 38093, 30110	
	You Sure Look Good to Me	CCO 4988	Co 38093, 30110	
	I'll Be Right Some Day	CCO 4989	Co 30142	
2/18/49	Get Her off My Mind	CCO 5029	Co 30174	Hillard Brown (d)
	I Ain't Gonna Be Your Monkey Man (w. Caston)	CCO 5030	Co 30166	

Date	Songs	Matrix	Original Release	Other Musicians
	I Feel Like Steppin' Out	CCO 5031	Co 30156	
	Big Three Stomp [inst.] (w. Caston and Crawford)	CCO 5032	Co 30166	
	Hard Notch Boogie Beat [inst.] (w. Caston and Crawford)	CCO 5033	Co 30156	
	No One to Love Me	CCO 5034	Co 30174	
5/4/49	**Don't Let That Music Die**-1	BU 6508	Delta 202 Delta 202, Co 30222	Charles Sanders (d)
	Till the Day I Die	BU 6509	Delta 208, Co 30329	
	Appetite Blues	BU 6516	Unissued	
	Dry Bones	BU 6517	Delta 205, Co 30228	
	Why Do You Do Me Like You Do	BU 6518	Delta 205, Co 30222	
	Goodbye Mr. Blues	BU 6519	Delta 208	
	Cigarettes, Whiskey, and Wild Women	BU 6531		
12/16/49	There's Something on My Mind	CCO 5094	Co 30228	Charles Sanders (d)
	Don't Let That Music Die-1	CCO 5095	Co 30190	
	Blip Blip	CCO 5096	Co 30329	
	Practicing the Art of Love-1	CCO 5097	Co 30190	
5/29/51	Blues Because of You	CCO 5265	OK 6863	Charles Sanders (d)
	It's All Over Now	CCO 5266	OK 6842	
	Tell That Woman-1	CCO 5267	OK 6842	
	Lonesome	CCO 5268	OK 6807	
	Violent Love-1	CCO 5269	OK 6807	
1/3/52	Got You on My Mind	CCO 5296	OK 6863	Buddy Smith (d)
	Etiquette [inst.]	CCO 5297	Co CK 46216	
	You Don't Love Me No More	CCO 5298	OK 6901	

Date	Songs	Matrix	Original Release	Other Musicians
6/16/52	Come Here Baby	CCO 5356	OK 6944	unk. (d)
	O. C. Bounce [inst.]	CCO 5357	Co CK 46216	
	Cool Kind Woman-1	CCO 5358	Co CK 46216	
	Juice Headed Bartender	CCO 5359	Co CK 46216	
	My Love Will Never Die-1	CCO 5360	OK 6901	
12/16/52	**Torture My Soul**	CCO 5393	Unissued	unk. (d)
	What Am I to Do	CCO 5394	Co CK 46216	
	Be a Sweetheart	CCO 5395	OK 6944	
	Too Late	CCO 5356	Unissued	

Pre-Chess Sessions Participated in by Willie Dixon (bass): From 1945 to 1948 (Chicago)

Date Artist	Songs	Matrix	Original Release	Musicians Involved
7/2/45 John Lee "Sonny Boy" Williamson (v/h)	G. M. & O. Blues We Got to Win Sonny Boy's Jump Elevator Woman	D5AB 339 D5AB 340 D5AB 341 D5AB 342	Vic 20-2369 RCA INT (E) 5099 Bb 34-0744 Bb 34-0744	Eddie Boyd (p) Big Sid Cox (g) Willie Dixon (b) unk. (d) Dixon says he played bass for this session.[1]
10/18/45 St. Louis Jimmy (v)	Mother's Day Trouble in the Land Dog House Blues Make Up Your Mind	D5AB 0392 D5AB 0393 D5AB 0394 D5AB 0395	Unissued Unissued Vic 20-2650 Unissued	J. T. Brown (as) Roosevelt Sykes (p) Willie Dixon (b)
Late 1946 Memphis Slim (v/p) and the House Rockers	Kilroy Has Been Here-1 Rockin' the House Lend Me Your Love Darling, I Miss You	UB2650 SS UB2651 SS UB2652 SS UB2653 SS	Miracle 102 Miracle 103 Miracle 103 (Fed 12033) Miracle 102 (Fed 12033)	Alex Atkins (as) Ernest Cotton (ts) unk. (d) Willie Dixon (b/v-1)
6/10/47 Rosetta Howard (v)	Ebony Rhapsody I Keep on Worrying When I Been Drinking Help Me Baby	CCO 4788 CCO 4789 CCO 4790 CCO 4791	Co 37573, 30053, 40494 Co 30127 Co 37573, 30053 Co 38029, 30105	The Big Three Trio: Leonard Caston (p) Bernardo Dennis (g) Willie Dixon (b) Charles Sanders (d)

Date / Artist	Title	Matrix	Issue	Personnel
2/12/47 Brother John Sellers (v)	Farewell Night Life Let Me Be Your Sidetrack Mama What You Gonna Do Play Around with My Head	D7VB 312 D7VB 313 D7VB 314 D7VB 315	Vic 20-2338 Vic 20-2418 Vic 20-2418 Vic 20-2338	James Clark (p) Leonard Caston (g) Willie Dixon (b) Charles Sanders (d)
2/18/47 Washboard Sam (v/wb)	You Can't Make the Grade You Can't Have None of That I Just Couldn't Help It Soap and Water Blues	D7VB-316 D7VB-317 D7VB-318 D7VB-319	Vic 20-2440 Vic 20-2297 Vic 20-2297 Vic 20-2440	J. T. Brown (ts) Roosevelt Sykes (p) Big Bill Broonzy (g) Willie Dixon (b)
3/28/47 John Lee "Sonny Boy" Williamson (v/h)	Mellow Chick Swing Polly Put Your Kettle On Lace Belle Apple Tree Swing	D7VB-374 D7VB-375 D7VB-376 D7VB-377	Vic 20-2369 Vic 20-2521 Vic 20-2521 Vic 20-2369	Blind John Davis (p) Big Bill Broonzy (g) Charles Sanders (d) Willie Dixon (b)
4/3/47 Little Eddie Boyd (v) w. J. T. Brown's Boogie Band	I Had to Let Her Go Kilroy Won't Be Back	D7VB-389 D7VB-390	Vic 20-2311 Vic 20-2311	Howard Dixon (as) J. T. Brown (ts) James Clark (p) Lonnie Graham (g) Willie Dixon (b)
9/3/47 Rosetta Howard (v)	It's Hard to Go thru Life Alone Where Shall I Go Too Many Drivers Why Be So Blue	CCO 4837 CCO 4838 CCO 4839 CCO 4840	Co 38145, 30113 Co 38145, 30113 Co 38029, 30105 Co 30127	The Big Three Trio: Leonard Caston (p) Bernardo Dennis (g) Willie Dixon (b) Alphonse Walker (d)

¹See Willie Dixon, with Don Snowden, I Am the Blues: The Willie Dixon Story (New York: Da Capo Press, 1989), 61.

Chess Sessions Participated in by Willie Dixon: From August 1948 to June 1972 (Chicago, unless otherwise indicated)

Date / Artist	Songs	Matrix	Original Release	Musicians Involved
Sept. '48 Robert Nighthawk (Robert Lee McCollum, v/g, exc. 1)	Down the Line-1 Handsome Lover-1 Return Mail Blues My Sweet Lovin' Man-1	U 7127 U 7128 U 7129 U 7130	Ch (E) LP 6641 125 Ch (E) LP 6641 125 Unissued Ch 1484	Ethel Mae Brown (v-1) Sunnyland Slim or Ernest Lane (p) Willie Dixon (b)
7/12/49 Robert Nighthawk aka The Nighthawks (v/g)	She Knows How to Love a Man Black Angel Blues (Sweet Black Angel) Annie Lee Blues (Anna Lee) Return Mail Blues Sugar Papa-1	U 7194 U 7195 U 7196 U 7197 U 7198	Blues Ball LP 2003, Blue Night 073 1669 Ar 2301 Ar 2301 Ch 1484 Ch (E) LP 6641 125	Ernest Lane (p) Ethel Mae (v-1) Willie Dixon (b)
1/5/50 Robert Nighthawk (v/g)	Good News-1 Six Three O Prison Bound Jackson Town Gal	U 7226[?] U 7227 U 7228 U 7229	Ch (E) 6641 125 Ar 413 Ch (E) 6641 125 Ar 413	Pinetop Perkins (p) Ethel Mae Brown (v-1) Willie Dixon (b)
8/12/52 Jimmy Rogers (v/g)	Mistreated Baby The Last Time-1 What's the Matter? Out on the Road	U 7444 U 7445 U 7446 U 7447	Ch (E) LP 6641 174 Ch 1519 Ch (E) LP 6641 174 Ch 1519	Henry Gray (p) Muddy Waters (g/2nd v-1) Willie Dixon (b) A. J. Gladney (d)
10/10/52 Eddie Boyd (v/p)	24 Hours Hard Time Gettin' Started Best I Could The Tickler [inst.]	U 7486 U 7487 U 7488 U 7489	Ch 1533 Ch CHD 4-9340 Ch (JP) PLP 6019 Ch 1533	Robert "Little Sax" Crowder (ts) Robert Jr. Lockwood (g) Willie Dixon (b) Percy Walker (d)
Mar. '53 Little Walter (v-1/h)	Don't Have to Hurt No More Crazy Legs Tonight with a Fool-1, 2 Off the Wall Tell Me Mama-1	U 4343 U 4344 U 4345 U 4348 U 4349	Ckr 767 Ckr 986 Ckr 767 Ckr 770 Ckr 770	Louis Myers (g) Dave Myers (g) Henry Gray (p-2) Fred Below (d) Willie Dixon (b)

Date / Artist	Title	Matrix	Issue	Personnel
Mar. '53 John Brim (v/g) and His Gray Kings	Rattlesnake	U 4350	Ckr 769	Little Walter (h) Louis Myers (g) Dave Myers (g) Fred Below (d) Willie Dixon (b)
	It Was a Dream	U 4351	Ckr 769	
May '53 Eddie Boyd (v/p)	That's When I Miss You So	4373	Ch 1552	Robert "Little Sax" Crowder (ts) Lee Cooper (g) Willie Dixon (b) Percy Walker (d)
	Third Degree	4374	Ch 1541	
	Four Leaf Clover	4375	Ch 1634	
	Back Beat [inst.]	4376	Ch 1541	
7/23/53 Little Walter (v-1/h)	That's It	U 4390	Unissued	Jimmy Rogers (g) Dave Myers (g) Willie Dixon (b) Fred Below (d)
	Blues with a Feeling	U 4931	Unissued	
	Quarter to Twelve	U 4394	Ckr 780	
	That's It	U 4397	Ch CHD 2-9357	
	Blues with a Feeling-1	U 4398	Ch 780	
	Last Boogie	U 4399	Ch (E) LP 6641 174	
	Too Late-1	U 4400	Ckr 825	
	Fast Boogie	U 4401	Ch (E) LP 6641 174	
	Lights Out	U 4402	Ckr 786	
	Fast Large One	U 4403	LRB (CN) 33. 2007	
	You're So Fine-1	U 4404	Ckr 786	
	My Kind of Baby-1	[?]	LRB (CN) 33. 2007	
9/24/53 Eddie Boyd (v/p)	Tortured Soul	U 7558	Ch 1552	Robert "Little Sax" Crowder (ts) Lee Cooper (g) Willie Dixon (b) Percy Walker (d)
	Rattin' and Runnin' Around	U 7559	Ch 1576	
	Just a Fool	U 7560	Ch 1634	
	Hush Baby, Don't You Cry	U 7561	Ch 1573	
1/7/54 Muddy Waters (v/g)	**(I'm Your) Hoochie Coochie Man**	U 7589	Ch 1560	Little Walter (h) Otis Spann (p) Jimmy Rogers (g) Willie Dixon (b) Fred Below (d)
	She's So Pretty	U 7590	Ch 1560	

Date / Artist	Songs	Matrix	Original Release	Musicians Involved
1/7/54 Jimmy Rogers (v/g)	Blues All Day Long (Blues Leave Me Alone)	U 7591	Ch 1616	Little Walter (h) Henry Gray or Johnny Jones (p) Muddy Waters (g) Willie Dixon (b) Odie Payne (d)
	Chicago Bound	U 7592	Ch 1574	
1/16/54 Leon D. Tarver (v/p) and the Chordones	Oo-wee What's Wrong with Me	U 7593	Ckr 791	unk. (ts) Willie Dixon (b) The Chordones (bv)
	I'm a Young Rooster	U 7594	Ckr 791	
	Why Do I Love You So (Baby Don't Go)	U 7595	Rarin' LP 777	
	Come Back to Me	U 7596	Rarin' LP 777	
2/17/54 The El Rays with Willie Dixon Orchestra	Darling I Know	U 7599	Ckr 794	The El Rays: Johnny Funches Marvin Junior Verne Allison Lucius McGill Michael McGill Charles Blackwell Willie Dixon (b/v-1) Harold Ashby (ts)
	Whing Ding All Night (Wang Dang Doodle)-1	U 7600	Ch CD 9353	
	So Long-1	U 7601	Ch CD 9353	
	Christine	U 7602	Ckr 794	
2/22/54 Little Walter (v-1/h)	Come Back Baby-1	U 7603	LRB (CN) 33. 2012	Robert Jr. Lockwood (g) Dave Myers (g) Willie Dixon (b) Fred Below (d)
	Rocker	U 7604	Ckr 793	
	I Love You So-1	U 7605	LRB (CN) 33. 2012	
	Oh Baby-1 (w. Jacobs)	U 7608	Ckr 793	
	Blue Light	U 7609	Unissued	
Mar. '54 Howlin' Wolf (v/h, exc. 1)	No Place to Go (You Gonna Wreck My Life)	U 7618	Ch 1566	Otis Spann (p) Lee Cooper (g)

Date / Artist	Title	Matrix	Release	Personnel
4/13/54 Muddy Waters (v/g)	Neighbors-1 I'm the Wolf Rockin' Daddy-1	U 7619 U 7620 U 7621	Ch LP 1512 Ch LP 1512 Ch 1566	Hubert Sumlin (g) Willie Dixon (b) Earl Phillips (d)
	Just Make Love to Me (I Just Want **to Make Love to You)** **Ooh Wee (Oh Yeah)**	U 7630 U 7631	Ch 1571 Ch 1571	Little Walter (h) Otis Spann (p) Jimmy Rogers (g) Willie Dixon (b) Fred Below (d)
4/13/54 Jimmy Rogers (v/g)	Sloppy Drunk	U 7632	Ch 1574	Little Walter (h) Otis Spann (p) Muddy Waters (g) Willie Dixon (b) Fred Below or Elga Edmonds (d)
5/22/54 Little Walter (v-1/h)	I Got Find My Baby-1 Big Leg Mama	7653 7654	Ckr 1013 LRB LP 2007	Dave Myers (g) Robert Jr. Lockwood (g) Otis Spann (p) Willie Dixon (b) Fred Below (d)
5/25/54 Howlin' Wolf (v/h)	Baby How Long? **Evil Is Goin' On (Evil)**	7657 7658	Ch 1575 Ch 1575	Otis Spann (p) Jody Williams (g) Hubert Sumlin (g) Willie Dixon (b) Earl Phillips (d)
6/10/54 Jimmy Witherspoon (v)	**When the Lights Go Out**-1 Danger **Live So Easy** **Big Daddy (I Can Make Love to** **You)**	U 7661 U 7662 U 7663 U 7664	Ckr 798 Ch LP 93003 Ch LP 93003 Ckr 798	Eddie Chamblee (ts) Lafayette Leake (p) Lee Cooper (g) Fred Below (d) Willie Dixon (b/v-1)

Date Artist	Songs	Matrix	Original Release	Musicians Involved
7/1/54 Little Walter (v-1/h)	**Mercy Babe**-1 (First run through of "My Babe." Re-recorded 1/25/55)	U 7669	Ch CHD 2-9357	Dave Myers (g) Robert Jr. Lockwood (g) Willie Dixon (b) Fred Below (d) Otis Spann (p)
	Last Night-1	U 7670	Argo LP 4042	
7/14/54 Little Walter (v-1/h)	You'd Better Watch Yourself-1	U 7673	Ckr 799	Dave Myers (g) Robert Jr. Lockwood (g) Willie Dixon (b) Fred Below (d) Otis Spann (p)
	Blue Light(s)	U 7674	Ckr 799	
9/1/54 Muddy Waters (v/g)	**I'm Ready**	U 7697	Ch 1579	Little Walter (h) Otis Spann (p) Jimmy Rogers (g) Willie Dixon (b) Fred Below (d)
	Smokestack Lightnin'	U 7698	Sunnyland (E) KS 100	
	I Don't Know Why	U 7699	Ch 1579	
	Shake It Baby	U 7700	Unissued	
1954 The Moonglows (v)	Shoo Doo Be (My Loving Baby)	U 7717	Ckr 806	Bobby Lester (v) Harvey Fuqua (v) Alexander Graves (v) Prentiss Barnes (v) Eddie Chamblee (ts) Johnny Young (p) Sir Walter Scott (g) Willie Dixon (b) Wesley Landers (d)
	Sincerely	U 7718	Ch 1581	
	So All Alone	U 7719	Ckr 806	
	Such a Feeling	U 7720	Unissued	
	Tempting	U 7721	Ch 1581	
10/5/54 Little Walter (v-1/h)	Untitled instrumental	U 4415	Unissued	Robert Jr. Lockwood (g) Luther Tucker (g) Otis Spann (p) Willie Dixon (b) Fred Below (d)
	Last Night-1	U 4416	Ckr 805	
	Mellow Down Easy-1	U 4417	Ckr 805	
	Instrumental	U 4418	LRB LP 2017	

Date / Artist	Song Title	Matrix	Release	Personnel
10/25/54 Otis Spann (v/p)	It Must Have Been the Devil-1 Five Spot	7738 7739	Ckr 807 Ckr 807	George Smith (h-1) B.B. King (g) Jody Williams (g) Willie Dixon (b) Earl Phillips (d)
Oct. '54 Howlin' Wolf (v/h)	I'll Be Around Forty Four	7740 7741	Ch 1584 Ch 1584	Otis Spann (p) Jody Williams (g) poss. Hubert Sumlin (g) Willie Dixon (b) Earl Phillips (d)
1954 Muddy Waters (v/g)	I'm a Natural Born Lover Ooh Wee	U 7746 U 7747	Ch 1585 Ch 1724	Little Walter (h) Otis Spann (p) Jimmy Rogers (g) Willie Dixon (b) Fred Below (d)
Nov. '54 Jimmy Witherspoon (v)	Time Brings About a Change Lovin' Man in Town Waitin' for Your Return T.W.A.	U 7748 U 7749 U 7750 U 7751	Ckr 810 Unissued Ckr 810 Ch LP 93003	Eddie Chamblee (ts) Lafayette Leake (p) Lee Cooper (g) Willie Dixon (b) Fred Below (d)
1/13/55 Lowell Fulson (v/g)	Lonely Hours Check Yourself Loving You (Is All I Crave) **Do Me Right**	U 7762 U 7763 U 7764 U 7765	Ckr 820 Ckr 812 Ckr 812 Ckr 820	Eddie Chamblee (ts) Earl Brown (as) unk. (bs) Otis Spann (p) Willie Dixon (b) prob. Fred Below (d)
1955 Rev. Robert Ballinger (v/p)	How I Got Over This Train	U7770 U7771	Ch 1590 Ch 1590	Willie Dixon (b) prob. Odie Payne (d)

Date Artist	Songs	Matrix	Original Release	Musicians Involved
1/25/55 Little Walter (v-1/h)	Thunder Bird-2 **My Babe**-1	7776 7777	Ckr 811 Ckr 811	Leonard Caston (poss. g-2) Robert Jr. Lockwood (g/v-1) Willie Dixon (b/v-1) Fred Below (d)
2/3/55 Muddy Waters (v/g)	**This Pain** **Young Fashioned Ways** **I Want to Be Loved**	U 7783 U 7784 U 7785	Ch (JP) PLP 6040/50 Ch 1602 Ch 1603	Little Walter (h) Otis Spann (p) Jimmy Rogers (g) Willie Dixon (b) Fred Below (d)
3/2/55 Bo Diddley (v/g)	I'm a Man Little Girl (Can I Go Home with You) Bo Diddley You Don't Love Me (You Don't Care)	U 7786 U 7787 U 7788 U 7789	Ckr 814 Ckr LP 1436 Ckr 814 Ckr LP 1436	Billy Boy Arnold (h) Otis Spann (p) Willie Dixon (b) Clifton James (d) Jerome Green (mrcs)
Mar. '55 Howlin' Wolf (v/h)	Who Will Be Next I Have a Little Girl Come to Me Baby Don't Mess with My Baby	U 7795 U 7796 U 7798 U 7799	Ch 1593 Ch 1593 Ch 1607 Ch 1607	Henry Gray (p) Jody Williams (g) Hubert Sumlin (g) Willie Dixon (b) Earl Phillips (d)
3/9/55 Muddy Waters (v/g)	My Eyes (Keep Me in Trouble)	U 7797	Ch 1596	Little Walter (h) Jimmy Rogers (g) unk. (g) Otis Spann (p) Willie Dixon (b) Francis Clay (d)

Date / Artist	Song	Matrix	Release	Personnel
Mar. '55 Jimmy Rogers (g)	You're the One	U7800	Ch (E) LP 6641 174	Little Walter (h) Otis Spann (p) Muddy Waters (g) Willie Dixon (b) Fred Below (d)
4/28/55 Little Walter (v-1/h)	Roller Coaster-2 I Got to Go-1, 3	U 7827 U 7828	Ckr 817 Ckr 817	Bo Diddley (g-2) Luther Tucker (g) Robert Jr. Lockwood (g-3) Willie Dixon (b) Fred Below (d)
May '55 The Moonglows (v)	Starlite Foolish Me No One Doubtful Slow Down In Love	U 7829 U 7830 U 7831 U 7832 U 7833 U 7834	Ch 1605 Ch 1598 Unissued Unissued Ch 1598 Ch 1605	Bobby Lester (v) Harvey Fuqua (v) Alexander Graves (v) Prentiss Barnes (v) Eddie Chamblee (ts) Oett "Sax" Mallard (bs) unk. (p) Billy Johnson (g) Willie Dixon (b) Leon Hooper (d)
5/15/55 Bo Diddley (v/g)	Diddley Daddy-1 She's Fine, She's Mine-2	U 7836 U 7837	Ckr 819 Ckr 819	Little Walter (h-1) Billy Boy Arnold (h-2) Clifton James (d) Jerome Green (mrcs/perc-2) Willie Dixon (b) The Moonglows (bv-1)
May '55 Willie Dixon (v/b) and the All Stars	**If You're Mine-1** **Alone**	U 7842 U 7843	Ckr 828 Ch (GER) LP 6.24802	Harold Ashby (ts) unk. v grp (bv-1) Lafayette Leake (p) Willie Dixon (v/b) Fred Below (d)

Date / Artist	Songs	Matrix	Original Release	Musicians Involved
5/21/55 Chuck Berry (v/g)	Maybellene-1 Wee Wee Hours	U 7844 U 7845	Ch 1604 Ch 1604	Johnny Johnson (p) Willie Dixon (b) Eddie Hardy (d) Leonard Chess (mrcs-1)
5/24/55 Muddy Waters (v)	Mannish Boy	U 7846	Ch 1602	Junior Wells (h) Jimmy Rogers (g) Willie Dixon (b) Fred Below (d) Fem. backup chorus
6/15/55 Jimmy Witherspoon (v)	It Ain't No Secret (What My Baby Can Do) Why Did I Love You Like I Do (That's Why I Love You So) I Got a Lot of Lovin' Cryin'	U 7847 U 7848 U 7849 U 7850	Ckr 826 Ckr 826 Unissued Ch LP 93003	Harold Ashby (ts) Willie Dixon (b) unk. (ts, p, d)
6/1/55[?] Willie Mabon (v/p)	He Lied-1 Someday You Will Have to Pay The Seventh Son Lucinda	U 7869 U 7870 U 7871 U 7872	Ch (GER) LP 6. 24806 Ch (GER) LP 6. 24806 Ch 1608 Ch 1608	Paul King (tp) Andrew Gardner (as) Herbert Robinson (ts) Bill Anderson (b) Oliver Coleman (d) Willie Dixon (v-1)
Jul. '55 Willie Dixon (v/b)	Walking the Blues	U 7873	Ckr 822	Lafayette Leake (p) Willie Dixon (b) Fred Below (foot tapping)
7/14/55 Little Walter (v/h)	Little Girl, Little Girl Crazy for My Baby Can't Stop Loving You	U 7874 U 7875 U 7876	LRB LP 2012 Ckr 986 LRB LP 2012	Luther Tucker (g) Robert Jr. Lockwood (g) Willie Dixon (b) Fred Below (d)

Date / Artist	Title	Matrix	Issue	Personnel
7/14/55 Bo Diddley (v/g)	**Pretty Thing** Heart-O-Matic Love Bring It to Jerome-1 Spanish Guitar [inst.]	U 7877 U 7878 U 7879 U 7880	Ckr 827 Ch CD 9331 Ckr 827 Ckr LP 2974	Lester Davenport (h) Clifton James (d) Willie Dixon (b) Jerome Green (v-1/mrcs)
8/12/55 Little Walter (v/h)	I Hate to See You Go	U 7888	Ckr 825	Bo Diddley (g) Luther Tucker (g) Willie Dixon (b) Fred Below (d)
8/12/55 Sonny Boy Williamson (v/h)	Work with Me Don't Start Me Talkin' All My Love in Vain Good Evening Everybody You Killing Me (On My Feet)	U 7889 U 7890 U 7891 U 7892 U 7893	Ch LP 417 Ckr 824 Ckr 824 Ch LP 417 Ch LP 417	Otis Spann (p) Muddy Waters (g) Jody Williams (g) Willie Dixon (b) Fred Below (d)
Sept. '55 Chuck Berry (v/g)	Thirty Days-1 Together (We Will Always Be)	U 7898 U 7899	Ch 1610 Ch 1610	Johnny Johnson (p) Ebby Hardy (d) Leonard Chess or Jerome Green (mrcs-1) Willie Dixon (b) Band chorus-1
9/14/55 J. B. Lenoir (v/g)	Natural Man Don't Dog Your Woman Let Me Die with the One I Love If I Give My Love to You Low Down Dirty Shame	U 7900 U 7901 U 7902 U 7903 U 7904	Ch LP 410 Ch LP 410 Ckr 844 Ckr 844 Ch 2ACMB 208	Alex Atkins (as) Ernest Cotton (ts) Joe Montgomery (p) Willie Dixon (b) Al Galvin (d)
	Unknown date session in 1955 Lenoir Blues-1 Everybody Wants to Know (Laid Off Blues) If You Love Me J. B.'s Rock [inst.]		Unissued Ch LP 410 Ch 2 ACMB 208 Ch 2 ACMB 208	Omit saxes-1

Date Artist	Songs	Matrix	Original Release	Musicians Involved
11/3/55 Muddy Waters (v)	**I Got to Find My Baby**	U 7937	Ch 1644	Little Walter (h)
	Sugar Sweet	U 7938	Ch 1612	Jimmy Rogers (g)
	Trouble No More	U 7939	Ch 1612	Francis Clay (d)
	Clouds in My Heart	U 7940	Ch 1724	Otis Spann (p)
				Willie Dixon (b)
Nov. '55 Willie Dixon (v/b)	**Youth to You**	U 7941	Unissued	Harold Ashby (ts)
	Crazy for My Baby	U 7942	Ckr 828	Ollie Crawford (g)
	I Am the Lover Man	U 7943	Ckr 828	Lafayette Leake (p)
	This Pain in My Heart	U 7944	Ckr 851	Fred Below (d)
11/10/55 Bo Diddley (v/g)	Dancing Girl	7945	Ckr LP 2974	Little Willie Smith (h-1)
	Diddy Wah Diddy-1 (w. McDaniel)	7946	Ckr 832	Jody Williams (g)
	I'm Looking for a Woman	7947	Ckr 832	Clifton James (d)
				Willie Dixon (b)
				Jerome Green (mrcs)
				The Moonglows (bv-1)
12/20/55 Chuck Berry (v/g)	You Can't Catch Me	7951	Ch 1645	Otis Spann or Johnny Johnson (p, exc. 1)
	Roly Poly (Rolli Polli) [inst.]	7952	Ch LP 1426	Willie Dixon (b)
	Berry Pickin' [inst.]	7953	Ch LP 1426	Ebby Hardy (d)
	Down Bound Train-1	7954	Ch 1615	
	No Money Down	7955	Ch 1615	
Dec. '55 Little Walter (v/h)	One More Chance with You	U 7966	Ckr 838	Robert Jr. Lockwood (g)
	Who	U 7967	Ckr 833	Luther Tucker (g)
	Boom Boom Out Goes the Lights	U 7968	Ckr 867	Willie Dixon (b)
	It Ain't Right	U 7969	Ckr 833	Fred Below (d)
Dec. '55 Jimmy Rogers (v/g)	You're the One	U 7970	Ch 1616	Little Walter (h)
				Robert Jr. Lockwood or Luther Tucker (g)
				Willie Dixon (b)
				Fred Below (d)

Date / Artist	Title	Matrix	Issue	Personnel
Unk. date in 1955 Willie Dixon (v/b)	**Violent Love**	[?]	CHD2-16500	Harold Ashby [?] Lafayette Leake (p) unk. (d)
1/24/56 Sonny Boy Williamson (v/h)	Let Me Explain I Know What Love Is All About I Wonder Why Your Imagination Don't Lose Your Eye	U 7980 U 7981 U 7982 U 7983 U 7984	Ckr 834 Ch LP 417 Ch LP 417 Ckr 834 Ch LP 417	Otis Spann (p) Robert Jr. Lockwood (g) Luther Tucker (g) Willie Dixon (b) Fred Below (d)
Jan. '56 Howlin' Wolf (v/h)	Smokestack Lightnin' You Can't Be Beat	U 7985 U 7986	Ch 1618 Ch 1618	Hosea Lee Kennard (p) Hubert Sumlin (g) Willie Johnson (g) Willie Dixon (b) Earl Phillips (d)
Jan. '56 Muddy Waters (v)	40 Days and 40 Nights-1 All Aboard-1	U 8012 U 8013	Ch 1620 Ch 1620	Little Walter (h) Otis Spann (p) Pat Hare (g) Hubert Sumlin (g) Willie Dixon (b) Fred Below (d)
2/9/56 Lowell Fulson (v/g)	It's All Your Fault Baby **Tollin' Bells** Smokey Room [inst.] (It) Took Me a Long Time	U 8018 U 8019 U 8020 U 8021	Ckr 841 Ckr 841 Ch (GER) LP 6.24809 Ckr 937	Eddie Chamblee (ts) unk. (as, bs) prob. Otis Spann (p) Willie Dixon (b)
3/9/56 Little Walter (h)	Flying Saucer [inst.]	U 8068	Ckr 838	Luther Tucker (g) Robert Jr. Lockwood (g) Willie Dixon (b) Fred Below (d)
Apr. '56 Billy Stewart (v/p)	Billy's Blues Pt.1 Billy's Blues Pt. 2	U 8071 U 8072	Ch 1625, Argo 5256 Ch 1625, Argo 5256	Jody Williams (g) Bo Diddley (g) Willie Dixon (b) Clifton James or Frank Kirkland (d)

Date Artist	Songs	Matrix	Original Release	Musicians Involved
4/5/56 John Brim (v/g)	I Would Hate to See You Go (Be Careful) You've Got Me Where You Want Me	U 8080 U 8081	Ch 1624 Ch 1624	Little Walter (h) Robert Jr. Lockwood (g) Willie Dixon (b) Fred Below (d)
4/16/56 Chuck Berry (v/g)	Drifting Heart Brown Eyed Handsome Man-1 Roll Over Beethoven Too Much Monkey Business	U 8108 U 8109 U 8110 U 8111	Ch 1626 Ch 1635 Ch 1626 Ch 1635	Leroy C. Davis (ts, exc. 1) Johnny Johnson (p) Willie Dixon (b) Fred Below (d)
6/29/56 Muddy Waters (v)	Just to Be with You **Don't Go No Further** Diamonds at Your Feet	U 8147 U 8148 U 8149	Ch 1644 Ch 1630 Ch 1630	Little Walter (h) Otis Spann (p) Pat Hare (g) Hubert Sumlin (g) Willie Dixon (b) prob. Odie Payne (d)
7/19/56 Howlin' Wolf (v/h)	I Asked for Water So Glad Break of Day The Natchez Burning	U 8175 U 8176 U 8177 U 8178	Ch 1632 Ch 1632 Ch (E) LP 6641 125 Ch 1744	Hosea Lee Kennard (p) Otis "Smokey" Smothers (g) Willie Johnson (g) Willie Dixon (b) Earl Phillips (d)
Jul. '56 Otis Spann (v/p)	I'm Leaving You I'm in Love with You Baby	U 8185 U 8186	Ch (JP) PLP 6022 Ch (JP) PLP 6022	Walter Horton (h) Robert Jr. Lockwood (g) unk. (g) Willie Dixon (b) Fred Below (d)
7/27/56 Willie Dixon (v/b)	**29 Ways**	U 8190	Ckr 851	Harold Ashby (ts) Lafayette Leake (p) Al Duncan (d) The Moonglows (bv)

Date / Artist	Title	Matrix	Release	Personnel
7/27/56 Little Walter (v, exc. 1/h)	(It's) Too Late Brother Teenage Beat-1 [inst.] Take Me Back Just a Feeling	U 8191 U 8192 U 8193 U 8194	Ckr 852 Ckr 845 Ckr 852 Ckr 845	Robert Jr. Lockwood (g) Willie Dixon (b) Fred Below (d)
8/7/56 Sonny Boy Williamson (v/h)	Keep It to Yourself Please Forgive (Keep It to Yourself) The Key (To Your Door) Have You Ever Been in Love	U 8205 U 8206 U 8207 U 8208	Ckr 847 Ckr LP 1437 Ckr 847 Ch LP 417	Luther Tucker (g) Robert Jr. Lockwood (g) Willie Dixon (b) Fred Below (d)
8/15/56 Jimmy Witherspoon (v)	Congratulations Ain't Nobody's Business Soda Crackers Cain Rivers	U 8215 U 8216 U 8218 U 8219	Ch LP 93003 Ch LP 93003 Unissued Unissued	unk. saxes Floyd Dixon (p) Jody Williams (g) Willie Dixon (b) Fred Below (d)
8/15/56 Floyd Dixon (v/p)	Alarm Clock Blues I'm Ashamed of Myself-1 Please Don't Go-1	U 8217 U 8220 U 8221	Ckr 857 Ckr 857 Ch CHD 4-9340	unk. saxes-1 Jody Williams (g) Willie Dixon (b) Fred Below (d)
Aug. '56 Earl Hooker (g)	Frog Hop [inst.] Guitar Rumba [inst.]	U 8252 U 8253	Argo 5256 Argo 5256	unk. (p, d) Willie Dixon (b)[?]
Oct. '56 Bo Diddley (v/g)	Cops and Robbers-1 Down Home Special (Down Home Train)-2	U 8272 U 8273	Ckr 850 Ckr 850	Otis Spann (p-1) Clifton James (d) Jerome Green (mrcs/effects, speech-2) Willie Dixon (b)
10/29/56 Chuck Berry (v/g)	Havana Moon	U 8303	Ch 1645	Willie Dixon (b) Jimmy Rogers (g)
10/29/56 Jimmy Rogers (v/g)	If It Ain't Me (Who You Thinking Of) Walking by Myself	U 8304 U 8305	Ch 1643 Ch 1643	Walter Horton (h) Robert Jr. Lockwood (g) Otis Spann (p) Willie Dixon (b) A. J. Gladney (d)

Date / Artist	Songs	Matrix	Original Release	Musicians Involved
12/15/56 Chuck Berry (v/g)	Rock and Roll Music [demo] Untitled Instrumental		Ch LP 9190 Ch LP/CD 9318	Johnny Johnson (p) Willie Dixon (b) Fred Below (d)
12/19/56 J. B. Lenoir (v/g)	Don't Touch My Head!!! When I Am Drinking I've Been Down So Long (Mama) What about Your Daughter Five Years	U 8360 U 8361 U 8362 U 8363 U 8364	Ckr 856 Ch 2ACMB 208 Ckr 856 Ckr 874 Ckr 874	Alex Atkins (as) Ernest Cotton (ts) Joe Montgomery (p) Willie Dixon (b) Al Galvin (d)
1/21/57 Chuck Berry (v/g)	Deep Feeling [inst.]-1 School Day (Ring! Ring! Goes the Bell) Lajaunda-2 Blue Feeling (Low Feeling) Wee Wee Hours	U 8378 U 8379 U 8380 U 8381 U 8382	Ch 1653 Ch 1653 Ch 1664 Ch 1671 Pye (E) NPL 28028	Johnny Johnson (p) Hubert Sumlin (g-1) Willie Dixon (b) Fred Below (d, bgs-2)
12/1/56[?] Muddy Waters (v)	**I Live the Life I Love, I Love the Life I Live** Rock Me	U 8388 U 8389	Ch 1680 Ch 1652	Little Walter (h) Otis Spann (p) Pat Hare (g) Hubert Sumlin (g) Willie Dixon (b) Francis Clay or S. P. Leary (d)
1/12/57 Muddy Waters (v)	Look What You've Done Got My Mojo Working	U 8392 U 8393	Ch 1758 Ch 1652	Little Walter (h) Otis Spann (p) Pat Hare (g) Hubert Sumlin (g) Willie Dixon (b) Francis Clay or S. P. Leary (d)

Date / Artist	Song	Matrix	Release	Personnel
12/1/56[?] Jimmy Rogers (v/g)	**I Can't Believe** **One Kiss** Can't Keep from Crying	U 8394 U 8395 U 8396	Ch 1659 Ch 1659 [lost]	Walter Horton (h) Otis Spann (p) Jody Williams (g) Willie Dixon (b) Fred Below (d)
Jan. '57 Jody Williams (v/g)	You May What Kind of Gal Is That?	U 8400	Argo 5274 Ch CHD 9330	Harold Ashby (ts) James "Red" Holloway (ts) Lafayette Leake (p) Willie Dixon (b) Phillip Thomas (d)
2/8/57 Sonny Boy Williamson (v/h)	Hurts Me So Much Fattening Frogs for Snakes I Don't Know Like Wolf This Is My Apartment	U 8408 U 8409 U 8410 U 8411 U 8412	Blues Ball LP 2004 Ckr 864 Ckr 864 Ch LP 417 Ch LP 417	Otis Spann (p) Luther Tucker (g) Robert Jr. Lockwood (g) Willie Dixon (b) Fred Below (d)
3/5/57[?] Little Walter (v/h-exc.1)	Nobody but You Temperature Shake Dancer-1 Everybody Needs Somebody	U 8433 U 8434 U 8435 U 8436	Ckr 859 LRB LP 2012 Ckr 1071 Ckr 859	Luther Tucker (g) Robert Jr. Lockwood (g) Willie Dixon (b) Fred Below (d)
2/8/57[?] Bo Diddley (v/g)	Hey! Bo Diddley-1 Mona (I Need You Baby)	U 8441 U 8442	Ckr 860 Ckr 860	Clifton James or Frank Kirkland (d) Lady Bo (v/g) Willie Dixon (b) The Moonglows (bv-1)
Mar. '57 Bernie Allen (v)	You Can Run, but You Can't Hide Too Late for Love	U 8443 U 8444	Ckr 862 Ckr 862	Willie Dixon (b) unk. (tp, saxes, d, fem. bv)
1/23/57[?] Jody Williams (g)	Lucky Lou [inst.] Hooked on Love [inst.]	U 8482 U 8483	Argo 5274 Blue Night 073 1669	Harold Ashby (ts) Lafayette Leake (o) Willie Dixon (b) Phillip Thomas (d)

Date Artist	Songs	Matrix	Original Release	Musicians Involved
Apr. '57 Willie Dixon (v/b)	**Jelly Jam** **Firey Love**-1 **All the Time**	U 8484 U 8485 [?]	Unissued Ch (GER) LP 6.24802 Ch CHD 9353	Jody Williams (g) unk. (ts, d, v grp-1)
5/15/57 Chuck Berry (v/g)	How You've Changed Rock and Roll Music Oh Baby Doll Thirteen Question Method	U 8498 U 8499 U 8500 U 8501	Ch LP 1432 Ch 1671 Ch 1664 Reelin' 001	Lafayette Leake (p) Willie Dixon (b) Fred Below (d)
Jun. '57 Muddy Waters (v)	Good News Evil-1 Come Home Baby, I Wish You Would Let Me Hang Around-1	U 8510 U 8511 U 8512 U 8513	Ch 1667 Ch 1680 Ch 1667 Ch LP 9180	Marcus Johnson (ts) unk. (ts) James Cotton (h-1) Otis Spann (p) Pat Hare (g) Robert Jr. Lockwood (g) Willie Dixon (b) prob. Fred Below (d)
6/20/57 Little Walter (v/h)	Temperature Ah'w Baby I Had My Fun	U 8525 U 8526 U 8527	Ckr 867 Ckr 945 Ckr 945	Jimmy Lee Robinson (g) Robert Jr. Lockwood (g) Willie Dixon (b) Fred Below (d)
8/15/57 Bo Diddley (v/g)	Say Boss Man-1 Before You Accuse Me (Take a Look at Yourself)	U 8566 U 8567	Ckr 878 Ckr 878	Lafayette Leake (p) Willie Dixon (b) Frank Kirkland or Clifton James (d) Jerome Green (mrcs) The Moonglows (bv-1)

Date / Artist	Song	Matrix	Release	Personnel
9/1/57 Sonny Boy Williamson (v/h)	Cross My Heart	U 8593	Ckr 910	Otis Spann (p) Luther Tucker (g) Robert Jr. Lockwood (g) Willie Dixon (b) Fred Below (d)
	Born Blind	U 8594	Ckr 883	
	Ninety Nine	U 8595	Ckr 883	
	Dissatisfied	U 8596	Ckr 910	
	Little Village	18030	Ch LP 1536	
	Unseen Eye	18031	Ch LP 1536	
9/18/57 Jimmy Rogers (v/g)	What Have I Done	8597	Ch 1687	Little Walter (v-1/h) Otis Spann (p) poss. Wayne Benett (g) Willie Dixon (b) Francis Clay (d) Margaret Whitfield (v-1)
	My Baby Don't Love Me No More	8598	Ch 2ACMB 207	
	Trace of You-1	8599	Ch 1687	
12/7/57 Lafayette Leake (p)	Slow Leake	[?]	Ch CD 4-9340	unk. (g) Willie Dixon (b) Odie Payne (d)
12/29/57 Chuck Berry (v/g)	Sweet Little Sixteen	U 8627	Ch 1683	Lafayette Leake (p) Willie Dixon (b) Fred Below (d)
	Rock at the Philharmonic [inst.]	U 8628	Ch EP 5121, LP 1432	
	Guitar Boogie [inst.]	U 8629	Ch EP 5121, LP 1432	
	Night Beat [inst.]	U 8630	Ch LP 1488	
	Time Was	U 8631	Ch LP 6-8001	
	Reelin' and Rockin'	U 8632	Ch 1683	
	Chuckwalk [inst.]		Ch CD 9170	
12/30/57 Chuck Berry (v/g)	Johnny B. Goode	U 8633	Ch 1961	Lafayette Leake (p) Willie Dixon (b) Fred Below (d)
Jan. '58 Little Walter (v, exc. 1/h)	The Toddle-1, 3	U 8644	Ckr 890	prob. Lafayette Leake (o-2, p-3) Luther Tucker (g) Jimmy Lee Robinson (g) Willie Dixon (b) Odie Payne (d)
	Confession the Blues-2	U 8645	Ckr 890	

Date Artist	Songs	Matrix	Original Release	Musicians Involved
Jan. '58[?] J. B. Lenoir (v/g)	Daddy Talk to Your Son	U 8728	Ckr 901	Alex Atkins (as)
	She Don't Know-1	U 8729	Ckr 901	Ernest Cotton (ts)
	Good Looking Woman	U 8730	Ch 2ACMB 208	Leonard Caston (o)
	Voodoo Boogie	U 8731	Ch 2ACMB 208	Joe Montgomery (p)
				Robert Jr. Lockwood (g)
				Willie Dixon (b)
				Al Galvin (d)
				unk. v grp (bv-1)
Jan. '58[?] Muddy Waters (v)	I Won't Go On	U 8732	Ch 1692	James Cotton (h)
	She's Got It	U 8733	Ch 1692	Otis Spann (p)
	Born Lover	U 8734	Ch LP 9180	Pat Hare (g)
				Willie Dixon (b)
				prob. Fred Below (d)
1/29/58 Bo Diddley (v-1/g/vl)	Say Man-2	U 8748	Ckr 391	Lafayette Leake (p)
	Hush Your Mouth-1	U 8749	Ckr 896	Lady Bo (g)
	Bo's Guitar [inst.]	U 8750	Ch LP 3-19502	Willie Dixon (b)
	The Clock Strikes Twelve	U 8751	Ckr 931	Frank Kirkland or
	Dearest Darling	U 8752	Ckr 896	Clifton James (d)
				Jerome Green (mrcs, v-2)
3/27/58 Sonny Boy Williamson (v/h)	Your Funeral and My Trial	U 8753	Ckr 894	Lafayette Leake (p)
	She Got Next to Me	U 8754	Ch LP 1536	Eugene Pearson (g)
	Wake Up Baby	U 8755	Ckr 894	Robert Jr. Lockwood (g)
	Keep Your Hand Out of My Pocket	U 8756	Ch LP 1536	Willie Dixon (b)
				Fred Below (d)
5/20/58 Jimmy Rogers (v/g)	Don't You Know My Baby-1	U 8797	Ch 2ACMB 207	unk. (ts-1)
	Don't Turn Me Down-1	U 8798	Ch CHD 2-9372	Otis Spann (p)
	Looka Here	U 8799	Ch CHD 2-9372	Mighty Joe Young (g)
	This Has Never Been	U 8800	Ch 2ACMB 207	Willie Dixon (b)
				Odie Payne (d)

Date / Artist	Title	Matrix	Release	Personnel
Aug. '58 Muddy Waters (v)	She's Nineteen Years Old **Close to You** Walking thru the Park-1	U 8979 U 8980 U 9140[?]	Ch 1704 Ch 1718 Ch 1718	Little Walter (h) Otis Spann (p) Pat Hare (g) Luther Tucker (g) Willie Dixon (b) Francis Clay (d) George Hunter (d-1)
Aug. '58 Little Walter (v/h)	Key to the Highway Rock Bottom (alt. Walkin' On)	U 8981 U 8982	Ckr 904 Ckr 904 Ch LP 416	Otis Spann (p) Muddy Waters (g) Luther Tucker (g) Willie Dixon (b) Francis Clay (d)
Aug. '58 Bo Diddley (v/g)	Willie and Lillie Bo Meets the Monster-1	U 8986 U 8987	Ckr 907 Ckr 907	Lafayette Leake (p) Lady Bo (g) Willie Dixon (b) Frank Kirkland or Clifton James (d) Jerome Green (mrcs, v-1)
9/28/58 Chuck Berry (v/g)	Anthony Boy Sweet Little Rock & Roller	U 9070 U 9072	Ch 1709 Ch 1729	Johnny Johnson (p) Willie Dixon (b) Fred Below (d)
Sept. '58 Chuck Berry (v/g)	Jo Jo Gunne Memphis (Tennessee)	U 9071 U 9073	Ch 1716 Ch 1709	Willie Dixon (b) Fred Below (d) Basic tracks were recorded at Chuck's office in St. Louis on June 7, 1958. Bass and drums were later overdubbed probably with 9070 and 9072.

Date / Artist	Songs	Matrix	Original Release	Musicians Involved
11/19/58 Chuck Berry (v/g)	Merry Christmas Baby Run Rudolph Run Little Queenie That's My Desire-1	U 9166 U 9167 U 9206 U 9207	Ch 1714 Ch 1714 Ch 1722 Ch 1716	Johnny Johnson (p) Willie Dixon (b) Fred Below (d) unk. (tamb-1)
Dec. '58 Bo Diddley (v/g)	Crackin' Up-1 Don't Let It Go (Hold on to What You Got) I'm Sorry-1 Oh Yea Blues, Blues The Great Grandfather	U 9168 U 9169 U 9170 U 9171 U 9172 U 7837	Ckr 924 Ch LP 1436 Ckr 914 Ckr 914 Ch CD 9331 Ckr 924	Lafayette Leake (p) Lady Bo (g/bv) Willie Dixon (b) Clifton James or Frank Kirkland (d) Jerome Green (mrcs) The Teardrops (bv-1)
2/17/59 Chuck Berry (v/g)	Do You Love Me Almost Grown Back in the U.S.A. Blue on Blue [inst.]	U 9235 U 9236 U 9237 U 9238	Ch (E) LP 6641 177 Ch 1722 Ch 1729 Ch LP 60028	Johnny Johnson (p) Willie Dixon (b) Fred Below (d) The Moonglows (bv)
prob. 2/25/59 Jimmy Rogers (v/g)	Rock This House My Last Meal-1	U 9241 U 9242	Ch 1721 Ch 1721	Otis Spann (p) Reggie Boyd (g) Willie Dixon (b) S. P. Leary (d) unk. v grp (bv-1)
2/25/59 Little Walter (v/h)	Baby **My Baby Is Sweeter** **Crazy Mixed Up World** Worried Life	U 9243 U 9244 U 9245 U 9246	LRB LP 2007 Ckr 919 Ckr 919 LRB LP 2007	Otis Spann (p) Luther Tucker (g) Freddy Robinson (g) Willie Dixon (b) George Hunter (d)

Mar. '59
Bo Diddley (v/g)

9353	Mama Mia-1	Ckr LP 2985
9354	Bucket	Instant (E) INSD-5038
9355	What Do You Know about Love-1	Ckr LP 3001
9356	Lazy Woman-1	Ckr LP 2985
9357	Come On Baby-1	Ckr LP 2974

Lafayette Leake (p)
Lady Bo (g-1/bv)
Willie Dixon (b)
Clifton James or
Frank Kirkland (d)
Jerome Green (mrcs)
The Teardrops (bv)

1959
Bo Diddley (v/g)

9458	Nursery Rhyme (Puttentang)	Ckr LP 2974
9459	Mumblin' Guitar [inst.]	Ckr LP 2974
9462	I Love You So-1	Ckr LP 2974

Lady Bo (g-1/bv)
Willie Dixon (b)
Clifton James or Frank Kirkland (d)
Jerome Green (mrcs)
The Teardrops (bv-1)

1959
Sonny Boy Williamson (v/h)

9479	Let Your Conscience Be Your Guide	Ckr 927
9480	Unseeing Eye	Ckr 927

Otis Spann (p)
Robert Jr. Lockwood (g)
Luther Tucker (g)
Willie Dixon (b)
Odie Payne (d)

1/4/59
Jimmy Witherspoon (v)

9482	**Everything but You** [Dixon's authorship of this composition is dubious. See chapter 5, note 3).]	CHV-412

Recorded in Kansas City. The master was later purchased.

Harold Ashby (ts)
Jay McShann (p)
unk. (tp, g, b, d)

Jul. '59
Billy "The Kid" Emerson (v/p) with Willie Dixon's Band

9575	I'll Get You Too	Ch 1740
9576	A Mighty Love	Unissued
9577	Um Hum, My Baby-1	Ch 1740
9578	When It Rains It Pours	Unissued

Joe Jones (ts)
Vincent Duling (Collins) (g)
Willie Dixon (b)
Phil Thomas (d)
The Dells (bv-1)

Date / Artist	Songs	Matrix	Original Release	Musicians Involved
Jul. '59 Howlin' Wolf (v)	**Howlin' for My Darling** (w. Burnett)	9584	Ch 1762	Willie Dixon (comp. only) Abb Locke (ts) Hosea Lee Kennard (p) Hubert Sumlin (g) Abraham Smothers (g) S. P. Leary (d)
Jul. '59 Larry Williams (v)	My Baby's Got Soul Every Day I Wonder I Wanna Know You Killing Me (On My Feet)	U 9605 U 9606 U 9607 U 9608	Ch 1736 Ch 1736 Ch 1761 Ch 1745	Willie Dixon (b) prob. Billy Emerson (p) unk. (fl, ts, bs, g, d, v grp)
7/21/59 Little Walter (v-exc.1/h)	Everything's Gonna Be Alright Mean Old Frisco Back Track	9619 9620 9621	Ckr 930 Ckr 1117 Ckr 930	Otis Spann (p) Freddy Robinson (g) Luther Tucker (g) Willie Dixon (b) Billy Stepney (d)
7/29 or 7/30 of 1959 Chuck Berry (v/g)	Betty Jean County Line-1 Childhood Sweetheart One O'Clock Jump-1,2 I Just Want to Make Love to You Broken Arrow-1 Let It Rock (Rockin' on the Railroad)-2 Too Pooped to Pop-1	9626 9627 9628 9629 9630 9631 9632 9633	Ch 1737 Ch 1700 [repress] Ch 1737 Reelin' LP 001 Ch LP 1480 Ch 1737 Ch 1747 Ch 1747	Leroy. C. Davis (ts-1) Johnny Johnson (p) Willie Dixon (b) Fred Below (d) The Educators (bv, exc. 2)

Date / Artist	Title	Matrix	Release	Personnel
Sept. '59 Bo Diddley (v/g)	The Story of Bo Diddley (My Story)	9727	Ckr 942	Lafayette Leake (p)
	She's Alright	9728	Ckr 936	Lady Bo (g/bv)
	Limber-2	9731	Ckr LP 2976	Willie Dixon (b)
	Say Man, Back Again-1	9732	Ckr 936	Clifton James or
	Run Diddley Daddy	9737	Ckr LP 2974	Frank Kirkland (d)
				Jerome Green (v-1/mrcs)
				unk. v grp-2
Dec. '59 Little Walter (v/h)	Going Down Slow	9889	LRB LP 2007	Robert Jr. Lockwood (g)
	My Desire	9890	Unissued	Freddy Robinson (g)
	You're Sweet	9891	Ch CD 2-9357	Luther Tucker (g)
				Willie Dixon (b)
				George Hunter (d)
1/30/60 Sonny Boy Williamson (v/h)	The Goat	9829	Ckr 943	Otis Spann (p)
	Cool Disposition	9830	Ch LP 417	Robert Jr. Lockwood (g)
	I Never Do Wrong	9831	Ch 2ACMB 206	Luther Tucker (eb)
	It's So Sad to Be Alone	9832	Ckr 943	Willie Dixon (b)
				Fred Below (d)
Jan. '60 Otis Rush (v/g)	So Many Roads, So Many Trains	9966	Ch 1751	Bob Neely (ts)
	I'm Satisfied	9967	Ch 1751	Lafayette Leake (p)
	So Close	9968	Ch LP 1538	Matt Murphy (eb)
	All Your Love	9969	Ch LP 1538	Willie Dixon (b)
	I Won't Be Worried No More	[?]	Blue Night 073 1669	Odie Payne (d)
	Ooh Wee Baby	[?]	Blue Night 073 1669	
2/12/60 Chuck Berry (v/g) Date of Mar. 29 is also given for this session.	Driftin' Blues-1, 2	10075	Ch LP 1448	Leroy C. Davis (ts-1)
	I Got to Find My Baby-1	10076	Ch 1763	unk. (ts-1)
	Don't You Lie to Me-1	10077	Ch LP 1456	Johnny Johnson (p)
	Worried Life Blues-1	10078	Ch 1754	Matt Murphy (g)
	Our Little Rendezvous	10079	Ch 1767	Willie Dixon (b)
	Bye Bye Johnny	10080	Ch 1754	Ebby Hardy or
	Run Around	10081	Ch LP 1456	Jasper Thomas (d)
	Jaguar and Thunderbird-2	10082	Ch 1767	The Galaxies[?] (bv-2)

Date Artist	Songs	Matrix	Original Release	Musicians Involved
2/15/60 Chuck Berry (v/g)	Diploma for Two-1, 2	10092	Ch 1853, LP 1456	Leroy C. Davis
	Little Star-1, 2	10093	Ch 1779, LP 1456	unk. (ts-1)
Date of Apr. 12 is also given for this session.	The Way It Was Before-1, 2	10094	Ch LP 1456	Johnny Johnson (p)
	Away from You-1, 2,	10095	Ch LP 1456	Matt Murphy (g-4)
	Down the Road a Piece-4	10096	Ch LP 1448	Willie Dixon (b)
	Confessin' the Blues-4	10097	Ch LP 1448	Eddie Hardy (d)
	Sweet Sixteen-4	10098	Ch LP 1456	The Galaxies[?] (bv-2)
	Thirteen Question Method-4	10099	Ch LP 1456	unk. fem. grp-3
	Stop and Listen-3, 4	10100	Ch LP 1456	
	I Still Got the Blues-4	10101	Ch LP 1480	
	I'm Just a Lucky So and So-4	10102	Ch LP 6-80001	
	Mad Lad [inst.]	10103	Ch 1763	
	Surfing Steel (Crying Steel)-3	10104	Ch LP 1480	
3/2/60 Buddy Guy (v/g)	**Slop Around** (w. Guy)	10043	Ch 1753	Willie Dixon (comp. only)
	Broken-Hearted Blues (w. Guy and Montgomery)	10044	Ch 1759	Jarrett Gibson (ts) Bob Neely (ts)
	I Got My Eyes on You (w. Guy)	10045	Ch 1735	Donald Hankins (bs) Little Brother Montgomery (p) Jack Meyers (eb) Fred Below (d)
4/23/60 Muddy Waters (v/g)	Read Way Back-1	10031	Ch 1752	Little Walter (h) Otis Spann (p) Jimmy Rogers (g) Andrew Stephens (b) Francis Clay (d) Willie Dixon (bv-1)

May '60 — Detroit Jr. (Emery Williams Jr. v/p)

Johnny Board (ts)
unk. (saxes)
Eddie King Milton (g)
Willie Dixon (b)
Fred Below (d)
Little Mac (Simmons)
Georgia Hinton (v-1)

Matrix	Title	Release
10194	Too Poor-1	Ch 1772
10195	No Other Girl but You	Unissued
10196	You Mean Everything	Ch 1772
10197	Respect My Baby	Unissued

6/1/60 — Sam Lazor (o)

Grant Green (g)
Willie Dixon (b)
Chauncey Williams (d)

Matrix	Title	Release
10214	Funky Blues	Argo 5365
10215	Big Willie	
10216	Space Flight	Chess (GER)
10217	Dig a Little Deeper	6.24802AG[?]
10218	Gigi Blues	
	Blues	All tracks are included in Argo LP 4002: Space Flight, unless otherwise noted.
10219	Caramu	
10220	Mad Lad	
10221	We Don't Know	
10222	Ruby	
10223	So Fine	Unissued
10224	Put on Your Old Grey Bonnet	Unissued
10225	My Babe	Unissued
10226	All or Nothing at All	
10227		

Jun. '60 — Howlin' Wolf (v)

Otis Spann (p)
Hubert Sumlin (g)
Freddy Robinson (g)
Willie Dixon (b)
Fred Below (d)

Matrix	Title	Release
10263	Wang Dang Doodle	Ch 1777
10264	Back Door Man	Ch 1777
10265	Spoonful	Ch 1762

Date / Artist	Songs	Matrix	Original Release	Musicians Involved
Jun. '60 Sonny Boy Williamson (v/h)	Temperature 110 Peach Tree Lonesome Cabin Somebody Help Me	10266 10267 10268 10269	Ckr 956 Ch LP 1503 Ckr 956 Ch LP 1509	Otis Spann (p) Eddie King (g) Luther Tucker (g) Willie Dixon (b) Fred Below (d)
6/7/60 Muddy Waters (v/g)	**Tiger in Your Tank** **I Got My Brand on You**	10293 10296	Ch 1765 Ch (JP) LPS 6040/50	Willie Dixon (comp. only) Otis Spann (p) Auburn "Pat" Hare (g) Andrew Stephens (eb) Francis Clay (d)
9/15/60 Sonny Boy Williamson (v/h)	Down Child Trust My Baby This Old Life Too Close Together-1	10415 10416 10417 10418	Ckr 1134 Ckr 963 Ch LP 1536 Ckr 963	Lafayette Leake (p) Robert Jr. Lockwood (g) Luther Tucker (g) Willie Dixon (b/v-1) Fred Below (d)
9/29/60 Otis Rush (v/g)	**You Know My Love** **I Can't Stop Baby** So Many Ways Love You Baby	10447 10448 10449 10450	Ch 1775 Ch 1775 Unissued Unissued	Bobby Neely (ts) Lafayette Leake (p) Matt Murphy (g) Willie Dixon (b) Odie Payne (d)
12/14/60 Sonny Boy Williamson (v/h)	Too Young to Die Don't Mean Maybe Stop Right Now The Hunt-1	10569 10570 10571 10572	Ch LP 1503 Ch LP 1509 Ckr 975 Ckr 975	Otis Spann (p) Robert Jr. Lockwood (g) Luther Tucker (g) Odie Payne (d) Willie Dixon (b/v-1)

Date / Artist	Title	Matrix	Release	Personnel
Dec. '60 Little Walter (v/h)	**I Don't Play**	10593	Ckr 968	Otis Spann (p)
	As Long As I Have You	10594	Ckr 968	Freddy Robinson (g)
	You Don't Know	10595	LRB LP 2012	Luther Tucker (g)
	Just You Fool	10596	Ckr 1013	Willie Dixon (b)
				George Hunter (d)
12/16/60 Buddy Guy (v/g)	**Let Me Love You Baby**	10622	Ch 1784	Willie Dixon (comp. only)
	I Got a Strange Feeling (w. Al Perkins)	10623	Ch LP 409	Jarrett Gibson (ts)
				Bob Neely (ts)
				Donald Hankins (bs)
				Otis Spann (p)
				Junior Wells (h)
				Jack Meyers (eb)
				Fred Below (d)
May '61 Howlin' Wolf (v/g-1)	**Little Baby**	10913	Ch 1793	Johnny Jones (p)
	Down in the Bottom-1	10917	Ch 1793	Jimmy Rogers (g)
				Hubert Sumlin (g)
				Willie Dixon (b)
				Sammy Lay (d)
Jun. '61 Howlin' Wolf (v/g-1)	**Shake for Me**	10937	Ch 1804	Johnny Jones (p)
	The Red Rooster-1	10938	Ch 1804	Hubert Sumlin (g)
				Willie Dixon (b)
				unk. (eb)
				Sammy Lay (d)
9/8/61 Sonny Boy Williamson (v/h)	Too Old to Think	11224	Ch LP 1503	Otis Spann (p)
	That's All I Want	11225	Ch LP 1503	Robert Jr. Lockwood (g)
	One Way Out	11226	Ckr 1003	Willie Dixon (b)
	Nine Below Zero	11227	Ckr 1003	Fred Below (d)

Date / Artist	Songs	Matrix	Original Release	Musicians Involved
Dec. '61 Howlin' Wolf (v/g-1)	**You'll Be Mine**-1 **Just Like I Treat You**-1 **I Ain't Superstitious** Goin' Down Slow-2	11377 11378 11379 11380	Ch 1813 Ch 1823 Ch 1823 Ch 1813	Henry Gray (p) Jimmy Rogers (eb) Hubert Sumlin (g) Sammy Lay (d) Willie Dixon (b/speech-2)
1962 The Lucky Three Trio	Back Home in Indiana-1 Wrinkles	11694 11695	Ch (GER) 6.24802AG Tuba Single 8002	Lafayette Leake (p) Clifton James (d) Willie Dixon (b) unk. v grp-1
6/27/62 Bo Diddley (v/g)	**You Can't Judge a Book by Its Cover**	11699	Ckr 1019	Willie Dixon (comp. only) prob. Frank Kirkland (d) Jerome Green (mrcs) unk. (eb)
6/27/62 Muddy Waters (v) Overdubbed to "Blue Guitar" (Age 29106) by Earl Hooker	**You Shook Me** (w. J. B. Lenoir)	U 11711	Ch 1827	Willie Dixon (comp. only) A.C. Reed (ts) John "Big Moose" Walker (o) Ernest Cotton (ts) Earl Hooker (g) Ernest Johnson (eb) Bobby Little (d)

Date / Artist	Song	Matrix	Release	Personnel
8/12/62 Buddy Guy (v/g)	**Hard but It's Fair**-1 **When My Left Eye Jumps**	11802 11804	Ch 1878 Ch 1838	Willie Dixon (comp. only) Sonny Turner (tp) Maury Watson (tp) Jarrett Gibson (ts) Abb Locke (ts) Lafayette Leake (o/p) William "Lefty" Bates (g) Jack Meyers (eb) Phil Thomas (d) unk. (bv-1)
9/27 to 9/28 of 1962 Howlin' Wolf (v)	**Mama's Baby** **Do the Do** **Tail Dragger** **Long Green Stuff**	11914 11915 11916 11917	Ch 1844 Ch 1844 Ch 1890 Blues Ball LP 2002	Willie Dixon (comp. only) J. T. Brown (ts) unk. (s) Johnny Jones (p) Hubert Sumlin (g) Jerome Arnold (b) Junior Blackmon (d) Dixon made a guide vocal track of "Tail Dragger" (Ch CD 9353).
10/12/62 Muddy Waters (v)	**You Need Love**	11836	Ch 1839	Willie Dixon (comp. only) Earl Hooker (g) John "Big Moose" Walker (o) Earnest Johnson (eb) Casey Jones (d) unk. (perc: overdubbed)

Date Artist	Songs	Matrix	Original Release	Musicians Involved
1/11/63 Sonny Boy Williamson (v/h)	**Bye Bye Bird** **Bring It on Home**	12114 12116	Ckr 1036 Ckr 1134	Willie Dixon (comp. only) Billy Emerson (o) Matt Murphy (g) Milton Rector (eb) Al Duncan (d)
2/5/63 Little Walter (v/h-exc.1)	**I'm a Business Man** (w. B. Emerson) **Dead Presidents** **Southern Feeling** [inst.]-1 (w. B. Emerson)	12169 12170 12171	Ckr 1081 Ckr 1081 Ckr 1043	Willie Dixon (comp. only) Billy Emerson (o/p) Jarrett Gibson (ts) Donald Hankins (ts) Buddy Guy (g) Jack Meyers (eb) Al Duncan (d)
2/8/63 Buddy Guy (v/g)	**American Bandstand** (w. Guy and Emerson)	12184	Ch LP2-92519	Willie Dixon (comp. only) Jarrett Gibson (bs) Bob Neely (ts) Lafayette Leake (p) Lacey Gibson (g) Jack Meyers (eb) Al Duncan (d)
5/2/63 Muddy Waters (v)	Five Long Years Brown Skin Woman Twenty Four Hours Coming Round the Mountain Let Me Hang Around	U 12442 U 12443 U 12444 U 12445 U 12446	Ch 1862 Ch (JP) PLP 6040/50 Ch 1862 Ch (JP) PLP 6040/50 Ch (JP) PLP 6040/50	James Cotton (h) Otis Spann (p) Luther Tucker (g) Willie Dixon (b) Willie Smith (d)

Date / Artist	Song Titles	Matrix	Label / Notes	Personnel
7/26/63 Willie Dixon (b/v)	**Wee Wee Baby (You Sure Look Good to Me)** Vocals: Muddy, Dixon, and Buddy	12574	Argo LP 4031: *Folk Festival of the Blues* Live recording at Copacabana Club, Chicago.	Jarrett Gibson (ts) Donald Hankins (bs) Otis Spann (p) Jack Meyers (eb) Fred Below (d)
Muddy Waters (v)	Got My Mojo Working Sitting and Thinking Clouds in My Heart Nineteen Years Old	12575		
Howlin' Wolf (v)	Sugar Mama May I Have a Talk with You	12576		
Buddy Guy (g/v)	**Let Me Love You Baby** Senior Blues Air Line Every Day Baby Don't You Love Me **Don't Know Which Way to Go** (w. Perkins) Worried Blues	12577 12578 12579 12580 12581 12582	Buddy Guy's tracks that are included in the album are only "Worried Blues" and "Don't Know Which Way to Go."	"Bring It on Home" by Sonny Boy Williamson in this album is a pseudo-live recording.
8/14/63 Howlin' Wolf (v)	**Hidden Charms** **Three Hundred Pounds of Joy** **Built for Comfort**	12617 12618 12619	Ch 1890 Ch 1870 Ch 1870	Willie Dixon (comp. only) J. T. Brown (ts) Donald Hankins (bs) Lafayette Leake (p) Hubert Sumlin (g) Buddy Guy (g) Jerome Arnold (eb) Sam Lay (d)

Date / Artist	Songs	Matrix	Original Release	Musicians Involved
Sept. '63 Muddy Waters (v/ acoustic g)	My Home Is in the Delta-2	12838	Ch LP 1483: Folk Singer	Buddy Guy (g, exc. 1)
	Long Distance-2	12839		Clifton James (d-2)
	My Captain	12840		Willie Dixon (b-2)
	Good Morning Little School Girl	12841		
	You Gonna Need My Help-2	12842		
	Cold Weather Blues	12843		
	Big Leg Woman	12844		
	Country Boy-2	12845		
	Feel Like Going Home-1	12846		
1/13/64 Walter "Shakey" Horton (h)	**Good Moanin' Blues**-1	12915	Argo 5476	Francis Bobby Buster (o)
	Gonna Bring It on Home-1	12916		Buddy Guy (g)
				Jack Meyers (eb)
				Willie Smith (d)
1/24/64	Hard Hearted Woman-1	12956	All tracks are included in LP 4037: *The Soul of Blues Harmonica*	Willie Dixon (v-1, prod)
	Wee Baby Blues-1	12957		
4/9/64 Muddy Waters (v/g)	**The Same Thing**	13150	Ch 1895	Otis Spann (p)
	You Can't Lose What You Ain't Never Had	13151	Ch 1895	Buddy Guy or James "Pee Wee" Madison (g)
				Willie Dixon (b)
				S. P. Leary (d)
4/30/64 Buddy Guy (v/g)	**I Dig Your Wig** (w. Guy)	13209	Ch 1899	Willie Dixon (comp. only)
				Sonny Boy Williamson (h)
				Lafayette Leake (p)
				Jack Myers (eb)
				Clifton James (d)

Date / Artist	Title	Matrix	Release	Personnel
4/30/64 Sonny Boy Williamson (v/h)	**(I Want You) Close to Me** Originally "Close to You" presented to Muddy Waters in 1958.	13211	Ckr 1080	Willie Dixon (comp. only) Lafayette Leake (p) Buddy Guy (g) Jack Myers (eb) Fred Below (d)
6/30/64 Koko Taylor (v)	**I Got What It Takes**	13306	Ckr 1092	Willie Dixon (prod) Walter Horton (h) Lafayette Leake (p) Buddy Guy (g) Robert Nighthawk (g) Jack Myers (eb) Clifton James (d)
Aug. '64 Howlin' Wolf (v/h-1)	Love Me Darlin' Killing Floor My Country Sugar Mama-1 Louise	13417 13418 13419 13420	Ch 1911 Ch 1923 Ch 1911 Ch 1923	Arnold Rogers (ts) Donald Hankins (bs) Lafayette Leake (p) Hubert Sumlin (g) Buddy Guy (g) Andrew McMahon (eb) Willie Dixon (b) Sammy Lay (d)
Sept. '64 Muddy Waters (v/g)	**My John the Conqueror Root**	13473	Ch 1914	Willie Dixon (comp. only) James Cotton (h) J. T. Brown (ts) Otis Spann (p) James "Pee Wee" Madison (g) Milton Rector (eb) S. P. Leary (d)

Date / Artist	Songs	Matrix	Original Release	Musicians Involved
1/20/65 Koko Taylor (v)	Love Sick Tears **Don't Mess with the Messer** Red Hot Daddy **Whatever I Am You Made Me-1**	13686 13687 13688 13689	Ch CD 112 519 Ckr 1106 Unissued Ckr 1106	Willie Dixon (prod) unk. (saxes) Lafayette Leake (p) Buddy Guy (g) Matt Murphy (g) Clifton James (d) unk. v grp-1
Apr. '65 Buddy Guy (v/g)	**Crazy Love (Crazy Music)** Every Girl I See (w. Michael P. Murphy) **Too Many Ways**	13896 13897 13898	Ch 1936 Ch LPS 1527 Ch LPS 1527	Willie Dixon (comp. only) Gene Barge (ts) unk. (saxes) Matt Murphy (g) Reggie Boyd (eb) Phil Thomas (d)
1965 Koko Taylor (v)	I'm a Little Mixed Up	13995	Ch LPS 1532	Willie Dixon (prod) unk. (sax) Gene Barge (ts) Lafayette Leake (p) Buddy Guy (g) Matt Murphy (g) Clifton James (d)
12/7/65 Koko Taylor (v)	**Wang Dang Doodle-1** **Blues Heaven-1** **(I Got) All You Need** Tell Me the Truth-1	14389 14390 14391 14392	Ckr 1135 Ckr 1135 Ckr 1174 Ckr 1148	Willie Dixon (prod/bv-1) Gene Barge (ts) Donald Hankins (s) Lafayette Leake (p) Johnny "Twist" Williams (g) Buddy Guy (g) Jack Myers (eb) Fred Below (d)

Date / Artist	Title	Matrix	Issue	Personnel
4/5/66 Johnny "Twist" Williams (v/g)	Nobody Knows Love but You Go Go Baby Knock on My Door	14637 14638 14639	Ckr 1139 Ckr 1139 Unissued	Willie Dixon (prod/v) unk. (ts, p, b, d)
5/17/66 Koko Taylor	Good Advice **When I Think of My Baby** **I'm Gonna**	14787 14788 14789	Unissued Unissued Unissued	Willie Dixon (prod) Gene Barge (ts) Lafayette Leake (p) Buddy Guy (g) Jack Myers (eb) Fred Below (d)
6/29/66 Koko Taylor (v)	Good Advice **He's a Good Un** That's All I Want	14891 14892 14893	Ckr 1148 Unissued Unissued	Willie Dixon (prod) Gene Barge (ts) Lafayette Leake (p) Johnny "Twist" Williams (g) Jack Myers (eb) Fred Below (d)
Dec. '66 Koko Taylor (v)	**What Came First the Egg or the** **Hen-1** **Love Me-2** All Money Spent (on Feeling Good)	15441 15442 15443	Ckr 1166 Ckr 1166 Ckr 1174	Willie Dixon (prod/bv-1) Gene Barge (ts) Lafayette Leake (p) Johnny "Twist" Williams (g) Rufus Crume (g) Dillard Crume (eb) Al Duncan (d) unk. fem. v grp-2
Mar. '67 Little Joe Blue (v)	Something Going On Me and My Woman She Knocks Me Out My Heart Beats like a Drum	15651 15652 15653 15654	Unissued Ckr 1173 Unissued Ckr 1173	Gene Barge (ts) unk. (tps, saxes) Bryce Robinson (g) Willie Dixon (b) Maurice White (d)

Date Artist	Songs	Matrix	Original Release	Musicians Involved
1967[?] Tommy Tucker (v/o/p-1)	Sitting Home Alone-1 A Whole Lot of Fun (Before the Weekend Is Done) I'm Shorty-1, 2 Real True Love-1	U 15797 U 15798 U 15799 U 15800	Ckr 1178 Ckr 1186 Ckr 1178 Ckr 1186	Willie Dixon (v-2) Walter Horton (h-1) unk. (g, eb, d)
1967 Muddy Waters (v)	**When the Eagle Flies**	15840	Ch 2018, LP 1553	Willie Dixon (comp. only) Otis Spann (p) Pinetop Perkins (o) James "Pee Wee" Madison (g) Sammy Lawhorn (g) Cash McCall (g) Earnest Johnson (eb) Willie Smith (d)
Jul. '67 Buddy Guy (v/g)	**I Cry and Sing the Blues** **Goin' Home**	15965 15966	Ch CHD 2-9337 Ch LPS 1527	Willie Dixon (comp. only) unk. (ts, p, g, eb, d)
Aug. '67 Koko Taylor (v)	**Fire** **Insane Asylum** I Ain't Gonna Tell	16132 16133 16134	Ckr 1191 Ckr 1191 Unissued	Willie Dixon (prod/bv) Gene Barge (ts) Lafayette Leake (p/o) Buddy Guy (g) Johnny "Twist" Williams (g) unk. (eb, d, bs)
Oct. '68 Koko Taylor (v)	**Separate or Integrate**-1, 2 **I Don't Care Who Knows**-1, 3 **Love You like a Woman**-1, 4 **Yes It's Good for You**	17365 17366 17367 17368	Ckr 1210 Ckr 1210 Ch LPS 1532 Ch LPS 1532	Willie Dixon (prod) poss. Donald Hankins (ts) poss. Johnny Shines (g) unk. (tp, sax-1, eb, d, v grp-2, fem. v grp-3, mixed v grp-4)

Date / Artist	Title / Tracks	Matrix	Issue	Personnel
Jan. '69 Muddy Waters (v/g)	**I Am the Blues**	17690	Cadet LP 320: *After the Rain*	Willie Dixon (comp. only) Paul Oscher (h) Otis Spann (p) Charles Stepney (o) Phil Upchurch (g) Pete Cosey (g) Louis Satterfield (eb) Morris Jennings (d)
4/21/69 Fathers and Sons	Sad Letter Walkin' thru the Park-3 Standin' Round Cryin' **I Love the Life I Live, I Live the Life I Love**	17782 17783 17784 17785	Unissued Exc. the cuts noted "unissued," all included in Chess 2LPS 127: *Fathers and Sons.*	Willie Dixon (adviser) Muddy Waters (v/g) Otis Spann (p) Michael Bloomfield (g) Paul Butterfield (h) Donald "Duck" Dunn (eb, exc. 1)
4/22/69	Twenty Four Hours Country Boy Sugar Sweet-3 Forty Days and Forty Nights-3 All Aboard-1 You Can't Lose What You Ain't Never Had I Wanna Go Home	17786 17787 17788 17789 17790 17791 17792	 Unissued	Sam Lay (d, exc. 2) Buddy Miles (d, only 2) Jeff Carp (chromatic h-1) Paul Absell (g-3) Phil Upchurch (eb-1)
4/23/69	**Oh Yeah** Mean Disposition Blow Wind Blow **I'm Ready** I Feel So Good Someday Baby	17793 17794 17795 17796 17797 17798	 Unissued	

Date / Artist	Songs	Matrix	Original Release	Musicians Involved
4/24/69 Fathers and Sons Live recording at The Super Cosmic Joy-Scout Jamboree, Chicago.	**Hoochie Coochie Man**	17799	Unissued	
	Long Distance Call	17800		
	Baby Please Don't Go	17801		
	The Same Thing	17802		
	Got My Mojo Working, Pt.1	17803		
	Got My Mojo Working, Pt. 2-2	17804		
	Honey Bee	17805		
4/23/69 Koko Taylor (v)	**29 Ways**	17773	Ch LPS 1532	Willie Dixon (prod/b-1)
	Nitty Gritty	17774	Ch LPS 1532	Walter Horton (h)
	He Always Knocks Me Out	17775	Ch CD 112 519	Lafayette Leake or Sunnyland Slim (p)
	I Love a Lover like You-1	17776	Ch LPS 1532	Buddy Guy (g)
				Matt Murphy (g)
				Jack Myers (eb)
				Fred Below (d)
3/12/70 Jimmy Reeves Jr. (v)	**Hoo Doo Blues**	18479	All tracks exc. "She's Doing Wrong" are included in Ckr LP 3016: *Born to Love Me.*	Willie Dixon (prod/bv)
	Born to Love Me-1	18480		M. T. Murphy (g)
	Shame, Shame, Shame	18481		Mighty Joe Young (g)
	Baby What's on Your Worried Mind	18482		Lafayette Leake (p)
	Bright Lights, Big City-1	18483		Walter Horton (h)
	Honest I Do	18484		Sylvester Boines (eb)
	Put It All in There-1	18485		Morris Jennings (d)
	She's Doing Wrong	18486		The Pick-Ups (bv)
	Don't Let the Music Die	18487		
	Love That Woman-1	18488		
	Baby, Watcha Want Me to Do-1	18489		
	I Love You Baby	18490		

11/24/71
Koko Taylor (v)

Title	Matrix	Issue	Personnel
Love Me to Death-1	2033	Ch 2132	Willie Dixon (prod/bv-2)
I Need You More and More-1	2034		Gene Barge (ts)
Um Huh My Baby	2035	All tracks exc. "Blue	Lafayette Leake (p)
It's a Poor Dog	2036	Prelude" are	Mighty Joe Young (g)
That's the Way Love Is	2037	included in Ch LP	Reggie Boyd (g)
Tears Your Man	2038	50018: *Basic Soul*.	Louis Satterfield (eb)
Violent Love	2039		Clifton James (d)
Bills, Bills and More Bills	2040		Brass overdubbed-1
Blue Prelude	2041		
Pollution-1, 2	2042		
Let Me Love You Baby	2043		

6/17/72
Lafayette Leake (p)
Live recording at Montreux
Jazz Festival, Switzerland

Title	Matrix	Issue	Personnel
Wrinkles	2479	Ch LP 60015	Willie Dixon (b)
Swiss Boogie	2480	Ch LP 60015	Fred Below (d)

6/17/72
Koko Taylor (v)
Live recording at Montreux
Jazz Festival, Switzerland

Title	Matrix	Issue	Personnel
Big Boss Man	2496	Unissued	Lafayette Leake (p)
One Day I'm Gonn' Get Lucky	2497	Unissued	Louis Myers (g)
Think I Got the Blues	2498	Unissued	Dave Myers (eb)
Wonder Why My Man Won't Treat Me Right	2499	Unissued	Fred Below (d)
Insane Asylum-1	2500	Unissued	Willie Dixon (v/b-1)
I Got What It Takes-2	2501	Ch LP 60015	Muddy Waters (v-2)
Wang Dang Doodle	2502	Ch LP 60015	

Dixon's Abco and Cobra Sessions: 1956–1958 (Chicago)

Date / Artist	Songs	Matrix	Original Release	Musicians Involved
1956 Arbee Stidham (v)	I'll Always Remember You Meet Me Halfway	3061 3062	Ab 100 Ab 100	unk. (ts, bs) Art Sims (p) Wayne Bennett (g) Willie Dixon (b) Odie Payne (d) Sonny Boy Williamson (h) Walter Horton (h)
1956 Freddie Hall	Can't This Be Mine Playing Hard to Get	U 3105 U 3106	Ab 103 Ab 103	Louis Myers (g) Dave Myers (g) Willie Dixon (b) Eugene Lyons (d)
1956 Louis (Louie) Myers (h) and the Aces	Just Whaling (Just Wailing) Bluesy	3126 3127	Ab 104 Ab 104	Dave Myers (g) Willie Dixon (b) Eugene Lyons (d)
1956 Arbee Stidham (v)	When I Find My Baby Please Let It Be Me	U 3207 U 3208	Ab 107 Ab 107	unk. (ts, bs) Art Sims (p) Wayne Bennett (g) Willie Dixon (b) Odie Payne (d)
Summer 1956 Otis Rush (v/g)	**I Can't Quit You Baby** **Sit Down Baby** (w. Howard Bedno)	U 3236 U 3237	Cb 5000 Cb 5000	Walter Horton (h) Red Holloway (ts) Lafayette Leake (p) Wayne Bennett (g) Willie Dixon (b) Al Duncan (d)

1956 Walter "Shakey" Horton (v/h)	Have a Good Time Need My Baby	U 3238 U 3239	Cb 5002 Cb 5002	Harold Ashby (ts) Lafayette Leake (p) Otis Rush (g) Willie Dixon (b) Al Duncan (d)
1956 The Clouds (v grp)	Rock and Roll Boogie I Do	[?] [?]	Cb 5001 Cb 5001	The Clouds: Sherrard Jones (v) Al Butler (v) William English (v) Bobby Walker (v) Red Holloway (ts) Harold Ashby (ts) Wayne Bennett (g) Otis Rush (g) Lafayette Leake (p) Willie Dixon (b) Al Duncan (d)
1956 The Calvaes	Mambo Fiesta Fine Girl	[?] [?]	Cb 5003 Cb 5003	The Calvaes: James "Zeke" Brown (v) Donald Handley (v) James Bailey (v) Donald "Duck" Coles (v) Paul Morgan (v) poss. Willie Dixon (b) unk. (saxes, p, d, g)

Date / Artist	Songs	Matrix	Original Release	Musicians Involved
Fall '56 Otis Rush (v/g)	**Violent Love** **My Love Will Never Die**	U 3331 U 3332	Cb 5005 Cb 5005	Lucius Washington (ts) Harold Ashby (ts) Walter Horton (h) Lafayette Leake (p) Wayne Bennett (g) Willie Dixon (b) Al Duncan (d)
1956 Harold Burrage (v/p)	One More Dance You Eat Too Much	U 3333 U 3334	Cb 5004 Cb 5004	Lucius Washington (ts) Harold Ashby (ts) Wayne Bennet (g) Willie Dixon (b) Al Duncan (d)
1956 Harold Burrage (v)	Hot Dog and a Bottle of Pop	tk3	Flyright (E) 579	poss. Johnny Jones or Henry Gray (p) Magic Sam (g) Willie Dixon (b) Billie Stepney (d)
1956 Sunnyland Slim (v/p)	It's You Baby Highway 61 Blues (Eli Toscano Blues)	C 1000 C 1001 [?]	Cb 5006 Cb 5006 Flyright (E) 594	Walter Horton (h) Jimmy Rogers (g) Poor Bob Woodfork (eb) Willie Dixon (b) S. P. Leary (d)
1956 Lee Jackson (Warren G. Hardin Lee) (v/g)	**Fishin' in My Pond** I'll Just Keep Walking	C 1002 C 1003	Cb 5007 Cb 5007	Walter Horton (h) Harold Ashby (ts) Lucius Washington or John Tinsley (ts) Sunnyland Slim (p) Jimmy Rogers (g) Willie Dixon (b) Jesse Fowler or Henry "Sneaky Joe" Harris (d)

Date / Artist	Title	Matrix	Catalog	Personnel
1957 Gloria Irving (v)	I Need a Man **For You and Only You**	[?] [?]	Cb 5008 Cb 5008	poss. Willie Dixon (b) unk. (as, ts, p, g, d)
Early 1957 Otis Rush (v/g)	**Groaning the Blues** **If You Were Mine**	U 1008 U 1009	Cb 5010 Cb 5010	Little Walter (h) Harold Ashby (ts) Lafayette Leake (p) Jody Williams (g) Willie Dixon (b) Odie Payne (d)
1957 Little Willie Foster (v-1/h)	Crying the Blues-1 Little Girl-2	C 1010 C 1011	Cb 5011 Cb 5011	Lazy Bill Lucas (p) Floyd Jones (v-2/g) Triolue High (g) prob. Willie Dixon (b) Ray Scott (d)
1957 Harold Burrage (v/p)	**Messed Up** **I Don't Care Who Knows**	C 1012 C 1013	Cb 5012 Cb 5012	Harold Ashby (ts) Jody Williams (g) Willie Dixon (b) Odie Payne (d)
1957 Magic Sam (Sam Maghett) (v/g)	Love Me with a Feeling All Your Love	1014 1015	Cb 5013 Cb 5013	Little Brother Montgomery (p) Mack Thompson (eb) Willie Dixon (b) Billy Stepney (d)
1957 The Calvaes (v grp)	Lonely Lonely Village Born with Rhythm	1016? 1017?	Cb 5014 Cb 5014	The Calvaes: James "Zeke" Brown (v) Donald Handley (v) James Bailey (v) Donald "Duck" Coles (v) Paul Morgan (v) Poss. Willie Dixon (b) unk. (saxes, p, d, g)

Date / Artist	Songs	Matrix	Original Release	Musicians Involved
Mid 1957 Otis Rush (v/g)	Love That Woman **Jump Sister Bessie**	C 1018 C 1019	Cb 5015 Cb 5015	Little Walter (h) Harold Ashby (ts) Little Brother Montgomery (p) Louis Myers (g) Willie Dixon (b) Odie Payne (d)
1957 Clarence Jolly (v)	Changing Love Don't Leave Me	C 1020 C 1021	Cb 5016 Cb 5016	Guitar Shorty aka David Kearney (g) Willie Dixon (b) unk. (ts, p, d)
1957 Guitar Shorty (v/g)	You Don't Treat Me Right Irma Lee	C 1022 C 1023	Cb 5017 Cb 5017	John Tinsley (ts) unk. (g) Lafayette Leake (p) Willie Dixon (b) Odie Payne (d)
1957 Harold Burrage (v/p)	Stop for the Red Light **I'm Satisfied** Hey Little Girl	C 1024 C 1025 [?]	Cb 5018 Cb 5018 Unissued	Harold Ashby (ts) Otis Rush (g) Willie Dixon (b) Billy Stepney (d)
Aug. 1957 Betty Everett (v)	My Life Depends on You **My Love**	C 1026 C 1027	Cb 5019 Cb 5019	poss. Harold Ashby (ts) James "Red" Holloway (ts) Little Brother Montgomery (p) Wayne Bennett (g) Willie Dixon (b) Billy Stepney (d)

1957
Eddie Kirkland (v/g)

Title	Matrix	Issue	Personnel
I Gave You Everything	[?]	Unissued	Johnny Hooks (ts)
He Just Went out the Back Door	[?]	Unissued	Joe Percival (p)
			Willie Dixon (b)
			Thomas Whitehead (d)

1957
Magic Sam (Sam Maghett) (v/g)

Title	Matrix	Issue	Personnel
Everything Gonna Be Alright	1030	Cb 5021	Little Brother Montgomery (p)
Look Watcha Done	1031	Cb 5021	Mack Thompson (eb)
Magic Rocker [inst.]	[?]	BH (E) LP 7-63223	Willie Dixon (b)
			Billy Stepney (d)

1957
Harold Burrage (v/p) with Willie Dixon Band

Title	Matrix	Issue	Personnel
Crazy about My Baby-1	C 1032	P-Vine (JP) PLP 9021	Harold Ashby (ts-exc.1)
She Knocks Me Out	C 1032	Cb 5022	Mack Thompson (g)
My Love Has Been in Vain	C 1033	Unissued	Willie Dixon (b)
A Heart (Filled with Pain)	C 1033	Cb 5022	Billy Stepney (d)

Late 1957
Otis Rush (v/g)

Title	Matrix	Issue	Personnel
Three Times a Fool	C 1034	Cb 5023	Lafayette Leake (p)
She's a Good Un	C 1035	Cb 5023	Reggie Boyd (g)
			Willie Dixon (b)
			Odie Payne (d)

Late 1957
Betty Everett (v)

Title	Matrix	Issue	Personnel
Ain't Gonna Cry	C 1036	Cb 5024	poss.
Killer Diller	C 1037	Cb 5024	Harold Ashby (ts)
I Want You	[?]	Unissued	James "Red" Holloway (ts)
			Little Brother Montgomery (p)
			Wayne Bennett (g)
			Willie Dixon (b)
			Billy Stepney (d)

1958
Magic Sam (v/g)

Title	Matrix	Issue	Personnel
All Night Long-1	C 1038	Cb 5025	Harold Burrage (p)
All My Whole Life	C 1039	Cb 5025	Odell Campbell (eb-1)
Love Me This Way	[?]	BH (E) LP 7-63223	Willie Dixon (b)
			Odie Payne (d)
			unk. (bv-1)

Date Artist	Songs	Matrix	Original Release	Musicians Involved
1958 Charles Clark (v) and Willie Dixon Band	Row Your Boat **Hidden Charms**	C 1040 C 1041	At 1500 At 1500	Sonny Boy Williamson (h) Harold Burrage (p) Otis Rush (g) Louis Myers (g) Willie Dixon (b) Billy Stepney (d)
1958 Buddy Guy (v/g)	**Sit and Cry (The Blues)**-2 Try to Quit You Baby-1	C 1042 C 1043	At 1501 At 1501	Bob Neely (ts-1) Harold Ashby (ts-1) McKinley Easton (eb-2) Harold Burrage (p) Otis Rush (g) Willie Dixon (b) Odie Payne (d)
1958 Harold Burrage (v/p)	**I Cry for You** Betty Jean	C 1044 C 1045	Cb 5026 Cb 5026	Harold Ashby (ts) Abb Locke (ts) Henry Gray (p) Otis Rush (g) Willie Dixon (b) Odie Payne (d)
1958 Otis Rush (v/g)	It Takes Time Checking My Baby	C 1046 C 1047	Cb 5027 Cb 5027	Harold Ashby (ts/bs) Little Brother Montgomery (p) Louis Myers (g) Fred Below (d)
1958 Shakey Jake (v) with Willie Dixon Band	Roll Your Moneymaker-1 Call Me (If You Need Me)	C 1048 C 1049	At 1502 At 1502	Magic Sam (g) Freddy King (g) Odell Campbell (eb) Willie Dixon (b) Junior Blackman (d) unk. v grp-1

Year / Artist	Title	Matrix	Release	Personnel
1958 Evangelist "Baby" Ballinger (p/v)	So Glad Let It Be	[?] [?]	At 100 At 100	poss. Willie Dixon (b) unk. (d)
1958 Magic Sam (v/g)	**Easy Baby** **21 Days in Jail**	1054 1055	Cb 5029 Cb 5029	Harold Burrage (p) Odell Campbell (eb) Willie Dixon (b) Odie Payne (d)
1958 Otis Rush (v/g)	Double Trouble Keep on Loving Me Baby	C 1056 C 1057	Cb 5030 Cb 5030	Eddie Jones (ts) Carlson Oliver (ts) Jackie Brenston (bs) Harold Burrage or Little Brother Montgomery (p) Ike Turner (g) Willie Dixon (b) Odie Payne (d)
1958 Betty Everett (v) and the Willie Dixon Band	I'll Weep No More-1 Tell Me Darling-2	C 1058 C 1059	Cb 5031 Cb 5031	Ike Turner (p-1/g-2) unk. (g-1) unk. (p-2) Willie Dixon (b) Odie Payne (d) Tommy Hodge (bv-1) Carlson Oliver (bv-1/ts-2) Fred Sample (bv-1) Jimmy Thomas (bv-1) Eddie Jones (ts-2)
1958 Buddy Guy (v/g-1)	You Sure Can't Do-2 This Is the End-1	C 1060 C 1061	At 1503 At 1503	Carlson Oliver (ts) Eddie Jones (ts) Jackie Brenston (bs) Harold Burrage (p) Ike Turner (g-2) Willie Dixon (b) Odie Payne (d)

Date / Artist	Songs	Matrix	Original Release	Musicians Involved
1958 Ike Turner (g/p-2) Kings of Rhythm	You Keep on Worrying Me I'm Gonna Forget about You-1 Matchbox (I Know) You Don't Love Me-2 Down and Out-2	[?] [?] [?] C 1062 C 1063	Flyright (E) 578 Flyright (E) 578 Flyright (E) 578 At 1504 At 1504	Jackie Brenston (v/bs-2) Tommy Hodge (bv) Carlson Oliver (bv/ts-1) Jimmy Thomas (bv) Eddie Jones (ts-1) Fred Sample (p) Willie Dixon (b) Odie Payne (d)
1958 Otis Rush (v/g)	All Your Love My Baby's Good 'Un	C 1064 C 1065	Cb 5032 Cb 5032	Eddie Jones (ts) Carlson Oliver (ts) Jackie Brenston (bs) Harold Burrage or Little Brother Montgomery (p) Ike Turner (g) Willie Dixon (b) Odie Payne (d)
1959 Ike Turner (v/g/p-1/eb-1) Kings of Rhythm	Walking Down the Aisle-1 Box Top	C 1066 C 1067	Cb 5033 Cb 5033	Tommy Hodge (bv) Carlson Oliver (bv) Willie Dixon (b) Odie Payne (d) Billy Gayles (bv/d-1)

Non-Chess and Non-Cobra Sessions from 1953–1990, including session works for Chief, Jewel, Spivey, States, and USA Records, AFBF, and Dixon's solo projects (Chicago, unless otherwise noted)

Date Artist	Songs	Label and Original Release	Matrix Number	Musicians Involved
11/30/53 Albert King (v/g)	Little Boy Blue Sweet Woman Hand Me Down Blues Be on Your (Merry Way) Bad Luck Blues Murder	Relic LP 8024 Blue Night 073 1669 Relic LP 8024 Parrot 798 Parrot 798 Ch LP 1538	P 53175 P 53176 P 53176-2 P 53177 P 53178 P 53179	Johnny Jones (p) John Brim (g) Willie Dixon (b) Grace Brim[?] (d)
4/15/54 Junior Wells (v/h)	'Bout the Break of Day Lord, Lord (Lawdy! Lawdy!) So All Alone Blues Hit Big Town	States 139 States 139 States 143 Delmark 640	1441 1442 1443 1444	Otis Spann (p) Muddy Waters (g) Louis Myers (g) Willie Dixon (b) Fred Below (d)
8/26/54 Tommy Brown (v)	Southern Woman Remember Me Card Game Nosey Neighbor	United 183 United 183 Pearl PL 12 Pearl PL 12	U-1476-7 U-1477-2 U-1478-1 U-1479-1	Walter Horton (h) Harold Ashby (ts) Memphis Slim (p) Lee Cooper (g) Willie Dixon (b) unk. (d)
11/1/54 Big Walter Horton (v/h) and His Combo	Hard Hearted Woman **Back Home to Mama**	States 145 States 145	S 1496-3 S 1497-4	James "Red" Holloway (ts) John Cameron (ts) Lafayette Leake (p) Lee Cooper (g) Willie Dixon (b) Fred Below (d)

Date / Artist	Songs	Matrix Number	Label and Original Release	Musicians [involved]
11/1/54 Harold Burrage (v/p)	I Feel So Fine You're Gonna Cry	U-1498 U-1499	States 144 States 144	prob. James "Red" Holloway (ts) John Cameron (ts) Lee Cooper (g) Willie Dixon (b) Fred Below (d)
1956 J. T. Brown (v/ts)	Going Home to My Baby It's a Shame to Tell the People Lonely (As a Man Can Be) Use That Spot	42-4311-5 42-4312-10 42-4313-5 42-4314-2	Pearl PL 9 [United] Pearl PL 9 Pearl PL 9 Pearl PL 9	Lafayette Leake (o/p) Jody Williams (g) Willie Dixon (b) Fred Below (d)
Sept./Oct. '57 Junior Wells (v/h-1)	**Two Headed Woman** Lovey Dovey Lovey One I Could Cry Cha Cha Cha in Blue (Cut My Toe Nail) [inst.]-1	25-111 25-112 25-113 25-114	Chief 7005 Chief 7005 Chief 7008 Chief 7008	Syl Johnson (g) David Myers (g) Willie Dixon (b) Eugene Lounge (d)
Oct. '57 Elmore James (v/g)	Cry for Me Baby Take Me Where You Go	25-117 25-118	Chief 7006 Chief 7006	J. T. Brown (ts) Eddie Taylor (g) Willie Dixon (b) Fred Below (d)
Jan. '59 Five Blind Boys of Mississippi	Our Father Coming Home Song of Praise Save a Seat for Me There's No Need to Cry Someone Watches		Peacock PLP-102: *Precious Memories*	Willie Dixon (prod)

Don't Give Up
Certainly Lord
Somebody's Knocking
Walk Together Children
Leaning on the Everlasting Arm
That Awful Hour

12/3/59		Prestige: Bluesville	Harold Ashby (ts-1)
Englewood Cliffs, NJ		BV LP 1003:	Memphis Slim (p)
Willie Dixon (v/b)		*Willie's Blues*	Wally Richardson (g-2)
			Gus Johnson (d, exc. 3)

Matrix	Title
1923-2	**Move Me-1**
1924	**Don't You Tell Nobody**
1925	**That's All I Want Baby-1**
1926	**Good Understanding**
1927	I Got a Razor-3
1928	**That's My Baby-2**
1929	Nervous-2
1930	**Sittin' and Cryin' the Blues-1, 2**
1931	**Built for Comfort-1, 2**
1932	**Youth to You**
1933	Slim's Thing [inst.]1, 2
1934	Go Easy-1, 2
1935	**Move Me-1**

1959		Folkways FA 2385:
New York City		*Joogie Boogie*
Willie Dixon (v/b)		
Memphis Slim (v/p)		

Stewball
John Henry
Kansas City 1
Kansas City 2
Kansas City 3
Have You Ever Been to
  Nashville Pen
Roll and Tumble
Beer Drinking Woman
Chicago House Rent Party
44 Blues
Unlucky

Date / Artist	Songs	Matrix Number	Label and Original Release	Musicians Involved
1959 Junior Wells (v/h-1)	Little by Little (I'm Losing You)-2 Come On in This House-1	25-119 25-220	Profile 401 Profile 401	Willie Dixon (v-2/b) Lafayette Leake (p) Earl Hooker (g) David Myers (g) Eugene Lyons (d) Mel London (bv-2)
Jan. '60 New York City Memphis Slim (v-1/p) Willie Dixon (v-2/b)	Choo Choo-1 4 O'Clock Blues Rub My Root-2 C Rocker Home to Mama-2 Shaky-2 After Hours One More Time-2 John Henry-1, 2 Now Howdy-1, 2		Verve MSV 3007: *The Blues Every Which Way*	
3/29/60 Jimmy Reed (v/h/g)	Come Love-1 Big Boss Man Meet Me	60-1417 60-1418 60-1419	VJ LP 1022 VJ 380, LP 1022 VJ LP 1022	Mama Reed (v-1) Lefty Bates (g) Lee Baker (g) Willie Dixon (b) Earl Phillips (d)
Apr. '60 Memphis Slim (v/p) Willie Dixon (v/b)	**Somebody Tell That Woman** **My Baby Don't Stand No** **Cheating** Stewball-1 Slop Boogie Misery Falls like Rain Wish Me Well		Folkways FA 2386: *At the Village Gate*	Pete Seeger (v-1)

T for Texas-1
I Just Want to Make Love to You
Try to Find My Baby
One More Time
Nobody Loves Me
We Are Going to Rock

1960
Junior Wells (v/h)

Willie Dixon (v-1/b), Otis Spann (p), Earl Hooker (g), Eugene Lyons (d), Mel London (bv)

Title	Matrix	Issue
You Don't Care-1	S 866	Profile 4013
Prison Bars All Around Me	S 877	Profile 4013

11/16/60
Bobby Stone (v)

unk. fem./Lucy[?] (v), Von Freeman (ts), Lafayette Leake (p), Matt Murphy (g), Willie Dixon (b), Al Duncan (d)

Title	Matrix	Issue
I Feel Strange	25-165	Chief 7025
It's Nothing	25-166	Chief 7025
On Bended Knee	25-167	Unissued
Hey Girl	25-168	Unissued

10/7/61
New York City
Big Joe Williams (v/g)

Larry Johnson (h, exc. 1), Willie Dixon (b, exc. 2)

Title	Issue
I'm a Fool about My Baby	Prestige: Bluesville BVLP 1056: Blues for Nine Strings
38 Pistol Blues	
Pearly Mae	
Walking Blues	
Highway 45	
Meet Me in the Bottom	
Skinny Mama	
Jockey Ride Blues	
Coal and Iceman Blues	
Army Man Blues	
Black Gal	
Pallet on the Floor	

Date / Artist	Songs	Matrix Number	Label and Original Release	Musicians involved
	Levee Camp Blues-1		Prestige: Bluesville BVLP 1083: Studio Blues	
	Low Down Dirty Shame			
	Gambling Man-1			
	Ain't Gonna Rain No More			
	Feel So Good-1			
	Prowling Ground Hog-1			
	Back Home Again-1, 2			
	Sugar Babe			
	Tell Me Mama-1			
	Studio Blues-1			
1962 Paris, France Memphis Slim (v-1, p) Willie Dixon (v-2, b)	Rock and Rolling the House-1, 2		Polydor (FR) 46.131: Live at the Trois Mailletz	Phillipe Combelle (d)
	Baby Please Come Home-1			
	How Come You Do Me Like You Do-1			
	The Way She Loves a Man-2			
	New Way to Love-2			
	African Hunch with a Boogie Beat-2			
	Shame Pretty Girls-2			
	Baby-Baby-Baby-2			
	Do De Do-2			
	Cold Blooded-2			
	Just You and I-1, 2			
	Pigalle Love-1			
	All by Myself-1, 2			

Apr./May '62 Roosevelt Sykes (v/p)			Sax Mallard (ts) Lee Jackson (g) Willie Dixon (b) Jump Jackson (d)
Slave for Your Love		Crown CLP 5287: *Sings the Blues*	
Gone with the Wind			
Wild Side			
Out on a Limb			
Honey Child			
Never Loved like This Before			
Last Chance			
Casual Friend			
You Will Is Mine			
Hupe Dupe Do			
Fall '62 J. B. Lenoir (v/g)			Willie Dixon (v-1)
Oh Captain (One of These Mornings)-1		1105?	These titles were recorded by Willie Dixon for audition purposes. First three titles were recorded for a film by Steve Seaberg.
Everything I Do-1			
Need Somebody's Help		Polydor LP 24-4011	
(My Mama Told Me)		Polydor LP 24-4011	
For Squirrel			
I Feel So Good		JSP (E) LP 1105	
Mumble Low		JSP (E) LP 1105	
When My Left Eye Jumps		JSP (E) LP 1105	
Mama Talk to Your Daughter		JSP (E) LP 1105	
		JSP (E) LP 1105	
		JSP (E) LP 1105	
9/20/62 AFBF (Place unk.)			Memphis Slim (p) Willie Dixon (b) Jump Jackson (d)
T-Bone Walker			
Don't Throw Your Love on Me So Strong		Hip-O CD 1003	

Note for J. B. Lenoir entry: Oh Captain (One of These Mornings)-1 is listed at Polydor LP 24-4011; the two titles Need Somebody's Help and (My Mama Told Me) are at Polydor LP 24-4011.

Date Artist	Songs	Matrix Number	Label and Original Release	Musicians involved
10/2 to 10/5 of 1962 AFBF (Place unk.)	T-Bone Walker Don't Throw Your Love So Hard on Me I'm in Love		Secret Records (GER) LP 12-8 Secret Records (GER) LP 12-8	Memphis Slim (p) Willie Dixon (b) Jump Jackson (d)
10/18/62 AFBF Hamburg	Memphis Slim (p/v) We're Gonna Rock	Brunswick (GER)	LP 9012 (mono)/10912(stereo): American Folk Blues Festival 1962	Jump Jackson (d)
	T-Bone Walker (v/g) I Wanna See My Baby I'm in Love			
	Sonny Terry (v/h) and Brownie McGhee (v/g) I'm Crazy about You Baby Crying at the Station Blues Was Money			
	Memphis Slim (v/p) and Willie Dixon (v/b) Stewball Wee Baby Blues			

John Lee Hooker (v/g)
Let's Make It (Baby)
Shake It Baby
Night Time Is the Right Time
Need Your Love So Bad

Shakey Jake (v/h)
Ah'w Baby
Love Me Baby

4/26/63
Jessie Fortune (v)

Too Many Cooks	778	USA 738	Walter Horton (h)
Good Things	779	USA 747	Lafayette Leake (p)
God's Gift to Man-1	780	USA 747	Buddy Guy[?] (g)
Heavy Heart Beat	781	USA 738	Jack Meyers (eb)
			Willie Smith (d)
			Willie Dixon (2nd v-1)

7/23/63
J. B. Lenoir (v/g) and African
Hunch Rhythm

I Sing Um the Way I Feel-2	789	USA 744	Donald Hankins (ts)
I Feel So Good-1	790	USA 744	Jarrett Gibson (bs-1)
			Lafayette Leake (p)
			Milton Rector (eb)
			Willie Smith (d)
			"Peeples" (bgs-2)
			Willie Dixon (bv-1/speech-2)

7/23/63
Koko Taylor/Cora Taylor (v)

Like Heaven to Me-1	791	USA 745	Willie Dixon (comp/prod)
Honky Tonk	792	USA 745	Jarrett Gibson (bs-1)
			Lafayette Leake (p)
			Milton Rector (eb)
			Clifton James (d)
			unk. (bgs-2)

Date / Artist	Songs	Matrix Number	Label and Original Release	Musicians Involved
Fall '63 AFBF				Matt Murphy (g) Willie Dixon (b) Billy Stepney (d) Sonny Boy Williamson (h-1)
9/20/63 (Place unk.) Muddy Waters (v)	Got My Mojo Workin'-1		Hip-O CD 1003	
9/21/63 (Place unk.) Otis Spann (v/p)	Skies Are Blue My Baby Is Gone Love Is a Miracle No No No	Unissued		
10/3/63 Hellborn Muddy Waters (v)	Blow Wind Blow Five Long Years I've Got My Mojo Workin'	Armando Curico Editore (IT) LP 13 (?)		
10/4/63 Frankfurt Muddy Waters (v)	Trouble No More Five Long Years Got My Mojo Workin'	Black Bear (E) LP 901		
10/13/63 AFBF Bremen	Memphis Slim (v/p) and Willie Dixon (v/b/g) The Blues Is Everywhere (Slim solo)	Fontana 681510 TL (mono) / 885403 ZY (stereo): *American Folk Blues Festival 1963* Evidence ECD 26100:		Additional musician: Billie Stepney (d)

Memphis Boogie (Slim solo)
John Henry
Wish Me Well
Sittin' and Cryin' the Blues
Crazy for My Baby
My Captain (Dixon solo w. guitar)

Muddy Waters (v/g)
Catfish Blues (solo)
Blow Wind Blow
My Home Is in the Delta

Eddie Boyd (v/p)
Five Long Years

Sonny Boy Williamson (v/h)
That's All I Want
Don't Misuse Me
I Don't Know
I'm Getting' Tired (solo)
Sonny Boy's Harmonica Blues (solo)

St. Louis Jimmy/Jimmy Oden (v)
Goin' Down Slow

Victoria Spivey (v)
Grant Spivey
T. B. Blues

*American Folk Blues Festival '62
to '65*

Above titles also include

Big Joe Williams (v/g)
Big Roll Blues (solo)
Back In the Bottom Blues (solo)
I Have No Friends (solo)

Lonnie Johnson (v/g)
Careless Love (solo)
C. C. Rider (solo)
It's Too Late to Cry (solo)

Dixon is not on bass for the above
performances.

Dixon is bass on all tracks exc.
marked "solo."

Date / Artist	Songs	Matrix Number	Label and Original Release	Musicians Involved
Matt Murphy (g)	Matt's Guitar Boogie			
Otis Spann	Had My Fun			
	Goin' Down Slow			
All Participants	Bye Bye Blues			
Oct. '63 AFBF Baden-Baden Muddy Waters (v/g-1)		Black Bear (E) LP 903		Otis Spann (p) Matt Murphy (g) Willie Dixon (b) Billy Stepney (d) Sonny Boy Williamson (h)
	Sonny Boy and Muddy's Mojo Captain, Captain (g-1)	Black Bear (E) LP 903		
Oct. '63 AFBF poss. Heilbronn Muddy Waters (v/g)		GSR (It) LP 13		Otis Spann (p) Matt Murphy (g) Willie Dixon (b) Bill Stepney (d)
	Got My Mojo Workin' Blow Wind Blow	GSR (It) LP13		
1963 AFBF (Place unk.) Otis Spann (v/p)		Black Bear (E) LP 902		Willie Dixon (b) Billy Stepney (d)
	What's Wrong with Me	JSP (E) LP 1070		
	Everything Gonna Be Alright	JSP (E) LP 1070		
	Love Me or Leave Me	JSP (E) LP 1070		
	Why Did She Have to Go	JSP (E) LP 1070		

Spann Boogie [inst.]
Why Should I Cry

The Blues Ain't Nothin'-1
T-99 (T.99-Lucky So and So)-1
Built Up from the Ground-1
I Got a Gal-1

3/26/64
Victoria Spivey Session

Sunnyland Slim (v/o)
Won't Do That No More
Drinking

John Henry Barbee/William George Tucker (v/g)
Early in the Morning
No Pickin' No Pullin'

St. Louis Jimmy/Jimmy Oden (v)
Goody, Goody, Goody
Going Down Slow

Willie Dixon (v/g)
Weak Brain! Narrow Mind!
So Long!

Homesick James (v/g)
Can't Hold Out
Queens Rock

Cocoa Taylor/Koko Taylor (v)
What Kind of Man Is This?-1
Which'a Way to Go-1

JSP (E) LP 1070	Matt Murphy (g-1)
JSP (E) LP 1070	poss. Muddy Waters (g-1)
Black Bear (E) LP 901	
Black Bear (E) LP 901	
Black Bear (E) LP 903	
JSP (E) LP 1056	
Spivey LP 1003:	Victoria Spivey (prod)
Chicago Blues: A Bonanza All Star LP	Len Kunstadt (prod)
	Willie Dixon
	(supervisor, tamb-1)
	Evans Spencer (g)
	Washboard Sam (wb)

Date Artist	Songs	Matrix Number	Label and Original Release	Musicians Involved
10/9/64 AFBF Hamburg			Fontana 885411: *American Folk Blues Festival '64*	Additional musician: Clifton James (d)
Sonny Boy Williamson (v/h) Dissatisfied			Evidence ECD 26100: *American Folk Blues Festival '62 to '65*	Dixon plays bass for all the tracks exc. marked "solo."
Sunnyland Slim (v/p) Everytime I Get to Drinkin'			Above titles also include	
Hubert Sumlin No Title Boogie [inst.]			Sonny Boy Williamson (v/h) w. Hubert Sumlin (g)	
Sugar Pie DeSanto (v) Slip-In Mules Baby What You Want Me to Do			I'm Trying to Make London My Home I Got to Cut Out	
Howlin' Wolf (v/g) Dust My Broom			Lightnin' Hopkins (v/g) Ain't It a Pity Baby Please Don't Go	
Willie Dixon (v/g) Weak Brain and Narrow Mind (solo) Big Legged Woman (solo)			John Henry Barbee (v/g) I Ain't Gonna Pick No More Cotton	
			Sleepy John Estes (v/g) w. Hammie Nixon Your Best Friend's Gone	
			Dixon is not on above tracks.	

11/1/64
AFBF Amiga Studio, Berlin

Sunnyland Slim (v/p)
It's You, My Baby
Levee Camp Moan (with only Dixon)
We Gonna Jump
Too Late for Me to Play

Hubert Sumlin (v/g)
Love You, Woman (solo)
When I Feel Better (solo)
Hubert's Blues

Willie Dixon (v/b/g)
Blues Anytime
My Babe
Big Legged Woman (solo with guitar)

Amiga (E) LP 8 50 043:
American Folk Blues

Evidence ECD 26052-2:
Blues Anytime!

Other musician:
Clifton James (d)

Dixon plays bass for all the tracks
exc. marked "solo."

1964
AFBF Germany[?]
Howlin' Wolf (v/g/h)

Shake for Me
Love Me
Dust My Broom
I Didn't Mean to Hurt Your
  Feelings
Rockin' the Blues
All My Life
Going Down Slow
Howlin' for My Darlin'
Forty-Four

Acrobat Music AMACD 019:
*Rockin' the Blues:
Live in Germany 1964*

Sunnyland Slim (p)
Hubert Sumlin (g)
Willie Dixon (b)
Clifton James (d)

1965
J. B. Lenoir (v/g)

Korea Blues

Spivey LP 1009:
Encore for the Chicago Blues

Willie Dixon (b)
Lafayette Leake (p)

Date Artist	Songs	Matrix Number	Label and Original Release	Musicians Involved
3/5/65 J. B. Lenoir (v/g)	Alabama Blue God's Word The Whale Has Swallowed Me Remove This Rope Alabama March Mississippi Road Good Advice (w. Lenoir) Vietnam The Mojo Boogie-1 I Feel So Good-2 Mama Talk to Your Daughter-1 I Want to Go-1		CBS(GER) LP 62593	Willie Dixon (supervisor/bv-2) Fred Below (d-1, 2)
Jul. '65 Newport Folk Festival, RI Lafayette Leake (p) Willie Dixon (b)	Wrinkles		Vanguard CD 77005	Pete Seeger (bj)
9/2/66 J. B. Lenoir (v/g)	Down in Mississippi-1 Voodoo Music Tax Paying Blues If I Get Lucky How Much More Feeling Good-1 Shot on James Meredith		Polydor LP 24-4011	Willie Dixon (supervisor/v-1) Fred Below (d)

	Matrix	Release	Personnel
Round and Round			
Slow-Down			
Vietnam Blues			
Leaving Here			
Born Dead			
1966			
George "Wild Child" Butler (v/h)			Willie Dixon (bv-1)
Hold Me Baby-1	TM 1723	Jewel 769	Walter Horton (h)
Do Something Baby	TM 1724	Jewel 769	Johnny "Twist" Williams (g)
Jelly Jam			Jack Meyers (eb)
Axe and the Wind	TM 2000	Jewel 793	Vince Chappell (d)
Open Up Baby	TM 2001	Jewel 793	
Big Momma, Little Momma	TM 2002	Jewel 780	
	TM 2003	Jewel 780	
1967			
George "Wild Child" Butler (v/h)			Willie Dixon (bv-1)
Put It All in There	SL 1504	Jewel 798	Lafayette Leake (p)
My 40 Year Old Woman	SL 1505	Jewel 798	Jimmy Dawkins (g)
She Walks like My Mary Ann		Polydor (E) 2941 006	unk. (saxes, b, d)
Harmonica Player-1		Polydor (E) 2941 006	
6/10/68			
Sunnyland Slim (v/p)			Walter Horton (h)
Heartache	SBH 10243	Unissued	Johnny Shines (g)
Get to My Baby	SBH 10244		Willie Dixon (b)
Heartache	SBH 10245	Others included in	Clifton James (d)
Stepmother	SBH 10246	Blue Horizon (E)	
Midnight Jump	SBH 10247	LP 7-63213:	
Depression Blues	SBH 10248	*Midnight Jump*	
Stella Mae	SBH 10249		
Layin' in My Cell Sleepin'	SBH 10250		
I Am the Blues	SBH 10251		
Sunnyland Special	SBH 10252		
Lowalnd Blues	SBH 10253		

Date Artist	Songs	Matrix Number	Label and Original Release	Musicians Involved
6/10/68 Johnny Shines (v/g)	Pipeline Blues-1 I Don't Know Baby Don't You Think I Know Mean Fisherman I Will Be Kind to You From Dark 'til Dawn Solid Gold I Had a Good Home Last Night's Dream Black Panther	SBH 10254 SBH 10255 SBH 10256 SBH 10257 SBH 10258 SBH 10259 SBH 10260 SBH 10261 SBH 10262 SBH 10263	Blue Horizon (E) LP 7-63212: Last Night's Dream	Walter Horton (h) Otis Spann (p-1) Willie Dixon (b) Clifton James (d)
6/10/68 Otis Spann (v/p)	Can't Do Me No Good Bloody Murder	SBH 10264 SBH 10265	Blue Horizon (E) LP 7-63217 The Biggest Thing since Colossus	Walter Horton (h) Johnny Shines (g) Willie Dixon (b) Clifton James (d)
6/27/68 Arthur "Big Boy" Crudup (v/g)	Strictly a Woman Can't You Make Rain Meant for Me (Make an Arrangement) Rambling on My Mind Got No One to Love Me Crazy House Blues Talking Peaches Is Her Name I Got to Find My Baby You're a Good Little Girl		Delmark DS 621: Meets the Master Blues Bassists	Willie Dixon (b)

Date / Artist	Tracks	Label	Personnel
1/4/69 David "Honeyboy" Edwards (v/g)	My Baby's Gone-1 Honey Boy Blues-2	SBH 10499 Blue Horizon (E) LP 7-66227: *Blues Jam at Chess*	Walter Horton (h-2) Peter Green (g-1) Mick Fleetwood (d) Willie Dixon (b)
May '69 Chicago Blues All Stars	Down in the Bass-Ment Blues Drove Me Out of My Mind-1 Three O'Clock in the Morning-3 Lonesome Bedroom Blues-2	Spivey LP 1011: *Victoria Spivey Presents the All Stars BLUES WORLD of Spivey Records in Stereo*	Sunnyland Slim (v-1/p) Johnny Shines (v-2/g) Marie Dixon (v-3) Willie Dixon (b) Clifton James (d) Shirli Dixon (tamb)
7/1/69 Cologne, Germany Chicago Blues All Stars	German Babies-5 Baby I Need Your Love-1 **29 Ways-4** Put It All in There-2 She Got a Thing Goin' On-2 Every Time I Get to Drink-2 Fat Mama-3 Little Boy Blue-1 C. C. Rider-3 I Love the World-3 Chicago Is Loaded with the Blues-5	MPS (GER) LP 15.224: *Loaded with the Blues*	Walter Horton (v-1/h) Sunnyland Slim (v-2/p) Johnny Shines (v-3/g) Willie Dixon (v-4/b) Clifton James (v-5/d)
Summer '69 Willie Dixon (v/b)	**Back Door Man** **I Can't Quit You Baby** **The Seventh Son** **Spoonful** **I Ain't Superstitious** **(I'm Your) Hoochie Coochie Man** **The Little Red Rooster** **The Same Thing**	Co PC 9987: *I Am the Blues*	Walter Horton (h) Lafayette Leake (p) Mighty Joe Young (g) Johnny Shines (g) Sylvester Boines (eb) Clifton James (d)

Date Artist	Songs	Matrix Number	Label and Original Release	Musicians Involved
	Big Boat	Unissued from this session		
	Bring It on Home			
	Country Style			
	Crazy for My Baby			
	Hidden Charms			
	Hoodoo Woman			
	I Am the Blues			
	I Don't Care Who Knows			
	I Just Want to Make Love to You			
	Little Baby			
	My Baby			
	My John the Conqueror Root			
	My Love Will Never Die			
	Tail Dragger			
	29 Ways			
	Wang Dang Doodle			
	When the Lights Go Out			
	You Can't Judge a Book by Its Cover			
Aug. '70 Koko Taylor (v)	**Peace**		Unissued	unk. (tps, saxes)
	Mighty Love	777-07	Yambo 107	Lafayette Leake (p)
	Instant Everything	777-08	Yambo 107	Mighty Joe Young (g)
	Like I Did Before		Unissued	Willie Dixon (b)
				Clifton James (d)

11/16/70
AFBF Frankfurt

Willie Dixon (v/b)
Crazy for My Baby
Sittin' and Cryin' the Blues

Lafayette Leake (p)
After Hours

Lee Jackson (v/g)
Juanita
Came Home This Morning

Walter Horton (v/h)
Hard Hearted Woman
That Ain't It

Champion Jack Dupree (v/p)
School Day
Going to Louisiana
Blues before Sunrise

Sonny Terry (v/h) and Brownie McGhee (v/g)
Hootin' the Blues
Back Water Blues
Walk On
When I Was Drinking

Scout (G) SC7:
American Folk Blues Festival '70

Above title also includes

Bukka White (v/g)
Maggie Lee
World Boogie
Old Lady

Dixon is not on bass for the above
tracks.

Other musician:
Clifton James (d)

Date Artist	Songs	Matrix Number	Label and Original Release	Musicians Involved
1970 Buster Benton/Arley Benton (v/g)	**Spider in My Stew** **Dangerous Woman**	777-104 777-105	Supreme 1004 Supreme 1004	Carey Bell (h) Lafayette Leake (p) Mighty Joe Young (g) Willie Dixon (b) Billy Davenport (d)
1970 Lucky Peterson (v/k)	**1-2-3-4** **Good Old Candy**	Yambo 777-3		Willie Dixon (comp/prod) rest unk.
1970 James Peterson (v/g)	All on Account of You Sing the Blues till I Die	Yambo 777-05		Willie Dixon (prod) Lucky Peterson (k)
1970 Boston Chicago All Stars		Wolf Records (AU) CD 120.291: *Chicago All Stars*		Other Musician Clifton James (b)

Willie Dixon (b/v)
29 Ways-1
I Just Want to Make Love to You
Crazy for My Baby
My Babe

Sunnyland Slim (v/p)
Every Time I Get to Drinkin'
Rock This House
Sunnyland Boogie
Won't Do That No More
It's You Baby
She's Got a Good Thing Goin' On

Johnny Shines (v/g)

Worried Life Blues
Fat Mama
High Road Blues
Hello Central

Walter Horton (v/h)

Hard Hearted Woman
Everybody's Fishin'
Baby I Need Your Love

prob. 1971
Willie Dixon (v)

Yambo 77715
Boot Records (CN) BOS 713:
Peace?

I'm Wanted
Peace?
It's in the News
I'd Give My Life for You
You Go to Move
Suffering Sun of a Gun
Jelly Jam
You Don't Make Sense or Peace
Blues You Can't Lose
If I Could See

Walter Horton (h)
Lafayette Leake (p)
Dennis Miller (g)
Buster Benton (g)
Joe Young (g)
Louis Satterfield (eb)
Phil Upchurch (eb)
Clifton James (d)
Frank Swan (d)

1973
Willie Dixon (v)

Ovation OVQD 1443
Catalyst

Bring It on Home
I Don't Trust Nobody
God's Gift to Man
Hoo Doo Doctor
My Babe
Wang Dang Doodle
When I Make Love
I Think I Got the Blues
But It Sure Is Fun
I Just Want to Make Love to You

Lafayette Leake (p)
Carey Bell Harrington (h)
Buster Benton (g)
Mighty Joe Young (g)
Phil Upchurch (g)
Morris Jennings (d)
Louis Satterfield (b)

Date Artist	Songs	Matrix Number	Label and Original Release	Musicians Involved
1973 Brooklyn, NY Maestro Willie Dixon and His Chicago Blues Band			Spivey LP 1016: *The All Star Blues World of Maestro Willie Dixon and His Chicago Blues Band*	
Willie Dixon (b)	Intro			
Lafayette Leake (v/p)	Leake's Trouble Trouble Fine Little Girl			
Larry Johnson (v)	My Hoodoo Doctor Put It All in There			
Victoria Spivey (v)	I'm Taking Over			
Carey Bell Harrington (v/h)	The Evening Sun Goes Down One Day You're Going to Get Lucky			
Buster Benton (v/g)	Everyday I Have the Blues The Thrill Is Gone			
Victoria Spivey	It's a Mighty Poor Rat That Ain't Got But One Hole			

Date / Artist	Titles	Label	Personnel
1974 McKinley Mitchell	**Last Home Run** **All Star Bougee**	Yambo 777-20	Willie Dixon (comp/prod) Chicago Blues All Stars (Detailed personnel unk.)
1974 McKinley Mitchelle	**Good Time Baby** **All Star Bougee**	Spoonful 777-26	Willie Dixon (comp/prod) Chicago Blues All Stars (Detailed personnel unk.)
1976 Libertyville, IL. Willie Dixon (v/b)	**Moon Cattin'** **What Happened to My Blues** **Pretty Baby** **Got to Love You Baby** (w. Ingram and Ingram) **Shakin' the Shack** **Hold Me Babe** **It's Easy to Love** (w. Harrington) **Uh Huh Baby** Put It All in There **Hey Hey Pretty Mama**	Ovation OV-175: *What Happened to My Blues*	Carey Bell Harrington (h) Dennis Miller (g) Buster Benton (g) Freddie Dixon (eb) Clifton James (d)
7/15/83 Montreux Jazz Festival Montreux, Switzerland Willie Dixon (v/b) with the Chicago Blues Allstars	**Closing Blues** **I Don't Trust Nobody** **It Don't Make Sense (You Can't Make Peace)** **Shakin' the Shack** **Wang Dang Doodle** **Built for Comfort** **Spoonful** I've Got My Mojo Working	Pausa PR 7183: *15 July 1983 Live! Backstage Access*	Sugar Blue (h) Clifton James (d) John Watkins (g/v) Freddie Dixon (eb/v) Arthur "Butch" Dixon (p)

Date / Artist	Songs	Matrix Number / Label and Original Release	Musicians Involved
unk. date Long Beach, CA[?] Willie Dixon (v-1/b) and the Chicago Allstars		Wolf International 120.700 CD: *Good Advice* The insert says recorded in 1991, but Carey Bell left Dixon's group by 1984.	Carey Bell (v-2/h) John Watkins (v-3/g) Arthur "Butch" Dixon (p) Freddie Dixon (eb) C. Jackson (d)
	Chicago Allstars Boogie [inst.] **Tellin' about the Blues**-1 **Good Advice**-1 **Built for Comfort**-1 Rock Me-1 I Don't Trust Nobody-1 So Hard to Leave You Alone-2 You Don't Have to Go-3 Rock the House [inst.]		
1984 Willie Dixon (v)	**Mighty Earthquake and Hurricane** **It Don't Make Sense (You Can't Make Peace)** **After Five Long Years** **Everything's Got a Time** **Wigglin' Worm** **Flamin' Mamie** **Grave Digger Blues** **Pie in the Sky**	Pausa PR 7157, Mighty Tiger MT 6002: *Mighty Earthquake and Hurricane*	Lafayett Leake (p) Billy Branch (h) Freddie Dixon (eb) Jimmy Tillman (d) John Watkins (g) Johnny B. Moore (g) The Lights: Mae Cohen (bv) Ayo Kason (bv) Ellen Samuels (bv) Zora Young (bv)

Date / Location / Artist	Songs	Album / Label	Personnel
1984 Sonny Terry (v/h)	I Want My Eyes on You Sonny's Whoopin' the Doop Burnt Child Whoee, Whoee Crow Jane So Tough with Me Whoo Wee Baby I Think I Got the Blues Ya, Ya Roll Me Baby	Alligator AL 514734: *Whoopin' (with Johnny Winter and Willie Dixon)*	Johnny Winter (g/p) Willie Dixon (b) Styve Homnick (d)
1986 Hollywood[?] Willie Dixon (v)	**Don't Tell Me Nothin'**	MCA MCAD-6189: *The Color of Money* [Original Motion Picture Soundtrack]	Robbie Robertson (prod) unk. (g, eb, k, d, h, bv)
1987 Hollywood[?] Bo Diddley (v/g)	Who Do You Love	Warner Bros/Slash Records 9 25605-1: *La Bamba* [Original Motion Picture Soundtrack]	Willie Dixon (prod) unk. (d, 2nd g, h, eb, bs)
1987 Northridge, CA Willie Dixon (v)	**Aids to the Grave**	As the B side of Vernell Jennings: *The Boogie Man (AIDS)*	Freddie Robinson (g) Cash McCall (eb) Al Duncan (d)
1988 Los Angeles Willie Dixon (v)	**Blues You Can't Lose** **I Don't Trust Myself** **Jungle Swing** (w. Caston) **Don't Mess with the Messer** **Study War No More** **I Love the Life I Live (I Live the Life I Love)** **I Cry for You** **Good Advice** (w. Lenoir) **I Do the Job**	Capitol/Bug CI 90595: *Hidden Charms*	Sugar Blue (h) Lafayette Leake (p) Cash McCall (g/v) T-Bone Burnett (prod/dobro) Red Callender (eb) Earl Palmer (d)

Date Artist	Songs	Matrix Number	Label and Original Release	Musicians Involved
1989 Los Angeles[?] Willie Dixon (v)	**Miseries of Memories** **Wigglin' Worm** **I Don't Trust Nobody** **Earthquake and Hurricane** **The Real Thing** **Move Me Baby** **Save My Child I** **I Just Want to Make Love to** **You** **Sittin' and Cryin' the Blues** **Save My Child II** **Shakin' the Shack** **That's My Baby** **Ginger Ale Blues** **Save My Child III** **Good Understanding-**[1]		MCA/Varese Sarabande VSD-5234: *Ginger Ale Afternoon*	Cash McCall (g, eb) Stanley Behrens (h, ts) Chucki Burke (d) Arthur "Butch" Dixon (p) Charlotte Crossly (bv-1)
1990 Los Angeles[? Willie Dixon (v/b)	**Dustin' off the Bass**		MCA/GRP MGD 4021 Rob Wasserman: *Trio*	Rob Wasserman (eb) Al Duncan (d)

Unknown Date Releases from Willie Dixon's Labels

1969 or 1970 Margie Evans (v)	**When I Make Love** **29 Ways**	Yambo 109	Willie Dixon (comp/prod) Chicago Blues All Stars (Detailed personnel unk.)
1969 or 1970 J. J. Taylor (v)	I'm Not Tired Tell Me the Truth	Yambo 1011	Willie Dixon (prod) (Detailed personnel unk.)
1969? Honey Duo Twins (v grp)	**Come On Baby** **Kiss Me**	Yambo 8915	Willie Dixon (comp/prod) Chicago Blues All Stars unk. (g/eb/d)
1968 or 1969 E. Rodney Jones (narrator) Lafayette Leake Trio	Might Is Right (side 1) (poetry reading) Soul Wrinkles (side 2)	Yambo 77701	Willie Dixon (prod) Lafayette Leake (p) (Other personnel unk.)
Early 1970s Modern Times (v grp)	Why Must I Live Such a Lonely Life Baby Just Maybe	Yambo 777-13	Willie Dixon (prod?) unk. (g/horns/eb/d)
Early 1970s Willie Dixon (v)	Petting the Baby You Got to Move (prob. composed by Dixon, but not registered for BMI)	Yambo 777-15	Willie Dixon (prod) Chicago Blues All Stars (Detailed personnel unk.)
Mid-1970s The Satagans (v grp)	**Smokin'** **Lovers to Friends**	Yambo 777-110	Willie Dixon (prod?) unk. (g/eb/d/fl/horns/perc)
1982 Willie Dixon (v)	**It Don't Make Sense (You Can't Make Peace)** It's in the News	WHY? 45s	Willie Dixon (prod?) (Detailed personnel unk.)

LP and EP Index

Acrobat Music AMACD 019 / Howlin' Wolf / *Rockin' the Blues: Live in Germany 1964*

Alligator AL 514734 / Sonny Terry (with Johnny Winter and Willie Dixon): *Whoopin'*

Amiga (E) LP 8 50 043 / VA: *American Folk Blues ('64)*

Argo LP 4002 / Sam Lazor: *Space Flight*

Argo LP 4031 / VA: *Folk Festival of the Blues*

Argo LP 4037 / Walter "Shakey" Horton: *The Soul of Blues Harmonica*

Argo LP 4042 / VA: *The Blues*, Vol. 4

Armando Curico Editore (IT) LP 13 / Muddy Waters: [no information available]

Black Bear (E) LP 901 / Muddy Waters: *Rare Live Recordings*, Vol. 1

Black Bear (E) LP 902 / Muddy Waters: *Rare Live Recordings*, Vol. 2

Black Bear (E) LP 903 / Muddy Waters: *Rare Live Recordings*, Vol. 3

Blue Horizon (E) LP 7-63212 / Johnny Shines: *Last Night's Dream*

Blue Horizon (E) LP 7-63213 / Sunnyland Slim: *Midnight Jump*

Blue Horizon (E) LP 7-63217 / Otis Spann: *The Biggest Thing since Colossus . . .*

Blue Horizon (E) LP 7-63223 / Magic Sam: *1937–1969*

Blue Horizon (E) LP 7-66227 / VA: *Blues Jam at Chess*

Blue Night 073 1669 / VA: *Chicago Guitar Killers*

Blues Ball LP 2002 / Howlin' Wolf: *Can't Put Me Out—Chicago 1956–1972*, Vol. 2

Blues Ball LP 2003 / VA: *Sultans of Slide Guitar*

Blues Ball LP 2004 / Sonny Boy Williamson: *Don't Make a Mistake*

Boot Records (CN) BOS 713 / Willie Dixon: *Peace?*

Brunswick (GER) LP 9012 (mono) / 10912 (stereo) / VA: *American Folk Blues Festival 1962*

Cadet LP 320 / Muddy Waters: *After the Rain*

Capitol/Bug Cl 90595/ Willie Dixon: *Hidden Charms*

CBS (GER) LP 62593 / J. B. Lenoir: *Alabama Blues*

Checker LP 1436 / *Go Bo Diddley Go*

Checker LP 1437 / Sonny Boy Williamson: *Down and Out Blues*

Checker LP 2974 / Bo Diddley: *Have Guitar Will Travel*

Checker LP 2976 / *Bo Diddley in the Spotlight*

Checker LP 2985 / *Bo Diddley and Company*

Checker LP 3001 / Bo Diddley: *The Originator*

Chess CD 088 112 519-2 / *Koko Taylor*

Chess CHD 9170 / Bo Diddley with Chuck Berry: *Two Great Guitars*

Chess CHD 9318 / Chuck Berry: *Missing Berries, Rarities*, Vol. 3

Chess CHD 9330 / VA: *The Blues*, Vol. 6

Chess CHD 9331 / Bo Diddley: *Rare and Well Done*

Chess CHD 9353 / Willie Dixon: *The Original Wang Dang Doodle*

Chess CHD 2-9337 / Buddy Guy: *The Complete Chess Studio Recordings*

Chess CHD 2-9357 / Little Walter: *Blues with a Feeling—Chess Collectibles*, Vol. 3

Chess CHD 2-9372 / Jimmy Rogers: *The Complete Chess Recordings*

Chess CHD 2-16500 / Willie Dixon: *The Chess Box*

Chess CHD 4-9340 / VA: *Chess Blues*

Chess CHV 412 / VA: *Shoutin' Singin' and Makin Love*

Chess EP 5121 / Chuck Berry: *Sweet Little Sixteen*

Chess LP 409 / Buddy Guy: *I Was Walking through the Woods*

Chess LP 410 / J. B. Lenoir: *Natural Man*

Chess LP 416 / Little Walter: *Confessin' the Blues*

Chess LP 417 / Sonny Boy Williamson: *One Way Out*

Chess LP 1426 / *After School Session with Chuck Berry*

Chess LP 1432 / Chuck Berry: *One Dozen Berrys*

Chess LP 1436 / *Go Bo Diddley*

Chess LP 1448 / Chuck Berry: *Rockin' at the Hops*

Chess LP 1456 / Chuck Berry: *New Juke Box Hits*

Chess LP 1480 / *Chuck Berry on Stage!*

Chess LP 1483/ Muddy Waters: *Folk Singer*

Chess LP 1488 / *Larry Williams*

Chess LP 1503 / Sonny Boy Williamson: *The Real Folk Blues*

Chess LP 1509 / Sonny Boy Williamson: *More Real Folk Blues*

Chess LP 1512 / Howlin' Wolf: *More Real Folk Blues*

Chess LP 1536 / Sonny Boy Williamson: *Bummer Road*

Chess LP 1538 / Albert King and Otis Rush: *Door to Door*

Chess LP 1553 / *They Call Me Muddy Waters*

Chess LP 9180 / Muddy Waters: *Rare and Unissued*

Chess LP 60028 / Chuck Berry: *Golden Decade*, Vol. 3

Chess LP 93003 / Jimmy Witherspoon: *Spoon So Easy*

Chess LPS 1527 / Buddy Guy: *I Left My Heart in San Francisco*

Chess LPS 1532 / *Koko Taylor*

Chess LPS 1535/ Little Walter: *Hate to See You Go*

Chess 2LPS 127 / VA: *Fathers and Sons*

Chess LP 2CH 60015 / VA: *Blue Rock Cookbook: Montreux Festival*

Chess LP 2-92519 / VA: *Chess Blues Rarities*

Chess LP 3-19502 / Bo Diddley: *The Chess Box*

Chess LP 6-80001 (8001)/ *Chuck Berry*

Chess 2ACMB 206 / *Sonny Boy Williamson*

Chess 2ACMB 207 / *Jimmy Rogers*

Chess 2ACMB 208 / *J. B. Lenoir*

Chess (E) LP 6641 125/ VA: *Genesis*

Chess (E) LP 6641 174 / VA: *Genesis III*

Chess (E) LP 6641 177 / *Chuck Berry's Golden Decade*, Vol. 3

Chess/P-Vine (JP) PLP 6019 / *The Best of Eddie Boyd*

Chess/P-Vine (JP) PLP 6022 /VA: *Chicago Piano-Ology*

Chess/P-Vine (JP) PLP 6040/50 / Muddy Waters: *The Chess Box*

Chess/Teldec (GER) LP 6.24802 / Willie Dixon: *Blues Roots Series*, Vol. 12
Chess/Teldec (GER) LP 6.24806 / Willie Mabon: *Blues Roots Series*, Vol. 16
Chess/Teldec (GER) LP 6.24809 / Lowel Fulson: *Blues Roots Series*, Vol. 19
Columbia CK 46216 / Willie Dixon: *The Big Three Trio*
Columbia PC 9987 / Willie Dixon: *I Am the Blues*
Crown CLP 5287 / Roosevelt Sykes: *Sings the Blues*

Delmark 640 / Junior Wells: *Blues Hit Big Town*
Delmark DS 621 / VA: *Meets the Master Blues Bassists*

Evidence ECD 26100 / VA: *American Folk Blues Festival '62 to '65*
Evidence ECD 26052-2 / Hubert Sumlin, Willie Dixon, and Sunnyland Slim: *Blues Anytime!*

Flyright (E) 578 / Ike Turner: *Kings of Rhythm*
Flyright (E) 579 / Harold Burrage: *She Knocks Me Out—Original Cobra Blues*
Flyright (E) 594 / Otis Rush: *The Final Takes and Others*
Folkways FA 2385 / Memphis Slim and Willie Dixon: *Joogie Boogie*
Folkways FA 2386 / Memphis Slim and Willie Dixon: *At the Village Gate*
Fontana 681510 TL (mono) / 885403 (stereo) / VA: *American Folk Blues Festival '63*
Fontana 885411 / VA: *American Folk Blues Festival '64*

GSR 13 (It) / VA: *Grande Storia Del Rock*, Vol. 13

Hip-O CD 1003 / VA: *The American Folk Blues Festival 1962–1966*

Instant (E) INSD-5038 / *Hey! Bo Diddley*

JSP (E) 1070 / Otis Spann: *Live at Newport Jazz Festival, Newport, Rhode Island, Sun. 3 July 1960*
JSP (E) LP 1105/ J. B. Lenoir and Willie Dixon: *One of These Mornings*
JSP (E) 1056 / VA: *Piano Blues Legends*

Le Roi Du Blues 33. 2007 / Little Walter: *Blue and Lonesome*
Le Roi Du Blues 33. 2012 / Little Walter: *Blue Midnight*

MCA MCAD-6189/ VA: *The Color of Money* [Original Motion Picture Soundtrack]
MCA/Varese SarabandeVSD-5234 / Willie Dixon: *Ginger Ale Afternoon*
MCA/GRP MGD 4021/ Rob Wasserman: *Trio*
Mighty Tiger MT 6002 / Willie Dixon: *Mighty Earthquake and Hurricane*
MPS (GER) LP 15.224 / Chicago Blues All Stars: *Loaded with the Blues*

Ovation OVQD 1443 / Willie Dixon: *Catalyst*
Ovation OV-175 / Willie Dixon: *What Happened to My Blues*

Pausa PR 7183 / Willie Dixon: *15 July, 1983 Live! Backstage Access*
Pausa PR 7157 / Willie Dixon: *Mighty Earthquake and Hurricane*
Peacock PLP 102 / Five Blind Boys of Mississippi: *Precious Memories*
Pearl PL 9 / J. T. Brown: *Windy City Boogie*
Pearl PL 12 / Tommy Brown: [no information available]
Polydor LP 24-4011 / J. B. Lenoir: *Crusade*
Polydor (E) 2941 006 / VA: *Harpin' on It*
Polydor (FR) 46.131 / Memphis Slim and Willie Dixon: *Live at the Trois Mailletz*
Prestige/Bluesville BVLP 1003 / Willie Dixon: *Willie's Blues*
Prestige/Bluesville BVLP 1056 / Big Joe Williams: *Blues for Nine Strings*
Prestige/Bluesville BVLP 1083 / Big Joe Williams: *Studio Blues*
P-Vine (JP) PLP 9021 / *Ike Turner's Kings of Rhythm/Harold Burrage—Rockin' Wild*
Pye (E) NPL 28028 / *More Chuck Berry*

Rarin' LP 777 / VA: *Doo Woppin' the Blues—Rare and Unreleased Recordings from 1949–1956*
RCA International (E) INT 5099 / Sonny Boy Williamson: [no information available]
Red Lightnin (E) 0012 / Billy Boy Arnold: *Blow the Back off It*
Reelin' 001 / Chuck Berry: *America's Hottest Wax*
Relic LP 8024 / VA: *Hand Me Down Blues: Parrot/Blue Lake*, Vol. 1

Scout (G) SC7 / VA: *American Folk Blues Festival '70*
Secret Records (GER) LP 12-8 / T-Bone Walker: [no information available]
Spivey LP 1003 / VA: *Chicago Blues: A Bonanza All Star LP*
Spivey LP 1009 / VA: *Encore for the Chicago Blues*
Spivey LP 1011 / VA: *Victoria Spivey Presents the All Star Blues World of Spivey Records in Stereo*
Spivey LP 1016 / *The All Star Blues World of Maestro Willie Dixon and His Chicago Blues Band*
Sunnyland (E) KS 100 / *Vintage Muddy Waters*

Vanguard CD 77005 / VA: *Blues with a Feeling—Newport Folk Festival 1965*
Vee-Jay VJ LP 1022 / Jimmy Reed: *Found Love*
Verve MSV 3007 / Memphis Slim and Willie Dixon: *The Blues Every Which Way*

Warner Bros/Slash Records 9 25605-1 / VA: *La Bamba* [Original Motion Picture Soundtrack]
Wolf International 120.700 CD / Willie Dixon: *Good Advice*
Wolf Records (AU) CD 120.291 / VA: *Chicago All Stars*

Yambo 77701 / E. Rodney Jones w. Lafayette Leake Trio: *Might Is Right*
Yambo 77715 / Willie Dixon: *Peace?*

~

Bibliography

Written Sources

Abrahams, Roger D. *Deep Down in the Jungle: Negro Narrative Folklore from the Streets of Philadelphia*. Hatboro, PA: Folklore Associates, 1964.

"Advanced Record Releases." *Billboard*, May 10, 1947, 122.

"Advanced Record Releases." *Billboard*, June 7, 1947, 117.

Aldin, Mary Katherine. "Liner Notes." *The Big Three Trio*. Recorded by Willie Dixon. New York: Columbia Records Inc., CK 46216, 1990.

———. "Liner Notes." *The Complete Chess Masters*. Recorded by Lowell Fulson. Tokyo: Chess/MCA Victor, MVCE 30011–2, 1998.

———. "Liner Notes." *The Complete Chess Recordings*. Recorded by Jimmy Rogers. Universal City: Chess/MCA, CHD2–9372, 1997.

Aldin, Mary Katherine, and Mark Humphrey. "Lowell Fulson." *Living Blues*, no. 115 (May/June 1994): 10–27.

Aldin, Mary Katherine. "Liner Notes." *Chess Blues* [CD]. Universal City: Chess/MCA, CHC4-9340, 1992.

Barlow, William. *Looking Up at Down: The Emergence of Blues Culture*. Philadelphia: Temple University Press, 1989.

Bastin, Bruce. *Red River Blues: The Blues Tradition in the Southeast*. Urbana: University of Illinois Press, 1986. Reprint, 1995.

Bernholm, Jonas. "Liner Notes." *I Feel Like Steppin' Out* [CD]. Recorded by the Big Three Trio. Czechoslovakia: Dr. Horse, RBD 804, 1985.

Berry, Chuck. *The Autobiography*. New York: Harmony Books, 1987.

Blues Heaven Willie Dixon: Wednesday, February 5, 1992 [funeral pamphlet]. Chicago: Metropolitan Funeral Parlors, 1992.

Bo Diddley and Robert Palmer. "Liner Notes." *Chess Box*. Recorded by Bo Diddley. Universal City, CA: Chess/MCA, CHD2–19502, 1990.

Bogdanov, Vladimir, Chris Woodstra, and Stephan Thomas Erlewine, eds. *All Music Guide to the Blues: The Definitive Guide to the Blues*. 3rd ed. San Francisco: Backbeat Books, 2003.

Botkin, Benjamin Albert, ed. *A Treasury of Southern Folklore: Stories, Ballads, and Folkways of the People of the South*. Introduction by Benjamin Albert Botkin. New York: Crown, 1949. Reprint, New York: Bonanza Books, 1980. Citations are to the Bonanza Books edition.

Brisbin, John Anthony. "Jimmy Rogers." In *Rollin' and Tumblin': The Postwar Blues Guitarists*, ed. Jas Obrecht, 115–52. San Francisco: Miller Freeman Books, 2000.

Cohn, Lawrence, ed. *Nothing but the Blues: The Music and the Musicians*. New York: Abbeville Press, 1993.

Cohodas, Nadine. *Spinning Blues into Gold: The Chess Brothers and the Legendary Chess Records*. New York: St. Martin's Press, 2000.

Collis, John. *Chuck Berry: The Biography*. London: Aurum Press, 2002.

———. *The Story of Chess Records*. London: Bloomsbury, 1998.

Cone, James H. *The Spirituals and the Blues: An Interpretation*. New York: Seabury Press, 1972. Reprint, Maryknoll, NY: Orbis Books, 2000. Citations are to the Orbis Books edition.

Connor, Anthony, and Robert Neff. *The Blues: In Images and Interviews*. Boston: D. R. Godine, 1975. Reprint, New York: Cooper Square Press, 1999. Citations are to the Cooper Square Press edition.

Corritore, Bob, Bill Ferris, and Jim O'Neal. "Willie Dixon (Part 1)." *Living Blues*, no. 81 (July/August 1988): 16–25.

———. "Willie Dixon (Part 2)." *Living Blues*, no. 82 (September/October 1988): 20–31.

Crawford, Margo G. "Willie Dixon Embodies 'Spirit of the Blues.'" *Chicago Defender*, March 4, 1978, 5.

Dalzell, Tom, and Terry Victor, eds. *A New Partridge Dictionary of Slang and Unconventional English*. Vol. 1, A–I. New York: Routledge, Taylor and Francis Group, 2006.

Danchin, Sebastian. *Earl Hooker: Blues Master*. Jackson: University Press of Mississippi, 2001.

Davis, Francis. *The History of the Blues: The Roots, the Music, the People from Charley Patton to Robert Cray*. New York: Hyperion, 1995.

DeCurtis, Anthony. "Willie Dixon and the Wisdom of the Blues." *Rolling Stone*, no. 548 (March 23, 1989): 109–14.

Department of Commerce, Bureau of the Census. *Fourteenth Census of the United States Taken in the Year 1920*. Vol. 3, *Population 1920, Composition and Characteristics of the Population by States*. Directors Sam. L. Rogers, W. M. Stewart. Washington, DC: Department of Commerce, 1922.

———. *Thirteenth Census of the United States Taken in the Year 1910*. Vol. 2, *Population 1910, Alabama–Montana*. Reports by States, with Statistics for Counties, Cities and Other Civil Divisions. Director E. Dana Durand, Wm. J. Harris. Washington, DC: Department of Commerce, 1913.

DeSalvo, Debra. "Otis Rush: Still Can't Quit You Baby." *Blues Revue*, no. 21 (February/March 1996): 24–31.

Dixon, Robert M. W., John Godrich, and Howard Rye. *Blues and Gospel Records, 1890–1943*. 4th ed. Oxford: Clarendon Press, 1997.

Dixon, Willie. *Willie Dixon: The Master Blues Composer*. Milwaukee: Hal Leonard, 1992.

———. With Don Snowden. *I Am the Blues: The Willie Dixon Story*. New York: Da Capo Press, 1989.

Donoghue, William E. *'Fessor Mojo's "Don't Start Me to Talkin'."* Seattle: Mojo Visions Productions, 1997.

Ellison, Ralph. *Shadow and Act*. New York: Random House, 1953. Reprint, 1964.

Erlewine, Michael, Vladimir Bogdanov, Chris Woodstra, and Cub Koda, eds. *All Music Guide to the Blues: The Expert's Guide to the Best Blues Recordings*. San Francisco: Miller Freeman, 1996.

Escott, Colin, with Martin Hawkins. *Good Rockin' Tonight: Sun Records and the Birth of Rock 'n' Roll*. New York: St. Martin's Press, 1991.

Evans, David. *Big Road Blues: Tradition and Creativity in Folk Blues*. Berkeley: University of California Press, 1982.

———. "Goin' up the Country: Blues in Texas and the Deep South." In *Nothing but the Blues: The Music and the Musicians*, ed. Lawrence Cohn, 33–86. New York: Abbeville Press, 1993.

Fancourt, Les. *Chess Blues: A Discography of the Blues Artists on the Chess Labels, 1947–1975*. Faversham, Kent, England: L. Fancourt, 1983. Reprint, 1989.

———. *Chess Blues/R&B Discography*. Faversham, Kent, England: L. Fancourt, 1983.

———. *Chess R&B Discography*. Faversham, Kent, England: L. Fancourt, 1984.

———. "Liner Notes." *The Chess Years, 1952–1963*. Recorded by Little Walter. London: Charly Records, CD RED BOX 5, 1992.

Fancourt, Les, and Bob McGrath. *The Blues Discography 1943–1970*. Canada: Eyeball Productions, 2006.

Filene, Benjamin. *Romancing the Folk: Public Memory & American Roots Music*. Chapel Hill: University of North Carolina Press, 2000.

Frantz, Niles. "Koko Taylor: Forever the Queen of the Blues." *Blues Revue*, no. 38 (June 1998): 14–16, 18–19.

Franz, Steve. "Magic Rocker: The Life and Music of Magic Sam." *Living Blues*, no. 125 (January/February 1996): 32–44.

Gart, Galen, ed. *First Pressings: Rock History as Chronicled in Billboard Magazine*. Vol. 1, *1948–1950*. Milford, NH: Big Nickel, 1986.

———, ed. *First Pressings: Rock History as Chronicled in Billboard Magazine*. Vol. 2, *1952*. Milford, NH: Big Nickel, 1992.

———, ed. *First Pressings: The History of Rhythm & Blues*. Vol. 3, *1953*. Milford, NH: Big Nickel, 1986.

———, ed. *First Pressings: The History of Rhythm & Blues*. Vol. 4, 1954. Milford, NH: Big Nickel, 1992.

———, ed. *First Pressings: The History of Rhythm & Blues*. Vol. 5, 1955. Milford, NH: Big Nickel, 1990.

———, ed. *First Pressings: The History of Rhythm & Blues*. Vol. 6, 1956. Milford, NH: Big Nickel, 1990.

Glover, Tony, Scott Dirks, and Ward Gaines. *Blues with a Feeling: The Little Walter Story*. New York: Routledge, 2002.

Goines, Leonard. "The Blues as Black Therapy." *Black World* (November 1973): 31.

"Golden Gloves Bouts Begin." *Chicago Defender*. February 27, 1937, 14.

Gordon, Robert. *Can't Be Satisfied: The Life and Times of Muddy Waters*. Boston: Little, Brown, 2002.

Green, Jonathon, ed. *Cassell's Dictionary of Slang*. London: Cassel, 1998. Reprint, 1999.

Greenburg, Roy. "Otis Rush Interview." *Cadence* 5 (December 1979): 9–14.

Gruver, Rod. "The Blues as a Secular Religion." In *Write Me a Few of Your Lines: A Blues Reader*, ed. Steven C. Tracy, 222–30. Amherst: University of Massachusetts Press, 1999.

Guralnick, Peter. *Feel Like Going Home: Portraits in Blues and Rock 'n' Roll*. New York: Outerbridge & Dienstfrey, 1971. Reprint, New York: Harper & Row, 1989. Citations are to the Harper & Row edition.

Haig, Diana, and Don Snowden, comp. "Liner Notes." *The Cobra Records Story*. New York: Capricorn/Warner Brothers, 9 42012–2, 1993.

Harris, Sheldon. *Blues Who's Who: A Biographical Dictionary of Blues Singers*. New York: Arlington House, 1979.

Hawkins, Martin. "Liner Notes." *A Shot in the Dark: Nashville Jumps: Blues & Rhythm on Nashville Independent Labels*. Hambergen, Germany: Bear Family Records, BCD 15864 HL, 2000.

Heide, Karl Gert zur. *Deep South Piano: The Story of Little Brother Montgomery*. London: Studio Vista, November Books, 1970.

Herzhaft, Gerard. *Encyclopedia of the Blues*. 2nd ed. Translated by Brigitte Debora. Fayetteville: University of Arkansas Press, 1997.

Hildebrand, Lee. "Liner Notes." *Windy City Blues*. Berkeley: Stax Records/Fantasy, 2004.

Hoffman, Larry. "Robert Lockwood, Jr. Interview." *Living Blues*, no. 121 (June 1995): 12–29.

Hollis, Larry, and Eddie Ferguson. "Koko Taylor Interview." *Cadence* 10 (May 1984): 17–20.

Hookstra, Dave. "Jimmy Rogers Gets in His Licks." *Chicago Sun-Times*, June 15, 1990, 62.

Humphrey, Mark A. "Bright Lights, Big City." In *Nothing but the Blues: The Music and the Musicians*, ed. Lawrence Cohn, 151–204. New York: Abbeville Press, 1993.

———. "Holy Blues: The Gospel Tradition." In *Nothing but the Blues: The Music and the Musicians*, ed. Lawrence Cohn 107–50. New York: Abbeville Press, 1993.

———. "Liner Notes." *The Essential Sonny Boy Williamson*. Recorded by Sonny Boy Williamson. Universal City, CA: MCA/Chess, CHD2–9343, 1993.

Jackson, Bruce. *Get Your Ass in the Water and Swim like Me: Narrative Poetry from Black Oral Tradition*. Cambridge, MA: Harvard University Press, 1974.

———. "Liner Notes." *Get Your Ass in the Water and Swim like Me! Narrative Poetry from Black Oral Tradition*. Cambridge, MA: Rounder Records, Rounder CD 2014, 1998.

Jones, LeRoi. *Blues People: Negro Music in White America and the Music That Developed from It*. New York: William Morrow, 1963.

Keil, Charles. *Urban Blues*. Chicago: University of Chicago Press, 1966. Reprint, 1970.

Koda, Cub. "Sonny Boy Williamson [II]." In *AMG All Music Guide to the Blues: The Experts' Guide to the Best Blues Recordings*, 2nd ed., ed. Michael Erlewine, Vladimir Bogdanov, Chris Woodstra, and Cub Koda, 484–85. San Francisco: Miller Freeman Books, 1999.

Koide, Hitoshi. "Liner Notes." *The Complete Cobra Singles*. Tokyo: P-Vine Records, PCD-18528/31, 2008.

Larrison, Red. "The Lion Monkey and Elephant." *The Lancer* 3, no. 3 (March 1946): 37.

Leadbitter, Mike, Leslie Fancourt, and Paul Pelletier. *Blues Records, 1943–1970: The Bible of the Blues*. Vol. 2, *L to Z*. London: Record Information Services, 1994.

Leadbitter, Mike, and Neil Slaven. *Blues Records, 1943–1970: A Selective Discography*. Vol. 1, *A to K*. London: Record Information Services, 1987.

Lester, Julius. *Black Folktales*. New York: Grove Press, 1969.

Lighter, J. E., ed. *Random House Historical Dictionary of American Slang*. Vol. 1, *A–G*. New York: Random House, 1994.

Lomax, Alan. *The Land Where the Blues Began*. New York: Pantheon Books, 1993.

Long, Worth. "The Wisdom of the Blues—Defining Blues as the True Facts of Life: An Interview with Willie Dixon." *African American Review* 29, no. 2 (Summer 1995): 207–12.

Maultsby, Portia K. "Rhythm and Blues." In *African American Music: An Introduction*, ed. Mellonee V. Burnim and Portia K. Maultsby, 245–91. New York: Routledge, 2006.

———. "The Impact of Gospel Music on the Secular Music Industry." In *We'll Understand It Better By and By: Pioneering African American Gospel Composers*, ed. Bernice Johnson Reagon, 19–33. Washington, DC: Smithsonian Institution Press, 1992.

Minton, John. "Cockaigne to Diddy Wah Diddy: Fabulous Geographies and Geographic Fabulations." *Folklore* 102 (1991): 39–47.

Morris, Chris, and Willie Dixon. "Liner Notes." *The Real Folk Blues*. Recorded by Sonny Boy Williamson. Universal City, CA: Chess/MCA Records, CHD-9272, 1987.

Morris, Chris, Dick Shurman, and Andy McKaie. "Liner Notes." *Chess Box*. Recorded by Howlin' Wolf. Universal City, CA: Chess/MCA, CH5–9332, 1991.

Murray, Albert. *Stomping the Blues*, 2nd ed. New York: Vintage Books, 1982.

Neal, Larry. "The Ethos of the Blues." *Black Scholar*, no. 10 (Summer 1972): 42–48.

Oakley, Giles. *The Devil's Music: A History of the Blues*. New York: Taplinger, 1976.

Obrecht, Jas. "Buddy Guy." In *Rollin' and Tumblin': The Postwar Blues Guitarists*, ed. Jas Obrecht, 255–74. San Francisco: Miller Freeman Books, 2000.

———. "Otis Rush." In *Rollin' and Tumblin': The Postwar Blues Guitarists*, ed. Jas Obrecht, 222–46. San Francisco: Miller Freeman Books, 2000.

Oliver, Paul. *Conversation with the Blues*. 2nd ed. Cambridge: Cambridge University Press, 1997.

———. "Lookin' for the Bully: An Enquiry into a Song and Its Story." In *Nobody Knows Where the Blues Come From: Lyrics and History*, ed. Robert Springer, 108–25. Jackson: University Press of Mississippi, 2006.

———. *Songsters and Saints: Vocal Traditions on Race Records*. Cambridge: Cambridge University Press, 1984.

O'Neal, Amy. "Koko Taylor." *Living Blues* (Winter 1972): 11–13.

O'Neal, Jim. "I Once Was Lost, but Now I'm Found." In *Nothing but the Blues: The Music and the Musicians*, ed. Lawrence Cohn, 347–87. New York: Abbeville Press, 1993.

———. "Junior Wells." *Living Blues*, no. 119 (January/February, 1995): 25–26.

———. "Willie Dixon, 1915–1992: A Tribute." *Living Blues*, no. 103 (May/June 1992): 46–49.

O'Neal, Jim, Amy O'Neal, and Dick Shurman. "Interview: Otis Rush." *Living Blues*, no. 28 (July/August 1976): 10–28.

O'Neal, Jim, and Amy van Singel. *The Voices of the Blues: Classic Interviews from Living Blues Magazine*. New York, London: Routledge, 2002.

O'Neal, Jim, and Tim Zorn. "Interview: Buddy Guy." *Living Blues* 1, no. 2 (Summer 1970): 3.

Palmer, Robert. *Deep Blues*. New York: Viking Press, 1981. Reprint, New York: Penguin Books, 1982. Citations are to the Penguin Books edition.

Pearson, Barry Lee, and Bill McCulloch. *Robert Johnson: Lost and Found*. Urbana: University of Illinois Press, 2003.

Pruter, Robert. *Chicago Soul*. Urbana: University of Illinois Press, 1991.

Reed, Teresa L. *The Holy Profane: Religion in Black Popular Music*. Lexington: University Press of Kentucky, 2003.

"Rhythm and Blues Tattler." *Billboard*, February 20, 1954, 42.

Robble, Andrew M. "Buddy Guy: You Got to Play That Thing Like You Was Flyin' a Plane." *Living Blues*, no. 112 (November/December 1993): 8–21.

Roberts, John W. *From Trickster to Badman: The Black Folk Hero in Slavery and Freedom*. Philadelphia: University of Pennsylvania Press, 1989.

Romano, Will. *Incurable Blues: The Troubles & Truumph of Blues Legend Hubert Sumlin*. San Francisco: Backbeat Books, 2005.

Rothwell, Fred. *Long Distance Information: Chuck Berry's Recorded Legacy*. York, England: Music Mentor Books, 2001.

Rowe, Mike. *Chicago Blues: The City and the Music* [originally entitled *Chicago Break-down*]. London: Eddison Press, 1973. Reprint, New York: Da Capo Press, 1975. Citations are to the Da Capo Press edition.

Rowe, Mike, and Bill Greensmith. "'I Was Really Dedicated': An Interview with Billy Boy Arnold, Part 3: 'Whatever I Did It Was Me and I'm Proud of It.'" *Blues Unlimited*, no. 128 (1978): 18–26.

Ruppli, Michael. *The Chess Labels: A Discography.* 2 vols. Westport, CT: Greenwood Press, 1988.

Santelli, Robert. *The Big Book of Blues.* New York: Penguin Books, 1993.

Segrest, James, and Mark Hoffman. *Moanin' at Midnight: The Life and Times of Howlin' Wolf.* New York: Pantheon Books, 2004.

Shapiro, Anne Dhu. "Melodrama." In *The New Grove Dictionary of American Music.* Vol. 3, ed. H. Wiley Hitchcock and Stanley Sadie, 202–204. New York: Grove's Dictionaries of Music, 1986.

Shurman, Dick, Billy Vera, and Jim O'Neal. "Liner Notes." *The Mercury Blues 'n' Rhythm Story, 1945–1955.* New York: Mercury Records, 314 528 292-2, 1996.

Slaven, Neil. "Liner Notes." *The Essential Otis Rush: The Classic Cobra Recordings 1956–1958.* Universal City, CA: Fuel 2000 Records/Universal Music, 2000.

Smith, Michael B. "Koko Taylor." *Goldmine* 27, no. 2 (January 26, 2001): 14–18.

Snowden, Don. "Liner Notes." *The Chess Box.* Recorded by Willie Dixon. Universal City, CA: Chess/MCA, 1988.

Spears, Richard A. *NTC's Dictionary of American Slang and Colloquial Expressions,* 3rd ed. Lincolnwood, Chicago: NTC Publishing Group, 2000.

———. *Slang and Euphemism.* New York: Jonathan David Publishers, 1981.

Spencer, Jon Michael. *Blues and Evil.* Knoxville: University of Tennessee Press, 1993.

Springer, Robert. "Willie Mabon Interview." *Blues Unlimited*, no. 143 (Autumn/Winter, 1982): 25–31.

Titon, Jeff. *Early Downhome Blues: A Musical and Cultural Analysis.* 2nd ed. Chapel Hill: University of North Carolina Press, 1994.

———. *From Blues to Pop: The Autobiography of Leonard "Baby Doo" Caston.* JEMF Special Series no. 4. Los Angeles: John Edwards Memorial Foundation, Folklore and Mythology Center, University of California, 1974.

———, ed. *World of Music: An Introduction to the Music of the World's Peoples.* 3rd ed. New York: Schirmer Books, 1996.

Tooze, Sandra B. *Muddy Waters: The Mojo Man.* Toronto: ECW Press, 1997.

"To Revive OKeh Label: Many Top Names on Discs." *Chicago Defender,* June 23, 1951, 21.

Ward, Ed. "Chester Burnett: The Man Who Became the Wolf." In *Bluesland: Portraits of Twelve Major American Blues Masters,* ed. Pete Welding and Toby Byron, 204–23. New York: Dutton Books, 1991.

Welding, Pete. "Howlin' Wolf: I Sing for the People." *Downbeat*, no. 61 (July 1994): 44.

414 ~ Bibliography

———. "An Interview with Bluesman Howlin' Wolf." *Downbeat* (December 14, 1967): 8–9.

———. "Muddy Waters: Gone to Main Street." In *Bluesland*, ed. Pete Welding and Toby Byron, 130–57. New York: Dutton Books, 1991.

Welding, Pete, and Toby Byron, eds. *Bluesland: Portraits of Twelve Major American Blues Masters.* New York: Dutton Books, 1991.

Whitburn, Joel. *Top Pop Singles. 1955–1996: Chart Data Compiled from Billboard's Pop Singles Charts, 1955–1996.* Menomonee Falls, WI: Record Research, 1997.

———. *Top R&B Albums, 1965–1998.* Menomonee Falls, WI: Record Research, 1996.

———. *Top R&B Singles, 1942–1995.* Menomonee Falls, WI: Record Research, 1996.

———. *Top R&B Singles, 1942–1999.* Menomonee Falls, WI: Record Research, 2000.

White, George R. *Bo Diddley: Living Legend.* Surrey, England: Castle Communications, 1995.

Wilcock, Donald E. *Damn Right I've Got the Blues: Buddy Guy and the Blues Roots of Rock-and-Roll.* San Francisco: Woodford Press, 1993.

Willie Dixon's Blues Heaven Foundation's Record Row Festival [concert brochure]. Chicago: Willie Dixon, 2002.

Winfield, Ed, and Hitoshi Koide. "Liner Notes." *Born to Love Me.* Recorded by Jimmy Reeves Jr. Chicago: Checker, LPS-3016, 1970; reissue, Tokyo: Universal Music, UICY-93317, 2007.

Woods, Clyde. *Development Arrested: The Blues and Plantation Power in the Mississippi Delta.* New York: Verso, 1998.

Work, John W., Lewis Wade Jones, and Samuel C. Adams, Jr. *Lost Delta Found: Rediscovering the Fisk University—Library of Congress Coahoma County Study, 1941–1942.* Edited by Robert Gordon and Bruce Nemerov. Nashville: Vanderbilt University Press, 2005.

Electronic Sources

BMI Repertoire. www.bmi.com (accessed December 3, 2004).

Dixon, Willie. "Walkin' the Blues." BMI Repertoire. repertoire.bmi.com/title.asp?blnWriter=True&blnPublisher=True&blnArtist=True&page=1&keyid=1602106&ShowNbr=0&ShowSeqNbr=0&querytype=WorkID (accessed October 11, 2004).

Dupree, William Jack, and Teddy McRae. "Walking the Blues." BMI Repertoire. repertoire.bmi.com/title.asp?blnWriter=True&blnPublisher=True&blnArtist=True&keyID=1602107&ShowNbr=0&ShowSeqNbr=0&querytype=WorkID (accessed October 11, 2004).

Exxon Mobil Corporation. "Tiger History." www.exxonmobil.com/Corporate/About/History/Corp_A_H_Tiger.asp (accessed February 5, 2005).

Gross, Terry. "Interview with Former Led Zeppelin Singer Robert Plant." *Fresh Air Audio,* August 24, 2004; retrieved from the National Public Radio website: www.npr.org/templates/story/story.php?storyId=3868283 (accessed August 26, 2004).

———. "Interview with Robert Gordon." *Fresh Air Audio*, October 3, 2002; retrieved from the National Public Radio website: www.npr.org/features/feature .php?wfId=1329547 (accessed October 5, 2002).

"Hoodoo." Wikipedia: The Free Encyclopedia. en.wikipedia.org/wiki/Hoodoo_%28 folk_magic%29 (accessed May 26, 2007).

LePage, Jamie, founder. Spectro Pop Express. www.spectropop.com/ (accessed September 28, 2009).

Nelson, Angela. "Rap Music and the Stagolee Mythoform." *Americana: The Journal of American Popular Culture 1900 to Present* 4, no. 1 (Spring 2005). www.american popularculture.com/journal/articles/spring_2005/nelson.htm (accessed September 25, 2007).

Audio Recordings

Compilations

American Folk Blues Festival. Notes by Bill Dahl. Conshohocken, PA: Evidence, ECD 26100, 1995.

Bill Wyman's Blues Odyssey. Notes by Bill Wyman and Richard Havers. Newton Stewart, UK: Document, DOCD-32–20–2, 2001.

The Blues, 1927–1946. Notes by Touyou Nakamura, Yasufumi Higure, and Hiroshi Suzuki. Tokyo: BMG Victor, BVCP-8733–34, 1994.

Boyd, Eddie, Lafayette Leake, Willie Mabon, and Otis Spann. *Chess Blues Piano Greats.* Notes by Don Snowden. Tokyo: Chess/MCA Victor, MVCE-30015~6, 1997.

Chess Blues. Notes by Mary Katherine Aldin. Universal City, CA: Chess/MCA, CHC4-9340, 1992.

Chess Rhythm & Roll. Notes by Peter A. Grendysa. Universal City, CA: Chess/MCA, CHC4-9352, 1994.

The Chess Story, 1947–1956. Vol. 1. Notes by Colin Escott. European Union: Chess/ MCA/Universal Music International, 1126942, 2001.

The Chess Story, 1957–1964. Vol. 2. Notes by Colin Escott. European Union: Chess/ MCA/Universal Music International, 1126952, 2001.

The Chess Story, 1965–1975. Vol. 3. Notes by Colin Escott. European Union: Chess/ MCA/Universal Music International, 1126962, 2001.

Chicago Blues: A Bonanza All Star Blues LP. Chicago: Spivey, Spivey LP 1003, 1964.

Chicago Blues: Complete Recorded Works and Alternate Takes. Vol. 2, *1939–1944.* Notes by Tony Russell. Vienna: Document Records, DOCD-5444, 1996.

Chicago Blues: A Quarter Century. Notes by Ysufumi Higure, Hiroshi Suzuki, and Akira Kouchi. Tokyo: P-Vine, PCD-2130–22.

Chicago Blues of the 1950s. Shreveport, LA: Paula/Sue Records, PCD-22, 1997.

Chicago Blues of the 1960s. Shreveport, LA: Paula/Sue Records, PCD-22, 1997.

Chicago Boogie. Notes by Kiyoshi Nagata and George Paulus. Tokyo: P-Vine Records, PCD-1888, 1993.

Classic African-American Ballads from Smithonian Folkways. Notes by Barry Lee Pearson. Washington, DC: Smithonian Folkways Recordings, SFW CD 40191, 2006.

The Cobra Records Story: Chicago Rock and Blues, 1956–1958. Notes compiled by Diana Reid Haig and Don Snowden. New York: Capricorn/Warner Brothers, 9 42012-2, 1993.

The Complete Cobra Singles. Notes by Hitoshi Koide. Tokyo: P-Vine, PCD-18528/31, 2008.

Fathers and Sons. Notes by Bill Dahl. Universal City, CA: Chess/MCA, 088 112 648-2, 2001.

Folk Festival of the Blues. n.p.: Chess, CD CHESS 1015, 1989.

Get Your Ass in the Water and Swim like Me! Narrative Poetry from Black Oral Tradition. Notes by Bruce Jackson. Cambridge: Rounder, ROUNDER CD 2014, 1998.

Goin' Down to Eli's: The Rhythm & Blues Anthology, 1956–1958. Notes by Neil Slaven. London: Westside, WESA 868, 2001.

The Jewel/Paula Records Story. Notes by Diana Haig and Wayne Jancik. New York: Capricorn/Warner Brothers, 9 42014-2, 1993.

The Mercury Blues 'n' Rhythm Story, 1945–1955. Notes by Dick Shurman, Billy Vera, and Jim O'Neal. New York: Mercury Records, 314 528 292-2, 1996.

A Shot in the Dark: Nashville Jumps: Blues & Rhythm on Nashville Independent Labels. Notes by Martin Hawkins. Hambergen, Germany: Bear Family Records, BCD 15864 HL, 2000.

Shoutin' Swingin' and Makin' Love. Notes by Joe Segall. Tokyo: Chess/MCA Victor, MVCM 22015, 1994.

The Swingtime Records Story. Notes by Jimmy Guterman. New York: Capricorn/Warner Brothers, 9 42024-2, 1994.

Windy City Blues. Notes by Lee Hildebrand. Berkeley: Stax Records/Fantasy, 2004.

Individuals and Groups

Berry, Chuck. *The Chess Years.* Notes by Adam Komorowski. London: Charly Records, CD Red Box 2, 1991.

———. *The Great Twenty-Eight.* Notes by Michael Lydon. Universal City, CA: Chess/MCA, CHD-92500, 1984.

The Big Three Trio. *I Feel Like Steppin' Out* [CD]. Notes by Jonas Bernholm. Czechoslovakia: Dr. Horse, RBD 804, 1985.

Blind Blake. *The Best of Blind Blake.* Notes by Steve Calt, Woody Mann, and Don Kent. Newton, NJ: Yazoo/Shanachie, YAZOO 2058, 2000.

Bo Diddley. *Chess Box.* Notes by Bo Diddley and Robert Palmer. Universal City, CA: Chess/MCA Records, CHD2-19502, 1990.

———. *I'm a Man: The Chess Masters, 1955–1958.* Notes by Chris Morris. Santa Monica, CA: Hip-O Select, Geffen, Universal Music, B0009231-2, 2007.

———. *Road Runner: The Chess Masters, 1959–1960.* Notes by George R. White. Santa Monica, CA: Hip-O Select, Geffen, Universal Music, B0011076-02, 2008.

Dixon, Willie. *Big Three Boogie*. Notes by Pat Harrison. Guildford, England: Catfish, KATCD 189, 2001.

———. *The Big Three Trio*. Notes by Mary Katherine Aldin. New York: Columbia/ CBS, CK 46216, 1990.

———. *Catalyst*. Glenview, IL: Ovation, OVQD-1433, 1973.

———. *The Chess Box*. Notes by Don Snowden. Universal City, CA: Chess/MCA, CHD2–16500, 1988.

———. *The Collection: 20 Blues Greats*. Italy: Déjà vu, DVLP 2092, 1987.

———. *Ginger Ale Afternoon*. Universal City, CA: Varese Sarabande/MCA, VSC 5234, 1989.

———. *Hidden Charms*. Notes by Don Snowden. Hollywood: Bug/Capitol, CDP 7 90595 2, 1988.

———. *I Am the Blues*. Notes by Hitoshi Koide. Tokyo: Sony, SRCS 6348, 1993. Original release, New York: Columbia, PC 9987, 1969.

———. *I Think I Got the Blues*. n.p: Preview, Classic Records, CD PR 17, 1998.

———. *Live! Backstage Access*. Glendale, CA: Pausa, PR7183, 1985.

———. *Mighty Earthquake and Hurricane*. Glendale, CA: Mighty Tiger/Chase Music, MTD 6002.

———. *Mr. Dixon's Workshop*. Notes by unknown. Los Angeles: UNI/Fuel 2000, 302 061 138 2, 2001.

———. *The Original Wang Dang Doodle: The Chess Recordings and More*. Notes by Mary Katherine Aldin. Tokyo: Chess/MCA Victor, MVCM-22087, 1996.

———. *Peace?* Mississauga, Ontario: Boot Records, BOS-7136, 1973.

———. *What Happened to My Blues*. n.p: Preview, Classic Records, CD PR 18, 1998.

———. *Willie Dixon's Blues Dixonary*. Notes by Famke Damste. Belgium: Roots, RTS 2576, 1993.

———. *Willie's Blues*. Notes by Dale Wright. Berkeley: Prestige/Bluesville/Fantasy, OBCCD-501–2, 1991.

———. *Working on the Blues*. Vol. 1. Tokyo: P-Vine Records, PCD-2346, 1992.

———. *Working on the Blues*. Vol. 2. Tokyo: P-Vine Records, PCD-2347, 1992.

Dixon, Willie, and the Chicago Allstars. *Good Advice*. Vienna: Wolf Records, 120.700 CD, n.d.

Dupree, Champion Jack. *Walking the Blues*. Notes by C. Young. Nashville: King Records, KSCD 1405, 1994.

Fulson, Lowell. *The Complete Chess Masters*. Notes by Mary Katherine Aldin. Tokyo: Chess /MCA, Victor, MVCE-30011–2, 1998.

———. *Hung Down Head*. Notes by Noboru Wada, Don Snowden, and unknown writer. Tokyo: Chess/MCA Victor, MVCM 22011, 1994. Original release, Chicago: Chess LP CHV-408, 1970.

Guy, Buddy. *The Complete Chess Studio Recordings*. Notes by Don Snowden. Universal City, CA: Chess/MCA, CHD2–9337, 1992.

Hooker, Earl. *Blue Guitar: The Chief/Age/U.S.A. Sessions 1960–1963*. Notes by Hitoshi Koide. Tokyo: P-Vine Records, PCD-24045, 2001.

Howard, Rosetta. *Rosetta Howard (1939–1947)*. Notes by Victor Pearlin. Vienna: RST, JPCD-1514-2, 1994.

Howlin' Wolf. *Ain't Gonna Be Your Dog*. Notes by Dick Shurman. Universal City, CA: Chess/MCA, CHD2–9349, 1994.

———. *The Chess Box*. Notes by Chris Morris, Dick Shurman, and Andy McKaie. Universal City, CA: Chess/MCA, CHD3–9332, 1991.

———. *The Complete Recordings, 1951–1969*. Notes by Les Fancourt. London: Charly Records, CD RED BOX 7, 1993.

———. *Rockin' the Blues: Live in Germany 1964*. Notes by Neil Slaven. n.p.: Acrobat Music, AMACD 019, 2008.

Lenoir, J. B. *Vietnam Blues*. Notes by Jonny Meister. Conshohocken, PA: Evidence Music, 1995.

Little Brother Montgomery. *Complete Recorded Works, 1930–1936, in Chronological Order*. Vienna: Document Records, DODC-5109, 1992.

Little Walter. *Blues with a Feelin'*. Chess Collectibles. Vol. 3. Notes by Mary Katherine Aldin. Tokyo: Chess/MCA Victor, MVCE-30001–2, 1997.

———. *The Blues World of Little Walter*. Notes by Hitoshi Koide. Tokyo: P-Vine Records, PCD-5634, 2001.

———. *The Chess Years 1952–1963*. Notes by Leslie Fancourt. London: Charly Records, CD RED BOX 5, 1992.

———. *Confessin' the Blues*. Notes by Pete Welding. Tokyo: Chess/MCA Victor, MVCM-22086, 1996.

———. *The Essential Little Walter*. Notes by Don Snowden. Universal City: Chess/MCA, CHD2–9342, 1993.

———. *Hate to See You Go*. Notes by Mary Katherine Aldin. Universal City, CA: Chess/MCA, CHD-9321, 1990.

———. *His Best: The Chess 50th Anniversary Collection*. Notes by Billy Altman. Universal City, CA: Chess/MCA, CHD-9384, 1997.

Magic Sam. *The Essential Magic Sam*. Notes by Bill Dahl. Universal City, CA: Fuel 2000 Records, 302 061 104 2, 2001.

———. *Out of Bad Luck*. Notes by Akira Kouchi. Tokyo: P-Vine/Blues Interactions, PCD-2123, 1989.

Memphis Minnie. *Hoodoo Lady (1933–1937)*. Notes by Paul Garon. New York: Columbia/Sony, CK 46775, 1991.

Memphis Slim. *The Complete Recordings*. Vol. 2, *1946–1948*. Notes by Jean Buzelin. Paris: Blues Collection/EPM, 159862, 2000.

Memphis Slim and Willie Dixon. *At the Village Gate*. New York: Folkways, FA2386, 1962.

———. *In Paris: Baby Please Come Home!* Notes by Mike Edwards. Berkeley: Battle/Fantasy, OBCCD-582–2, 1996.

Muddy Waters. *After the Rain*. Tokyo: Universal Music, UICY-93294, 2007.

———. *At Newport 1960*. Notes by Mary Katherine Aldin and Jack Tracy. Universal City, CA: Chess/MCA, 088 112 515–2, 2001.

———. *The Best of Muddy Waters*. Chicago: Chess Records, Chess LP-1427, 1957; Universal City, CA: MCA/Chess, CHD31268, 1987.

———. *The Chess Box*. Notes by Robert Palmer. Universal City, CA: Chess/MCA, CHD3–80002, 1989.

———. *The Complete Muddy Waters, 1947–1967*. Notes by Les Fancourt. London: Charly Records, CD Red Box 3, 1992.

———. *Electric Mud*. Notes by Mark Humphrey. Universal City, CA: Chess/MCA, CHD-9364, 1996.

———. *Folk Singer*. Notes by Mary Katherine Aldin and Ralph Bass. Universal City, CA: Chess/MCA, CHD-12027, 1999.

———. *Hoochie Coochie Man: The Complete Chess Masters*. Vol. 2, *1952–1958*. Notes by Mary Katherine Aldin. Hip-O Select/Chess/Geffen, B 0002758–02, 2004.

———. *One More Mile: Chess Collectibles*. Vol. 1. Notes by Mary Katherine Aldin. Universal City, CA: Chess/MCA, CHD2–9348, 1994.

———. *Rollin' Stone: The Golden Anniversary Collection*. Notes by Mary Katherine Aldin. Universal City, CA: Chess/MCA, 088 112 301–2, 2000.

Reeves Jr., Jimmy. *Born to Love Me*. Notes by Ed Winfield and Hitoshi Koide. Chicago: Checker, LPS-3016, 1970; reissue, Tokyo: Universal Music, UICY-93317, 2007.

Rogers, Jimmy. *The Complete Chess Recordings*. Notes by Mary Katherine Aldin. Universal City, CA: Chess/MCA, CHD2–9372, 1997.

Rush, Otis. *The Essential Otis Rush: The Classic Cobra Recordings, 1956–1958*. Notes by Neil Slaven. Universal City, CA: Fuel 2000 Records, 302 061 077 2, 2000.

Sumlin, Hubert, Willie Dixon, and Sunnyland Slim. *Blues Anytime!* Notes by Bill Dahl. Conshohocken, PA: Evidence, ECD 26052–2, 1994.

Taylor, Koko. *Koko Taylor*. Notes by Bill Dahl. Universal City, CA: Chess/MCA, 008 112 519–2, 2001.

———. *What It Takes: The Chess Years*. Notes by Don Snowden. Universal City, CA: Chess/MCA, CHD-9328, 1991.

Tharpe, Sister Rosetta. *The Gospel of the Blues*. Notes by Mary Katherine Aldin. Universal City, CA: Decca/MCA, B0000533–02, 2003.

Wells, Junior. *1957–1963*. Shreveport, Los Angeles: Paula Records/Sue Records, PCD 03, 1992.

Williams, Robert Pete. *Poor Bob's Blues*. Notes by Elijah Wald. El Cerrito, CA: Arhoolie Records, Arhoolie CD 511, 2004.

Williamson, Sonny Boy. *Bummer Road*. Notes by Pete Welding. Universal City, CA: Chess/MCA, CHD-9324, 1991.

———. *The Essential Sonny Boy Williamson*. Notes by Mark Humphrey. Universal City, CA: MCA/Chess, CHD2–9343, 1993.

———. *The Real Folk Blues*. Notes by Chris Morris and Willie Dixon. Universal City, CA: Chess/MCA, CHD-9272.

Witherspoon, Jimmy. *Spoon So Easy*. Notes by Mary Katherine Aldin. Tokyo: Chess/MCA Victor, MVCE-22037, 1997.

Visual Recordings

Documentaries

Bluesland: A Portrait in American Music [VHS]. New York: BMG, 72333–80087–3, 1993.

Chicago Blues [DVD]. Produced and directed by Haley Cokliss. Tokyo: P-Vine Records, BMG Fun House, PVBP-953, 2003. Original produced in London: IRIT Film Production, 1970.

The Full Moon Show with Robbie Robertson [broadcast]. Hollywood: One Heart Productions, Video Arts Japan, Japan Satellite Broadcasting, 1991.

Howlin' Wolf. *The Howlin' Wolf Story* [DVD]. New York: BMG Music, 82876-56631-9, 2003.

Muddy Waters. *Can't Be Satisfied* [VHS]. n.p.: Wellspring/Tremolo Productions, WHE 71315, 2002.

Sweet Home Chicago: Story of Chess Records [VHS]. Notes by Tadashi Igarashi. Tokyo: Videoarts Music, Imagica Media, VAVZ-2129, 1993.

Live Performances

The American Folk Blues Festival, 1962–1966. Vol. 1 [DVD]. Notes by David Pack and Jon Kanis. Santa Monica, CA: Reelin the Years Publications, L.L.C., Experience Hendrix, L.L.C., Universal Music Enterprise, UMG Recordings, B0000750–09, 2003.

The American Folk Blues Festival, 1962–1966. Vol. 2 [DVD]. Notes by David Pack and Jon Kanis. Santa Monica, CA: Reelin the Years Publications, L.L.C., Experience Hendrix, L.L.C., Universal Music Enterprise, UMG Recordings, B0000751–09, 2003.

The American Folk Blues Festival, 1962–1966. Vol. 3 [DVD]. Notes by David Pack and Jon Kanis. Santa Monica, CA: Reelin the Years Publications, L.L.C., Experience Hendrix, L.L.C., Universal Music Enterprise, UMG Recordings, B0002937–09, 2004.

The American Folk Blues Festival: The British Tours, 1963–1966 [DVD]. Notes by Mike Rowe. Santa Monica, CA: Reelin the Years Publications, L.L.C., Experience Hendrix, L.L.C., Universal Music Enterprise, UMG Recordings, B0008353–09, 2007.

Devil Got My Woman: Blues at Newport 1966 [DVD]. Cambridge: Rounder Records, Vestapol 13049, 2001.

Dixon, Willie. *I Am the Blues* [DVD]. Huntingdon Cambs, England: CJ Productions and Quantum Leap Group, DRB-1345, 2002.

———. *Maintenance Shop Blues* [VHS]. Newton, NJ: Yazoo Records, Yazoo 511, 1981.

Howlin' Wolf. *In Concert 1970* [DVD]. Cambridge: Rounder Records, Vestapol 13099, 2007.

Masters of the Blues [VHS]. Los Angeles: Rhino Records, R3 2313, 1997.

Memphis Slim and Sonny Boy Williamson. *Live in Europe* [DVD]. Notes by Bill Wasserzieher. Santa Monica, CA: Reelin the Years Publications, L.L.C., Experience Hendrix, L.L.C., Universal Music Enterprise, UMG Recordings, B0003135–09, 2004.

Interviews

Branch, Billy. Interview by the author. Chicago, September 27, 2002.
Dixon, Arthur "Butch." Interview by the author. Chicago, September 23, 2003.
Dixon, Marie. Interview by the author. Chicago, September 25, 2004.
Dixon, Shirli. Interview by the author. Chicago, September 23–24, 2002.
Dixon, Willie. Interview by Jim O'Neal. Chicago, December 6, 1978.
Koester, Bob. Interview by the author. September 20, 2004.
O'Neal, Jim. Interview by the author. Kansas City, September 18, 2003.
Taylor, Koko. Interview by the author. Chicago, September 27, 2002.

Personal Correspondences

Evans, David. "A Review for Mitsutoshi Inaba's Manuscript." June 10, 2008.
Jennings, Vernell. E-mail correspondence with the author, July 11, 2005.
O'Neal, Jim. E-mail correspondence with the author, June 2, 2005.

Subject Index

walking-bass (pattern), 16, 32, 37, 40, 43, 78, 82, 83, 91, 96, 99, 109, 114, 121, 122, 126, 144, 148n37, 174, 176, 205, 224, 251, 272, 273, 279

Washboard Sam (Robert Brown), 28, 39, 52n19, 213

Waters, Muddy. *See* Muddy Waters

WDIA, 247

Weaver, Lucious Porter, 171, 182n39

Weir, Bob, 295

Welding, Pete, 68

What's Happened to My Blues?, 293

"Where the Lion Roareth and the Wang-doodle Mourneth" (African American toast/sermon), 118, 255. *See also* African American toast

White, Arthur, 181n30

White, Bukka, 172

White, Josh, 221

Williams, Big Joe, 212

Williams, Buster, 58

Williams, Fred, 28

Williams, Jody, 144

Williams, Mayo "Ink," 27, 28, 29, 51n7, 51n15, 77

Williams, Robert Pete, 55n56

Williamson, John Lee "Sonny Boy," 27, 28, 40, 41, 55n57, 73, 104, 150n84, 243, 256

Williamson, Sonny Boy (Rice Miller), xxv, 104, 174, 179, 184, 185, 205, 207, 208, 243–247, 256, 268, 287n117, 287n119, 288n124, 288n125. *See also individual song titles*

Willie Dixon: The Chess Box, 123, 295

Willie Dixon: The Master Blues Composer, xxvi, 219

Willie's Blues, 26, 287n110

Wills, Bob and His Texas Playboys, 62

Wilson, Edith, 118

Wilson, Jackie, 169

Witherspoon, Jimmy, 57, 71, 96, 127–131, 135, 152n132, 169

Woods, Clyde, xxvii

work songs, 13n45, 15, 16

The Wrecking Cru, 298

Wyoma, 58

Yambo Records, 264, 293

Young, Mighty Joe, 266, 289n156

Song Index

About the Author

Mitsutoshi Inaba was born in Kure, Hiroshima, Japan. He earned his Ph.D. in musicology and ethnomusicology at the University of Oregon. Dr. Inaba has taught courses on blues history, African American music history, and rock history.